THE SHAMBA RAIDERS

memories of a game warden

Revised Edition

BRUCE KINLOCH

Ashford Press Publishing
Southampton
1988

First published by Collins and Harvill Press, 1972

Revised edition published by   Ashford Press Publishing 1988
1 Church Road
Shedfield
Hampshire
SO3 2HW

British Library Cataloguing in Publication Data

Kinloch, Bruce
    The shamba raiders : memories of a game
    warden.
    1. Wildlife conservation — Africa
    I. Title
    639.9'092'4   QL84.6

    ISBN 1-85253-035-9

Cover design and new typesetting by Jordan and Jordan, Fareham, Hampshire

Printed and bound by Robert Hartnoll (1985) Ltd., Bodmin, Cornwall

Contents

Illustrations List

Acknowledgements

In the first edition of *The Shamba Raiders*, published in 1972, I said that for me the writing of this book had been a compulsion from the beginning, but that for my wife, Elizabeth, it had been sheer purgatory! I went on to emphasise that in the production of *The Shamba Raiders* my wife's practical help and support (although often strained to the limit!) had been not merely invaluable but indispensible, and I concluded by saying that, to Elizabeth, both this book and myself owe a very deep debt of gratitude. These words of appreciation are even more applicable now, in view of the additional work and problems which were involved in the production of this new edition of *The Shamba Raiders*, a revised version incorporating a substantial extra section which covers the period of twenty three tumultuous years of East African history that followed the original story that I told in the book.

I have not forgotten the patience, kindness and encouragement of my original publishers, Sir William Collins and Marjorie Villiers, both of whom, sadly, have since departed this troubled world; now, with this revised edition, their place has been taken by Jane Tatam and Lindsey Charles, respectively Managing Director and Editor of Ashford Press Publishing, for whose kindly help and interest I am also very grateful. However, I must add that, with this new edition, I am particularly indebted to Tony Jackson, former Editor of *Shooting Times and Country Magazine*. Over the last ten years I have often been asked why *The Shamba Raiders* has not been reprinted; by recommending the book to Ashford Press, Tony Jackson is the only person to have done anything about it!

A man to whom I owe a specially deep debt of the saddest gratitude is my old friend the late Charles Astley Maberly, whose line drawings do much to enliven the pages of this book. Charles, a charming and eccentric naturalist who lived alone, and who with typical generosity refused to accept any material reward for the painstaking work he had done for me, died a month before the book was published, brutally murdered by an intruder in his farmhouse in the North Eastern Transvaal.

Most of the photographs in this book were taken by myself; the obvious exceptions are those in which I myself appear and in these cases an obliging companion pressed the button. However, I again have to thank Captain K.B. ("Robbie") Robson for his courtesy in allowing me to use his excellent photograph of a horrifying collection of poachers' snares and traps; and Tom Chorley, one of my honorary game wardens in Uganda, for the equally telling picture of a snared rhino. Acknowledgements are also due to the Tanganyika (now Tanzania) Information Service for the photographs of the Arusha Conference, of the Students at the college of African Wildlife Management, and of the elephant tusks in the Ivory Room, Dar es Salaam; and to *Shooting Times and Country Magazine* for their courtesy in permitting me to conclude the 'Afterword' with my verses, *An African Night*, which were originally published in that magazine.

Another person to whom I am particularly grateful is the late Richard Owen (T.R.H. Owen, C.B.E.), another old friend and former colleague who wrote the brilliant and amusing poem, *The Triumph of Science*, which appears in Chapter Sixteen. In my interests, Richard resisted numerous requests for the poem to be published in other books.

The writing of the additional 'Afterword' for this edition entailed a considerable amount of detailed research, work in which I received a great deal of very valuable and sympathetic help from a number of experienced and knowledgeable people to whom I owe my sincere and very grateful thanks. In particular, I have to thank my two old friends and former colleagues, Dr. Keith Eltringham and Dr. Hugh Lamprey, both of whom are very experienced wildlife research scientists who have spent many years in Africa and both of whom took endless trouble to provide me with the information I needed. In this respect, my grateful thanks also go to Dr Eric L. Edroma, Chief Research Officer of the Uganda Institute of Ecology; to Dr Esmond Bradley-Martin, Vice-Chairman of the Survival Service Commission's 'African Elephant and Rhino' Group'; to Richard Fitter, Chairman of the Fauna and Flora Preservation Society; to Tony Mence, my former deputy when I was Chief Game Warden of Tanganyika and an old friend who later became the second Principal of the College of African Wildlife Management before joining I.U.C.N.; to Colin Imray, British High Commissioner in Dar es Salaam; and last, but by no means least, to John ('Steve') Stephenson, a former District Commissioner who for twelve years was Senior Park Warden of Tanzania National Parks, and who gave me full access to his recent and very comprehensive printed report entitled *Rehabilitation of The Selous Game Reserve,* from July to September, 1986.

Finally, there are the many game wardens and others who, at my request, took the time and trouble to send me particulars of themselves, their experiences and similar relevant details, to ensure the accuracy of this book. A number of them are named in the following pages, but although, to my regret, it has proved to be impossible to mention them all, this unavoidable omission is no indication of any lack of appreciation of their most willing assistance and friendly interest; indeed, it is them to whom I have dedicated this book.

To the Game Wardens of Africa

'They hear on the wind, as it passes,
The Call of the Veld.'

MARY BRYON
The Call of the Veld

by the same author:

SAUCE FOR THE MONGOOSE

Painting the Backdrop

The scream came from the deep shadows of the forest; wild and savage, it was so close that I was awake and on my feet in one scrambling movement. One moment I was dozing, sprawling in the loose sand by the side of the track. The next second I was on my feet, every sense alerted, my heart pounding against my ribs.

It was hot in the forest, the humid, clammy heat that clings like treacle and syphons the moisture from the human body in steady streams of salty sweat. There was hardly a breath of air and the stillness was almost ominous. In the far distance a troop of baboons broke the quiet as they squealed and squabbled over the fruits of a giant fig-tree. At the side of the track there was an illusion of coolness. I eased my left foot into a more comfortable position in the sand and, with quick irritation, slapped wildly at the lone mosquito that circled my head with a supersonic whine.

Suddenly a whisper of wind stirred the fine dust in the rutted path; immediately another scream of such venom and intensity that it seemed to tear the stillness of the forest apart burst from the gloom of the nearby trees.

The silence that followed was electric. The hairs on my nape rose as a cold shiver coursed up my spine. Even the distant baboons had been shocked into a timorous, watchful quiet.

Hardly daring to move, I turned my head slowly around towards my companion. Clad in the khaki uniform of a tribal police *askari**, he was standing motionless on the forest path, slightly behind me and to my right. What had made that blood chilling sound? What manner of beast could produce a cry of such power and savagery? Or was it a beast at all? I raised my eyebrows in an unspoken query, while my lips mouthed the single word –'Ngoloko?'

Masha Makatha jumped like a bush-buck stung by a tsetse fly. He was a well disciplined constable in the Giriama Tribal Police, chosen by the District Commissioner of Kilifi, on the Kenya coast,

* Strictly speaking 'a soldier'.

'A great grey head…'

to be my orderly, but he was still a superstitious peasant at heart. His dusky, sweat-streaked face was troubled, and at the sound of the ominous word 'Ngoloko' his eyes widened until the whites gleamed like beacons in the dark. The 'Ngoloko', the legendary, manlike beast of the dense forests and swamps of the East African coast, at the mention of whose dreaded name men huddle closer round their camp fires at night and women lash the doors of their huts at dusk, is scoffed at at one's peril. For a moment Masha the sophisticated, cynical askari reverted to Masha the simple, witchcraft-fearing peasant. But the lapse was brief. Discipline and training prevailed. With an obvious effort he braced himself and grinned – still rather nervously, baring a large expanse of gleaming white teeth as he shook his head in negation.

'Ndovu', he breathed, pointing into the forest with a forward jerk of his chin.

Of course, I should have remembered. I had heard the noise before. Not quite the same, nor quite so overpoweringly close, but there was no mistaking it. The same enraged, blood-chilling scream had sent shivers down my back in the far-off jungles of Burma and northern India long before I had come to East Africa as a district officer in the Colonial Administrative Service.

Scarcely had Masha spoken when, without a sound and only a few yards distant, the wall of the forest parted and towering above us appeared a great, grey head backed by mighty, spreading ears. Scarred and wrinkled, it looked like the massive, weathered bows of some ancient barque with her tattered sails billowing in the breeze. Framed between two great tusks of gleaming ivory, vicious, pig-like eyes searched myopically in every direction, while a trunk like some monstrous snake curled and twisted, striving to locate the faintest trace of man-tainted air. There before me was the first wild animal I had seen in Africa – a giant bull elephant.

For a moment nothing moved. Even the massive trunk was still, poised aloft in the shape of a question mark. Then in a split second the spell was broken. The echoing crash of a powerful rifle sounded nearby and in a flash the big bull whirled in his tracks and vanished, noiselessly as a shadow, into the depths of the Arabuko Forest.

The speed and silence of the great elephant's disappearance left me almost as stunned as his dramatic arrival, and it was some seconds before I recovered my senses and remembered where I was and for what purpose – the control of raiding elephant. I glanced down at the heavy double-barrelled rifle clasped limply in my sweating hands and then turned and raced towards the bend in the track where the game ranger had been waiting.

Turning the corner, I was confronted by an enormous, inert mass sprawling across the path and into the forest. It was as if some massive and ancient oak tree had been felled to block the route, but the slowly spreading pool of blood brought hard reality to the scene. For a moment I was appalled. Then I remembered the peasant shambas* I had seen the day before. Acres of cultivation flattened, eaten or wantonly destroyed. Women weeping quietly in hopeless despair. Men with a look of stunned disbelief in their eyes as they gazed at the scenes of future famine. A year's food supply for one whole village destroyed overnight by a herd of rampaging elephants.

I glanced at Jack Bonham, the Game Ranger of Kenya's Coast Province. He was tense and listening intently, rifle poised for instant use. Suddenly there was another wild and angry scream in the forest and a noise as of a mighty rushing wind through the tree tops, fading slowly into the distance. Jack relaxed, lowering the butt of his rifle to the ground.

'They've gone,' he said laconically.

*

There are milestones in everyone's life, crossroads where either decisions are made or impressions gained that alter the whole future of the person concerned. Many is the time that I have been asked how I became a game warden, and I have always replied that the story is a long one. However, it was this incident, when I was assisting the Game Department with elephant control, only a very few days after I first arrived in Africa, as a district officer on the Kenya coast, which I now firmly believe decided my fate, although I did not realise it at the time I could scarcely have had a more dramatic introduction to the African bush and the impression it made on me was profound. From that moment on, I joined the ranks of those who are held in thrall by the fascination of the mightiest and most majestic animal in the world, the African elephant.

* Cultivated areas

That twenty-fifth day of January, 1948, saw my wandering feet finally and firmly planted on the uncertain path that led to my becoming a game warden. Although all that had gone before provided much of the training and experience that was needed, at the age of twenty-eight my fate could not be foreseen.

In those days the conservation of wildlife was not the fashionable and widely-known subject it is today. There were no training facilities designed to produce a stereotyped, professional guardian of wild animal life. The game wardens of that era were individualists by nature and game wardens by chance – and choice. Coming from many walks of life and varied social backgrounds, they shared one common denominator – an all consuming love of the wild coupled with a strong sense of adventure. They formed a select but loosely knit company of dedicated men. Their material rewards were meagre; this they accepted in return for the freedom of the life they enjoyed.

More than forty years have now passed since that day in the Arabuko, the dense tropical forest that cloaks much of the land lying close to the coral-fringed shores of the District of Kilifi, on the coast of Kenya. During this time I have known many game wardens and, thinking back, I am struck by the number who became wardens through their association, in one capacity or another, with two particular living things which, from the earliest times, have exerted a profound influence on the African scene. One of these animals is a small but vicious insect, the other the largest of the world's land mammals. The one is the tsetse fly, the other is the elephant.

The tsetse fly, the carrier of the various forms of sleeping-sickness that can be lethal to either human beings or their domestic stock, has been somewhat cynically described as the most effective game preservationist in Africa. Certainly, by its very presence, it has long discouraged the often destructive and frequently wasteful use by humans of extensive regions of scenically beautiful, unspoilt wilderness, the natural home of the great game herds that form the essential but unwilling hosts of the blood-sucking fly. Sadly, since the Second World War, this very fact has many times been used as the excuse, in the name of human progress, for the otherwise senseless mass destruction of countless numbers of magnificent wild animals and their habitat, in the often vain attempt to starve out the tsetse fly. But this tenacious insect has defended its wild domain long enough to see much of it not only saved from human greed and vandalism, but transformed into famous national game parks and reserves, the almost impregnable wildlife sanctuaries of the present day – for which no animal has greater cause to be thankful than the elephant.

The management of the African elephant has always been a mammoth task in more senses than one. Fearing no living thing, except man, and having no peer in strength and sagacity among the wild animals of the forest and veld, since time immemorial these great beasts have roamed in their thousands, free and untrammelled, across vast areas of the African continent. In fact, to those who know and understand him, the elephant is the true 'King of Beasts', the real 'Lord of the Forest', of whom Topsell wrote: 'There is no creature among al the beastes of the world which hath so great and ample demonstration of the power and wisdom of almighty God as the Elephant.'*

But the elephant, the mightiest of the land mammals, is burdened by two things – massive tusks and a prodigious appetite. In his tusks he carries the valuable ivory long coveted by man, and to nourish his huge frame he must find anything up to a quarter of a ton of food per day. These things he cannot help, but, to his detriment, he is also an immensely destructive and terribly wasteful feeder. In consequence the elephant has been in conflict with human beings ever since man began to hunt the mammoth and till the soil, while in the last hundred years or so in particular, modern man has harried the elephant mercilessly whenever he has had the chance and the ability to do so – although the conflict has been far from entirely one-sided.

In the opinion of an old friend of mine, Professor Irven Buss**, a learned scientist who has been making a close study of the African elephant in recent years, the elephant is second only to man as the potentially dominant animal on earth. Thus, it is scarcely surprising that as the numbers of both elephants and humans rapidly increased in certain parts of Africa, as a result of the introduction of 'Pax Britannica' and the rule of law, their interest almost inevitably clashed with steadily mounting frequency and violence. In some areas acres of African peasant crops were

* Edward Topsell *The Historie of Four-Footed Beastes*, 1607.
** Professor of Wildlife Biology, Washington State University, USA.

xiv

devastated by raiding elephants; in others whole herds of these great beasts were butchered by the most barbarous methods. On the one hand human famine threatened; on the other an animal carrying valuable ivory (one of Africa's traditional exports since time immemorial) was faced with the long-term danger of extermination. Haphazard punitive measures, coupled with money-saving ivory-hunting schemes, either proved ineffectual or made matters worse. As often as not they merely succeeded in chivvying the frightened and angry animals from one cultivated area to the next. Finally, each of the British colonial administrations concerned was reluctantly forced to the inevitable conclusion – the responsibility for the protection of African shambas from crop-raiding elephants, and the general preservation and control of these mighty and troublesome animals had to be vested in a properly organised department of government. Thus with one outstanding exception, Kenya (whose game department dates back to the turn of the century), some years after the First World War the game departments of East and Central Africa came to be formed – in the first place as elephant control departments pure and simple.

Despite the creation of the game departments of East and Central Africa, charged with the primary task of protecting man from the unwelcome attentions of wild animals and the secondary task of protecting wild animals from the destructive urges of man, wildlife continued to disappear from the land in the face of human encroachment.

The process of attrition was slow but remorseless, until the Second World War, when it was accelerated alarmingly by the demands for more meat and increased agricultural production dictated by total war. Only after victory had been won, however, did officialdom at last really begin to sit up and take notice of the situation and listen to the angry pleas of game wardens and other individuals with a dedicated interest in wildlife. It is therefore with profound relief that I can now write, with an easy conscience, that the years since the Second World War have seen a revolutionary change in the status of wild animal life throughout the world. On balance this change has been very much for the better, for the mounting flood of destruction has finally been blocked by the solid breakwater of hard economic reality – the rapidly growing realisation, by those most intimately concerned, that wildlife has a considerable economic potential, as well as an intrinsic aesthetic value. As a result, in many countries where its future was previously in jeopardy, wildlife is now regarded as a primary national asset, a valuable natural resource to be displayed with pride and conserved and managed with scientific care.

Nowhere has the revolutionary change been more noticeable and dramatic than in East and Central Africa, the last and greatest stronghold of wild animal life, blessed with far larger numbers and varieties of spectacular and interesting species than any other quarter of the globe. East Africa, in fact, is now recognised as the 'cradle of man' and the greatest 'factory' and 'store-house' of wild animal life that the world has ever seen.

In this scenically magnificent region, since the Second World War, new national parks and reserves, many of them covering thousands of square miles, have sprung up like a carpet of veld flowers after a spring shower.

Urgently needed wildlife research has been introduced and has made spectacular progress.

The attitude to wild animal life of both officialdom and a rapidly increasing percentage of the general public has changed from apathy, even hostility, to active support.

And last, but not least, a flourishing and economically valuable tourist industry, now officially recognised as one of East Africa's primary economic exports, has not only blossomed from the development of the wildlife resource but is still expanding. None of this happened by accident and there is documentary evidence to show that the first real concern for the future of Africa's incomparable wildlife, and the first positive steps to protect it from destruction, date back to the closing years of the last century. In those distant days little more than a handful of widely scattered, but luckily powerful, influential and imaginative men was involved.

In 1884, far away in southern Africa, alarmed at the rapid disappearance of game in his beloved Transvaal, Stephanus Johannes Paulus Kruger, then President of the South African Republic, (but in his younger days famous as a hunter 'Paul Kruger the lion hunter'), in a speech to the Volksraad, warned the burghers that game would not last for ever unless it was afforded adequate protection. Remembering the days of his youth, when wildlife was abundant in the South African bushveld, he pleaded for the establishment of sanctuaries in which wildlife would be totally protected.

Initially, Paul Kruger's eloquent appeal fell on deaf ears. But the old hunter was a determined and stubborn man and eleven years later the Volksraad formally approved the establishment, in the area between the Sabie and Crocodile rivers, in the north-eastern Transvaal, of a complete game reserve, the first of its size and kind in Africa.* It was named the Sabie Game Reserve.

Thanks to that visionary and now legendary character, the late Colonel James Stevenson-Hamilton, its Warden for over forty years, the Sabie, like so many game reserves in Africa, eventually became a national park, the famous Kruger National Park. This development did not take place for many years, but about the time that the reserve was first approved, thousands of miles to the north, in East Africa, certain celebrated administrators, hunters and naturalists had also begun to express concern at the wildlife situation in that part of the 'Dark Continent'.

Outstanding among these early British pioneers of game conservation in East Africa, who successfully pressed for official action, were the names of Sir Harry Johnston and, later, Sir Frederick Jackson and Lord Delamere, with the Marquis of Salisbury (then British Foreign Secretary) as a stalwart and active ally in British Government offical circles. But perhaps the person most deserving of mention, in connection with the earliest efforts to conserve wildlife in East Africa, is Major Hermann von Wissmann, the Imperial Commissioner for German East Africa, a man who was particularly interested in elephant.

According to Noel Simon**, Hermann von Wissmann was one of the prime movers in the creation of German East Africa (now Tanzania) and stands forth not only as a great administrator but as perhaps the most far-sighted conservationist of that period. In fact, the late Colonel Ewart Grogan, himself one of Africa's immortal pioneers, described him as 'one of the great men of East Africa'.

*The first true game reserve in Africa was established in Natal in 1887, but it was a comparatively small area.

The picture is also not complete without mention of the fact that in 1890 King Leopold II of the Belgians created special game reserves in the Congo Free State, but these were for the protection of elephants from ruthless destruction.

** Noel Simon *Between the Sunlight and the Thunder*, 1962.

Certainly, many of von Wissmann's ideas were far ahead of his time and it seems that it was largely due to him, in conjunction with the Marquis of Salisbury, that the Governments of Great Britain and Germany convened a conference, in London, in May 1900, which the Governments of France, Italy, Belgium, Portugal, Spain, Turkey and Egypt were also invited to attend.

The declared object of this Conference was to establish agreed principles and methods to protect the fauna of Africa, in the territories controlled by the signatories, 'from the destruction which has overtaken wild animals in Southern Africa and in other parts of the globe'.

The Conference achieved a fair measure of success, but what has always intrigued me is that the biggest problems that arose from its ratification were mainly in connection with Africa's valuable and age-old ivory trade. In fact, in considering the history of wildlife conservation in Africa, it is important to remember the extent to which the elephant has dominated the scene. Had it not been for the elephant, few, if any, of the game departments of East and Central Africa might ever have been created; and without the initiative of the game departments it is problematical whether the now famous and popular national parks would ever have seen the light of day.

*

The years between the two world wars can best be described as the era of the great game wardens of East Africa, most of them much decorated ex-soldiers of outstanding ability. In fact, this period can well be regarded as the halcyon days of game conservation in East Africa.* Problems there certainly were, but time was not at a premium and political pressures were minimal. It was an era of happy feudalism, respected and unchallenged, and in the field of wildlife conservation in Africa it was a period of steady progress. It saw the creation of the high principles and ideals of the London Convention of 1933** – finally ratified in 1937, and when the world blew up in 1939, important developments were afoot in the wildlife sphere in East Africa, including plans for the creation of national parks. By that time many great game reserves had been created and small but efficient game departments had long been in

* It was also the period during which the famous national parks of the Belgian Congo were created at the instigation of King Albert of the Belgians.

existence, backed by comprehensive game laws and staffed by dedicated and experienced enthusiasts. It was the hey-day of the game departments, an élite force whose reputation and morale were high and whose authority was unchallenged.

The events of the years 1939 to 1945 shook the world, and in the immediate post-war years ominous cracks appeared in the very foundations of East Africa's wildlife citadel. Menacing political pressures, involving vociferous demands for development and the freeing of reserved land, soon threatened to destroy much, if not all, that had been so carefully planned. It was a time of steadily mounting emergency, a time for new ideas, reappraisals and fresh thinking

A few years after the Second World War the prospect of independence for the African colonial territories ceased to be a remote possibility. Almost overnight, what had long been a vague spectre dimly seen in the mists of the future, appeared, with all the inevitable attendant problems, as a dark, menacing and rapidly growing cloud on the near horizon. The pessimists gloomily predicted the gathering storm. They forecast the disintegration of the great game reserves and the wholesale massacre of the teeming herds of game. They described the era as 'the twilight of the great beasts'.

At this time most Europeans, government officials and civilians alike, accepted the premise that there was a certain moral obligation to preserve game – where it was convenient to do so. Their attitude to wild animals was traditionally one of sentiment, but sentiment strongly tempered by the dictates of economic land-use. To them game was a nice thing to have around when on safari, to look at, or sometimes to hunt for sport or for food for the pot. But in general they classified it as a hindrance to economic development rather than as being in itself a valuable natural resource, of positive economic worth, just waiting to be developed wisely.

The African attitude was different. The majority of Africans

**The signing of this Convention was the final act of the International Conference for the Protection of the Fauna and Flora of Africa, called by the British Government and held in London in 1933, under the chairmanship of the Earl of Onslow, President of the Sociey for the Preservation of the Wild Fauna of the Empire (later renamed the Fauna Preservation Society). In a Protocol to the 1933 Convention provision was made for further Conferences, and the first of these was held in London in 1938.

regarded game as a nuisance, a dangerous menace to their crops and stock, or as a welcome free meat supply – when they could get it. To them the game reserves and early national parks were little more than government 'game-farms'. The animals in these reserves they rated as being government 'cattle', while the areas themselves they looked upon as having been set aside for the exclusive use and enjoyment of Europeans, something they greatly resented. The game laws they counted as merely another irksome restriction imposed by an alien government, conceived and designed for the sole purpose of impeding or preventing the exercise of their legitimate rights to live, cultivate and hunt when, where and how they pleased.

It was a critical period for time itself was short and going fast. To save the situation both Europeans and Africans first had to be convinced that their countries' wildlife was a true natural resource of potential economic value. They then had to be shown how this theoretical value could be translated into hard economic fact. Finally, the Africans, in particular, had to be persuaded that in their wildlife they possessed a renewable natural resource not only of great economic value, if properly managed, but also of great scientific and aesthetic value – in fact a spectacular national heritage of which they could justly be proud, for it was unmatched by anything to be found in the more advanced countries of the world.

One thing, above all else, saved the day. This was the explosive development of international tourism that occurred after the Second World War, coupled with the rapid, post-war expansion of world-wide air-travel. This was the peg on which the wildlife enthusiasts hung their main plans and hopes. Dedicated and determined, and undeterred by the pessimists, as independence approached they redoubled their efforts to enlist the support of all races.

The measure and speed of their success surprised not only the doubters, both at home and abroad, but the enthusiasts themselves. In a short time the latter had got rid of the old concept, which regarded the large game animals merely as an attractive sporting asset and a convenient fresh meat supply on safari in areas where there could be no possible use for the land these beasts occupied, but which condemned all game animals uncompromisingly as a direct obstacle to development in virtually every other region. Instead, there was a growing body of opinion, among people of all races, that, as the basis of a rapidly expanding tourist industry, wildlife could become one of the great economic assets of the African countries. Coupled with this was a steadily mounting national pride in the possession of something that was unique and the envy of the outside world.

Even during the painful birth-pangs of independence the faith and hopes of the enthusiasts were justified. Contrary to the gloomy predictions of the pessimists, the new African governments accepted with alacrity the fact that their countries' wildlife was one of their most valuable natural assets. They recognised its economic importance as the basis of a tourist trade that was capable of enormous expansion. In Kenya alone, at that time, the most conservative estimates placed its annual value to that country at £8 million. Five years later it was calculated that East Africa's tourist industry was worth £20 million per year to Kenya, Uganda and Tanzania – and it is still increasing*.

Politically, the new governments were able and willing to take strong and rapid action to counteract any misguided local opposition to wildlife conservation: much stronger action than their colonial predecessors, hobbled and hamstrung as they were by overseas policy directives and shallow purses, had dared to consider.

Financially, the emergent countries were boosted by generous foreign aid, both economic and technical. And so they gave enthusiastic support to ambitious plans for the further development of their wildlife resources.

What has been the result? Many more national parks have been created. Game departments have been expanded. Wildlife research has been intensified. And more game management schemes have been introduced. Even in the strife-torn, blood-soaked lands of the Congo and Rwanda, the famous, game-rich areas of the Albert National Park and the Kagera National Park have miraculously survived, virtually unscathed, like islands in a flooded river.

As I write these words, in the wildlife world of East and Central Africa, arising from the inevitable dicates of political development, one serious problem yet remains, the need for suitably qualified Africans progressively to take over in a field

*Up-to-date figures are given in Chapter 18.

still largely dominated by dedicated Europeans. The latter are the devoted and experienced game wardens, with years of service in the game departments and national parks of both East and Central Africa, who, despite the uncertainty of their future, have elected to serve on as long as they are wanted. To them their work is calling. It is a sobering thought when one considers that this final problem, so vulnerable to the unpredictable whims and pressures of African politics, is probably the most vital one of all. Despite all that has so far been achieved, on its safe solution will depend the future of the most valuable game areas of Africa, for this in turn must depend on maintaining the efficiency and dedicated traditions of their long established guardians – the game departments and their off-spring, the national parks.

Those concerned with the creation and later development of these game departments (initially often caustically referred to as 'stunt departments' but finally culminating in the introduction of national game parks and extensive wildlife research schemes) were, until recently, mainly ex-soldiers with an inborn love of the wild. Most of them countrymen, nurtured in an atmosphere of traditional field sports, and all of them members of that vanishing breed, the sportsman-hunter-naturalist, it is they who can be thanked for laying the ground-work and setting the course of so many of the successful wildlife conservation developments of today. It is their place that the young African game wardens, from such sources as East Africa's recently created College of African Wildlife Management, now have to take. And, even as their predecessors did, these young Africans will find that the rational control of elephants and other animals, and the training of their game scouts to carry out the arduous duties involved, both humanely and efficiently, will still remain as one of the most important and demanding of their tasks.

It is not always sufficiently widely recognised that game control is exacting work which calls for knowledge and experience of hunting, and an understanding of the habits and reactions of animals, that cannot be learnt from the text-book or black board alone, it also calls for a degree of respect and sympathy, if not actual affection, for the quarry which is inherent in the true hunter-naturalist who in the past, has been brought up to observe a certain strict code of sporting ethics. With the granting of independence to the newly emergent, game-rich African states, these are some of the more intangible things that, henceforth, will somehow have to be instilled into the very varied raw material that will be trained and influenced at institutions such as the College of African Wildlife Management.

While lovers of the wild must welcome the fact that mass game slaughter as a means to control the tsetse fly has generally fallen into disrepute, they should be less ready to rejoice that restricted big game hunting as a true sport, disciplined by stern laws and a strict ethical code, has been to a great extent discredited in recent years by a wave of well meaning, but not always well informed and balanced, public sentiment. It is true that much of this public hostility has been aroused by the use and abuse of moderm 'armchair' methods of commercially organised hunting, involving the four-wheel drive, go anywhere hunting car, luxury food, iced drinks and valet service in the bush. Such hedonistic refinements are equally abhorrent to the rather more ascetic sensibilities of the true hunter-naturalist. But it should not be forgotten that until now the hunting of big game has been the only practical field training available for Africa's potential game wardens, and where it has involved the traditional elements of danger, austerity and physical endeavour it has been a training not to be despised. As in many walks of life the hard school of experience is often the best teacher, though not always the fastest or the most refined.

In contrast to the present antipathy to big game hunting as a sport, it is at last becoming widely though reluctantly recognised that properly planned and controlled killing, carried out by competent and experienced persons, does form a sad but essential part of the planned management of wild animal populations. This acceptance of a painful truth is based on the realisation that, when the grim alternative is mass mortality through starvation or disease, control of numbers by careful shooting is often the only really humane and practical way to help those expanding wild animal populations which are struggling to exist under the increasingly cramped and artificial conditions of the present day. On the other hand, the only way by which people can really learn to become thoroughly efficient at this often arduous and distasteful task, and thus carry it out humanely, is to have gained experience through actual hunting. Despite this inescapable fact, big game hunting is still widely condemned as a barbarous pastime. Here we have a real paradox!

'The truth of the matter is that hunting is a stage in the evolution of the man who is absorbed in wildlife. He goes through it, and usually grows out of it.' This is the considered view of many practising conservationists, here lucidly expressed by C.J.P. Ionides, one of the last of the old-time game wardens, who died in Nairobi in 1968 at the age of sixty-seven. 'Ionides, the Snake Man of East Africa' was a colourful and engaging character, famous both as a herpetologist and as a philosopher. Not only was he an expert charmer of both snakes and humans, he was also a friend and colleague of mine for whose opinions I had the greatest respect. But in supporting Ionides' wise pronouncement I would go further and say that hunting is also a stage through which any person must pass if he is to become a competent and balanced game warden. No matter what other experience and training he may have had, in no other way can any person learn all that a game warden has to know about wild animals and their habits and reactions in the bush under varying conditions and circumstances. And in no other way can he learn to use his rifle as a game warden must – with the unerring precision and humane certainty of the surgeon's knife.

The old-time game wardens served their apprenticeship as hunters. Many of them were primarily elephant hunters. Few of them were mere killers. There is a clear-cut difference between disciplined and restricted killing, as a part of hunting, when the final objective is to obtain food, scientific specimens or carefully selected trophies, and compulsive killing for the sheer love of slaughter. It is an important difference that all those actively concerned with the true welfare of wild animal life would be wise not to ignore. And it should always be remembered that the modern swing to the camera, in place of the rifle, was only made feasible with the comparatively recent advent of the precision miniature camera.

Many people have been and still are attracted to the pursuit of big game by the very nature of the life that it offers – the glorious feeling of freedom that envelops a person when he is camped on his own in the vastness of the African bush, or in the remote vastness of some distant mountain range. This was the fascination that lured so many of the old-time hunters and game wardens into the wilderness. They were true pioneers, ignoring hardship, danger and disease, and glorying in solitude. Not for them the protection of modern drugs, the convenience of tinned provisions, and the safety of civilised government. They depended on the strength of their constitutions, the power of their personalities and, in particular, their accuracy with a rifle, for they obtained their food by a mercifully placed bullet instead of hard cash on the marble slab of a butcher's shop. Many of them were also keen observers and fine naturalists, for which we have much cause to be thankful. Unfortunately on the other hand, the great majority of them have always shunned personal publicity and to this day have fought shy of placing their hard-won knowledge and often unique experiences on permanent record. The fact that the same can be said of even the most recent of this vanishing breed is one of the reasons that have inspired this book.

'The past is dead,' the Arabs say, but they do not infer that experience and historical facts are not valuable guides and teachers. Thus the true history of the development of wildlife conservation in Africa needs to be kept well to the fore when considering the soundness and value of new managment ideas, schemes and policies. The years when the game departments quietly got on with their job, despite totally inadequate staff and funds and little or no moral support, tend to be forgotten in the fanfares of trumpets that herald the bright new wildlife conservation schemes of the present day. A lot can be learnt from the hard-earned experiences of the game departments, and the old-time game wardens, without whose years of untiring effort few, if any, of the spectacular wildlife conservation developments of today would ever have materialised.

*

What I have related is the broad history of the evolution of wild life conservation in East and Central Africa. The story of my own life as a game warden* fits into this complex picture as one of the pieces in an intricate jigsaw puzzle. It started nearly two years after my first encounter with an African elephant in the Arabuko Forest, on that hot January day in 1948. But during those two

---

* During 25 years in Africa, the author was successively Chief Game Warden of Uganda, Tanganyika, and Malawi, and Wildlife Adviser to the governments of Botswana and Rwanda.

years, when I was a District Officer in Kenya, I had served an exacting apprenticeship pursuing both the shamba raiding elephants and the elusive ivory poachers and smugglers who flourished in the dense, tropical bush of the Kenya coast. And before that, as a soldier and hunter-naturalist in India and Burma, after a childhood dominated by an all enveloping interest in natural history, I had learnt much that was to be of value to me as a game warden in Africa.

The Tsetse Fly

PART ONE

To Pastures New

*

East Africa – 1964

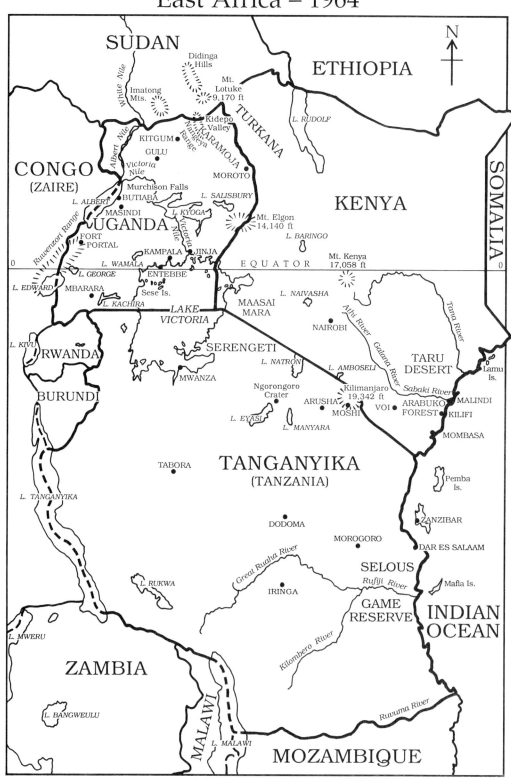

N

SUDAN

ETHIOPIA

Didinga Hills

Imatong Mts.

Mt. Lotuke 9,170 ft

White Nile

TURKANA

L. RUDOLF

SOMALIA

Kidepo Valley

KARAMOJA

Dodinga Range

Nangeya Range

KITGUM

GULU

Victoria Nile

MOROTO

Albert Nile

Murchison Falls

BUTIABA

L. ALBERT

L. SALISBURY

KENYA

CONGO (ZAIRE)

MASINDI

L. KYOGA

UGANDA

FORT PORTAL

Mt. Elgon 14,140 ft

L. BARINGO

Ruwenzori Range

KAMPALA

JINJA

EQUATOR

Mt. Kenya 17,058 ft

L. WAMALA

ENTEBBE

0

L. GEORGE

Victoria Nile

0

L. EDWARD

MBARARA

Sese Is.

L. NAIVASHA

L. KACHIRA

LAKE VICTORIA

MAASAI MARA

Athi River

Tana River

L. KIVU

RWANDA

NAIROBI

Galana River

TARU DESERT

Lamu Is.

BURUNDI

SERENGETI

L. NATRON

L. AMBOSELI

Sabaki River

MWANZA

Ngorongoro Crater

Kilimanjaro 19,342 ft

ARABUKO FOREST

MALINDI

ARUSHA

VOI

KILIFI

L. EYASI

MOSHI

L. MANYARA

MOMBASA

TABORA

TANGANYIKA (TANZANIA)

Pemba Is.

L. TANGANYIKA

DODOMA

ZANZIBAR

MOROGORO

DAR ES SALAAM

SELOUS

Great Ruaha River

Rufiji River

Mafia Is.

L. RUKWA

IRINGA

GAME RESERVE

INDIAN OCEAN

Kilombero River

L. MWERU

ZAMBIA

L. BANGWEULU

MALAWI

Ruvuma River

L. MALAWI

MOZAMBIQUE

CHAPTER 1

Opportunity Knocks

THE waiting room that served the offices of the Protectorate Agent in Kampala was depressing. The old-fashioned, green-painted shutters kept out the worst of the heat and glare that shimmered beyond the wide verandah, but the resulting gloom was enough to dampen the most ebullient spirit. Half a dozen, hard, straight-backed chairs lined the walls and in the middle of the floor stood a square, wooden table on which were scattered a few, dog-eared magazines. The only decoration was a commercial calendar, issued by an optimistic oil company; hanging limply on one wall in the humid heat it displayed a colourful picture of a cheerful African girl bearing a bulging basket of freshly picked cotton – one of Uganda's staple crops. Below the smiling dusky belle, the almanac proudly proclaimed that the Uganda Protectorate was the 'Pearl of Africa', that 'Mobtex' products were indisputably the best, and that the date was the 3rd of August 1949.

There were three men in the room; I was one of them. Conversation was friendly on the surface, but guarded, for we were all competing for the same job. Like three strange dogs meeting, by chance, on neutral ground, we eyed one another warily, each trying to establish a moral ascendancy over the other two and each attempting the while to discover the strength of the opposition with which he was faced.

For the umpteenth time I took the soiled copy of the official gazette from my pocket and studied the advertisement. 'Vacancy – Assistant Game Warden, Uganda Protectorate', it read, and then went on to detail the salary scale, the duties, and the qualifications required by any optimist who might summon up the courage to apply. What chance *had* I got? Doubtfully I scrutinised my two opponents. We were the 'short list' of applicants from which the final selection for the game warden post would be made and my newly met acquaintances were both obviously older and presumably also more experienced than I.

One of my rivals was a Kenya veteran with impressive scientific qualifications which he disclosed with airy but studied casualness. He was thick-set, heavily bearded, and strikingly sun-tanned. When I had first seen him, on the train from Nairobi the day before, he had been wearing an old sports coat, khaki shorts and a checked shirt. Then, with his powerful, sunburnt legs thrust purposefully into khaki stockings and well-worn desert boots, he had been so much the popular image of an African game warden or big game hunter that my heart had sunk and my hopes had dropped to zero when, in the dining car, I had overheard him loudly proclaiming the purpose of his journey. With memories of Allan Quartermain, Trader Horn, Selous and other similar heroes of my boyhood, both fictional and real, I had felt like taking the next train back to the Kenya coast, with my tail between my legs, for this man had looked ready-made for the job for which I had had the temerity to apply.

Now all this had suddenly changed. For the interview the man had abandoned the traditional garb of the East African pioneer. Instead, in honour of the occasion he had donned a very tight, blue, pin-striped suit and a pair of pointed, highly-polished, black leather shoes. With his luxuriant beard hiding his sober tie the metamorphosis was complete. Gone was the previous day's story book image of a game warden with the expected air of solid dependability and rugged self-confidence. In its place was a figure that could easily have been mistaken for a rather worldly off-duty priest. Looking at him again my spirits slowly began to rise. Had he committed a tactical error? First impressions are important at interviews and I felt that in my tweed jacket, Bedford-cord trousers and buckskin boots, sartorially speaking at least I was one up on 'Blackbeard'.

My other rival was a local candidate, a fact which I was sure gave him a distinct advantage. He was a determined looking character, a senior officer in Uganda's Department of Tsetse Control and an Honorary Game Warden, as well as being (as I later found out) a very experienced hunter. I couldn't help liking him; in fact, both my opponents seemed pleasant enough. But with his local experience and reputation, and his easy manner, I felt that the tsetse man would be certain to have friends at court. This would give him a flying start in itself, and even in the matter of dress I had no advantage over him. Reluctantly I decided that my money was on the tsetse man with myself probably a poor third.

'Major Kinloch?'

A door to an adjoining room had opened silently and in the gap was a young man wearing horn-rimmed glasses and a worried frown. His left hand clasped a bundle of papers, his right was pointed hesitantly in my direction.

'Yes?' I replied, trying to sound cool and confident.

'Would you come this way, please. The Board is ready for you.'

I braced myself. This was it. At least I was going in first and getting the ordeal over. But I have always dreaded interviews and as I reached the open door my mind went numb, my last conscious thought being a surge of self-pity as I realised what Daniel must have felt as he was about to enter the lions' den, alone and unarmed.

Slowly the contents of the room swam into focus and the mumbling in my ears began to form into words. Four men were seated at a long table; three were close together, the fourth sat slightly apart. The tall, commanding man in the centre of the group of three was speaking. I realised that he had just finished introducing himself and his two companions and was now indicating the fourth man.

'. . . and this is Captain Pitman, the Game Warden* of Uganda,' he said in a pleasant voice. 'We three are what you might call "the inquisition"! Captain Pitman is here to advise and guide us. You might also describe him as an interested party,' he continued with a smile, 'for he's the Director of the Game and Fisheries

* The title of the post was later changed to Chief Game Warden when Game Rangers were re-named Game Wardens.

Department of Uganda and our task today is to choose a deputy for him. Please be seated Major Kinloch.'

As I sat down I stole a quick glance at the Game Warden. He was a tall, distinguished looking man with fine features, conspicuously bushy eyebrows and greying hair brushed fiercely back from a high intelligent forehead. He gave me an encouraging smile.

'I think we should explain to Major Kinloch that this is a new post,' he said quietly, 'and one to which we attach great importance as far as the future of the Game Department is concerned.'

'I agree,' replied the Chairman, 'and I hope that Major Kinloch will not hesitate to ask us to clarify any matters about which he is in doubt. But perhaps it would be best if we first asked him to help us by answering a few questions. We are most grateful to him for coming all the way from Mombasa to see us. Therefore, we must take full advantage of this opportunity not only to discuss his qualifications and suitability for the post, but to ensure that he is fully aware of what the job entails.' It was clear that the Chairman was human and an expert at putting nervous candidates at their ease. I felt myself consciously relaxing and I warmed towards him.

'I see that you were in the Indian Army, Major Kinloch,' the Chairman said, removing his glasses after a quick glance at the papers in front of him. 'Were you a regular officer?'

'Yes, sir,' I answered.

'You were at the Royal Military College, Sandhurst then?'

'Yes, sir.'

'I was in the Indian Army myself,' the Game Warden volunteered, a note of quickening interest in his voice, '27th Punjabis. What was your regiment?'

'3rd Gurkha Rifles, sir,' I replied proudly. 'My family regiment.'

'*Magnificent* soldiers the Gurkhas,' said the Game Warden with emphasis. 'I knew them in the first war, in France – and Mesopotamia. I saw a lot of them later in Palestine,' he concluded slowly.

For a moment I thought of asking him if he recalled the epic battle of Nebi Samwyl in Palestine, in 1917, when the 3/3rd Gurkhas, commanded by my uncle – having run out of ammunition and suffered crippling casualties – had attacked and routed the Turks with their *kukris** and lumps of rock.

'Where were you in the war, Major Kinloch?' the Chairman's voice interrupted my thoughts.

'In India and Burma, sir.'

'Could you give us a few more details? It will help us if we can first get a clear picture of your background.'

'I had two years on the North West Frontier with the 1/3rd Gurkhas and then two years in Burma with the same Battalion. After that I was a jungle warfare instructor for a time before joining the 4/9th Gurkhas.'

'Why the 4/9th Gurkhas?'

Memories of war in the jungle flooded back – The uneasy quiet of a teak forest in the early morning with jungle fowl, like farmyard bantams, scratching busily in the fallen leaves beside the path. The same forest blazing fiercely during a low-level air attack; tired men kneeling, scorched and blackened by the flames and smoke; crouching in the treacherous, flimsy shelter of smouldering trees at the side of the track, while converging streams of tracer bullets from the multi-gunned fighters scythed savagely through the branches with a high-pitched, tearing snarl that merged into a continuous, ear-splitting crescendo of sound as the planes screamed over, again and again, just skimming the tree tops, strafing and bombing without a moment's respite; in their wake a tinkling shower of blistering hot cartridge cases, and torn leaves slowly falling. The earth heaving and shuddering under the muffled thud and roar of fragmentation bombs; the screaming of injured mules ripped and torn by the jagged pieces of flying steel; the cries and groans of sorely wounded and dying men; an ambulance burning furiously in the dusty track, its Sikh driver cut in half by a machine-gun burst, its occupants dead, the bright red cross on its white painted roof turning to a blistered brown as the hungry flames licked up and over the roasted bodies. Two young Gurkha soldiers standing stolidly in the open behind the funeral pyre of the ambulance, manning a tripod-mounted Bren-gun, sending a steady stream of tracer bullets into the fiercely flickering gun-teeth of the howling fighters that swooped low along the track like sparrow hawks after a bewildered pigeon; beside the Gurkhas their British officer, mouthing curses

* Heavy Gurkha slashing knives.

7

as he fired another Bren-gun, swinging it from the shoulder as if he was shooting at flighting duck on a mist-swathed Norfolk marsh; all around them the grey, powdery earth in the rutted road leaping in tiny, gouting fountains like erupting volcanoes as the hail of bullets from the strafing planes tore savagely into the ground, until the three lonely figures were hidden in the mounting cloud of swirling dust. Miraculously they had not been hit, nor had they ever been attacked from the air before – but they had seen the ambulance and the cold rage that consumed them left no room for fear.

And what else? Seven thousand feet and more up in dense mountain jungle; soaked with monsoon rain and shivering with cold as the clinging misty tendrils of low-lying cloud swirled through the silent, dripping forest; no shelter and one blanket per man; leeches in their legions, thin, thread-like and menacing, crawling on the soggy forest floor, draining an exhausted man of his life-blood overnight. And then the finding of our own men, a patrol that had been ambushed, some dead, the unlucky ones wounded and captured, tied to trees and their living bodies used for bayonet practice, sport for the heroic soldiers of the Japanese Imperial Army; cutting the pathetic, broken corpses down while the silent, merciless jungle watched unmoved.

And finally the sight of a great river, half a mile wide, once spanned by a bridge now lying torn and twisted in the swirling, yellow torrent, blown up by a retreating army – our own. Ourselves a rear guard obeying orders; doomed men sacrificed in the common cause. No food, ammunition almost gone. In front of us swarming hordes of jungle-trained Japanese. On each side more Japanese. At our backs the river – half a mile wide, no bridge, no boats. 'Hold the high ground', our orders had said, and we had – until all the rest had gone.

Yes, I had had many old scores to settle with the Japanese. Then the tide of the war in the jungle had well and truly turned and this had seemed to be my last chance to get even. I had jumped at it. But how could I explain all this, in a few simple words, to the expectant faces around the table?

'The 4/9th were a "Special Force" battalion, "Chindits", glider-borne,' I replied slowly. 'They were training for the final assault on Malaya and they needed a column commander. I lost a lot of my friends at the hands of the Japs. I wanted to be in at the kill.'

'And what happened?'

'Nothing!' I said, ruefully. 'The Americans dropped the atom bomb first.'

The Chairman smiled, but I noticed that the other two members of the Board appeared to be getting a little restive. One of them was a small, thin, wiry man with a balding head and a prominent, hooked nose. The other was his exact opposite, large, paunchy and florid, with dark, curly hair and thick horn-rimmed glasses. He looked as if he had been born in an office chair. Neither of them had yet spoken.

'I feel that it's time we heard a little more about Major Kinloch's *administrative* experience, Mr Chairman,' the florid one now interjected. 'I've been given to understand that there will be a *great* deal of administrative responsibility attached to this new post.

'With due respect for your interesting military career, Major Kinloch,' he went on, 'I *personally* feel that what is required for this post is, first and foremost, an able administrator. Can you please tell me what administrative qualifications you have?'

'Well, sir,' I replied slowly, 'just after the war I qualified at the Staff College, Quetta.'

'Oh!' said the florid man, sitting back suddenly as if I had punched him in the solar plexus without fair warning. I looked at him with mounting satisfaction. I felt that I had scored a point, but that I might lose my advantage if I revealed the manner in which fate had ordained that I should achieve the coveted status of a Staff College graduate.

After the war my wife had insisted that I should go to the Staff College. 'You'll get nowhere unless you do,' she had said, wisely but reprovingly, despite my protestations that the only reason I had joined the army was to enjoy an outdoor life and all the shooting and fishing that I could cram into it.

My Gurkha battalion was in Delhi at the time, guarding Japanese prisoners in the Red Fort, and, by a twist of fate – a freak accident to my Colonel – I was in command; so it had not been difficult for me to find an excuse to visit GHQ.

I had marched purposefully into the GHQ office that dealt with the Staff College. My first surprise had been to find that the

Laden with illegal ivory, a dhow slips away from a lonely beach at dusk

Poached ivory recovered in the case of Rex versus Jafferali Daudji

Bull elephants resting at midday

Waliangulu elephant bow and poisoned arrows

Girl of the Giriama tribe, a cheerful, colourful people

Staff Captain behind the desk was an officer of my own regiment whom I knew well. Surprise number two had been the discovery that he was in the very act of selecting the names of officers for the next Staff College Course. The unfinished list had been lying on the desk in front of him as I entered his office.

'Put my name down will you, there's a good chap?' I had asked, after explaining my predicament.

'Certainly, *sir!*' he had said, with a grin, casting a sardonic glance at my very new lieutenant-colonel's insignia as he reached for his pen – I was not quite twenty-six.

'The fact that you qualified at a military staff college is certainly to your credit, Major Kinloch,' purred the florid man, 'But I am still anxious to establish the extent of your administrative experience *outside* the armed services. After all, the duties of the post we are now considering are concerned with the problems of *civil* administration. I am sure you will agree with me therefore, that we must keep this thought very much to the fore in our deliberations? So now perhaps you could tell us what experience you have had in civilian life? I mean, of course, experience which might *reasonably* be considered to enhance your suitability for this post.'

'Well sir,' I replied brightly, 'since I left the Indian Army I have been in the Colonial Administrative Service. I'm a District Officer in Kenya now.'

'What actual duties have you performed?'

This was a poser, inasmuch as it was a question that could not be covered by a simple answer. Kilifi, in the Coast Province of Kenya, where I was the Senior District Officer, was classified as a 'backward' district; in such areas a district officer had to be a 'Jack of all trades' and a pocket 'Solomon', very similar to the famous fictional character created by Edgar Wallace – 'Sanders', the District Commissioner in the classic story *Sanders of the River*.

At the time of my interview in Uganda, my District Commissioner was away in England on eight months extended home leave. In his absence I was officially responsible for the maintenance of law, order, progress and well-being in a wild area of some five thousand square miles of forest, bush and scattered cultivation, populated by nearly seventy thousand mainly primitive people.

The inhabitants of Kilifi District are the Giriama, a pleasant, cheerful tribe of shifting cultivators and inveterate hunters. They are a colourful lot, particularly the women. High breasted and bronze of skin the ladies of the tribe seldom wear more than a voluminous, flouncing kilt of pleated, white cloth, reminiscent of the 'Evzones' of Greece, while the men favour the *kikoi*, a length of brightly patterned cloth that is wrapped sarong-wise about the waist. In the coastal areas there are small settlements of Arabs and Swahilis, mainly traders and fishermen, and a handful of Europeans who operate plantations of sisal, coconuts, cashew and pineapples, while a few have just retired to pass the autumn of their days gazing at the ever-changing colours of the Indian Ocean. These then are the varied wards for whose health, wealth, prosperity and progress Kilifi's District Commissioner and his assistants are required to account, but during my time there had been an additional problem – elephants and the poachers who hunted them and traded in their ivory.

There have always been small herds of elephants in the dense forests and arid bush of the Kenya coast, and many more in its hinterland, but during the two years that I was in Kilifi District these mighty beasts went on an extended rampage. Driven to desperation by drought and the poisoned arrows of the Waliangulu* in the interior, they invaded the coastal belt in their hundreds in search of food, water and freedom from incessant persecution. In the process they became a dangerous menace to both the people and their crops. Men were killed, huts destroyed and cultivation laid waste by the restless, ever-moving herds that descended on the shambas like raiders in the night, and disappeared, like great, grey ghosts, deep into the forests in the dim light of dawn.

The District Commissioner was magistrate, policeman, and in charge of the local gaol. He had a force of tribal police known as *askari kanga* (*kanga* meaning guinea fowl) and a section of regular Kenya police, Africans of various tribes, under his personal command, as well as a number of African prison warders. He was required to be a road engineer and a minor builder of such essential public works as dispensaries, latrines and staff lines. He was the local 'Receiver of Revenue' and on safari he and his district officers collected taxes and settled disputes on matters varying from land claims to adultery, which they judged according to native law and custom. Officially he was 'Receiver

* A Kenya hunting tribe famous for their prowess as elephant hunters.

of Wrecks' and 'Collector of Customs'. He supervised, directed and led the local District Council and in the process of this, and many other things from agricultural development to tsetse fly control, he was engaged in a never-ending paper war with a distant and mysterious oligarchy called 'The Secretariat'. And finally he was the local representative of His Britannic Majesty and everyone's guide, counsellor and general bottle-washer. I myself had become involved in one more most demanding and time-consuming task, the control of the elephant hordes that harassed the district and of the ivory poachers and smugglers who harassed the elephants.

All this I had to try to explain in a few concise sentences in order to convince my interrogator of my administrative experience and ability. I did my best, but shorn of detail it did not sound very impressive to me and when I had finished I felt depressed. But I noticed that the Game Warden was looking at me with renewed interest and the small, bald-headed man was regarding me keenly. The florid man alone sat poker-faced, then nodded curtly to the Chairman indicating that his cross-examination was finished. It was now the turn of the bald-headed man.

'You seem to have had some valuable experience with elephants, Major Kinloch – as well as some very varied administrative experience,' he added, 'but why did you leave the army? From your record you appear to have had a promising military career ahead of you.'

'When the old Indian Army was broken up in 1947, my Gurkha regiment was handed over to the new Republic of India,' I replied. 'I was offered a transfer to the British Army, but after serving with the Gurkhas I couldn't bear the idea of soldiering with any other troops. So I resigned.'

'I see,' commented the bald-headed man, his voice thoughtful. 'And what made you choose to come to East Africa?'

'Because it's the finest game country in the world.'

'So you were interested in wild animals before you came to Africa?'

I was surprised for it had never occurred to me that there could be any doubt about such a basic fact. The truth of the matter was that I had never had much interest in anything that was not in some way connected with what Victorian novelists were fond of describing as 'the wide open spaces'. It had been my primary reason for joining the Indian Army, although my relations fondly believed that I had done so out of respect for family traditions, a praiseworthy sense of duty and an ambition to emulate the example of my two grandfathers, both of whom had become Generals after distinguished military careers. Instead, it had been my fond hope that I would have the opportunity to follow in the footsteps of my paternal grandfather, General Kinloch, who had successfully organised his army career with one object in mind – the hunting of big game in the wilder parts of India and the Himalayas. He became a renowned hunter-naturalist and his imposing book on the game animals of India, the Himalayas and Thibet is a classic.

I didn't think that the Selection Board would want to hear a long-winded story about my family history, but I tried to explain that, like my paternal grandfather, ever since I could remember my life had been dominated by my interest in natural history and that I had had some experience of hunting dangerous game in India and Burma long before I found myself in Africa.

'There's one thing I'm not quite clear about,' the bald-headed man continued. 'You seem to have got very involved with elephant control at Kilifi, but isn't that the responsibility of the Kenya Game Department? Here, in Uganda, elephant control is one of the most important duties of our Game Department.'

The bald man was right but the circumstances had been exceptional. Prolonged drought and remorseless poaching in the hinterland had driven the elephants right into the cultivated areas of the coastal strip. They were appearing in places where they had not been seen for nearly twenty years. They had even wandered into Kilifi *boma* itself, strolling silently between the houses and offices in the still of the night to gorge themselves on the ripening fruit that hung, in heavy clusters, from the great mango trees planted by the early Arab traders. The Kenya Game Department had been desperately short of staff. Jack Bonham, the Game Ranger of the Coast, was responsible for a vast area stretching from the Somaliland border in the north to the Tanganyika border in the south. 'I'd be glad of your help, Bruce,' he had said in answer to my eager offer of assistance.

'You're quite right, sir,' I replied. 'But the elephant situation on the coast has been abnormal for the last two years. The Kenya Game Department just haven't had enough staff to cope with it and they welcomed my help. I must admit that the Provincial Commissioner was getting a bit worried about the amount of time I was spending chasing elephants and poachers,' I added frankly. 'I tried to start a carrier-pigeon service to get early information of raiding elephants from the remoter parts of the district, but the Provincial Commissioner put his foot down over that. He said the Giriama would eat them all!'

The Chairman smiled and looked at the Game Warden. 'Have you any questions you would like to ask, Captain Pitman?'

The Game Warden shook his head. 'Major Kinloch has produced a letter of recommendation from the Game Warden of Kenya, Captain Ritchie. I think that tells me all I want to know.'

'In that case I feel we can let you go, unless you have any questions you would like to ask the Selection Board?' said the Chairman, turning to me.

I shook my head. 'No thank you, sir.'

'Right,' he said, rising and shaking me by the hand. 'You'll be notified of the Government's decision shortly. We'll put you out of your misery as soon as we can!' he finished with a smile.

My wife was waiting for me in the ante-room. 'How did you get on?' she asked, anxiously.

I glanced at my two opponents. They were looking tense and expectant. 'Oh! All right,' I said, as we walked out into the brilliant sunshine.

*

A week later, as I was sitting in my office overlooking the blue waters of Kilifi Creek, a telegram arrived on my desk. I opened it. 'Congratulations and welcome to the Department,' it read. 'Official letter follows.' It was signed 'Pitman'.

Slowly and thoughtfully I folded the telegram and replaced it in the buff envelope. New and exciting vistas began to appear before my eyes. For a time I gave my imagination free rein. Then I shook myself and came down to earth. There was still an elephant problem in Kilifi District and now I only had about three months left to try to deal with it.

CHAPTER 2

The Hand of Fate

LESS than a month after my return from Uganda there started a chain of events which culminated in the most interesting illegal ivory case in which I have ever been involved. But the most intriguing part of it was the strange way in which 'Fate' stepped in at the crucial point to influence the issue; as James Shirley wrote: 'There is no armour against fate,'* and certainly, in my last ivory case in Kenya, the 'Hand of Fate' was the deciding factor and it happened like this.

I was sitting in my office in Kilifi trying to clear up a backlog of paper work. It was late and everyone else had long since left. The light was fading rapidly and through the window I could just see the silhouettes of the *ngalawas* – the outrigger fishing canoes with their small, lateen sails – drifting quietly home up the creek on the glassy surface of the flooding tide. In the distance was the dim, white line of the reef and the muted roar of the surf. Suddenly I noticed a shadowy figure hovering by the open door.

'*Hodi, Bwana!*' a voice said quietly.

* James Shirley (1596–1666), *The Contention of Ajax and Ulysses.*

18

For a moment I hesitated, my pen poised in my hand, uncertain what to do. There was no electric light in Kilifi in those days and I had been finishing my work with the aid of a powerful safari torch; on impulse I seized it and aimed the beam at the doorway. To my relief the light shone on the uniformed figure of one of my Giriama Tribal Police askaris.

'*Karibu* – come in,' I replied, giving the traditional welcoming response to the formal Kiswahili greeting.

The man who entered was a tall, well built African, a Giriama from the dry, bush country of the hinterland, his face decorated with the fancy cicatrices that revealed his tribal origins. Like my orderly, his first name was also Masha, but his second name was Iha, after his father, and it will avoid confusion if henceforth I refer to him only as Iha.

'Well, what do you want, Iha?' I asked, speaking in Kiswahili.

The figure in front of me came smartly to attention. 'Leave, *Effendi*,' he replied, his eyes focused rigidly on a point some six inches above my head.

'*Leave!*' I snapped indignantly. 'But you've only just come back from leave.'

Iha had obviously anticipated my initial reaction. He lowered his eyes until they met mine. '*Ndio* – yes, Effendi,' he said. 'But I have a reason.'

I looked at him with mounting puzzlement. Not only had he just returned from long leave in his home village, but he was also an askari of some years service; as such he was fully aware of the correct procedure when applying for leave. Discipline had to be maintained and a tribal policeman was not permitted to side-track the regulation formalities and make personal, informal application for leave direct to a district commissioner, or even a district officer, during normal duty hours, let alone outside them. There was something strange about the whole manner in which he had approached me and my curiosity began to get the better of my annoyance.

'All right,' I said, slowly. 'Tell me. What is your reason?'

The man relaxed, conscious that he had won the first round. Without answering he strode quickly to the door and glanced outside. Apparently satisfied that no one was there, he returned and bent over my desk with the air of a conspirator. 'Ivory,

Effendi,' he hissed in my ear, and then stepped back with a look of triumph on his face.

I stared at him reflectively. Was this a try-on? All the tribal police askaris knew of my fanatical interest in elephant. Iha had returned from his village in the hinterland only a few days before. Was his request really concerned with ivory or was he in woman trouble, perhaps? It was a common reason for requests for compassionate leave among the tribal police. I was intrigued despite myself.

'Ivory?'

'*Ndio*, Effendi.'

'Well, tell me more, Iha,' I said testily. 'I can't give you leave just because you say "ivory" like that.'

Iha looked at me in pained surprise. The illegal ivory racket on the East African coast is so riddled with spies and informers working for both sides, that anyone who is in any way involved or interested always speaks of it with the greatest caution. As a man whose tribe had traded ivory and hunted elephant with poisoned arrows since long before these activities were first labelled as poaching, Iha was genuinely shocked at my curt reaction. Besides which, he had a strong sense of the dramatic and, like most Africans, he enjoyed spinning any story out to its uttermost limits. There was a moment's silence, then he spoke again – this time rather huffily.

'On my leave I went to Goshi, Effendi. I have a brother there; he brings charcoal to Mombasa. While I was at Goshi there was a big *ngoma**. Many people got drunk and their tongues were loosened. I heard talk of ivory, Effendi.'

Despite myself I sat up sharply and leant forward in my chair with quickened interest. I knew Goshi; it was then a small collection of huts deep in the thorn-scrub country of the hinterland, about fifty miles from Kilifi.

The people who lived at Goshi were ostensibly charcoal burners, but the village, if one could call it that, was within easy striking distance of some of the finest elephant country in Africa. It was only twenty miles from the eastern boundary of the newly created Tsavo National Park, and exactly equidistant between the two was a large, permanent water-hole called Garibete.

Garibete water-hole, which nestles at the foot of a high,

* Dance.

rounded rock, was – and for all I know still is – a favourite camp-site of a small, amorphous tribe of bush people called the Wasanya. Better known now as the Waliangulu, the Wasanya are a tribe of renowned hunters. Using massive bows that no ordinary man can pull, and arrows tipped with deadly acokanthera* poison, they are dedicated to the almost exclusive pursuit of one animal – the elephant.

I knew the Wasanya. More than once, when I had been hunting shamba-raiding elephants, they had suddenly appeared from the coastal forest like dusky gnomes, and as trackers they had proved themselves brilliant. Where there were Wasanya, elephant ivory could not be far away, however well hidden, of that I was certain.

'Go on,' I said.

'Effendi, at Goshi there is a man called Pekeshi; he acts as an agent for ivory deals between the Waliangulu and the merchants in Mombasa.'

'So?'

'At the *ngoma*, Effendi, I heard this Pekeshi boasting about a big ivory sale that he had planned for this coming week.'

'Where?' I asked.

'That I know not, Effendi. Though Pekeshi was drunk still he would not talk much. But if you give me leave, Effendi, I think I can find out.'

I continued to stare at Iha, saying nothing but thinking hard. Was this information accurate or was it a cock and bull story? If it was genuine what was Iha's object in approaching me in this secretive manner? Was it purely on security grounds, or was he, or were his relations, involved in some way perhaps? If so, he could be trying to get his own back on someone for having been double-crossed, or for refusing to pay him 'hush money', or for a quarrel over a woman. Finally, and this was what I hoped, he could conceivably be doing his duty as a conscientious police constable with ambitions for promotion.

The Game Ranger for the Coast, Jack Bonham, was up north in the wild bush-country beyond the Tana River, somewhere

* This poison is made by prolonged boiling of slivers of the acokanthera tree. The black, pitch-like residue contains a highly toxic glucoside called Oubain which affects the action of the heart. The detailed recipe varies but several poisonous irritants are usually added.

near the Somaliland border, at least two hundred miles away. It was hopeless trying to get in touch with him and if his own informers had picked up this information and passed it to him he would be back in time anyway. If not, and if I myself didn't act on it, a rare opportunity of catching some of the key men in the ivory racket – the receivers – might be missed. There was nothing to lose in trusting Iha and giving him a chance to prove his worth.

'All right, Iha,' I said. 'I'll give you ten days special leave. You can collect a bus warrant from my office in the morning. But, I warn you, if you don't produce some results I'll cut ten days off your next earned leave.'

Iha relaxed. The look of tense expectancy faded from his face to be replaced by a wide, white-toothed grin. '*Asante* – thank you, Effendi!' he beamed, and with a smart salute turned and faded quietly into the night.

*

Early in the morning of the 10th of September, a week after Iha had departed on leave, I received an urgent telegram. It was in Kiswahili and it said 'Come Mariakani immediately.' It was dated the 9th of September and it was signed 'Masha Iha'.

Mariakani is a small township and trading centre, situated on the main Mombasa to Nairobi railway line and road, about thirty miles inland from the sea port of Mombasa. It lies on the southern boundary of Kilifi District and it is a collecting post for much of the charcoal and scrub cattle from the hinterland that are destined for the Mombasa markets. It is also on a direct route to Bamba, in the north, and Goshi.

I wasted no time. Within half an hour I was speeding on my way in my official, three-ton Bedford lorry, with an escort of half a dozen well armed tribal police askaris: and shortly after eleven o'clock in the morning I reached the police post at Mariakani. Iha was waiting for me, his face wreathed in smiles. 'All is well, Effendi', he grinned, and then gave me a long, detailed account of his actions since leaving Kilifi.

As his tale unfolded, and well before it had finished, it became clear that Iha had redeemed his promise to the full. But I shall tell the story from the beginning, in the manner of its happening and as it eventually came to light when all the dust had settled.

*

On the evening of the 8th of September 1949, a box-body van set out from Mombasa. In the van were three Indians; one of them was the driver and owner of the vehicle, his name was Jafferali Taibali Mulla Daudji, who with commendable foresight had fitted his van with false number plates.

Shortly after dark the party arrived at Mariakani where they turned off northwards along the road to Bamba. Ten miles further on they reached the crossroads at Gotani, where there was a well established barrier supervised by tribal police askaris. This barrier was designed to stop the illicit traffic in rice – a commodity in short supply at the time – between the coastal areas and the lucrative black market in Mombasa. After a brief inspection the askaris, having satisfied themselves that the vehicle was empty, let it through. But in the background was Iha. He had a good look at the Indians and when he saw their van drive off in the direction of Bamba he began to wonder.

The night was showery and overcast, a fact that pleased Jafferali Daudji and his companions, for the fewer the people who observed their movements on that particular journey, the better as far as they were concerned. They drove confidently on to Bamba, where they halted at a hut on the outskirts of the trading centre.

Carrying a shaded torch, Jafferali Daudji went to the door of the hut and knocked three times, a pause, then twice. A moment later an African appeared at the door of the hut, pulling on a coat against the late night chill. After a whispered conversation he and Daudji returned to the van, where Daudji introduced him to the others as Mutole, a local Giriama who was a contact man for illegal ivory. They then drove on together along the bush track leading north-westward into the hinterland.

Shortly before midnight the van reached Goshi. It was still raining slightly and the village was deserted, but Mutole knew where to go.

'Drive on to the third hut,' he said to Daudji. 'Pekeshi will be waiting for us.'

Any motor vehicle arriving in a remote bush village, even with dimmed lights in the darkest hours of the night, will normally very soon be the centre of curious attention. But the inhabitants of Goshi were long used to such strange, nocturnal comings and goings, for the village was a clearing centre for much of the Waliangulu ivory and Pekeshi, another Giriama, was one of the main agents. So the villagers merely stoked up their fires, pulled their blankets over their heads, and went back to sleep.

Pekeshi greeted his visitors affably. He had dealt with Jafferali Daudji on previous occasions, to their mutual satisfaction. Nevertheless, the bargaining was shrewd and prolonged before a price was agreed for the twenty-six pieces of fine ivory that lay, gleaming dully, in the dim light of the smoky oil-lamp that flared and flickered in the dark interior of Pekeshi's hut.

When Daudji and his party left, Pekeshi accompanied them. He wanted to buy some new clothes in Mombasa, he said. This was partly true, but a more important reason was that he didn't entirely trust Daudji and his friends. They had paid him only half the agreed price on the spot and he wanted to collect the balance from them as soon as possible.

By the time the van again arrived at the crossroads at Gotani it was four o'clock in the morning. The night had cleared and a full moon shone brightly on the barrier. This did not please Daudji, but he had timed his arrival with care and cunning and he did not think he would have much trouble. He knew that the sentry at the barrier would not be relieved until dawn, and from past experience he had reckoned that, by four o'clock in the morning, this askari, having been on duty since midnight, would be too drowsy to bother even to look at a small van. This time, however, things were different.

As Daudji drove up to the barrier he saw to his horror that it was a scene of quite abnormal activity. A local bus had been halted just ahead of him and it was in the process of being thoroughly searched by four tribal police askaris with torches. One of them was Iha.

Jafferali Daudji was a man of resource. He was used to rising to meet an emergency. He knew that the seven sacks of ivory in the back of his van would not escape discovery in this sort of search, and that his only hope of avoiding detection was to bluff his way past the barrier. Heaving his bulk out of his driving seat and leaving the engine running, he went up to the nearest askari.

'Bwana,' he said, in great agitation, which was only partly feigned, 'Please let me through quickly. My friends have to catch the train at Mariakani and there is little time.'

He had chosen the wrong man. Iha looked at him coldly, but with growing interest. 'Have patience, Bwana, have patience,' he replied. 'You must take your turn. Some of these good folk on the bus are also catching the train. They are not worried for they know there's plenty of time. What is your hurry?'

Daudji did not answer; instead he turned on his heel, walked rapidly to the van, clambered in and slammed the door.

By this time Iha's suspicions were fully aroused. He had not known what sort of vehicle to expect, but through his bush contacts he had obtained a lot of other useful information. He had learnt that the ivory deal would take place at Goshi about the time of the full moon. He had also received a rather unflattering, but cruelly accurate, description of a large, fat Indian from Mombasa, with a heavy pendulous paunch and quivering jowls, who had visited Goshi before and was expected again.

Iha had used his intelligence. It had taken him longer than he had expected to get all this information; in fact he had received it too late to warn me in time. He hadn't the resources necessary to lay an ambush at Goshi itself, or to launch a raid there. In any case he knew that such action would have had a very limited chance of success. Most of the people in that area were involved in the ivory racket in one way or another, and the trap would almost certainly have been sprung before the desired quarry had walked into it.

After much thought, Iha had decided that there was only one course open to him and that was to wait at the long established barrier at the Gotani crossroads. There were several alternative routes that a vehicle from Mombasa could take when heading for, or returning from, Bamba and Goshi, but the only feasible ones all passed through Gotani. Furthermore, if arrests had to be made, there was a small force of tribal police askaris permanently stationed at Gotani to man the barrier. Warned by Iha, these askaris were now searching every vehicle coming from the direction of Bamba, with unusual zest and thoroughness. They were looking for ivory – and a large, fat Indian.

When Jafferali Daudji turned away without answering his question, Iha sensed, with growing excitement, that he had at last found the man for whom he had been patiently waiting; but his feeling of triumph was short lived. Daudji was as crafty as a fox. He had far too much initiative and astuteness to allow himself to be caught in an obvious trap. As Iha quietly warned the askaris, who had almost completed their search of the bus, there was the roar of an engine and the crash of gears hastily engaged. Iha swung round just in time to see the van do a rapid U-turn. Then, with a scream of tyres and Daudji crouched low over the wheel, it roared off into the moonlit night, back up the road to Bamba.

Iha thought fast and again showed that he was a man of resource and initiative. He remembered that a few miles away, in the direction of Bamba, a rough bush track led westwards off the road to head deep into the interior. Regularly used by lorries collecting charcoal, it swung in a wide arc through the bush country of the hinterland, before curving southwards to rejoin the Gotani to Mariakani Road at a place called Mnyenzeni, some four miles to the west of the Gotani crossroads. Iha knew that by following this track Daudji and his companions could by-pass the Gotani barrier and drive on unhindered through Maria-kani to Mombasa, unless he could intercept them at Mnyenzeni. There was no time to be lost.

Calling to three other askaris to accompany him, Iha leapt on the bus and urged the driver forward. 'To Mnyenzeni, Bwana, quickly!' he shouted, as the sleepy, startled driver blinked at him in surprise. In a few moments, the remaining askaris had herded the bewildered, grumbling passengers back on board, and as the last one scrambled cursing into his seat the ancient bus lumbered rapidly away into the pre-dawn mist.

Iha's guess had been right. Shortly after seven o'clock in the morning the van appeared at Mnyenzeni, travelling on the bush track from the interior. Jafferali Daudji and his two Indian com-panions drove brazenly up to the barrier of oil drums that the four askaris had hastily erected. Daudji's beaming face leant out of the driver's window to greet them. '*Jambo*, Bwana!' he said affably to Iha. 'May we pass, please?'

Watched by the three grinning Indians, the four askaris searched the van with minute care. They found nothing. Baffled by their failure, and irritated by the smug smiles of the Indians, they then cross-examined Daudji. He had turned back from the Gotani barrier because he and his companions had forgotten something, he explained airily, in answer to the askaris' questions. They had a charcoal contract, he went on, and when they got to Gotani they had suddenly remembered that they had failed to see some of their suppliers who lived in the back country behind Mnyenzeni. So his friends had decided to catch a later train.

26

And now, if the askaris had no more questions, would they *please* let them through the barrier as they were weary and hungry and wanted to get home.

Reluctantly, the tribal policemen let the Indians pass, but not before they had made a careful note of the van's registration number and had memorised the features of its occupants. Iha then thought again. Something had happened between the time that the van had escaped from the Gotani barrier and the moment it had driven up at Mnyenzeni. He was certain that there had been ivory aboard when the vehicle had appeared at the Gotani crossroads in the moonlight. Where was the ivory now? There was only one answer; it must have been dumped in the bush somewhere along the charcoal track between Mnyenzeni and the Bamba road.

Deep in thought, Iha stared down the charcoal track, his eyes following its twisting, uneven course until it disappeared into the dense tangle of thorn-bush to the north. The heavy rain during the early part of the night had given the track a thick coating of brown, glutinous mud. Cutting deep into this sticky surface, and weaving and winding as they followed the course of the track, were two sharply defined, parallel lines; they were the tyre marks of Jafferali Daudji's van. Iha turned to his companions. 'Come on!' he said, pointing at the tyre marks. 'We'll back-track them.'

*

While the four tribal policemen followed the car tracks deep into the bush, loping along the clear-cut trail like a pack of eager fox-hounds on a fresh, dawn scent, things had been happening at a small, bush hamlet called Makwala, some seven miles ahead of them.

Makwala was at the junction of two charcoal tracks; one led deeper into the interior, the other swung eastwards to connect with the Gotani to Bamba road about four miles to the north of the Gotani crossroads. Along this latter track, wet and greasy from the previous night's rain, shortly after dawn a box-body van had appeared. Swaying and swerving, its engine roaring as its wheels spun wildly on the slippery surface, its driver clinging grimly to the bucking steering-wheel, the van had finally come to a slithering halt outside Makwala's solitary shop, a tiny, mud-walled *duka* owned by a simple African shopkeeper called Nzioka.

Nzioka had only just opened the rough, wooden shutters of his little, wayside store when the van had arrived. Rubbing his eyes he had stared at it in surprise. With mounting curiosity he had watched while two Africans had leapt out and dragged seven, heavy sacks from the rear of the van. Then, after a hasty exchange of words between the two men and someone in the front seat, the vehicle had roared off again in the direction of Mnyenzeni. As it had driven rapidly away, the shopkeeper had caught a glimpse of the driver's features; the face was that of a large, fat Indian with heavy, pendulous jowls – Jafferali Daudji had been in a hurry.

When the van had disappeared the two Africans had entered Nzioka's shop. He had recognised them immediately, for both Pekeshi and Mutole were well known in the neighbourhood. Could Nzioka help them? Pekeshi had asked. They had some sacks of provisions which they had to take to Mariakani, but the police were stopping all vehicles on the main road and he and Mutole were afraid that their stores would be confiscated by over zealous askaris. Could they please leave the seven sacks in Nzioka's store, while they went off into the bush to find some of their friends who would help them carry the bags across country to Mariakani? Nzioka had agreed readily. He was a simple, kindly man, always ready to assist an acquaintance who was in trouble, besides which he himself had had difficulty in the past with the askaris at the barrier. From bitter, personal experience he knew that the policemen were often inclined to exceed their authority and query the passage of quite legitimate goods. And so, leaving the seven sacks in Nzioka's trusting care, Pekeshi and Mutole had walked off into the bush in search of enough able-bodied men to help them move the sacks to a safe hiding place close to Mariakani. Only after their departure, and at about the same time as Jafferali Daudji's van was being searched by Masha Iha and his colleagues at Mnyenzeni, had Nzioka examined the bulky gunny bags. It was then, to his horror and alarm, that he had discovered that the heavy sacks were packed tight with freshly sawn sections of elephant tusks.

While Nzioka sat in his shop, wondering what to do, and Daudji and his Indian friends drove happily on to Mombasa, Iha and his three companions made good time. The back trail of the van was easy to follow for there had been no lorries over the track since the previous night's rain. Moving at a jog trot for most of the way, the askaris reached Makwala in under two hours; and as they entered the tiny village they saw that the tyre marks of the van swung in towards a small, wayside shop.

Nzioka saw the askaris coming. For once in his life he was thankful to see them and a few moments after their arrival he blurted out his story, omitting no details. So, an hour later, when Pekeshi and Mutole walked unsuspectingly into the shop, the askaris were waiting for them; and in a matter of seconds the two ivory agents were sitting on the floor, handcuffed together, glowering at their captors.

*

'Well done! Well done, indeed!' I said to Iha when he had concluded his story. Then I glanced in the direction of the Mariakani police post manned by Kenya Police regulars. 'And where are the prisoners now?' I queried, expecting to be told that they were in the nearby cells.

'They're at Makwala, Effendi; with the other askaris,' Iha replied, rather evasively I thought. He then went on to a long-winded explanation as to how he had had to wait at Makwala until late afternoon for a lift in to Mariakani on a charcoal lorry. It had been so full that it could only take one passenger, he said, and he had only just got to the telegraph office as it was closing. In fact, he had had to order the clerk to take his telegram, which had ended in a row. He was quite sure that this was why I had not received his message until the following morning. Everyone knew that the clerk, who was a foreigner from up-country, was idle and untruthful, he added loftily; and no doubt the despatch of the telegram had been deliberately delayed out of sheer spite, he himself was quite sure about that.

While Iha was rambling on, I wondered why the tribal police-man had not enlisted the help of the Kenya Police post to send his message and collect the prisoners and the ivory. Then I remembered the fierce professional rivalry that existed between the lower ranks of the two forces. Iha was clearly quite determined that no Kenya Police askari should have the slightest chance of stealing *his* thunder over this ivory case, particularly after all the effort he had put into trying to solve it!

29

'All right, we'll collect them now,' I cut in, bringing Iha's rambling indictment of the telegraph clerk to an abrupt end. 'But first I must telephone the CID in Mombasa to get them to check the number of the van and trace the owner,' I added; and ignoring the tribal policeman's black looks I walked into the Kenya Police post.

Late that afternoon found us on our way back to Kilifi. In the back of the lorry, carefully guarded by the askaris, were seven sacks full of sections of elephant tusks and the Giriama ivory agents Pekeshi and Mutole. The two prisoners, still firmly handcuffed, had refused to talk, which alone indicated that they were old hands at the game. However, a number of people had seen them arrive at Makwala and dump the sacks of ivory at Nzioka's store, while two willing witnesses had also overheard their conversation with the shopkeeper. All in all, I had collected more than enough evidence to put Pekeshi and Mutole out of circulation for quite a long time. But the person I really wanted to see behind bars was the receiver – the fat Indian from Mombasa.

I had first considered driving back through Mombasa to discuss the case with CID Headquarters there, but on second thoughts I had decided against it. I wanted to get Pekeshi and Mutole put away safely in a place where there was little chance of their being got at. I was quite sure that the Indian receiver would have his own informers keeping a sharp look out for the two ivory agents. Furthermore, there was little doubt in my mind that all our movements in and around Mariakani had already been reported to the Indian, and that he had long since realised that the two agents must have been arrested. He would obviously spare no effort to ensure their continued silence and I therefore deemed it best to keep a big gap between them and Mombasa for as long as possible. It was thus with a feeling of some relief that I watched Pekeshi and Mutole finally being locked away in the remand cells of Kilifi's prison at the end of the day.

The next morning brought a message from the CID in Mombasa. A check of the vehicle register had revealed that the van's number plates had been false, it said, and since there were literally hundreds of box-body vans in and around Mombasa answering to the same general description, the CID considered the chances of tracing it and its owner to be small. This was a set-back, but one that I had rather expected. It was aggravated by Pekeshi's and Mutole's continued refusal to talk.

According to the two ivory agents the people at the village of Makwala were lying. Nzioka had panicked when he saw the askaris coming, they said. He, Nzioka, was the ivory agent not they, but when he realised that he was going to be found in possession of seven sacks of illegal ivory, he and his friends and accomplices in the village had tried to place the blame on them, helpless strangers from a distant hamlet. They were merely innocent travellers seeking food and shelter who, without cause or warning, had been assaulted by the askaris, handcuffed and finally bound hand and foot; and all this had happened the moment they had stepped unsuspectingly into Nzioka's shop to buy food.

Yes, they had certainly seen a van drive up to the shop earlier on, they admitted when questioned. The driver had been an Indian whom they did not know, but whom Nzioka obviously did for he greeted him like a friend. In fact, Nzioka and the other villagers had then opened the back of the van and dragged out the seven sacks which seemed to be the cause of all the trouble and misunderstanding. They themselves had then gone off into the bush to relieve the call of nature. On their return they had noticed that the van had departed, which was a great disappointment to them as they had hoped to get a lift to Mariakani, where they were going to look for work. So they had gone to Nzioka's shop to buy food and seek his help to get a lift on a charcoal lorry. It was then that the askaris had jumped on them from the dark interior of the store.

This was Pekeshi's and Mutole's story and they were sticking to it. I knew they were lying, but they were belligerent and watchful and nothing I tried would get them to change a word or, more important, to reveal the name of the Indian. Since their attitude indicated that they were expecting help of some sort from somewhere, I decided that the best thing I could do was to arrange for them to be remanded in custody and join them in the waiting game – a cat and mouse affair with myself in the role of the cat.

A week passed with no developments. Then, one evening, as I was sitting on the wide verandah of my old-fashioned bungalow, a familiar figure appeared in the drive. It approached with a swagger and an almost nautical roll, and ended with a crash of horny bare feet stamped hard into the gravel, followed by an exaggerated, parade ground salute. Masha Makatha, my Giriama Tribal Police orderly, always staged this dramatic entrance whenever he had news to divulge which he considered to be of major importance.

'Jambo, Effendi!' he bellowed.

'*Sijambo*, Masha!' I replied. 'What do you want?'

'Effendi, I have brought someone to see you,' he boomed, indicating a figure lurking in the shadows behind him.

'So I see,' I observed, noticing for the first time a young African in a faded blue shirt and tattered khaki shorts. 'What does he want?'

Masha Makatha prodded the youth in the ribs with the tip of his swagger cane. 'Go on!' he growled. 'Tell your story to the Bwana *Mkubwa*.' The youth winced but remained silent.

'He is afraid, Effendi,' Masha said scornfully, giving the young man a withering look. 'But I will tell you and then you can ask him questions.' 'Well?' I prompted, glancing from Masha to the youth and back again.

'Effendi, his name is Katana. He works for an Indian in Mombasa.'

'So?' I said.

'This Indian, Effendi, has sent this miserable Katana to Kilifi to deliver a message.'

'To whom, Masha?'

'To the two prisoners, Pekeshi and Mutole, Effendi.'

I sat up with a jerk. 'What is the message?' I snapped.

'Effendi, Katana was told to go secretly to the prison fence and speak to Pekeshi and Mutole through the wire in the evening rest time. He was ordered to tell Pekeshi and Mutole not to talk, and that if they did not do so their families would be well looked after and they themselves would be richly rewarded when they came out of prison.'

'What does this Indian do?' I snapped again as the tension mounted.

'He is an ivory dealer, Effendi, and this Katana works in his shop as a cleaner and messenger.'

I hesitated before putting the final, crucial question. Then – 'What is the Indian's name?' I asked with studied carelessness.

'Go on, tell him yourself,' Masha growled, again prodding the youth in the ribs with his cane. The youngster looked terrified, then muttered something under his breath.

'Speak up, Katana!' I said kindly. 'I can't hear you.'

The youth glanced wildly around like a trapped animal seeking desperately to escape. Then he braced himself, stared at me with wide, frightened eyes, and spoke. His voice was clear but little more than a whisper.

'Bwana Mkubwa, his name is Jafferali Daudji,' he said miserably.

'A-a-a-a-ah!' I responded, letting out my pent-up breath in a long-drawn sigh of relief and satisfaction. At last I had the missing piece of the jig-saw puzzle, the key to the solving of the case. But one thing still mystified me.

'Masha,' I said, turning to my orderly, 'you have done well. But tell me, where did you arrest Katana? At the prison?'

'Effendi, I did not arrest him. He came to see me to ask what he should do. He was too frightened to go near the prison.'

Masha's reply only made the mystery deeper. 'Why did he go to see you?' I asked, bewildered.

The tribal policeman studied me with amused eyes, pausing to savour the full drama of the situation. At last he spoke.

'Effendi,' he announced, his voice triumphant, 'Katana is my brother!'

For a moment or two there was dead silence, then the full irony of the situation struck me like a blow between the eyes. Jafferali Daudji had covered his tracks well. He had been sitting in Mombasa, safe and unknown as far as the ivory case was concerned; and, with the very minimum of luck, he could have stayed that way indefinitely. Then 'Fate' had sown a seed of doubt in his mind, a doubt which led him to decide to send a warning to the only two men who might reveal his identity. And of all the people he could have chosen to act as his special messenger, he had selected the brother of the tribal policeman who was orderly to the district officer who was trying to track him down!

*

Early the following morning, I telephoned the CID in Mombasa. The African police constable operating the exchange, at the other end of forty miles of sagging wire, was either a little slow on the up-take or else he had had a heavy night. 'Police Headquarters speaking,' he said, when he had plugged my call into his switch-board.

'Give me CID, please – Mr Wright,' I requested briskly.

'Sir, this is Police Headquarters. There is no Mr White here.'

'Get me Inspector WRIGHT – WRIGHT,' I roared, spelling out each letter. 'Criminal Investigation Department.'

'Oh, you mean *Inspector Wright!*' the voice at the other end said, in a tone of profound relief now that the mystery had been solved.

'Yes,' I sighed. 'That's right – correct I mean,' I added hastily, fearful that this breakthrough might again become confused.

'Ah yes, sir; Inspector Wright, Criminal Investigation Department; I will put you through to him now.' A moment later Inspector Ernest G. Wright's voice came on the line.

'This is Bruce Kinloch. I'm speaking from Kilifi. Can you hear me all right, Ernie?'

'Yes, I can hear you, Bruce. Good morning!'

'Remember that van I asked you to trace ten days ago, the one in the ivory case?'

'Yes. What about it?'

'Well,' I said, trying to hide the note of triumph in my voice. 'I think I've got the name of the owner, or the driver – he may be both. Anyway, I believe he's the fat Indian we're looking for.' I could almost feel the tense expectancy at the other end of the line. 'Wait for it!' I said, mockingly. 'According to information received, the name of the wanted man is Jafferali Daudji.'

There was a sharp intake of breath, clearly audible even over the telephone. 'Why, do you know him?' I asked, in surprise.

'Yes,' replied the Detective Inspector slowly. 'Yes, I do. He's a general merchant who dabbles in ivory. He has been in trouble before. Thanks, Bruce. We'll check on this and I'll ring you directly I've got anything worth reporting.'

I put the phone down, confident that the case was in good hands. Inspector Ernest Wright of the Kenya Police was a first class detective and all-round policeman. In later years he made a name for himself on Kenya's Northern Frontier. On one occasion, with only one platoon of armed police under his command, he fought a long, running battle with a heavily armed raiding party of some three hundred Merile tribesmen. The Merile raiders, who were absconding with large numbers of Turkana livestock which they had rustled after murdering the owners, outnumbered the police party by more than ten to one. For hours the battle raged in broiling heat over endless miles of sun-scorched bush. By the end of it several policemen had been killed, but all the stock were recovered and the Merile fled in disorder leaving many of their warriors lying dead in the thorn-scrub.

This action did not pass unnoticed and among the awards for gallantry was a well-earned George Medal for Inspector Ernest Wright – and later the hand of a governor's daughter. But all that was yet to come when, on that hot September day in 1949, he and I planned the outwitting and downfall of Jafferali Taibali Mulla Daudji, the Indian ivory dealer.

Late that afternoon my telephone rang; it was the Inspector himself back on the line. 'The bird's in the bag,' he said quietly. 'We picked him up this afternoon. He's inside now on two charges of being in illegal possession of ivory and for buying it without authority.'

'Well *done!*' I said. 'What happened?'

Ernie Wright chuckled. 'It was all quite simple. I got a search warrant and went straight to Jafferali Daudji's shop. In a lock-up garage at the back I found the van, which is registered in his name. The false number plates were under the front seat – very careless of him!' He chuckled again.

'Did he talk?' I asked.

'Not he. He went as white as a sheet when I found the number plates and I thought he was going to collapse. But when I charged him he said he was saying nothing without his lawyer.'

'Who is his lawyer – O'Brien Kelly?'

'That's right.' Ernie Wright replied dryly. 'The usual!'

I whistled softly.

J. O'Brien Kelly was a particularly astute, and expensive, advocate who specialised in protecting the interests of Mombasa's varied Asian community. He was adept at getting his clients acquitted on legal technicalities.

'That means we'll have to make the case really watertight,' I said thoughtfully. 'What's the next step?'

'Identification parade,' the Inspector answered briskly. 'I've already sent a truck out to Makwala to bring in the shopkeeper and your supporting witnesses from that village, but I also need

Iha and the other tribal policemen concerned. The sooner you can get them into Mombasa the better. Daudji's lawyer is already agitating to get him out on bail.'

'Right,' I said. 'I'll send them in on the lorry straight away.'

From then on things appeared to go smoothly, although at one time it seemed that there might be a hitch over the question of hearing the case. As the crimes were committed in Kilifi Dictrict the case came under the jurisdiction of the Kilifi Magistrate's Court. I myself was a Second Class Magistrate, but I could not preside because I was personally closely involved in the investigations, while the two, newly joined, young district officers under me were only Third Class Magistrates. Luckily, John Stringer, the substantive District Commissioner and a First Class Magistrate, returned from overseas leave just in time to save the situation.

When the case came to court the evidence against Jafferali Daudji appeared unchallengeable. At the identification parade all the vital witnesses had picked out Daudji without hesitation as the driver of the box-body van, while Pekeshi and Mutole – charged as Daudji's accomplices – faced in court by overwhelming evidence, both lost their nerve, pleaded guilty, and confessed in full.

During the course of the court proceedings it came out that Jafferali Daudji had twice before been convicted of major offences involving illegal trafficking in game trophies, and John Stringer, as presiding magistrate, ruled that the case was far too serious to be dealt with by the District Magistrate's Court. Instead, Jafferali Daudji was remanded, on bail, to appear in the Supreme Court of Kenya, at Mombasa, on a date to be notified.

When it was all over, Daudji's advocate, O'Brien Kelly, came up to me. 'Do you always have a case sewn up as tightly as this one?' he asked with a rueful grin.

A few days later Jack Bonham, Game Ranger for the Coast Province, arrived back from his long safari in the Tana River region. He listened attentively while I told him the story of the tracking down and arrest of Jafferali Daudji and the two Giriama ivory agents. 'This is the third time Daudji's been charged with game trophy offences in the last few years,' he commented grimly, when I had finished. 'On the first occasion I got a tip-off that he was exporting rhino horn hidden in sacks of gum copal.

That time I got a crane driver to drop one of the bags on the Mombasa docks – by accident! It burst open and there were the pieces of rhino horn for all the world to see. Daudji was convicted on two counts and fined three thousand shillings.

'The second time I caught him,' the Game Ranger went on, 'exactly the same sort of thing happened except, just for a change, it was elephant ivory hidden in tins of ghee. That cost him fifteen thousand shillings on two counts. Now this is the third time. It just shows you what a profitable and well organised racket it is. The only thing that'll teach him and his like a real lesson is a bloody stiff stretch in the cooler,' he concluded. 'And I sure hope he doesn't wriggle out of it in the Supreme Court. It wouldn't surprise me if he did though, there's big money involved.'

As I listened to Jack Bonham's words my heart sank. After all our efforts it would be a major set-back if our chief prize should slip through the meshes of our net, at the last minute, merely due to the persuasive tongue of a slick lawyer. Yet there was nothing more we could do but wait in patience until the case came up for hearing.

CHAPTER 3

Dispute for the Water-hole

IT was my old friend Edward Rodwell, then Editor of the *Mombasa Times* and one of the outstanding characters of a region that was full of colourful personalities, who one day reminded me of what Major C. H. Stigand – one of the truly great among the old-time hunters of East Africa – had said about the East African coast.

'Stigand it was, Bruce,' Roddy said, puffing clouds of rank smoke from his black Mutolere cheroot, as we sat on the white coral sand by the blue waters of Kilifi Creek. 'Stigand it was who declared the coast of East Africa to be the best hunting ground in the world. In the first place, Stigand said, a man has to really "hunt" in coastal bush; he must know how to stalk; he must be an excellent shot; and as tough as rope. There the hunted and the hunter have a much more even chance.'

I often remembered Stigand's words after that; I thought of them with some feeling when I was tracking shamba raiders in the almost impenetrable coastal bush; and I thought of them ruefully when I was trying to intercept the elusive, but determined, poachers, whose continual harassing of the great elephant herds in the hinterland was driving more and more of these mighty animals seawards, to cause havoc in the cultivated areas near the shores of the Indian Ocean. I was not to leave Kilifi District without one last encounter in the bush, an encounter which served as a final reminder, not only of many of the lessons I had already learnt, but of how much I still had to find out. It was like discovering another key piece in a jig-saw puzzle, a missing section which completes the picture.

Unexpectedly, I found myself having to carry out a routine official safari only a few days before my family and I were due to travel to Uganda. The young district officer who had been detailed to do it fell sick and I had to substitute for him. Being a safari for the collection of tax and the payment of wages to government employees at various isolated places in the hinterland, it could not be postponed. I would not have minded had it not been for the fact that, during the time that I would be out of touch in the bush country, the case of Jafferali Daudji was scheduled for hearing in the Supreme Court at Mombasa. I had particularly wanted to attend the case to watch developments.

The second day of my safari I reached the small trading centre of Bamba, in the west of Kilifi District. I completed my duties there much sooner than I had planned. So, instead of driving straight on down the road to the township of Mariakani, where I was not expected until the following afternoon, I decided to take my lorry further westwards along the charcoal tracks to have a last look at the elephant country of the interior, and camp for the night at one of the few, scattered water-holes in the bush. On a sudden whim, when we reached a fork in the track, I ordered the driver to turn south and head for the tiny, remote village of Makwala. With the case of Jafferali Daudji uppermost in my mind, I thought I would like to see what was happening in the region of the village, which was on one of the main ivory smuggling routes regularly used by the Waliangulu and the Giriama.

When I reached Makwala I was greeted by the village headman with a long face. 'Bwana Mkubwa we are in great trouble,' he said dolefully.

'What is wrong?' I asked.

The old man launched into a long and highly coloured story. A huge and evil tempered elephant was terrorising the village.

The twice yearly ivory
auction in 'The Ivory
Room', Mombasa

The Giriama
Headman of Makwala
village

It had taken up residence by the nearest water-hole, he said, and for the past week it had been chasing anyone who went near the spring. Not only were the women terrified and refusing to collect water, but several cattle which had gone to drink had been killed. The people were suffering much. Could I not help them?

With variations, I had heard similar stories before. As often as not they were inspired by an insatiable craving for meat. But this time there was a ring of truth in the old man's tale. Evening was approaching but there might be time to have a quick look at the water-hole before darkness fell. Through force of habit I had brought my rifles with me and I called to my orderly, to get them out of the back of the lorry.

A few moments later Masha approached me. There was a worried look on his face and his voice was hesitant as he spoke. 'Effendi,' he said, holding out the old, canvas haversack in which I always kept my ammunition ready for safari, 'there are no cartridges for the big rifle.'

Seizing the haversack from him I hastily emptied the contents on the grass – a tin of rifle oil; some cleaning materials; a hunting knife; and two packets of 7 mm – or ·275 – cartridges for the light magazine rifle that I used to collect the occasional buck for meat on safari. In the flurry of my departure I had not thought to check to see that the haversack still contained some packets of cartridges for my heavy rifle.

My Mauser actioned ·275 rifle, made by John Rigby of London, was a beautiful and deadly accurate little weapon. But – and it was a big 'but' – it fired a bullet weighing a mere 173 grains, compared with the four to five hundred grains normally regarded as essential for elephant hunting. It would certainly kill an elephant, and humanely, if its well designed bullet – of high sectional density – was placed in exactly the right spot, but such a light, small-bore weapon lacked stopping power. In fact, no one in their right senses would think of regularly using such a rifle for the exacting, and sometimes dangerous, task of elephant control. Nevertheless, in times of urgency, or emergency, calculated risks have to be taken.

Removing four of the glistening brass cartridges from one of the packets, I looked at them ruefully, sensing their inadequacy. Then I opened the bolt of the ·275 and pressed them into the magazine. 'Come on,' I said to Masha. 'We must go.' So saying, I started along the well-worn path leading to the water-hole, the headman stepping warily ahead of me to show the way. After a few paces I glanced back. Masha was at my heels. I suppressed a desire to laugh. From sheer force of habit he was carrying my now quite useless heavy rifle.

The distance to the water-hole was scarcely a quarter of a mile. There were others in the vicinity but none so near or so permanent. The path wound its way through thick clumps of thorn bush and *sansevieria* – the wild, sisal-type plant whose long, fibrous, spear-tipped leaves are so greatly relished by elephant. Everywhere there were signs of the great beasts – balls of chewed fibre; strips of torn bark; broken branches; and droppings of all sizes, some old, some fresh. It seemed to me that numbers of elephant were using the water-hole regularly, not merely one rogue bull, and I began to wonder whether my first suspicions were not correct. Then the headman halted abruptly at a bend in the track; reaching back to grip my arm as he did so, he pointed excitedly at something ahead of him.

Slowly and quietly I eased alongside the old man, until I could see what he was pointing at. Thirty yards away the bush opened into what, at first glance, appeared to be a clearing fringed with longish grass and backed by a high bank. Then I saw that it was a sand river, and under the high bank on the opposite side of the clearing, standing motionless, apparently dozing in the slanting rays of the evening sun, was a massive bull elephant.

'That's him, Bwana, that's him,' the old headman croaked excitedly, continuing to hold my arm in a vice-like grip. '*Piga*, Bwana, *piga* – shoot him, quickly, *upesi*, Bwana,' he pleaded in a hoarse whisper.

I put a restraining hand on his shoulder. 'Quiet, *mzee**, he'll hear us,' I hissed. But it was too late; the headman's penetrating whisper had already reached the dozing elephant. Roused from his reverie, the old bull swung majestically round until he was facing us. Then, with his mighty ears spread wide, he raised his massive trunk aloft with ponderous deliberation, moving it gently from side to side with almost sinuous grace, the nostrils at its tip flared wide to catch and pin-point the slightest hint of human scent. With his head raised high as he stared imperiously but

* Old man – a polite form of address in Kiswahili.

short-sightedly in our direction, his towering mud-caked body glowing red, and the great sweep of his heavy tusks shining cream-ily in the evening sun, he looked magnificent.

I turned to the headman. 'How do you know this is the one?' I breathed in his ear.

He pointed. 'Look at his tusks, Bwana. Look at his tusks,' he whispered. 'See the blood on them? See the blood of the cow he killed this morning?'.

As always when hunting, my binoculars were slung round my neck on a short strap, ready for instant use. With one hand I raised them to my eyes and adjusted the focus until the image of the old elephant's gleaming tusks filled my vision, magnified eight times and etched as clear as a line drawing by the delicate prisms.

I stared at the tusks fascinated. They were certainly a fine pair, long, smooth and apparently flawless, the tip of the right one being rather the blunter of the two through greater use. But what interested me more were the dark streaks and blotches that stained the tusks for some two feet or so from their tips. Was it blood, caked hard and dried black by the searing heat of the sun? It certainly looked like it, but it was difficult to be certain merely by peering through a pair of binoculars. There was only one thing I could do – test the elephant's reaction to human presence. By using myself as a guinea pig, I should soon find out if the old bull really was a vicious rogue.

Signalling the old headman to retire down the path – which he did with alacrity – I advanced slowly and cautiously to the edge of the clearing, Masha clinging to my heels like a faithful gun-dog. Pushing through the thin fringe of grass I halted, with some twenty-five paces of open sand still separating me from the now thoroughly alert elephant. I glanced back along the trail to make sure of our quickest line of retreat and nodded to Masha to check that he understood my plan; then I acted.

'Hrrr-hm,' I said, clearing my throat loudly and ostentatiously. The old bull stiffened visibly. His whole body seemed to swell; his ears became rigid; his trunk, the last foot or so still glistening darkly and dripping water from the muddy pool at his feet, curled across his chest; and his tail slowly twisted like a tensed spring – a sure sign of anger and impending trouble. Still he couldn't scent us for we were down wind from him, but his short-sighted eyes had located two, blurred, upright objects that could be men – his hated enemies – and his ears had heard noises that only the human animal would make.

For a moment the scene was a frozen tableau. Then I poised myself for instant flight and spoke. 'Go on,' I shouted. 'Get the hell out of it!' Without a moment's hesitation the elephant lowered his head and came at us in a silent, vicious rush. There was not the slightest doubt as to his intentions, and in a split second Masha and I turned and sprinted back along the curving path the way we had come, finally halting for breath when a good hundred yards separated us from the water-hole. We stopped and grinned at each other weakly as the tension eased. The headman's flying figure had long since disappeared in the direction of the village. From the vicinity of the clearing we could hear the elephant crashing about angrily in the thorn-scrub searching for his tor-mentors, from time to time venting his rage in blood-curdling screams as he picked up lingering traces of our scent. But slowly even this noise faded into the distance and we were left alone in the all enveloping silence of the bush.

I glanced at the sun. Its slanting rays were touching the tops of the thorn trees and the shadows were lengthening fast. There was little time left before darkness fell. I stared at my little ·275 rifle. Given a steady shot I knew that I could deal with the rogue bull even with this comparatively puny weapon. After all, the ·275 is noted for its penetration and one of the most famous ivory hunters of all time had used nothing else; but then he had been a brilliant marksman and he had also been lucky – two all important factors to ensure survival in the uncertain business of elephant hunting. I jerked my head in the direction of the water-hole. '*Twende*, let us go,' I said to Masha, and walked rapidly back along the path to the clearing.

Below the bank, close to a small pool dug deep into the sand, I found what I was looking for – the bony carcass of a freshly killed cow, its back broken by a smashing blow from an elephant's trunk. The ground around it was stained dark with the blood that had drained into the sand, and in the animal's side were two gap-ing holes buzzing with a swarm of glistening blue-bottle flies. Here was the final confirmation of the headman's story.

Scouting rapidly around we soon picked up the elephant's tracks. After tearing up bush and grass at the point where we had stood by the edge of the clearing, he had headed off up-wind, moving along a well-worn game trail. His tracks, clearly imprinted in the sandy soil, showed that he was moving slowly, the occasional torn branch revealing that he was feeding as he went and was therefore not unduly alarmed. With luck, he might not go far and we had a chance of catching up with him before nightfall. But it was an uncomfortable feeling following the winding path through dense bush in rapidly fading light, knowing that an alert and savage elephant – a proven killer – was only just ahead of us. Carefully scrutinising every clump of bush we came to, we moved along the trail, stepping very, very slowly and very, very cautiously.

Suddenly I felt my right shoulder gripped fiercely from behind. I halted abruptly in my tracks and turned my head gently round. Masha was staring fixedly at a thick clump of thorn scrub on our right, his eyes wide and bulging, his mouth half open. Following his gaze, for a moment I could see nothing; then, between the tangled branches, the outline of an elephant's head began to take shape. It was broadside on to us and absolutely motionless, in its mouth a long branch that it had previously been chewing. It was obviously listening intently, poised for instant action; and standing less than ten paces from the path it was almost certainly waiting in ambush for anyone who might follow it from the water-hole. We had walked right into the trap. Even fractions of a second counted and my hunter's reflexes reacted immediately.

Without pausing I raised the little ·275. Before the butt reached my shoulder I had already begun to squeeze the trigger and the instant the silver tip of the foresight centred on the leading edge of the orifice of the elephant's ear I fired. The whip-like crack of the little weapon scarcely disturbed the intense stillness of the surrounding bush, but its effect was breath-taking. Almost in slow motion the back legs of the great bull collapsed, his massive head reared skywards until, for a brief moment, his long, sweeping tusks were silhouetted against the pink glow of the evening sky; and then, with a rending crash of crushed foliage, he subsided gently on his chest with his forelegs folded neatly under him, the long, creamy pillars of his gleaming tusks propping him upright as if asleep. The grey dust cloud of his falling settled slowly on the branches of the clustering thorn trees and all was still. The rogue bull was dead.

For a few moments I waited, rifle at the ready. Then, with a sigh of relief, I stepped the few paces that separated us and examined the body closely. There was a tiny trickle of blood and a scarcely discernible hole on each side of the massive head. The small, high-velocity bullet had drilled its deadly way clean through the brain causing instantaneous and merciful death.

As I ran my hand over the blood stains on the shining and beautifully symmetrical ivory – which later weighed out at seventy-six pounds a side – I heard an exclamation from Masha. He had drawn his hunting knife and was slashing hard at the thick hide on the elephant's left hip. In a moment he straightened and handed me something that he had cut from a pocket of stinking, maggot-ridden flesh; it was a broad-bladed arrow head with traces of tarry acokanthera poison still clinging to it. 'Waliangulu, Effendi,' he growled and spat expressively in the dust.

This explained a lot. The poison must have been stale, for fresh acokanthera poison is deadly and kills quickly once it has entered the blood stream. But, stale as it was, it would have been enough to make the old elephant desperately ill; with high fever and a raging thirst he would naturally have laid up near water, as he had done, until he recovered, or died. In the meantime, tortured by the racking pain in his body, he had attacked anything, human or animal, that came near him.

So, there it was; another link in the chain of evidence that was revealing to me the complex story of the ancient ivory trade. The story that started with the great elephant herds in the wild thorn-scrub country of the Nyika, and their age-old enemies the Waliangulu, the tribe of traditional elephant hunters, with their mighty bows and deadly poisoned arrows, who lived for nothing but the pursuit of the elephant. The story that continued with the middle-men, of various tribes but largely Giriama, for the Giriama were the Borgias of the Nyika, the tribe who, above all others, were the experts at making the most virulent brew of acokanthera poison known, a poison which they bartered with the Waliangulu for ivory. And finally the receivers, Indians and Arabs on the coast, who flourished and waxed fat on the handsome profits they made from buying tusks cheaply from the Giriama middle-men and smuggling them across the Indian Ocean hidden deep in the holds of the great, sea-going dhows.

That night I slept at Makwala amidst scenes of revelry and

rejoicing. Throughout the hours of darkness the sky was lit by the flickering flames of cooking fires as men, women and children camped around the carcass of the elephant, laughing, singing and gossiping as they carved and hacked at the mountain of free meat. By morning little was left except a few massive bones and strips of tough, grey hide. The tusks I took to register as government control ivory, and as I set off for Mariakani, on the same route that Jafferali Daudji had followed a few weeks before, I wondered to myself whether or not the Indian ivory dealer had finally evaded the true course of justice in the Supreme Court at Mombasa.

In Mariakani I called to say goodbye to Dr Ahmed, the little Indian veterinary officer who was in charge of the government milk production scheme. Ahmed was a good friend of mine, a conscientious and hard-working officer whose heart was as big as his body was small. As usual, he and his smiling wife gave me a warm welcome, chattering away like magpies as they dispensed large cups of hot, sweet tea and spicy local gossip in equal proportions. Sadly, not so very long after, poor little Ahmed was killed by lightning while carrying on with his work in a savage, tropical storm – a tragic waste of a really good man. But, on the day of my last visit to Mariakani, he was bubbling over with excitement at an item of news that had caused a considerable stir among the dovecots of the Asian community of Mariakani.

'You have not seen today's *Mombasa Times*, I take it, Major Kinloch?' he asked, his eyes gleaming like those of a child bursting to reveal a secret.

'Ah ha! I thought not,' he cried triumphantly, when I shook my head. 'It came on the early train. You will be pleased. Here, let me show you.' And with a flourish he laid a carefully folded copy of the *Mombasa Times* on the table by the side of my steaming cup of tea.

INDIAN GAOLED FOR TRYING TO BUY IVORY.
SMART WORK BY TRIBAL POLICE LED TO ARREST.

The headlines seemed to stand out in three dimensions before my wondering eyes. Rapidly, and with growing excitement, I glanced down the page.

'In the Supreme Court of Kenya at Mombasa,' the newspaper account continued, 'has been unfolded during the last three days a fascinating tale of illicit ivory dealing, pursuit and escape, final capture and retribution.'

'Before Mr Justice M. C. N. de Lestang appeared Jafferali Taibali Mulla Daudji on charges of buying and being found in possession of twenty-six pieces of ivory without authority.'

Steadily I read on until I reached the last two paragraphs. 'His Lordship remarked,' the penultimate paragraph said, 'that Daudji's accomplices were now in prison; if there were no receivers there would be no poachers and it was therefore only fair that the accused should be treated no more leniently than they.'

The last paragraph riveted my attention. The twenty-six pieces of ivory were from the tusks of ten separate elephants, it revealed, and on all counts Jafferali Daudji had been sentenced to six months hard labour plus fines totalling four thousand shillings – or another six months in default.

I stared at the paper long and hard, my thoughts racing over the curious twists of 'Fate' and circumstance that had led to this final retribution. Slowly a sensation of profound relief replaced my long pent-up feeling of taut expectancy.

At last I put the paper down and looked up. Ahmed had been watching me with eager eyes.

'Major Kinloch,' he said severely, 'this is good! Justice has been done.'

I rose to my feet to go. 'Good-bye, Ahmed,' I said, shaking him by the hand. 'You know I'll come back some day.' I kept my promise, but I never saw Ahmed again.

*

A few days later I was on the train from Mombasa, heading westwards for Nairobi and on to Uganda; and it was over eight years before I again set foot on the sandy soil of Kilifi District. During my absence there had been many changes. Little Ahmed had long since joined his ancestors and several other old friends had also gone, while the elephant situation had changed considerably – but for the better.

The year of my return was 1958, and the Kenya Game Department had just published a report covering the period from the 1st of January 1956 to the 31st of December 1957. Included in this official document was a brief report by the Game Warden

48

in charge of what had, by then, become known as the 'Kilifi Range'. For me it made fascinating reading.

'This range had been the worst poached area in the Colony', the Game Warden wrote. 'It was in this area that the anti-poaching campaign was waged with such signal success. An idea of the ravages of the poachers is conveyed by the discovery *by one team* of one thousand, two hundred carcasses of elephants killed by poachers, from many of which the tusks had not been removed. . . . As has already been stated, the campaign had cleared up the area in and around the Tsavo East National Park by the end of 1957. Little control of game had to be carried out in this area as there was no migration of elephant to the cultivated coastal belt. Some people attribute this to the cessation of the harrying of elephant by poachers in the hinterland.'

The Game Warden's concluding words rang in my brain. My own, amateur efforts some eight years before had done little more than lift the corner of the heavy lid that concealed the buzzing termites' nest of the illeagl ivory trade. It had taken specially organised and equipped, radio-controlled teams of combined Game Department, National Parks, and Police personnel, assisted by spotter aircraft of the Police Air Wing and supported by the Administrative Service, nearly two years of intense, concentrated, and closely co-ordinated effort to take the lid right off. What was revealed shook the game world, and what was achieved undoubtedly saved the great elephant herds of the Nyika.

These intensive operations caused repercussions in the illegal ivory trade which reached as far afield as Uganda and beyond. But when I departed for Uganda, in November 1949, the extensive ramifications of this ancient trade were still a closely guarded secret. Certainly, at that time, I myself was blissfully unaware of the problems that lay ahead of me, and of the magnitude of the tasks with which I would be faced as a game warden in the heart of one of the major elephant countries in Africa.

Ripon Falls

CHAPTER 4

Revelations

I THINK it was when the train clattered slowly over the long bridge across the historic River Nile, at Jinja, on the morning of the 8th of November 1949, that I was first really conscious of feeling that I was entering a new life and I recalled the words of Sir Richard Burton: 'Of the gladdest moments in human life, methinks, is the departure upon a distant journey into unknown lands . . . man feels once more happy. The blood flows with the fast circulation of childhood. . . . Afresh dawns the morn of life . . .'*

On our left, sparkling in the brilliant sunshine, were the gleaming rapids of the Ripon Falls, where Lake Victoria spilled over its containing rim to form the mighty river that wanders majestically northwards through Uganda, the Sudan and Egypt, until it finally enters the Mediterranean Sea on the northernmost shores of the African Continent – a journey of over four thousand miles, the longest river in the world.

The foaming, white waters of the rapids were dotted with leaping fish – barbus, the close cousin of the great Indian mahseer, seeking their spawning grounds in Lake Victoria, as they had done for countless years. As they jumped high through the drifting spray, they reminded me of salmon fighting their way against the turbulent waters of some broad Scottish river, a thought that must have occurred to the famous explorer, John Hanning

* Sir Richard Burton, Journal entry, 2nd December 1856.

Speke, when he first set eyes on the Ripon Falls on the 28th of July 1862, and realised that, at last, he had discovered the source of the Nile.

Leaving the river, the lush greenness of Buganda closed softly round us, a land of banana trees, tall elephant grass, broad papyrus swamps, dense rain-forest and humid heat. The contrast with the greys and browns, the arid thorn-scrub and dry savannah of Kenya, was striking. We had reached a new land.

The previous three months had been sad ones for us. My family and I had been happy on the Kenya Coast, how happy we had only realised when the news of my new appointment had arrived and the slow parting had begun. We had made many good friends on the coast and the first we had wanted to tell were the Game Warden of Kenya, Captain Archie Ritchie, and his charming and gracious wife, Queenie. The Ritchies were then living at Malindi, in the north of Kilifi District, in a typical beach house overlooking the blue sea and the reef; it was there I had gone to say good-bye.

The rough road through the dense coastal bush had ended in a graceful clump of casuarina trees that sighed gently in the cool, on-shore breeze. In their shade the long, low bungalow had seemed to nestle like a sleeping animal. Through the wispy branches of the casuarinas I had been able to see the breakers crashing on the outer reef, the deep aquamarine of the translucent, curling waves, their frilly lips sparkling in the bright sunlight, turning to seething white foam as they hurled themselves on the jagged coral, the roar and hush of their passing muted by distance.

As I had approached the wide verandah, a fat and aged dachshund had risen wheezily on its short, bandy legs, wrinkling its greying muzzle to reveal worn, yellow fangs in a silent snarl, before waddling slowly into the house. Then came the yelps, high-pitched, querulous and resentful. 'Dog Trog' had always been allergic to strangers.

'Shut *up*, Trog!' a voice had roared from the dark interior, and with a last defiant yelp, the dachshund had galloped into the garden at a speed that belied its age, closely followed by a massive, sun-tanned, white-haired figure clad in faded blue shorts and an old pair of gym shoes.

'*Hullo*, Bruce!' the bronzed giant had boomed. 'What's the news?'

51

'I made it, Archie,' I had said, settling myself into an old, leather armchair from which the big man had forcibly removed a loudly protesting lilac-breasted roller.

'Now Chirpy, keep *quiet* – or I won't catch you any more grasshoppers. Sorry, Bruce! That damned bird acts as if he owns the house. Sometimes I think he may be right! You were saying?'

'I got the job, thanks to your recommendations.'

'Nonsense. You're just the person for it. Well done and congratulations!' His bright blue eyes had twinkled with genuine pleasure.

Archie Ritchie, was a big man in every way. With his mane of white hair, his bristling white moustache, and his massive, powerful frame, he had always reminded me of a cross between an old and regal lion and a majestic bull elephant. At that time it had been hard to believe that he, the 'Grand Old Man' of East African game, was on the brink of retirement through ill-health.

A few weeks later, as the train rumbled slowly through the Mabira Forest, the tall, dense, tropical rain-forest that lies between Jinja and Kampala, a region which I remembered was the home of such rarities as the beautifully coloured but deadly gaboon viper and the equally venomous Jameson's green mamba, I was reminded of Archie's parting words.

'Charles Pitman's a very old friend of mine,' Archie had said. 'His chief interest is snakes. As a matter of fact he's a world authority. Take him some specimens and he'll be your friend for life!'

I had followed Archie Ritchie's advice; few people who knew him didn't, for he was a great man, a *very* great man. His career had been colourful enough to inspire even the most cynically minded, let alone a romantically-inclined brother Celt like myself, and as my own life entered a new phase I found myself recalling what I knew of his.

Archibald Thomas Ayres Ritchie had been born near Dublin in the year 1890. Blessed with a fine physique, a brilliant brain, and with a silver spoon planted firmly in his mouth, it was not long before he revealed that he also had a strong character and a likeable personality; and over the years he made good use of the generous physical and material talents with which he had been endowed.

At Harrow, he became head of the school and captain of the shooting eight, as well as excelling on the rugby field. At Mag-

Doyen of East Africa's Game Wardens—
the late Captain Archie Ritchie with lilac-breasted roller

dalen College, Oxford, he became President of the Junior Common Room and, shortly before the start of the First World War, he left the University with an honours degree in zoology.

When War broke out Archie enlisted in the famous French Foreign Legion, with whom he fought in France until, in 1915, 'Caporal Ritchie' was commissioned in the equally famous Grenadier Guards of the British Army. That year he was wounded at Loos, and again on the Somme in 1916, and yet again near Ypres in 1917. For his exploits he was mentioned in despatches, awarded the Military Cross, and made a Chevalier of the Légion d'Honneur.

In his memoirs, *Winds of Change*, Harold Macmillan tells how he and another badly wounded officer of the Brigade of Guards were evacuated from the great Battle of the Somme, on the night of the 15th of September 1916. Severely wounded though they were, these two gallant Guards' Officers dismissed their stretcher-bearers – to save them from the intense shelling – and, alone and unaided, staggered and crawled their way back in the dark. Macmillan describes his companion as – 'an officer by the name of Ritchie, commonly known as "Dog" Ritchie, who subsequently became a distinguished game warden in Kenya.'

It was nearly twenty years after I went to Uganda that I read this story, but on that day in November 1949, while the train puffed slowly but steadily on through the Mabira Forest towards Kampala, I thought a lot about Archie Ritchie's long and impressive subsequent career as a game warden. He did more for wildlife in East Africa than any other single person. A game warden's job is to protect animals from humans and humans from animals – and the humans are always the more awkward side of any game problem. However, Archie had a knack of handling people, of all kinds. I once saw him deflate a pompous and very senior government official in a matter of seconds, with a few pithy and biting observations, when the man was being thoroughly nasty at an important conference that Archie and I were attending. In contrast, I remember seeing a tough and very angry farmer, with a very real grievance, go into Archie's office in Nairobi threatening to tear him apart unless he got immediate satisfaction. Half an hour later he came out beaming and saying 'old Archie's a grand chap!' although all Archie had done for him was to persuade him that he didn't really have a grievance at all! Archie had a silver tongue when he wanted to use it and he always kept an old bongo-skin bag by the side of his desk. He referred to it as his 'medicine bag'. It contained two glasses and what he called 'Dr Ritchie's miracle cure for dissatisfied customers' – a large bottle of gin! The combination worked wonders.

By the time the train pulled fussily into Kampala station, to the accompaniment of hissing clouds of steam and the welcoming shouts of barefooted, khaki-clad African porters, I was keyed-up and expectant. Followed by my wife, Elizabeth, our five year old daughter, Bydie, two large Labrador dogs – one black, one yellow – and a mountain of mixed baggage, I stepped nonchalantly onto the platform, at least as nonchalantly as I could with a seven-pound sweet-jar of assorted, pickled snakes under each arm!

In a second I was surrounded by a struggling throng of eager dusky faces as the owners pushed and fought for my custom and the privilege of carrying my travel-worn boxes. Suddenly, as if struck by a lightning-bolt, they fell back, eyes wide, mouths agape, quivering fingers pointing at my chest to a mounting chorus of horrified grunts.

For a moment I was puzzled, then the light dawned and the devil entered my soul. With a dramatic gesture, like some pagan high-priest offering up a ritual sacrifice, I thrust the jars of tightly-coiled, multi-coloured serpents towards the ring of nervous, troubled faces and uttered the one word – *mchawi*!

At the sound of this dreaded word, the name for the most evil type of African witch-doctor, there was instant silence and the porters recoiled as if stung. Puzzled at the ever-broadening grin on my face, they continued to stare at me doubtfully. Then, all at once, the penny dropped. Realising that their legs had been slyly pulled, with a crescendo of high-pitched guffaws the porters doubled up and danced around, slapping their thighs in delight, before descending on me *en masse* to seize my luggage.

Fighting my way through the milling throng, still grimly clutching my seven-pound sweet-jars and followed closely by my anxious family, I came face to face with a tall, familiar figure. Captain Pitman was standing, staring in surprise at the strange scene. On his face was a look of bewilderment.

'Hullo, sir!' I said breathlessly. 'I brought you these. Archie Ritchie said you would like them,' I added hopefully, showing him the sweet-jars, like a small child offering a Christmas present.

Charles Pitman stared at the snakes and at me in undisguised astonishment, then he broke into a roar of laughter. 'Good old Archie!' he said eventually. 'And thank *you*, Bruce, for your trouble. That's a fine specimen of a boomslang you have there, and a lot of other useful material I think. Where did you get them?'

'Around Kilifi,' I replied proudly. 'We were doing a lot of bush clearing.'

'You collected them yourself?'

'Some of them,' I answered guardedly. 'But I also had a tame snake-charmer, or snake *catcher* rather. He was a Giriama who seemed to be able to call them up!'

I thought it best not to add that after an unpleasant experience in the Burmese jungle, during the war with the Japanese, when I was bitten by a snake and came close to losing my life, I had become allergic to serpents in any shape or form. However, following Archie Ritchie's advice, before I left Kilifi I had steeled myself to collect some specimens to please my new boss, although the cold, clinging clutch of the writhing coils of every snake I handled sent icy shivers up my spine. At last Mohammed bin Ali had come to my rescue.

Mohammed bin Ali was an old friend of mine. He was an elderly Arab who ran a small trading store in the tiny, dusty trading centre of Bamba, in the hinterland of Kilifi District, surrounded by the interminable Nyika – the arid waste-land of tangled thorn-scrub and sharp-spined succulents, that stretched far beyond the hazy horizon in all directions. He traded *posho** and sugar, beans and salt, *pangas*† and hoes, cooking pots, cloth, and other essentials of life in the bush, for cattle hides and goat skins, charcoal and – I suspected – the odd elephant tusk, rhino horn or leopard skin brought in by wandering Waliangulu poachers.

On my last safari to Bamba, I had sat with Mohammed bin Ali on the shady verandah of his wooden store, drinking hot, sweet tea mixed with thick condensed milk and flavoured with cinnamon, while we exchanged local gossip and discussed our

* Mealie-meal.
† Broad-bladed slashing knives.

Masha Makatha, the author's Giriama Tribal Police orderly and gun-bearer with a monster puff-adder

mutual problems. Outside, in the dusty, sun-scorched road, naked, brown-skinned children had stared at us in wide-eyed interest.

In the dark interior of the store, from the corrugated iron roof of which the heat was reflected in shimmering waves, three nubile young Giriama girls, their satiny bronze skins and plump, round breasts shining with excitement and sweat, had chattered like magpies as they fingered a pile of gaily-patterned kikois. Giggling self-consciously while they displayed their choice, they had draped themselves coyly in the brightly coloured cloths before posing provocatively for the benefit of their admiring audience of young men, who leant against the rough, wooden counter in attitudes of studied carelessness. Alone in its misery, unaffected by the warm, sensual atmosphere and the arch glances of the dusky sirens, a mangy cur, little more than a living skeleton, had sat on a heap of sun-dried hides, surrounded by piled sacks of charcoal, its eyes half closed, scratching incessantly at its tortured skin. The scene had been a vignette of the old, unsophisticated Africa and as such it had remained fixed in my mind.

'Why are you leaving us, Effendi?' Mohammed bin Ali had asked me sadly, when I had told him, that I was moving to Uganda in a few weeks' time.

'So you prefer animals to people?' Mohammed had queried severely, after I had replied that I was joining the Game Department. Such an all-consuming interest in the beasts of the field was something that no true Arab found easy to understand. A spirited horse, or a good riding camel – they were different; or even a falcon, or a saluki which, after all, was not really a dog as everyone knew; all these had been honoured in the country of his ancestors, but the massive beasts of the African bush, whose throats were often too big to be cut in the manner required by strict Moslem rites – well, they fell in a different category altogether!

I had tried to explain that his assumption was not strictly correct, but that as I had been raised as a hunter the call was irresistible. Mohammed had nodded sagely, pretending out of courtesy to comprehend, and I had then gone on to tell him of my snake-collecting problem.

'With that I can help you, Effendi,' the old Arab had smiled, adjusting the finely embroidered Moslem cap on his head with one lean, brown hand as he waved the other towards the interior of the store and shouted 'Charo!' in a stentorian voice.

Out of the shadows had appeared an ancient, wizened Giriama clad in tattered shorts and a faded khaki shirt. Despite his age his eyes were bright and intelligent. At a word from Mohammed, he had slipped a hand inside his dusty shirt to produce a small, black, wriggling snake, clasped firmly behind its head.

'Charo is a *fundi** with snakes,' Mohammed had said simply.

Recovering from my surprise, I had asked the old Giriama if he would collect snakes for me. 'It is *most* important that their heads are undamaged,' I had emphasised, speaking in Kiswahili.

The old man had looked at me pityingly, his bright eyes glistening with tolerant amusement, his jaws working slowly and rhythmically as he chewed on a quid of strong tobacco. 'I will bring them to you alive, Bwana,' he had said in a husky voice. 'And if you wish to kill them it is simple – See!' As he spoke he had pressed the snake firmly behind the head with a horny finger and thumb forcing its jaws to gape wide, revealing the sharp poison fangs. Then, with a quick jerk of his chin and lips he had sent a thin stream of dark brown tobacco juice straight into the gaping mouth of the twisting serpent.

For a moment the snake had writhed as the nicotine took effect, but in a few seconds it was still, and with the triumphant flourish of a conjuror concluding a dramatic trick, the old man had tossed the limp and lifeless body at my feet. From then on, and for my last few weeks in Kilifi District, Charo had become my professional snake catcher.

My tale delighted Charles Pitman. 'Pity you didn't bring Charo with you!' he chuckled, as we climbed into his car outside Kampala railway station and set off for Entebbe, Uganda's administrative capital on the shores of Lake Victoria. Closely followed by our dogs and baggage and three uniformed game guards, all piled high on a government lorry driven by Paulo, an enormous, coal-black Acholi, we wove our way slowly and carefully through milling hordes of bicycles.

A Baganda bicycle seldom carries less than two persons – one usually a fat woman in long, flowing robes who is looped, buttocks bulging, over the cross-bar, or as dead-weight over the groaning back wheel – and at least one enormous bunch of green bananas

* Expert or highly skilled artisan.

that sways and thumps between the rider's knees. This clumsy load, combined with the obstructing bulk of the fat lady, forces the bicycle's rider to peddle with his legs straddled so far apart that he looks as if he were suffering agonies from some painful and unmentionable complaint.

The sight of these swarms of over-loaded, Baganda-owned bicycles blocking the road was too much for Paulo, who had driven an armoured carrier during the war. Leaning out of his cab to bellow imprecations and abuse in guttural Lwo, echoed by the furious, fist-shaking game guards on the back – Acholi like himself who had served in the war – with horn blowing constantly at full blast, and deviating not one inch from his chosen path, he drove his lorry straight through the milling throng. Not until Charles Pitman turned his car onto the open road to Entebbe did the noise and the tumult fade into the distance behind us; and only then could normal conversation be resumed.

'As you can see there's a certain amount of inter-tribal rivalry in Uganda,' Captain Pitman observed dryly as we gathered speed, a remark which seemed to me to be the understatement of the year. 'Very roughly, the Nile divides the Nilotic tribes of the north from the Bantu of the south,' he continued, commencing a colourful running commentary that lasted all the way to Entebbe and was so full of interest and dry humour that I remember it vividly to this day. 'The northerners think that the southern tribes are soft and decadent, and the southerners regard the darker-skinned northern tribes as being uncivilised and ignorant. Both views are based mainly on prejudice arising from their very different social customs and background. Neither side is really right about the other!

'Some of our most astute politicians, as well as many of our best soldiers, come from the north. On the other hand, very much the same could be said of our southerners! The north is certainly a much harsher country and living conditions there are more difficult; that encourages initiative and breeds a hardy race, although the Acholi are warriors by tradition in any case. Life in the south is easy by comparison, but the Baganda peasants are by no means soft and they don't lack shrewdness and intelligence. Furthermore, they are proud of their history. When Speke and Grant reached Buganda in 1862 – the first Europeans to do so – they were astonished to find that the Baganda were, even then,

well organised and comparatively civilised, with their own hereditary king, the 'Kabaka'. We have some excellent Baganda game
guards and, in my opinion, anyone who makes a regular habit
of riding a bicycle for twenty miles or more a day, in hilly country,
loaded up with a fat woman and heavy bunches of bananas, can
hardly be described as soft!'

Charles Pitman then began to reminisce about Archie Ritchie.
'Like all game wardens I know,' he said, 'Archie has a deep-seated
aversion to bureaucracy and for twenty-five years he has fought
a successful diplomatic guerilla action against small-minded
officials who have tried, time and again, to 'clip the wings' of the
Kenya Game Department. A good many of these attacks have
been based on petty jealousy – green-eyed envy of the aura of
romantic glamour with which the general public surrounds any
game department – but some of them have been directed at
Archie himself. His opinions carry considerable weight in very
influential international political and scientific circles, where it's
not forgotten that he's an honours graduate in zoology and speaks
with the authority conferred by many years of wide practical
experience. In fact, his prestige and influence have often been an
embarrassment to senior government bureaucrats, some of whom
regard him as a threat to their own authority and a major obstacle
to their policies and plans!

'A few years ago certain high officials of the Kenya Secretariat
decided that it was high time that the Game Department, the
black sheep of the Civil Service flock, was brought properly into
the bureaucratic fold. The first phase of their plan to reform the
non-conformist organisation, and curb its rebellious tendencies,
was to remove the Game Department's headquarters from its
historic old raised wooden building, I think you know the one I
mean? It's tucked away on a secluded hill in Nairobi, next to
the Coryndon Museum, partly hidden behind a thin screen of
blue gum trees. Instead they arranged for the Department's
headquarters to be installed in a modern, streamlined, soulless
office-block surrounded by real, died-in-the-wool civil servants –
loyal, sober and reliable men who studied, filed and implemented
official instructions with meticulous care, instead of using them
to light a camp-fire on a rainy night in the bush before they'd even
been read – or worse, on occasions, before they'd even been
removed from their buff official envelopes!

'The game rangers were horror-struck at the idea. Archie himself, who realised the sinister intentions and ulterior motives behind this menacing proposal, was particularly incensed and concerned at the plan. He called it "genocide for the Game Department" and he resisted it for as long as he could, using every stratagem in the book – and a few more that he had learnt during his service in the Legion. But he was up against "the big guns"; the "top brass" in the Civil Service formed into a solid phalanx, determined to assert their authority. They were out for Archie's blood and they were not going to let him thwart their plan to bring the Game Department to heel. Finally, the Chief Secretary, furious at being defied for so long, gave him a direct, personal order to move – or else! But he had underestimated Archie Ritchie!'

'What happened?' I prompted.

Charles Pitman chuckled 'Obeying his orders to the letter, Archie moved all his office furniture, files and books into the new building. Then he opened the old trophy stores behind the Game Department office and loaded their contents on to two three-ton lorries. It was the accumulation of years, most of it junk and much of it pretty smelly junk at that! Badly-cured buffalo hides, partly eaten by rats and insects; pieces of rotten elephant tusk, unsaleable in the ivory auctions; sacks of badly-cured, mildewed, sun-dried game meat, confiscated from poachers and awaiting destruction after being used as evidence in court cases; other sacks of rotting, half-cooked game meat being held as exhibits in poaching cases that were still pending; piles of rusty wire snares, massive steel gin-traps, and bows with arrows the tips of which were still thickly coated with black, tarry-looking acokanthera poison – all this and more he took with him and dumped in the narrow corridors of the hygienic office-block, outside the door of his new, poky little office. Then he settled himself behind his shiny new desk, took the bottle of gin out of his bongo-skin bag, poured himself a stiff drink, and awaited results!

'It wasn't long before his telephone was ringing and people were banging at his door. Irate civil servants, their olfactory senses outraged by the mounting stench in the narrow confines of the new building, their ankles cut and bruised and their trousers soiled and torn by the coils of jagged wire snares and the gaping, sharp-toothed jaws of rusty gin-traps piled in the dark corridors, angrily demanded that the offending objects be re-moved. Archie blandly replied that he was very sorry but this would not be possible. Most of the items had to be immediately available, he said, for study or reference purposes, for the pre-paration of court cases, and for other work that formed an im-portant part of the duties of the Game Department – and, as everyone could see, and as he had protested all along, there was *nowhere* in his new office where he could store them.

'After two days a steady stream of furious, complaining letters began to circulate around the Secretariat like a swarm of angry hornets. And within one week Archie Ritchie received an urgent, written instruction from the Chief Secretary himself, personally ordering him to move back to his old office immediately!

'I thought that story would appeal to you,' Charles Pitman grinned as we wiped tears of mirth from our eyes. 'But you'll find that it also contains some valuable warnings that will be of help to you in your new job, Bruce. You'll soon discover that the general public has a very distorted idea of the life of a game ranger. Most people think that it's one long, glorious, camping holiday in the bush, with shooting and fishing ad lib and occa-sional exciting encounters with poachers to add a little more zest to an already Utopian existence, free of any serious respon-sibility. The popular attitude is one of envy that a game ranger not only has all this, but is even *paid* for it as well! Sometimes the envy is mixed with a certain grudging admiration, for which one can thank the influence of the over-dramatised films and books of today.

'Even the average civil servant, and certainly those who have spent a long time away from field stations, seems to forget at times that a game ranger is on duty twenty-four hours a day and seven days a week; that he often has to live and work under conditions of extreme discomfort and sometimes real physical danger; that he usually has to operate on his own far from any source of physical aid or moral support; that he's frequently away from his family and home comforts for weeks at a time; and that he belongs to one of the most poorly paid branches of the govern-ment service.

'To virtually all game rangers and wardens their work's a vocation worth a good many sacrifices, and most cynically-minded governments are not slow to take advantage of this

S.R.

63

fact when it comes to fixing salary scales, for there's never any shortage of applicants for jobs in game departments. And as a fair number of the more senior posts are filled by ex-army officers, they are widely regarded as sinecures for retired members of the armed services who are comfortably off and merely want a little light work to occupy their time between the club and the golf-course!

'You may think I'm exaggerating,' Charles Pitman said severely, 'but I can assure you I'm not. The Uganda Game Department for one, has a good many very good friends and willing allies among the members of all government departments – more particularly those who are in the field – and we would indeed find it difficult to manage without their valuable help, but there's still a high percentage of the more hide-bound government officials who dislike the Game Department and seem to think that it can and should operate exactly the same as any other governmental department. These are the type who cannot get away from the idea that a civil servant normally works in an office on a fixed schedule from eight till five, with an hour's break for lunch and regular tea intervals to clear his brain and refresh his flagging energies. They are the ones who look down their noses and write "stiff" reminders, with hints of "disciplinary action" to follow, when a game ranger fails to submit his routine returns on time, in quadruplicate, and signed and witnessed in strict accordance with regulations.

'These are the hard-core bureaucrats who are quite unable to take into account that poachers and shamba-raiding elephants don't work to a time and date schedule,' Charles Pitman went on grimly. 'They just cannot visualise the exasperating burden that official returns can be to a game ranger in the field. When the average civil servant is sitting in a comfortable office, with a clerk diligently preparing the necessary documents for his signature, the wretched game ranger may well be huddled in a small, leaky tent in the bush, with the rain deluging down outside, squatting on a kerosene tin, frustrated, wet and exhausted, vainly trying to battle with sodden official forms and damp carbon paper in the dim light of a smoking hurricane-lantern. And more than likely he'll be anything up to a hundred miles from the nearest postal facilities, having been called out, at a moment's notice, to deal with a herd of elusive, rampaging elephants that have retired into dense bush after destroying much of the food-crops of an entire village.

'I remember Archie Ritchie telling me how he was once pestered with irate official letters demanding an explanation for the delay in submitting Jack Bonham's vehicle log-book. At the time Jack Bonham, who was the Game Ranger of the Coast Province, was way up on the Tana River, miles from anywhere, dealing with elephant who were troubling the Pokomo. Eventually, Archie sent him a police signal via Garissa, which was finally delivered by a runner sent by the District Commissioner. Jack, whose lorry had got stuck in the flooded Tana, leaving him temporarily stranded, wirelessed in reply "Full fathoms five my log-book lies. New one in pressure-cooker". That went up on the board in Archie's office among other classic messages, while the bureaucrats howled for Jack Bonham's head on a charger!

'You see,' Charles Pitman smiled, 'you just cannot expect a game department to conform exactly with all the rigid procedures that are designed to ensure the better administration of more conventional government organisations, but which are often a positive hindrance to a game department's work. By the very nature of its duties, it's essential that a game department should retain its individuality and freedom of action and not lose its identity by being swallowed up in an amorphous body like the Civil Service. The morale of his men in the field must be the Game Warden's primary concern, for they are often operating under very difficult and frustrating conditions and get small recognition for their efforts. In consequence, he's forced to spend a lot of his time trying to protect his game rangers from the petty slings and arrows of unimaginative officialdom.'

Charles Pitman sighed. 'I remember the outcry when the Uganda Game Department was started in 1924. It was referred to then, by many outraged people, as a "stunt" department, a waste of the tax-payer's money! In fact, it was created to deal primarily with the very serious elephant control problem – it was called the "Elephant Control Department" initially – and over the quarter of a century of its existence it has actually paid for itself several times over from the sale of elephant-control ivory alone. But the official attitude to the Department has remained very much the same, which is pretty clearly revealed by the status accorded to its officers in Government Standing Orders.'

Seeing my puzzled expression, Charles Pitman smiled again. 'Perhaps I should explain,' he said. 'On the whole, the Colonial Civil Service is a surprisingly efficient organisation and, despite its human weaknesses, it has done a remarkably good job with very little money, although you wouldn't think so if you believed all the sarcastic abuse that's heaped on its head by its detractors, most of whom have never been anywhere near Africa and have gained their so-called knowledge from the mouths of political agitators. However, in some ways the Colonial Service can certainly be regarded as archaic. For instance, its formal dress-uniform is Victorian and would look more appropriate in a Gilbert and Sullivan opera; while its rules of protocol are truly feudal. At the head of the table, as it were, are the senior officers of the Administrative Service – the Chief Secretary and other worthy and exalted officers of the Secretariat, and the Provincial and District Commissioners; they are the "chosen few" – the "lords", the "barons" and the "knights" – the local representatives of His Majesty the King. Then, descending in order of precedence, come the heads of various "important" departments, followed by the Deputy Commissioners of this and the Assistant Directors of that. Finally, well "below the salt", right among the yeomen and serfs at the bottom of the table, as it were, one comes to the Government Printer and the Game Warden, sitting side by side!

'You can guess that this theoretical status doesn't give game wardens and their rangers many sleepless nights, but they do resent the fact that it's reflected in the scale of pay that's considered to be appropriate to their official station in life. And when it comes to honours and awards – what that famous professional cynic, Malcolm Muggeridge, once described as "the school colours of later life" – the game departments are at the wrong end of the bread-line. Presumably, as with their pay, the official attitude is that their work in itself is sufficient reward; and, strangely enough, I believe that most game wardens and rangers secretly share this view! Anyway, the net result is that there is a tremendous *esprit de corps* in the game departments, who regard themselves as being an exclusive force little more than *attached*

to the Civil Service for the convenience of government administration!

'Well, I seem to have been lecturing you rather a lot,' Charles
Pitman said, with a laugh, 'but I'm certain it will help you when
you come to have dealings with the Secretariat and various
government departments here. Changing the subject, you'll
all be staying with us, my dear,' he said, turning to Elizabeth,
'until your new home is ready. We have a pleasant little house,
overlooking the Botanical Gardens and Lake Victoria, and I'm
sure you'll be comfortable there.' As he spoke, the car topped a
rise and there before us was a placid bay, its limpid, reed-fringed
waters shining blue in the late afternoon sun. Through the trees,
surrounded by beds of gay flowers and bright green lawns sloping
down to the lake, was a small, white bungalow.

An elderly African, in khaki uniform, greeted us courteously
as we arrived. 'This is John Tamusange, my gun-bearer,' said
Captain Pitman, by way of introduction. 'Take the Game Warden's rifles and lock them in the store, please John,' he instructed.
I started; 'the Game Warden', he had said. The words gave me an
unexpected thrill of pleasure. I really was a game warden at last!

*

On his retirement, a year later, after twenty-five years as Game
Warden of Uganda, in the 1950 'Birthday Honours List' Captain
Pitman was awarded the C.B.E. to add to his D.S.O. and M.C. –
decorations which he had earned for gallantry as a soldier. When I
congratulated him on the well-deserved recognition of his work,
I could not resist reminding him of his remarks about people who
had served with game departments very seldom ever being considered for honours and awards. In his reply he commented
dryly that, although he was reluctant to disillusion me, in fact,
he had been awarded the C.B.E. primarily for his work during the
war years, 1941 to 1946, when he had been seconded from the
Game Department to act as Director of Security Intelligence in
Uganda!

In the same year, Archie Ritchie also retired, after twenty-
seven years as Game Warden of Kenya. For more than twenty
years he had campaigned incessantly for the establishment of
inviolable wildlife sanctuaries, but without losing his sense of
proportion. None knew better than he that game also had to be

controlled, for if it was allowed to become a nuisance public and official support for its conservation would be lost. Finally, in 1946, his persistent efforts had been rewarded for, in December of that year, Kenya's first national game park was gazetted, followed very shortly by several more, including the famous Tsavo National Park in the great elephant country of the Nyika. They were the first true national parks in the British territories of East and Central Africa.

Typical of his selfless attitude, after working for so many years for the creation of national parks, when this aim was achieved Archie Ritchie declined to take charge of them. He felt that, at that time, when national parks were in their infancy, and much private apathy and official opposition had only just been overcome after a long struggle, national parks would be in a stronger position if divorced from direct government control. So Archie withdrew tactfully into the background, leaving the field to his friend and compatriot Mervyn Cowie, who had been one of the most active leaders in the final stages of the campaign to establish national parks in Kenya.

When he finally retired four years later, in 1950, Archie Ritchie deliberately faded even further into the background of wildlife affairs. He must have realised that any successor would have a hard task to fill the enormous gap created by the removal of his own powerful and respected personality. So he withdrew quietly to his peaceful home on the Kenya coast, with his years of devoted service for the conservation of wildlife in Africa apparently not officially recognised. But, despite his self-effacement, he continued to be a major influence behind the scenes in wildlife matters, never forcing his opinions or thrusting himself into the limelight, but always readily available for those who sought his wise counsel and astute guidance, as I myself did on many occasions.

In 1959, when Sir Evelyn Baring – the Governor of Kenya – got into difficulties while rescuing an Indian girl from drowning at Malindi, Archie Ritchie, then in bad health with a weak heart, plunged to their help through heavy seas. But for this gallant act, by a man who had been ordered to avoid exertion of any kind, the Governor of Kenya and the young Indian girl might have lost their lives. For his courageous deed Archie received the Queen's Commendation for Bravery.

When Archie Ritchie died in 1962, at his own wish he was

buried at sea, beyond the thundering waves of the coral reef, in the deep, blue waters of the Indian Ocean, within sight of his last home among the whispering casuarina trees that he loved so much. To the end he remained the undisputed oracle, the 'Grand Old Man' of East African wildlife; and the great national parks of Kenya, with their teeming herds of tranquil game, remain as a living monument to the memory of one of Africa's greatest game wardens.

CHAPTER 5

Pearls and Pachyderms

In 1949, when I first arrived in Entebbe, the capital of the lush and beautiful land which the famous Emin Pasha, escaping from the arid Sudan, described as 'the pearl among the countries all round here', the Uganda Game Department was still only a department in miniature faced with a gigantic task and quite inadequate staff, equipment and funds to meet its steadily mounting commitments, responsibilities and problems. At that time, for the whole country – an area the size of the British Isles – there was a total field force of only two permanent European game rangers, forty-four African game guards, eight game scouts, and seven gun-bearers. A third European game ranger was under training and there was one temporary game ranger – an experienced Asian hunter – employed on special buffalo control duties.

There was no separate national parks organisation, nor were there any national parks as such; but for the development and supervision of Uganda's fourteen thousand square miles of lake fisheries, the Department did have two recently recruited European fisheries officers and forty African fish guards. Finally, the headquarters' staff at Entebbe consisted of the Game Warden, myself in the newly created post of Assistant Game Warden, one Asian head clerk of many years' service, two African clerks, and two lower grade African office workers somewhat euphemistically described as 'clerical assistants'. The 'turn of the tide' did not really become apparent until towards the end of 1951.

Even now, the average layman has a very hazy and sometimes distorted idea of the nature and extent of the problems with which game departments in Africa are faced; nor does the general public always appreciate that the fluctuating fortunes of wild animal life are closely interwoven with the long term process of human development. In fact, to really understand even the necessity for the existence of a government game department in virtually every African country, as well as to be able to grasp the difficult and diverse nature of its work, it is essential, in each and every case, to have a clear picture of the country concerned – its topography; the characteristics, way of life, population densities, and particularly the distribution of its peoples; and even something of its history; as well as the numbers and varieties of wild animals to be found within its boundaries. Nowadays there is a better general understanding of these things, thanks to books, films and television, but twenty years ago when I wrote home to my relations and friends, telling them that I had forsaken all else to follow the stony path of a game warden's life, many of them wrote back saying 'Congratulations, but what do you have to do?' It would almost have been easier if they had asked what a game warden did *not* have to do!

In modern, scientific jargon a game warden's job is summarised in the term 'Wildlife Management'. Reduced to its simplest terms wildlife management is the science of keeping animals and humans out of each other's hair. In fact, this is an over-simplification for it also involves such matters as the artificial and carefully calculated control of wild animal numbers, and even the manipulation of their habitat.

However, many of the basic principles of wildlife management have been known and practised since time immemorial without the reasons for them always being clearly understood. Some are enshrined in the age-old traditions, taboos and codes of venery. Only in recent years has modern science become involved. Hither-to, in parts of Africa and a few other fortunate regions of the world, space and sheer weight of animal numbers have often – but unfortunately by no means always – been sufficient to absorb a good many of the more irresponsible and thoughtless attacks on wild animal populations.

Today it is recognised that although overcrowding of any given species finally inhibits its breeding, by the time this climax has been reached the species concerned may already have caused irreparable damage to its own habitat and that of other species also. Natural controls, such as normal predation, disease and shortage of food or water, may not always be sufficient to brake or halt the process in time. This is particularly the case with large, long-living, steady-breeding, wide-ranging, highly adaptable and immensely destructive species such as the elephant which, after a very early age, has no natural enemies except man, and is also remarkably resistant – and often immune – to most epizootic diseases. These factors, aggravated by the elephant's natural instinct to roam vast distances in search of food, variety of diet, essential minerals, and water, and the steady occupation of more and more of the previous range of this mighty pachyderm by man's exploding population, for the past fifty years or more have produced a steadily increasing and ever present problem in Uganda in particular – the problem of elephant control.

To the peripatetic visitor to Africa's spectacular game parks and reserves, the elephant, usually observed from the compara-tive safety of a comfortable car, is an exciting, interesting and lovable animal. But to the peasant farmer that same elephant, when it wilfully crosses the reserve boundary to feast upon fields of maize and millet, cotton or cassava, or plantations of bananas, is nothing more than a dangerous menace – public enemy number one.

*

Straddling the equator, Uganda is a little larger than the total land area of the United Kingdom of Great Britain and Northern Ireland, or the American states of Utah or Kansas. Nearly fourteen thousand square miles – or over one-seventh of its total area – are water, for Uganda is liberally endowed with lakes, swamps and rivers of all sizes and shapes, including the mighty, life-giving Nile. Yet, despite its comparative smallness, Uganda encompasses an extraordinary variety of country and vegetation, from the cold, misty tops of forest-clad, snow-capped mountains – the romantic Ruwenzori, Ptolemy's 'Mountains of the Moon' of ancient legend, rising to heights of over sixteen thousand feet above sea level – to the lushness and humid, tropical heat of the western Rift Valley whose floor drops down to an altitude of only two thousand feet; from the rolling, grassy savannah and thorn-scrub semi-desert of the wild country bordering the southern Sudan, to the dense, verdant rain forests, which are the extremity of the great tropical forest belt that extends eastwards across the waist of Africa from the near impenetrable jungles of the Congo to the shores of Victoria Nyanza, a lake the size of Ireland and the second largest in the world.

As can be imagined this diversity of terrain and climate provides ecological conditions suited to a bewildering variety of fauna, both large and small, from the mighty African elephant – occasionally standing as much as eleven feet or more at the shoulder and sometimes weighing upwards of six tons – to the tiny, wide-eyed Demidoff's galago, or bushbaby, one of the smallest of the primates, which can nestle in the palm of your hand. And there are three great beasts of particular rarity and interest – the giant (or Lord Derby's) eland, the largest and most magnificent of the antelopes; the massive white rhinoceros, the second largest of the land mammals; and man's nearest relative in the animal kingdom, the great, shaggy mountain gorilla from the mist-swathed, bamboo-clad slopes of the Virunga Volcanoes, the lonely jungle-covered mountains that straddle the border between Uganda and Rwanda. In fact, Uganda can be likened to the hub of a wheel: encircled by the Sudan and Kenya to the north and east – with Ethiopia close by – Tanzania in the south, and Rwanda and the Congo on the south-west and west, Uganda has some of the climate, the topography, the flora and the fauna of each of her neighbours.

In this small country, with its wealth of wildlife, game conservation problems have become increasingly more acute and complex with the rapid increase of the African population resulting from the establishment of 'Pax Britannica' and improved medical services. If you can imagine the states of either Wyoming or Oregon with a human population as big as that of New Jersey, or the state of Kansas with three times its present number of citizens, then you can visualise the difficulty of also fitting into this area an animal population including some 25,000 elephants and probably four times as many buffalo in addition to a multitude of various antelopes, gazelles and other ungulates, plus carnivora and primates. All this, mark you, in a country of just under 94,000 square miles, whose human population of over six and a half million gives it a greater density of persons per square mile than the United States of America!

To understand the picture properly one has to remember that Uganda's wealth of wildlife has long been largely confined to less than half the territory, for the economy of the Republic is mainly dependent on agriculture. Between three and four thousand bales of cotton and some hundred and twenty-five thousand tons of coffee are produced each year, as well as more than a hundred thousand tons of sugar and large quantities of tea, tobacco and other cash crops, while much of the country is cultivated for subsistence crops of bananas or millet, cassava and maize, beans and ground nuts. It is not therefore surprising that the problem of reconciling the basic daily needs of the peasant farmers with the sensible conservation of game has become increasingly difficult and complicated over the years, for the one frequently clashes with the other. In one single area of some fifteen hundred square miles in central Uganda, the elephant population alone has fluctuated between eight and ten thousand animals in recent years, and individual herds as large as twelve hundred and more of these mighty beasts, giving an appearance of an elephants' convention, have actually been counted. This region is surrounded by areas of dense human population and extensive agriculture, and forgetful or malicious elephant or buffalo are frequently in trouble when they, literally, over-step the mark.

The one saving grace in Uganda – from the wildlife point of view – has been the presence, over the years, of *Glossina*, the tsetse fly, the greatest game conservationist in Africa! Tsetse fly still deny a good third of the country to domestic stock, for the protozoal blood parasites – named trypanosomes – carried and transmitted by this biting, blood-sucking fly, cause a disease called *nagana* which is death to other than the wild animals which have developed a hereditary immunity. This is one of the main reasons why spectacular concentrations of many species of game have survived in regions of Uganda which might otherwise have been swamped long ago by rapidly increasing herds of often useless scrub-cattle. However, the tsetse fly is now slowly re-treating before the spread of human habitation, bush-clearing and cultivation, and the march of science, and Uganda's cattle population currently numbers some three and a half million head, with an equivalent number of sheep and goats.

But the tsetse is a tenacious, resilient and insidious foe, a past-master at silent infiltration. Like a determined and well-disci-plined guerilla army, the hosts of the tsetse fly seldom miss an opportunity to invade suitable country, or to re-occupy areas from which they have previously been driven, if the human defences have not been properly consolidated. To carry the mili-tary analogy a stage further, the 'army' of the genus *Glossina* is comprised of a number of specialised species each designed to live and operate efficiently in a given set of physical conditions. Thus, in Uganda, *Glossina morsitans* is the wide-ranging skirmisher, the 'game-fly' of the savannah, the main carrier of *nagana*, while *Glossina palpalis* is the waterside tsetse that lies in ambush in thick cover by rivers, lakes and swamps, and is the chief vector of the type of trypanosome that causes sleeping sickness – the human version of *nagana*. It was *Glossina palpalis* in fact, that was the cause of a human disaster which, in turn, led to the creation of Uganda's elephant control problem.

The late Sir Apolo Kagwa, the great Katikiro (or Prime Minister) of Buganda from 1900 to 1926, is on record as having stated that in pre-European days elephants were not a problem because the various human population groups were more con-centrated – for purposes of self-protection – and also because when elephants dared to appear near cultivation they were remorselessly hunted. The British brought peace, law and order to the land; they introduced medical services and the cultivation of new crops; and they put a stop to the crueller and more destructive traditional methods of killing elephant, such as the long lines of pitfalls, and the terrible technique of ring-firing by which whole herds of elephant were either burnt to death or blinded and so badly injured that they could safely be butchered by serried ranks of eager spearmen.

Sir Harry Johnston, the Protectorate's first Commissioner and a keen naturalist, was particularly concerned at the sorry state of Uganda's elephant herds when he arrived in that country late in December 1899. For years the elephants of East and Central Africa had been slaughtered in their thousands by the Arab slave traders, ruthless, avaricious men who used their newly captured slaves as porters to carry the ivory to the coast, and armed local Africans with muzzle-loading guns to do their hunting for them. The resulting carnage had been terrible. According to my old friend David Blunt*, between 1850 and 1890, nearly 47,000 elephants were killed *annually* in Africa to supply the London ivory market alone, and many more were wounded by the slugs of primitive weapons fired indiscriminately into the frightened, angry herds.

In the latter part of the nineteenth century the brutal slave trade, with all its horrors, had been finally suppressed, and with the passing of this evil traffic in human lives the predatory Arab slavers had slowly disappeared from the scene. But there had been no reprieve for the elephants, for the world's age-old appetite for ivory had remained and hard in the wake of the departing slavers, lured by the inexorable law of demand and supply, had followed a tough and adventurous body of men, mainly Europeans, who were professional elephant hunters. The intensive pursuit of ivory by these determined hunters had come close to sounding the final death knell of the elephant in Uganda – apart from the great herds that then roamed the wild, unadministered and virtually unknown no-man's-land of Karamoja – and one of Sir Harry Johnston's first moves was to enact legislation to curtail severely the previously unrestricted killing of elephant and to create game reserves for their protection in the most heavily hunted areas of Bunyoro and Toro. This alone may have had the desired effect of turning the tide – for the African bush elephant is a remarkably adaptable and resilient animal – but coincidental with the introduction of these protective measures

* Commander D. E. Blunt, R.N. (Rtd); ex-submarine commander of the Royal Navy; ex-Elephant Control Officer, Tanganyika; Honorary Game Warden, Kenya; author of the book *Elephant* – a hunter's classic, published in 1932.

Huge elephant tusks from Uganda, 173 lbs. and 155 lbs.

nature herself also took a hand in a totally unexpected and un-welcome way, by means of the tsetse fly.

At the turn of the century sleeping sickness began to make its presence felt in the newly created Uganda Protectorate and, by 1905, thousands of people were dying from the dread disease. To combat the deadly scourge, Sir Hesketh Bell, the Governor who had succeeded Sir Harry Johnston, took drastic measures. Whole villages and populations were moved permanently from lacustrine and riverine areas in many parts of Uganda, to break the human link with the tsetse flies that transmitted the disease, and even human travel within these areas was severely restricted or banned altogether. As a result, in addition to their newly created reserves, the elephants gained great natural sanctuaries, rich in food and abundant water – in fact the elephant version of 'a land flowing with milk and honey'. And it is not surprising that the elephants – to continue in biblical terms – 'rejoiced and multiplied ex-ceedingly'!

At that time few, if any, responsible people had the slightest conception of the truly remarkable powers of recovery of an elephant population. We now know that if suddenly freed from intensive persecution by man, and offered not only an over-abundance of readily available food and water but also virtually unlimited space in which to roam unmolested, it is possible for populations of the African bush elephant (*Loxodonta africana africana*) to double themselves in as little as ten to twelve years. Admittedly, these are ideal conditions but, thanks to Sir Harry Johnston, the tsetse fly and Sir Hesketh Bell, such conditions existed in several major regions of Uganda during the greater part of the first two decades of the present century. The result was an elephant population explosion of such alarming and disastrous proportions that not only was the economy of the country seriously endangered but the basic livelihood of the people also. In less than twenty years the status of the elephant in Uganda had changed from that of the bulwark of the country's economy, through its ivory, to being not merely a hindrance but a grave and direct threat to the Protectorate's economic development.

*

By about 1920, damage to shambas in Uganda by raiding ele-phants had become so serious and widespread that the authorities were forced to take positive action to remedy the situation. Various money-saving expedients were tried in a desperate endeavour to reduce and control the elephant herds, but all the measures tested were ill-conceived and in most cases only made matters worse. The first experiment was the arming of African peasant farmers to defend themselves. This resulted in large numbers of elephants being wounded, and the herds becoming more troublesome and vicious in consequence, for although the elephant is a big target, its few vital spots are not; furthermore, it is a dangerous animal, particularly when wounded, and the hunting of the elephant is not a suitable task for the poorly-armed, timorous novice. The majority of the peasant farmers shared this view. Few of them were hunters either by tradition or inclination and with typical improvidence they preferred to expend most of their free ammunition on other edible but far safer targets, such as antelope and wild pig. And when they did shoot at an elephant it was, as often as not, at such a range that wounding was almost inevitable.

There was no shortage of experienced elephant hunters in Uganda at that time for many of the old ivory poachers were still in the country. So, when the arming of the peasant farmers proved a dangerous fiasco, the Government tried issuing, to selected professional elephant hunters, bulk permits that author-ised the killing of large numbers of elephants in return for one tusk of each animal shot. This scheme was also a failure. The permit holders were only interested in quick profits and they therefore went for the big ivory and the herds that could be most easily hunted. The latter were seldom the elephants which had been causing trouble by raiding shambas and the net result of these operations was an undesirable loss of heavy tuskers coupled with the driving of innocent herds out of remote, uninhabited regions and towards the cultivated areas that the scheme had been designed to protect.

It was at this stage that the Uganda Government finally, but reluctantly bowed to experienced professional advice. In 1923 three of the old-time European ivory hunters were appointed as game rangers. The following year an 'Elephant Control Depart-ment' was conceived and Captain Keith Caldwell – deputy to Archie Ritchie – was seconded to Uganda to organise the adminis-tration of the new department. Almost immediately he was recalled to Kenya, to take charge of a four-month safari for the then Duke and Duchess of York (later to become King George VI and Queen Elizabeth) who were on their honeymoon. The creation of the Uganda Game Department was thus delayed and only finally came into being in February 1925, when Charles Pitman arrived in Entebbe as Uganda's first Game Warden, a post he was to hold for over twenty-five years.

Captain Charles Robert Senhouse Pitman, D.S.O., M.C., late 27th Punjab Regiment, was not only a distinguished soldier but an experienced big game hunter and a very knowledgeable naturalist. When he arrived in Uganda he was faced with a challenging task. To get the elephant herds under proper control, without destroying them in the process, was in itself a major and priority problem which had to be dealt with before general wildlife conservation measures could be considered. It was a problem aggravated by the hostility to the Game Department that was voiced in many quarters during its formative years.

As late as June 1931, a comment published in the *Uganda News* stated that 'The starting of "stunt" departments has been the greatest scandal in Uganda in recent years. Game Rangers where there is no game'. Forty years ago many people were of the opinion that game departments were an expensive and totally unnecessary luxury – and did not hesitate to say so! Even pragmatic officialdom considered that there was a constant need to justify the Game Department's existence by demonstrating, every year, that the Department was not a drain on the exchequer but, on the contrary, more than paid its way through the revenue obtained from the sale of control ivory and hunting licences. These factors inevitably coloured the Game Department's policy, and restricted the scope of its activities, during the long years of financial austerity that prevailed between the wars. In fact, it was not until the era of colonial development, which blossomed from the ashes and debris of the Second World War, that the Game Department was actually able to abandon the defensive. Then, conscious of the fact that the threat of the financial axe, which had for so long hung poised above its head, had finally been removed, the Department began to realise, with growing relief, that at last it could afford to drop its guard, flex its muscles and attempt to expand its activities into long neglected fields. But again it was no easy task, for opposition arising from anti-

S.R.   H

quated and deep-seated policies and attitudes was hard to break.

It was at this point that I myself entered the act in the role of Uganda's first Assistant Game Warden. It was a humble enough title but one in keeping with the Game Department's traditional dislike of ostentation and flamboyance. Later we were to learn that such modesty and reticence could be a positive disadvantage when the Game Department was in competition with other government departments for cuts of the annual 'financial cake', or the resolving of inter-departmental policy clashes, or the official evaluation of conflicting expert opinion. Thus a *'Chief* Game Warden' is in a much stronger position when in official competition with say, a 'Chief Conservator of Forests' than he was under his old title of 'Game Warden'; likewise a 'Deputy Director of Veterinary Services', or of 'Agriculture', or of 'Tsetse Control' for instance, has a built-in titular advantage over an 'Assistant Game Warden', yet the latter post is also that of the deputy director of a specialised professional and technical department. Nevertheless, during the eleven years that I was in Uganda, the Game Department, despite expansion, proudly stuck to its old traditional titles. For thirty-five years there was only *one* 'Game Warden' in Uganda. *The* 'Game Warden' was the director, head, leader – or whatever you prefer to call it – of the Department. He was the Government's official adviser on all wildlife matters, including fisheries, and his field officers were 'Game Rangers' – with the welcome addition, in later years, of a number of specialised 'Fisheries Officers'.

I think it was Captain Denis Zaphiro – an ex-*Bimbashi** of the Sudan Defence Force, a gifted artist, an expert bush pilot, and one of Kenya's Senior Game Rangers – who started the rot which finally led to the break with tradition. One day in 1959, he walked into the Game Warden's office in Nairobi with an idea in his head.

The old, wooden building that houses the headquarters of the Kenya Game Department, the oldest game department in Africa, a building preserved – as I have told – by Archie Ritchie, literally reeks of tradition. Memories of by-gone days are epitomised in the faded, sun-bleached photographs and humorous newspaper cuttings that adorn the walls, surrounded by the slowly decaying mortal remains of selected man-eaters, cattle-killers and shamba-

* Captain.

81

raiders, and a few of nature's stranger aberrations. From time to time these story-linked relics of the past are supplemented, while the shabbiest are removed when the ravages of time have done their worst and they have added their physical quota to the all-pervading aura of dusty romance that fills the building. The atmosphere is redolent of dust, the dust of countless safaris, carried on the travel-soiled clothes of visiting game rangers and hunters, millionaires and poachers. Over the years this dust has become ingrained in the wooden floors, in the worn, old-fashioned furniture, and in the grooves of the panelled walls; you can smell it as you enter, just as your nostrils will catch the faint but musty odour of aged elephant tusks and pieces of old rhino horn, and the unmistakable aroma of ancient, rough-cured lion and leopard skins.

It was in these hallowed precincts that Denis Zaphiro dropped his bomb-shell. Leaning across the Game Warden's desk, and fixing him with a gimlet eye, he said in a quiet voice – 'Tell me, Willie, *why* are we called "Game Rangers"?'

William Hale – Archie Ritchie's successor – looked surprised. He leant back in his chair, thought for a moment, and then re-plied hesitantly – 'I . . . I really don't know. I suppose it's tradi-tional!'

'Well,' Denis continued firmly, 'I think it's all wrong. We don't *range* game, we *ward* it. *I* think that "Game *Rangers*" should be called "Game *Wardens*" and you yourself should have the title of "*Chief* Game Warden".'

William Hale looked deeply shocked – and he was. To him the opinion that Denis had just voiced amounted to heresy; and to have uttered it in the office of the Game Warden himself was tantamount to sacrilege! After a moment's stunned silence he glanced wildly round the room. From the photographs on the walls, the ghosts of past game rangers and wardens seemed to lean forward with bulging, horrified eyes. 'It was all very like a Bateman cartoon,' Denis Zaphiro recalled, with an impish grin, when he told me the story several years later.

But William Hale was a good administrator and like all good administrators he was receptive to new ideas. As he thought about Denis Zaphiro's suggestions, the farcicality of the situation dawned on him. The newly created National Park Organisations of East Africa had given the rank title of 'Ranger' to their most junior field staff whose responsibilities were only equivalent to those of a game scout or game guard – the most humble rank in the Game Department – while a 'Ranger' in the Game Department was a senior field officer equivalent in status to a 'Warden' in the National Parks! To cap it all, in the Game Department the label of 'Warden' was reserved for the head of the Department, a position for which the National Parks had chosen the title of 'Director'. These contradictions in the naming of the various ranks of wildlife conservation staff had often caused confusion, particularly among tourists. There had been petty irritations and misunderstandings, as well as comical incidents that might not have been so funny if those concerned had not been blessed with a keen sense of humour – the most valuable asset that a game warden or a tourist can possess! So William Hale acted; his 'Game Rangers' became 'Game Wardens', while for his own post he chose the rather more impressive title of 'Chief Game Warden', as Denis Zaphiro had suggested; only for the subordinate field staff of the Game Department did he retain the time-honoured rank of 'Game Scout'.

In due course, the Game Departments of both Uganda and Tanganyika followed Kenya's example by replacing their old, traditionally modest, rank titles with the more impressive sounding ones adopted by the Kenya Game Department. But this change did not occur until shortly after I transferred from Uganda, in 1960, to become 'The Game Warden of Tanganyika'.

I have always been proud of the fact that I am the only person who was ever Chief Game Warden of two* African countries (Uganda and Tanganyika) during the colonial era, quite apart from subsequent short-term appointments as 'Wildlife Adviser' to two other African countries – a harmless enough vanity and a morale booster during this age of 'one-upmanship' in nearly every sphere and profession. But until the prefix of 'Chief' was officially added to my title I frequently experienced muddles over my true status and responsibilities. For the sake of clarity therefore, as I have done in one or two places earlier in this book, I shall henceforth refer to all game rangers, whatever their place in history, under the more-up-to-date title of 'Game Warden', while to the various people who were directors of game depart-

* Subsequently, the author became Chief Game Warden of a third African country – Malawi.

ments during the same period, I shall attach the now popular label of 'Chief Game Warden'.

Personally, I still prefer the old titles, just as I far prefer to hear a rat-catcher described as a 'Rat-catcher' and not as a 'Vermin Extermination Officer', and a dustman called a 'Dustman' and not a 'Refuse Disposal Officer'; but perhaps I am too old-fashioned, too much of a traditionalist! However, old fashioned or not, I am sincerely grateful that I have never yet had to live up to the *official* title of 'Director'. To me such a label smacks of a Civil Service uniform of bowler hats and dark, sober suits. In a proper African game department it would be regarded as a sinister sign that the Chief Game Warden was expected to spend the greater part of his time at his desk, or in the conference room, rather than on safari where he should belong.

I went to Africa to be with animals and I moved to Uganda to work with animals. For me the main lure was, and always has been, the elephant; and I had hardly arrived in Entebbe before I discovered that I was in the heart of a country which was a true 'elephant kingdom', a small, compact land which, in terms of relative game population densities and variety of sub-species, could still lay claim to being the greatest elephant and buffalo country in Africa.

Demidoff's Galago—or Bushbaby

PART TWO

The Year of the Apprentice

*

CHAPTER 6

The Shamba Raiders

My introduction to Uganda's elephant control problems was precipit. Scarcely a week after my arrival, I was sitting in the old Game Department headquarters in Entebbe when the ancient telephone on the Chief Game Warden's desk rang stridently, its shrill, persistent tone sounding a jarring note in the cool, quiet interior of the old-fashioned, book-lined office.

With a venomous look at the angrily vibrating receiver, Charles Pitman raised it gingerly to his right ear. I could not distinguish the words, but I could hear the disembodied voice at the other end of the line. It reminded me of a tape-recording being played at too high a speed. Whoever and wherever he was, its owner was clearly upset. Charles Pitman listened carefully. 'Whereabouts?' he queried, swivelling round in his chair to study the large map of Uganda that hung on the wall above his head.

'I see,' he said thoughtfully after a brief pause, his eyes focussed on a point on the map somewhere to the west of Kampala and Entebbe. 'How long have they been there?'

The reply was unintelligible to me but it evidently surprised the Chief Game Warden. His bushy eyebrows arched towards the ceiling.

'What on *earth* is the game guard doing?' he queried angrily.

There was more excited chattering on the telephone. It sounded like the scolding of an irate squirrel. From the tone I gathered that, whatever the unfortunate game guard in question was meant to have done or be doing, he had not exactly covered himself with glory. 'I see,' repeated Charles Pitman grimly. 'All right, George, I'll send someone to deal with them. What? Of *course*! I'll have him there by tomorrow morning.'

Replacing the now silent receiver, the Chief Game Warden glanced at me quizzically over the top of his spectacles. 'How would you like a break from the office, Bruce?'

My reaction must have been clearly reflected on my face for, without waiting for my reply, Charles Pitman smiled and said 'I thought so! Well, there's a job for you to do. That was the Protectorate Agent's office in Kampala on the telephone. Apparently the Saza* Chief at Mityana is complaining about serious elephant damage around Lake Wamala. Come over to the map and I'll explain.'

Using an ink-stained wooden foot-rule as a pointer, and with the assured air of a seasoned commander briefing the leader of a fighting patrol, the Chief Game Warden quickly and concisely explained the problem and what he wanted me to do.

'Here's Mityana,' he said, pointing to a cluster of tiny, black rectangles straddling the thick, red line that marked the course of the main Kampala-Mubende-Fort Portal road. 'And this is Lake Wamala,' he added, tapping a large, blue-hatched area on the map, lying to the south-west of the little township. 'In fact, it's a bit misleading to call it a lake; it's really a papyrus swamp, a big one, with some open water in the middle. It's about twenty-five miles long and roughly twelve broad at its widest point. The water level varies with the rains, but the papyrus is always about ten foot high or more, and as dense as a field of sugar cane. The country around is fairly thickly populated and covered with cotton and banana shambas. There *are* a few hippo and a fair number of sitatunga (marsh antelope) in the swamps, but apart from these and the odd duiker and bushbuck all the game

* County.

in the area was killed off years ago. Too many people,' he frowned regretfully.

'Lake Wamala drains southwards into the Katonga,' Charles Pitman went on, drawing the ruler slowly down the map until it was pointing at a broad river valley that seemed to run from west to east across Uganda, appearing to link the shallow waters of Lake George – nestling at the foot of the jagged gash of the western Rift – with the vast expanse of Lake Victoria. 'But the Katonga is not what it looks to be on the map,' the Chief Game Warden smiled. 'In fact, it's mainly a great, slow-flowing, papyrus-choked river with a very shallow watershed just about *here*,' he said, tapping the map smartly with the tip of the ruler, indicating a point roughly mid-way along the Katonga valley. 'When it flows, if it flows at all, it runs both east and west from that point. But, more important to us, the Katonga valley, for most of its length, is wonderful game country. It's stiff with buffalo and there are several large herds of elephant which are more or less permanent residents. They move a lot, of course, up and down the Katonga and its tributaries. And sometimes the big herds split up for a time into smaller groups which wander further afield along their old migration routes. Then we get trouble.' Charles Pitman paused thoughtfully.

'Every now and then,' he went on slowly, 'one of these smaller herds leaves the Katonga, heads northwards up the Nabakazi valley and then sneaks through the cultivated areas at night, across country eastwards, to hide up in the swamps of Lake Wamala. From there they sally forth, after dark, and systematically raid the cotton and banana shambas all around for night after night. Sometimes they stay in the Lake Wamala area for a few days, sometimes for as long as a couple of weeks, always returning to the sanctuary of the swamps before daylight. As you can imagine the damage they do is considerable. And once they're back in the swamps they're as safe as rats in a haystack; and they know it,' he added grimly.

'I would like you to have a go at dealing with the problem,' Charles Pitman said, giving me a searching look. 'I could send another game warden or game guard from somewhere else but it would take time to organise. In any case it will be a good chance for you to have a look at the country. I haven't told you before, but this time next year I shall be on leave pending retirement; and

I want you to see as much of the country as possible before I go.

With a start, I realised that I was being put on my mettle. Elephant control had been the chief preoccupation of the Game Department for twenty-five years and I was being given the chance to prove my worth. I remembered Neumann's comment – 'Elephant hunting is the most arduous and exacting of all field sports and, when persistently followed up, entails a tremendous strain on the system.'*

I glanced at the map. 'Lake Wamala's very close isn't it?'

'Yes. It's only forty miles from here; rather less from Kampala. Get yourself properly organised and make a really early start to-morrow morning. You'll need camp kit and food for at least four days. You'll have Firipo, your gun-bearer, with you; but he's a Madi so you'd better take John Tamusange as well; he knows the area and speaks Luganda, he's a Mganda himself. In any case I'll ring the Mukwenda – that's the title of the Saza Chief at Mityana – to tell him you're coming. I'll ask him to have the latest news of the elephants and some local guides ready for you. So you'd do best to go straight to the Saza Headquarters at Mityana first.'

I nodded, 'I think you mentioned something about a game guard at Mityana on the telephone just now, what's happened to him?'

'He's in hospital,' he said grimly. 'Got himself surrounded by the herd in thick elephant grass and tried to get out. A cow caught him and threw him into a tree. Broke his right arm and half a dozen ribs and then tried to tusk him. His porter saved him by firing a spare rifle before running for it. He's lucky to be alive but his rifle's smashed to bits.'

'Don't take any chances with this lot, Bruce,' he concluded. 'They're vicious. They killed an old woman last week.'

I smiled wryly, memories of the savage elephant herds in the Kenya coastal bush still fresh in my mind. I had learnt my lesson there and it was not likely that I should forget the smashed huts, the wrecked lorries, elephants tearing out of head-high maize at night, screaming with rage, and the pitiful bloody remains of what once had been living, breathing human beings buried under piles of torn branches.

As I rose to leave the office the Chief Game Warden fired his

* Arthur H. Neumann *Elephant Hunting in East Equatorial Africa*, 1898.

parting shot. 'Get a good night's sleep,' he said meaningly. 'You'll probably need it!'

*

Three fruitless days and four almost sleepless nights later, I remembered Charles Pitman's parting words with feeling. The view from my tent, pitched in the cool shade of a great, gnarled, wild-fig tree, on a small ridge of low rising ground, commanded a wide sweep of the great papyrus swamp of Lake Wamala. To the east of my vantage point the swamp stretched to the horizon like a vast, green sea of swaying, tufted reeds. Northwards and southwards the cracked, grey mud of its shores, baked hard in the blazing sun, curved away into the shimmering haze of the blue distance like a rim of crazy-paving stones around a suburban goldfish pond.

It was late in the afternoon. The sun was low in the sky warming my back with its slanting rays as I sat in a camp chair, slowly and methodically searching the swamp with a pair of powerful 10×50 binoculars.

The Mukwenda had been courteous and helpful, but obviously worried, when I had called at his office in Mityana three days before.

'Major Kinloch I can assure you that these animals are very dangerous, *very* dangerous,' the old Saza Chief had repeated, shaking his head in disapproval, his precise English lending emphasis to his words. 'Every year, about this time, they come to Lake Wamala and bring fear and hardship to my people. But your game guards cannot deal with such animals. Elephants like these are too cunning. The swamp is their fortress. Once they are inside it no human being can reach them unless he has wings. I have tried to hunt them myself and I know.'

The old, grizzle-haired Chief had paused at this point to take a large pinch of snuff before continuing. 'The reeds are so tall and thick, that no man can see or move unless he follows the paths of the elephants; but by day they stand still in the water to rest and wait and listen. And so silent do these elephants remain that no ordinary man can get within rifle shot of them without their being aware of his approach. The noise of his splashing in the water alone will warn them, but they will have sensed his presence long before that for the wind does strange things in the reeds. And to be smelt out and attacked by such elephants in that swamp is a very frightening experience, I can assure you.' The old Chief shuddered. 'I myself have been chased by these elephants in the swamp. I was a much younger man then, strong and fleet of foot, but I narrowly escaped with my life and my rifle was lost in the water. I would *not* like to repeat the experience I can assure you, no I would *not!*'

Looking at the venerable and rather portly Mganda aristocrat in the spotless white gown and smart, black waist-coat, the refined, courteous and remarkably sophisticated product of an old and relatively advanced African culture, I had found it hard to imagine him floundering through a muddy swamp after a herd of bad-tempered elephants. But his words had had the ring of truth, and he certainly had not exaggerated over the cunning and elusiveness of these elephants and the dangers and frustrations of trying to follow them into the vast, green papyrus jungle that was Lake Wamala.

As my vision, magnified ten times by the powerful binoculars, swept slowly from left to right, up, and then from right to left across the swamp and back, time and again, I thought not only of the old Chief's warning words but of my own abortive and frustrating experiences of the previous seventy-six hours. There before me stretched two hundred square miles of dense papyrus swamp. Hidden somewhere in this great water-borne jungle was a herd of about thirty obviously very determined, exceptionally cunning, and particularly savage elephants.

For ten days these astute and belligerent animals had used the swamp as their raiding base. For ten nights they had debouched from it as darkness fell, never using the same route twice, to devastate the banana shambas somewhere within a dozen miles of the perimeter of Lake Wamala. For three nights we had waited for them, but invariably in the wrong place since there was no set pattern to their raiding, and we always seemed to be on the wrong side or at the wrong end of the swamp when they emerged.

On the last night I had been luckier for we had heard them in the distance and had come on their fresh tracks close to the swamp in the grey light of dawn. But it had been too late. Although we had been able to hear the rhythmic swish and hush of displaced reeds and water as they surged ponderously through the swamp ahead of us, like some great, grey battle fleet, we had had

93

to abandon the chase when the water reached our waists and was clearly getting deeper.

After returning dejectedly to camp and drying our sodden clothes in the sun, we had fallen asleep through sheer exhaustion. And now John Tamusange, Firipo and the Mganda guide were huddled over their cooking pot, while I sat in my camp chair, slowly and carefully searching the swamp with my binoculars. Where were these elusive beasts and, more important, when and at what point would they again emerge from their impregnable fortress? It had a shoreline oɪ nearly seventy miles and the choice was theirs. I shook my head in despair.

And then a movement caught my eye and my binoculars centred on a large flight of pink-billed teal swinging wide over the swamps in a tight, speeding arc. As I watched them, they suddenly banked, and with a flash of wings and light belly-feathers caught by the sun, they dived headlong to the open water that was hidden from me by the tall, waving papyrus. They were a good half-mile away; too far for me to hear the noise of their passage. But I could imagine the sizzling hiss of the wind through their pinions as they scythed through the towering reeds, to land with a sharp clatter of furled wings on the still surface of some silent pool.

In the secret, nerve-tense world of the swamps, the explosive arrival of the teal was as unexpected and unwelcome as the bursting of a fire-cracker in a crowded living-room. When the speeding birds hit the water like a spatter of spent bullets, chestnut-coloured lily-trotters scattered squawking in clumsy, spindle-legged panic; a pair of sleepy hippo crash-dived with sudden snorts of alarm; a lone sitatunga ram plunged headlong through the reeds in instant flight; and a cluster of great, grey shapes, standing motionless and belly-deep in the cool, clear water, swung wildly round, mighty ears spread wide, massive trunks questing, pig-eyes gleaming, angrily prepared to repel the intruder. And from their broad, mud-caked backs there rose a dense cloud of snow-white egrets, the elephant's and buffalo's almost constant companions in country of this nature.

All that I had observed of this hidden drama was the flashing dive of the teal into the reeds; the rest was imagination. But seconds later, when I saw a flock of snow-white birds erupt from the tall papyrus at the precise point where the teal had vanished,

I knew at once exactly what had happened. There, a mere half-mile away, were the shamba raiders – the casual killers of a harmless old woman who had chanced to cross their path; the deliberate ravagers of poor men's crops; outlaws every one. But for the moment they were as safe from retribution as if they had been a hundred miles away, the water and the reeds made sure of that.

I cursed silently to myself, the gall of frustration bitter in my mouth, as I watched the ruffled egrets glide gently back to their mammoth perches. There was nothing I could do but watch and wait.

Slowly, and then with gathering speed, the sun sank towards the western horizon, bathing the swamp in a warm, red glow that gleamed like fire where the rays were reflected from the hidden pools. At last the colour was gone, and as everything turned to a uniform grey in the short tropical twilight, the egrets again rose from their living day-time perches to wing their way shorewards in a shifting white cloud against the gathering darkness. With them went my last chance of knowing in which direction the elephants would move under the cloak of the night.

I slept fitfully during the next eight hours, lying fully clothed on my camp-bed, one ear open for any sounds or signs of elephant movement. The night was particularly still and moonless and in the hush of the velvety darkness the high-pitched whine of countless mosquitoes seemed to be accentuated. Sound travels far across the swamps under these conditions and once I heard the distant bark of an alert sitatunga, thrice repeated, while from time to time the raucous, laughing bellow of a hippo sounded in my brain through the swirling mists of sleep.

Shortly after nightfall there had been one angry scream from the place where the egrets had earlier risen from the swamp, but after that, as far as the elephants were concerned, there had been silence. No distant drums or beating of kerosene tins signifying shambas that were being raided or about to be; no more savage trumpeting; just a deep, significant silence.

By the time the pale grey light of the false dawn washed the eastern horizon, I was sure I knew what had happened, and within a few minutes of leaving my tent in the morning I found the evidence that confirmed my suspicions. There, within thirty yards of my camp, was the broad, beaten trail of an elephant herd that

Bull elephant in papyrus swamp, Uganda

'The Patriarch', a really old elephant

was on the move. The meandering tracks of feeding animals were absent. In their place was a single, wide, flattened swathe, cutting through grass and bush alike, leading purposefully westwards.

What I found was no surprise to me, nor was the fact that not one of us had heard a sound. Elephants, with their great cushioned feet like giant, crepe-soled shoes, can move as quietly and as stealthily as cats if they wish, and at night they appear to become almost contemptuous of the proximity of humans. They seem to realise that man is almost helpless in the dark and that a sleeping man constitutes no danger whatsoever. In fact, if there is any incentive for them to do so, even the most timid and heavily hunted of elephant herds will readily pass close to sleeping humans at night, which explains the apparent boldness and persistence of many shamba-raiding herds.

A rapid search along the shore, the four of us questing like a pack of eager hounds, soon revealed that the herd must have headed directly out of the swamp very soon after darkness fell, passing just beyond the flickering light of our camp fire as we slept. The fact that they had not begun to move in the late afternoon, as elephants usually do when they are starting on a night's steady gorging, had in itself been an indication that they had just been waiting to start on a long, cross-country trek; and this was now confirmed.

I turned to my gun-bearer. 'Get the camp packed up Firipo,' I said. 'We're moving too.'

The lanky, coal-black Madi looked blank, he was not at his best in the early morning, but the Mganda guide shrugged, muttered something pithy in Luganda, spat expressively, and turned gloomily on his heel.

'What did he say, John?' I queried angrily, sensing the tone but not understanding the dialect.

John Tamusange grinned weakly, glancing doubtfully from the guide to me before translating. 'He said that you'll never catch these elephants, Bwana, for this is their country and they're laughing at you.' He hesitated and then looked serious 'He said that if you follow them further they will get angry.'

'So?'

John Tamusange appeared troubled. His brow was furrowed and his broad, chocolate-brown face was beaded with sweat.

Again he hesitated before answering. At last he spoke. 'Then they will kill you, Bwana,' he said simply, looking me straight in the face.

There was a moment's tense silence. Then Firipo let out a guffaw of laughter.

'*Hapana!*' he snorted derisively, in a tone of withering scorn, at the same time smacking the butt of my heavy, double-barrelled, ·470 rifle that he was carrying over his right shoulder.

The idea that we, well-armed members of the Game Department, had anything to fear from a lot of thick-skulled, flat-footed pachyderms had suddenly struck Firipo as being extremely funny. As a Madi from the north he did not have a very high opinion of the courage and hunting prowess of the Baganda. 'After all,' he once said to me in a tone of lofty condescension, 'they're not warriors, Effendi. What can you expect from a lot of banana-eating peasants?'

I did not share Firipo's uncharitable views on the Baganda, and I certainly did not encourage him to express them openly, but this time I was thankful for his abrupt interjection. I had been getting worried about the morale of my small force, and his blunt and contemptuous reaction to the dire forebodings of our Mganda guide was as effective as the shock of a cold shower. In a breath it swept away the atmosphere of oppressive gloom that had descended on us like a dark thunder-cloud when we discovered that, after all our weary efforts, our quarry had slipped through our fingers.

John Tamusange shook himself like a dog emerging from the water. 'Twende, Bwana,' he said briskly. glancing at the morning sky to fix the position of the sun. 'We must go. They're already far ahead.'

*

It must have been at about three o'clock in the afternoon that we first heard it, a deep resonant rumble, like distant, muted thunder rolling in the mountains, or the passing of a subway train far beneath the crowded pavements of a bustling, modern city. It was the sonorous, bass, purring rumble of a contented, drowsy elephant. It is a noise which is quite unmistakable, made in the throat and amplified a dozen times in its passage through the great nasal channels of the long, sinuous trunk.

To the alert and expectant elephant hunter, patiently and cautiously following the fresh tracks of a moving herd, often through dense cover, with visibility sometimes down to a few feet, his nerves keyed up like taut violin strings, every sense strained to the limit, this sound, when it finally comes, is always like a sudden, though long awaited electric shock. It sends a thrill through his body, his heart leaps and, for a moment, the adrenalin-charged blood pumps wildly through his veins. There is a sudden release of long pent-up feelings, followed by a sense of both elation and relief. Then, if he is experienced enough, he becomes icy calm, a tensed up, calculating machine, all his faculties concentrated on the task in hand. And so it was on this occasion, for all except our Mganda guide.

After hurriedly breaking camp in the early morning, we had bumped slowly across country in my old Chevrolet truck, following the footpaths and well-worn cattle trails that headed westwards towards the Nabakazi valley. To save time we had not attempted to follow the fresh tracks of the elephants. There was little doubt where they were heading and we had expected to pick up news of their movements and whereabouts from the hut dwellers in the scattered shambas that lay ahead.

Sure enough, shortly after midday, we had met a disconsolate shamba owner who had lost half a dozen banana trees which the herd had sampled in passing; and at two o'clock we had come upon another peasant farmer whose crops had been systematically devastated as if they had been hit by a cyclone. The herd had dallied there long enough to take a hearty meal of plantains, cotton plants and a few sticks of sugar cane, before moving on, just before dawn, into the high stands of elephant grass and spear grass that grew in wide, unbroken belts along the ridges overlooking the Nabakazi valley.

Within a half mile of leaving the shambas the herd, probably hot and thirsty after its long night march and its substantial feed in the small hours, had hurried down the slopes of the Nabakazi valley to drink its fill and wallow blissfully in the cool, refreshing waters of the papyrus swamp.

The tracks and fresh droppings in the soft mud at the edge of the swamp had been easy to read. The herd was obviously a mixed one of between thirty and forty elephants, with a high percentage of fully adult animals. In fact, we had only found signs of two young calves. The rest appeared to be females or young bulls in uncertain proportions, with about half a dozen fully adult bulls – always the worst shamba raiders – in attendance.

On leaving the swamp, the herd had wandered slowly back up the slopes of the valley, fanning out to feed leisurely on the long grass as they went, the big bulls moving out to a flank to travel on their own. On the high ground the herd had again converged, travelling purposefully southwards along the rim of the valley in the direction of a small, distant clump of large, spreading shade trees.

The country through which the herd had been moving can best be described as savannah woodland, dominated by small trees of mainly *Combretum* and *Terminalia* species growing in tall *Hyparrhenia* – or spear grass – sometimes far higher than a man's head. In patches, where the soil was suitable, there were great stands of *Pennisetum purpureum*, the giant elephant grass, towering up to fourteen feet and more and as thick-stemmed as a young bamboo.

Following elephant in this type of country is hot and nerve-wracking work, for it is only feasible for a man to move along the elephant trails where the grass has been beaten down by the moving animals; furthermore, the wind is invariably erratic and visibility is seldom more than a few yards at the most. Under these circumstances it is possible almost to walk into a resting elephant, or even pass it within touching distance, before one realises that it is there at all. And it was under such conditions, on that hot, sultry afternoon, that we first heard, close ahead, the contented rumbling of the resting herd.

The deep, muted noise reached our ears when we were in the middle of a wide area of once tall grass that had been extensively flattened by circling elephants. The whole patch of churned-up ground was littered with fresh droppings of all sizes – a clear indication that the herd had milled around quietly in the area for some time, sleeping and occasionally browsing, until the mounting heat of the morning sun had driven them to seek the comforting shade of the nearby trees – or so I guessed.

The four of us came to an abrupt halt. In fact, when our guide heard the ominous rumble, he stopped so suddenly in mid-stride that he was left with his right foot raised in the air like an alarmed hen. Slowly and gently he lowered it to the ground, at the same time turning his wide-eyed, nervous face in my direction. '*Ndovu!* – elephant!' he breathed, in a totally superfluous comment.

About forty yards ahead, over the tall screen of elephant grass that fringed the clearing, we could just see the dark, leafy crowns of a cluster of massive shade trees, the same trees which we had first sighted in the far distance from the bottom of the valley. I took my double-barrelled ·470 from Firipo, checked to see that it was loaded, and nodded to him to climb into the straggling branches of the nearest *Combretum*.

In a moment he was down again, slithering quietly on the smooth bark.

'*Yuko* – they're there, Bwana,' he whispered with a broad grin.

'How many?'

'I couldn't see.'

'Take my rifle,' I hissed. 'I'll look for myself.'

I couldn't match Firipo's agility and silence, but with a certain amount of scrabbling I soon found myself with my feet wedged precariously in a narrow fork some twelve feet from the ground. Steadying myself with my left hand, I glanced in the direction of the group of giant fig-trees, and then, at last, my long pent-up feelings were released in a deep sigh of excitement and relief. There, under the wide, spreading branches, deep in the dark, cool shade, was a restless, gently shifting mass of elephants – the elusive, cunning shamba raiders that we had pursued so relentlessly but fruitlessly for five exhausting days.

Using my binoculars with my right hand, I studied the herd carefully, or as much of it as I could see. Under one big fig-tree there was a tightly packed group of eight elephants dominated by a very tall, very old cow. They appeared to be dozing for, apart from the constant, slow movement of their ears and the occasional shifting of a fore-foot, they were virtually motionless. The old cow's head drooped, her ears were tattered, her features were gaunt and her wrinkled, weathered skin hung in loose folds on her ancient bony frame like a damp, well-worn blanket draped over a hard, wooden clothes-horse. They were all huddled together with their heads inwards, almost touching the massive bole of the giant tree.

Beyond them and to the left were more elephants. Some were just standing; others were shifting slowly and ponderously into the long grass and out again, occasionally idly plucking, with their sensitive, ever-questing trunks, a choice bunch of leaves, or a juicy tuft of grass. The latter they tapped fastidiously on their forelegs to remove the clinging earth before leisurely stuffing the carefully selected morsel into their cavernous mouths; and with the slow, rhythmic chomping of their mighty jaws, their half closed eyes, and the dreamy, far-away look on their wrinkled faces, they reminded me, as always, of a lot of old and corpulent gourmets lovingly demolishing a vast plateful of hot, buttered asparagus, delicately savouring every juicy mouthful.

One young bull was behaving very differently. He was away to one side, on his own, and had apparently found a rich store of fallen fruit, a discovery that he was obviously trying to keep to himself. I couldn't see what the small fruit were, they might even have been seed-pods, but he was hurriedly picking them up, as fast as he could, and throwing them, one by one, into his open mouth with rapid flicks of his ever-searching trunk. On his face there was a look of such intense concentration that I could hardly refrain from laughing. He reminded me of an excited spectator at a football match, absent-mindedly tossing peanuts into his mouth as he watches the scoring of the winning goal.

Swinging my binoculars to the right, I steadied them on another group under a lone *Kigelia*, or sausage tree. As I focussed on this group I stiffened. There, huddled together under the great, pendant fruits of the Kigelia, sleepily picking up handfuls of loose dust in their trunks to blow in soft, red clouds over their massive bodies, were six, big bulls.

*

Through long association, I have developed an almost exaggerated interest in, and fondness for, elephants, but I have few illusions about these great animals. Because of their immense strength and undoubted intelligence, elephants are always potentially very dangerous beasts for, like all intelligent animals, individuals vary tremendously in character without such differences being obvious on the surface.

As with the human race there are those elephants which appear to be placid and are, while in others a seemingly calm exterior may hide a quick and savage temper. And, again as with human beings, there are those who seem to be born thieves and trouble-makers, who steal not from necessity but because it is the easiest way to get what they have taken a fancy to – which is not necessarily also what they need! Like humans such individuals can lead whole groups astray, teaching them to adopt vicious, anti-social habits. Some again are ready to kill if thwarted or even without any provocation. So, like those human beings who become enemies of society – the individuals and organised gangs who pillage and murder with no compunction and little hesitation – crop-raiding elephants have to be severely punished to teach them that, in this so-called civilised world, crime is not meant to pay.

As I watched the elephant herd, enthralled as always, I forcibly reminded myself of these facts, and of the presence, a mere mile ahead, of yet more peasant shambas, which I was quite certain the herd was just waiting to raid as soon as darkness fell. I also remembered what Charles Pitman had recorded in some of his official annual reports, the documents I had read immediately prior to setting out after the Lake Wamala raiders. 'The Uganda Protectorate is still literally over-run with elephants – big, dangerous, destructive beasts,' were his very words written a few years before the war; while, in the following year, when the total elephant wastage in Uganda from all causes was estimated at the prodigious total of two thousand three hundred beasts, he had recorded in his report the sobering and significant statement – 'We are just holding our own and no more.'

'You must hammer this herd, Bruce,' Charles Pitman had said to me grimly before I finally left Entebbe for Lake Wamala. 'They're an evil-tempered lot and incorrigible crop raiders. They've got to be well and truly frightened and driven right out of the district. Don't be squeamish about killing as many of them as you find necessary to get them really moving. Remember, it's in the long-term interests of the elephants themselves. If they stay where they are we'll be forced to kill the whole lot. And don't forget we've still got twenty-five thousand of these problem animals in Uganda!'

Watching and waiting, high in the tree, I remembered Charles Pitman's sage and experienced words, and I thought of the ravaged shambas, the badly injured game guard, and the old woman who had been little more than a smear of bloody rags on the ground when they found her. Staring at the six big bulls I knew what I had to do; like it or not I had to try to kill most of them for these animals were outlaws. And as I looked and remembered, the steely excitement of man's inborn hunting instinct mounted steadily in my veins, while a deep bank of cloud, dark, menacing and heavy with rain, rolled slowly but inexorably across the face of the sun.

*

The arrival of the rain clouds seemed like a silent signal to the elephants. As the sun disappeared and the temperature dropped with the deep shadow that fell across the land, they suddenly became restless. Those that were dozing began to move; those that were already moving quickened their pace; the close-packed groups stirred; the old cow shook herself, her tattered ears slapping against her sides with a noise like the beating of a dusty carpet; and under the fig-tree the group that surrounded her broke up with deep, throaty grumbles of discontent, like elderly club-members rudely awakened from a post-prandial snooze. Only the six large bulls remained where they were, and even they were showing signs of alertness, one or another raising his trunk tentatively to test the light breeze that had sprung up, carrying with it the scent of rain.

The wind had me worried; it was fitful and gusty. I took a little linen bag of wood ash from my pocket and shook it; the small cloud of fine, grey particles, that burst through the coarse weave of the cloth, swirled in the air like a puff of smoke and blew straight back into my face. I was relieved; we were still down-wind of the elephants but, at any moment, a chance eddy might give them our scent. Should this happen then our days of concen-trated efforts would all have been wasted.

I glanced at my watch. With a shock I realised that it was past four o'clock. The elephants were already restless. At any moment they would start to move towards the shambas, probably to lie-up in some dense patch of cover close to the cultivation, there to wait until darkness fell, after which another group of poor peasants would have their basic food supply destroyed in one concentrated raid.

There was no time to lose. Sliding quietly to the ground I seized my double-barrelled ·470 from Firipo, loosened some spare cartridges in the loops in my waist belt, and signalled to

John Tamusange to hand my reserve heavy rifle – a ·416 Rigby – to Firipo. Then, slowly and carefully, with Firipo at my heels and John and the guide a few paces behind, I moved through the grass towards the sausage-tree under which the six bulls were still clustered.

In a few moments I reached the opposite edge of the tall grass that fringed the open ground under the shade trees, and there I crouched, my rifle half-raised, rapidly checking the position of the herd.

With a few lightning glances the whole picture was fixed in my brain, like the instant image that forms in a flash on a photographic plate. The old cow was already on the move, at her heels a well-grown bull calf approaching maturity; she was clearly the herd leader, for the other elephants, apart from the six large bulls, were slowly beginning to converge on her. The whole concourse was swinging into formation to move up-wind away from where I was crouched at the edge of the long grass. The six bulls remained where they were; in due course they would follow, behind or to one flank, but with dignified independence and at their leisure.

The group of bulls was only twenty paces from me. The nearest was broadside on, partially obscuring the others but offering an easy brain shot. He had small tusks, weighing not more than twenty-five pounds apiece, and I had already noted, with satisfaction, that none of the remaining bulls were carrying ivory heavier than forty pounds a side.

It was the Game Department's policy to try to spare elephants carrying heavy ivory, for big tusks do not grow overnight and old bulls are seldom persistent shamba raiders. Like elderly gentlemen, these patriarchs prefer a quiet, easy life in some secluded spot away from trouble and strife. However, just occasionally they would be led astray by their younger companions, or be seized with a nostalgic urge to return to the scenes of their youthful wanderings. I was relieved that on this occasion I did not have to worry about the safety of one of these absent-minded patriarchs. The bulls in front of me were all in their prime and active, aggressive shamba raiders. They wouldn't remain still much longer. It was time for me to act.

In one smooth, continuous movement I rose to my full height, at the same time bringing my rifle to my shoulder and lifting the twin barrels until the silver bead of the foresight centred on the leading edge of the ear orifice of the nearest bull. Gentle and unhurried as my movements were, at that short range even an elephant could not fail to notice something. While the barrels of my rifle came slowly up I saw his body stiffen, but before he could react further my gun-sights were aligned on his brain. At that instant I squeezed the front trigger.

There was a roar and a flash, and as the heavy recoil of the powerful rifle kicked viciously backwards, forcing the walnut butt hard into my shoulder and flipping the barrels skywards, the massive body of the bull collapsed like a house of cards.

The sudden death of an elephant is a dramatic and awe-inspiring, but sometimes a rather terrible, spectacle; like the sight of an ancient, historic building crumbling to a heap of smoking rubble on the firing of demolition charges, it arouses instant but momentary feelings of high excitement, followed by a sense of overwhelming sadness and regret. But this time there was no place for morbid thoughts. Inevitably some regrets would come later, but these animals had murdered and pillaged. They had been judged and condemned. It was my job to carry out the sentence humanely and efficiently, and in the heat of the action there was no time to think of anything else.

The first bull died instantly when the heavy, high-velocity bullet crashed into his brain. I knew he was dead long before his great body lay still on the ground, for at the shock of the bullet he had flung up his head and his hindquarters had collapsed first – sure signs of a clean brain-shot. In fact, I didn't even lower the rifle from my shoulder to check, but swung its sights on to the next bull.

But this was a sophisticated, battle-salted herd. Like trained and seasoned soldiers their reaction to the shot had been immediate and controlled. One second they were just standing or strolling slowly in the open; the next moment they were in full flight, diving for cover.

The second bull swerved wildly just as I pulled the trigger of my left barrel and the bullet, instead of driving into his brain, hit him somewhere in the neck. It neither killed nor stunned him but the force of the blow of a heavy, blunt-nosed, 500 grain, steel-jacketed bullet, travelling at over 2,100 feet per second, and striking with 5,000 foot-pounds of concentrated energy, at a moment when he was moving fast and off-balance, knocked all four and a half massive tons of him clean off his feet. He disappeared in a cloud of grey dust as he fell, out of sight, behind the bole of the sausage-tree.

Without pausing for an instant I lowered my rifle, snapped open the breech, flicked out the fired cartridge cases and dropped two fresh rounds into the gaping mouths of the empty chambers. They slid home with a solid, comforting, metallic *plonk, plonk*, and as I snapped the rifle shut again I breathed a sigh of relief. I knew from experience that in thick cover full of wild elephants an empty rifle is not a reassuring instrument. In such conditions speed in reloading is essential. I had had a couple of spare rounds held ready between the fingers of my left hand and my rifle was primed for further action within seconds; it proved lucky that it was.

Scarcely had I closed the breach when there was a scutter of feet behind me and a yell of warning from John Tamusange – '*Nakuja* – it's coming, Bwana!' he shouted as he and the guide dived out of the grass and past me in panic.

I swung round, my rifle half-raised, to see the tops of the long grass whipping down in a fast, straight line. Something was ploughing through the grass at the speed of a running man. It was heading straight for where I was standing, and there was a swishing, crushing noise like the sound of a reaping machine through a cornfield.

I ran back a few paces into the clearing under the trees to obtain a better field of fire. The next moment the screen of tall grass was torn apart and a cow elephant burst into the open not more than fifteen paces from me. Her ears were spread, her trunk raised, and her pig-like eyes were gleaming viciously. The instant she saw me she let out a savage scream, dropped her trunk across her chest, and came straight for me in a silent, crouching rush.

Everything happened so quickly that I reacted automatically. As the cow screamed my rifle butt thudded into my shoulder, and the moment she dropped her trunk the shining bead of my foresight was centred between her eyes. I hesitated just long enough to lower the sight to the level of the third wrinkle in her trunk, and a split second after she got into full stride I fired.

The crash of the powerful rifle, the wildly leaping barrels, and the sudden spurt of dust from the charging elephant's head were almost simultaneous. The shock effect of the heavy, high-velocity bullet smashing into her skull at point-blank range was dramatic. The force of the impact checked the cow in mid-stride, her forelegs buckled beneath her, and she plunged forward, slithering along on her belly under the momentum of her massive body, until her long, thin tusks, driving deep into the ground, brought her to a halt as abruptly as a locomotive against the buffers of a railway terminus. The tip of her extended trunk, stretched along the ground in front of her like a length of giant fire-hose, was only four feet from me. And there she lay, quite still. But I was taking no chances. As the dust slowly settled I took three quick strides towards the cow's motionless head and from the side I fired my second barrel into her right ear. She didn't move; she was stone dead.

Frontal brain shots on elephants are notoriously difficult and the results often unpredictable. The brain of an elephant – about the size and shape of a rugby football – is set far back in its head, almost on a level with an imaginary line drawn between the external orifices of its ears. From the front the brain is protected first by the mass of powerful muscle at the base of the trunk and then by two or three feet of heavy, cellular, shock-resistant bone structure that looks like a giant honeycomb. For a bullet to pierce all this bone and muscle, and still reach the brain, not only must it possess exceptionally good penetrating power but the angle of entry must be exactly right. The correct point of aim is therefore seldom easy to judge and certainly not with a quick snap-shot at a charging elephant at almost point-blank range. Under these conditions, a frontal head shot as often as not results in the elephant merely being stunned, and too many careless hunters have been killed by apparently dead elephants suddenly and unexpectedly coming to life!

On this occasion my second shot may not have been necessary, but I had a job to do and it would have been criminal folly to have taken any unwarranted chances. So, standing by the dead cow, I rapidly reloaded and trained my ears for any sound of further elephants behind me. There was nothing in that direction, but in the thick grass and bush beyond where the second bull had fallen I could hear the remainder of the herd moving rapidly and noisily away.

I had momentarily forgotten about the second bull in the heat of the action with the vicious cow; and as I studied the latter's long, thin tusks – one of which had a peculiar upward slant – I wondered idly if she could have been the cow that had attacked and nearly killed the game guard near Lake Wamala. Then I heard the rest of the elephants moving and I suddenly remembered the second bull that I had knocked over. At that time I was not at all certain whether he was alive or dead. He had fallen in long grass in the shadows behind the big sausage-tree, all of which would have effectively screened his body from us if he was still lying there, and it was beyond that point that we could now hear the herd moving.

I glanced at my companions. John Tamusange was wide-eyed, sweating profusely and breathing hard; his chocolate skin seemed several shades paler than before, while our guide's face had taken on the colour of dark wood-ash and he appeared dazed. Even Firipo was perspiring heavily, and when I raised my eyebrows enquiringly he responded with a half-hearted and rather tremulous grin. Then I noticed that my own hands were not quite so steady as usual! It had been a close enough call with the cow and the inevitable reaction had set in. I shook myself. 'Twende, let's go,' I said to my companions, and, with my rifle held ready, I walked quickly but cautiously towards the sausage-tree.

*

The bull had gone. The bush and grass beyond the sausage-tree were flattened and trampled over a wide area, but of the elephant itself there was no sign, except for a few, widely scattered splashes of rapidly congealing blood.

From the flattened area a broad, freshly made elephant trail cut through the tall grass towards the Nabakazi valley. We could still hear the herd ahead travelling steadily in the same direction. One quick look at the track was enough and we raced along the trail in the wake of the herd.

Five minutes later we reached a point where the track started to drop down into the valley. Still shut in by the long grass, we halted briefly to listen to a new noise – a sound of distant splashing – before running on to another point where the path slanted more steeply and the grass shortened giving a clear view of the valley bottom. There, far below us, was the herd streaming across the papyrus swamp in a long extended line. Leading the column, wading steadily through the reeds and shallow water, was the old cow. At the tail, and far behind the rest, was a small group of five elephants moving at half the pace of the others. I sat down on a termite mound, rested my elbows on my knees, and trained my binoculars on them.

As the picture swam into focus, my eyes were greeted with a sight that few people, even experienced elephant hunters, have ever actually seen. In the middle of the lone group of elephants was the injured bull. There was no mistaking him for he towered above the others. On either side of him, leaning inwards to support him with their powerful shoulders, were two big cows. Behind him, their massive foreheads against his rump, were two more cows. The whole group was moving slowly but steadily through the water, throwing up a small bow-wave that fanned out through the swamp in a broad arrow of muddy ripples, on which the reeds swayed and tossed like wind-blown corn.

I watched fascinated. Only once before had I seen a similar sight. On that occasion it had been at night in the district of Kilifi on the Kenya coast. We had caught a small herd of bulls raiding a maize shamba in pitch darkness, and in the dim light of our torches we had seen them lift a mortally wounded bull to his feet and attempt to carry him away. Now I was being lucky enough to observe another gallant elephant rescue, but this time in the broad light of day. And all I could do for the moment was to watch and see what the herd would do once it had crossed the swamp.

At this point the swamp was about a quarter of a mile wide. Despite its breadth we could see that the water was comparatively shallow, reaching only half way up the elephants' legs even in the deepest places. In five minutes the whole herd was across and spread out among the tall grass and bushes that grew on the steep slope of the opposite hillside. They did not seem to be unduly alarmed, or else they were waiting for the injured bull which had halted in a thick clump of reeds growing in the shallow water at the far edge of the swamp. Even with my binoculars I could only just see the line of his back and his rescuers seemed to have temporarily left him to seek shelter themselves in the shade of some tall bushes not far from the water's edge.

I paused to consider the situation. I had killed two of the raiders, but the herd had not yet been frightened sufficiently to make them forsake the cultivated country and return to the Katonga valley. But of more immediate importance there was a wounded elephant which, for humanitarian reasons alone, I had to destroy as soon as I possibly could. On all counts we had no choice but to continue to follow and harass the herd, yet the swamp presented a formidable, although not impossible, obstacle.

Should we try to cross the swamp higher up the valley where the water might be shallower? After a moment's thought I dismissed the idea. It might take us some time to find an easier crossing place, and any delay could well result in us losing touch with the elephants. Furthermore, evening was fast approaching. Time had become a critical factor. I hesitated no longer. There was only one thing for us to do – we had to try to cross the swamp by wading along the channel freshly cut by the herd. Nodding to my companions, I rose to my feet, slung my cartridge belt round my neck, shouldered my rifle, and set off down the hill towards the near shore of the swamp.

*

Scarcely had we entered the swamp when the first heavy rain-drops began to fall and in a few moments we were in the middle of a real tropical deluge. Very soon the water was up to our waists. By the time we were half way across the swamp it was up to our chests, and every now and then, when we stepped into a hidden elephant track, it came up to our armpits. The cold rain, caused by soaring tropical thermals, soon turned to solid hail, and as the surface of the swamp was churned into a froth by the lumps of ice that lashed and stung our unprotected faces, we struggled grimly on, wading slowly and carefully, our rifles held far above our heads.

Soaked and chilled to the bone, we finally reached the opposite shore. The hail was still lashing down as hard as ever, and when, at last, we stepped thankfully on to comparatively dry land, we could not see more than a few yards in any direction. There was nothing we could do but seek shelter, and we huddled together under a clump of bushes, recently vacated by some of the herd, vainly trying to restore a little warmth to our numbed limbs. We were soaked from head to foot and our thin, sodden clothes clung clammily to our shivering bodies like wet bathing suits.

At last the hail stopped, as suddenly as it had begun. The sun broke through the swirling clouds and wisps of steamy vapour began slowly to rise from the surface of the swamp and the surrounding hillsides. It was time for action again.

Rising to my feet I surveyed the scene. The herd was scattered across the nearby hillside as before, most of them grouped under clumps of trees. The four cows which had helped the wounded bull had not moved from their position near the water's edge. The bull himself was still standing in the swamp, almost completely hidden by tall, dense papyrus. Although he was only about forty yards away, he was so well screened by the thick reeds that I could still see no more than the line of his back. To approach him direct through the swamp was impossible; I would have had to advance to within a few feet of him before I could have had the slightest chance of a clear shot at a vital spot. And even if he had failed to scent me first, he would have heard me wading through the water towards him. The only thing I could do was to try to get a clear view down on him from some suitable spot on the hillside above. It would mean a long shot, always to be deplored in elephant hunting, but there was no feasible alternative.

I climbed up the hill and soon found a vantage point from where, looking down at an angle of about thirty degrees, I could see the wounded bull through a small gap where the reeds were lower. He was a good 120 yards below me and I remembered, ruefully, the wise old elephant hunter's advice to the tyro – 'Git as close as ye can, son – then git ten yards closer!' But on this occasion I *had* to attempt a long shot; I had no other choice. Luckily the elephant was standing quite still and broadside on to me. At short range it would have been an easy shot.

I handed my double-barrelled ·470 to Firipo and took the ·416 magazine rifle from him. The ·470 was an old friend and an excellent weapon for dealing with dangerous animals at close range in thick cover, but for longer shots in the open I preferred the superior accuracy and penetration of the Rigby ·416.

Sitting down on the ground, I rested my elbows on my knees and attempted to take a steady aim. In a moment I realised that it was hopeless. I was so cold that my teeth were literally chattering and I was shivering so much that the sights of my rifle were jumping all over my target. I lay down in what was left of the evening sunlight, sheltering from the wind behind a termite mound, and tried to get some warmth back into my body.

It was a good twenty minutes before I had recovered sufficiently to try again. Then, rising to my feet once more, I stared anxiously downwards towards the place where I had last seen the injured elephant. Breathing a sigh of relief, I saw that he hadn't moved. He was still standing in the same spot, motionless and broadside on to me as before. I raised my rifle, rested my left forearm against a convenient tree, and took careful aim. The range was too great to attempt a brain shot, so I steadied my sights on a point one-third of the way up his body on the line of the back of his foreleg; then I raised them a few inches to allow for the bullet's steep, downhill angle of entry. The sound of the shot rolled across the swamp, echoing and re-echoing from the surrounding hills. A pair of old, grey herons rose clumsily from the reeds with harsh squawks of alarm and flapped slowly across the valley, their long legs trailing. A flight of yellow-bill duck sprang from a hidden pool and sped swiftly out of sight around the curve of the hill. For a long moment the wounded bull showed no reaction. Then, almost in slow motion, his great legs gave way under him and, with scarcely a splash, his massive body rolled gently over on its side to lie, half submerged, in the shallow water. The long, 410 grain, ·416 bullet, still travelling at nearly 2,200 feet per second, had hit him squarely in the heart. I breathed a sigh of relief. For him it was all over.

Signalling to my companions to follow, I walked rapidly down the hill and waded out into the swamp. In a few minutes I reached the fallen elephant. Thigh deep in water, I examined the body carefully to make absolutely certain that no sign of life remained. Then I looked about me to find out what had happened to the rest of the herd.

Surrounded by the tall, waving papyrus, and standing deep in the water, I could see nothing, but from close-by came the deep, growling rumble of alerted, angry elephants. It is a noise so similar, yet with a subtle difference in timbre, to the purring rumble made by these great animals when they are contented and undisturbed, that the tyro is often misled – lulled into a false sense of security. To the experienced hunter, however, the difference is unmistakable. It tells him that his quarry is wakeful, suspicious and liable to take aggressive action at any moment, particularly if provoked.

To get a better view I clambered up on to the top of the dead, mud-smeared elephant and stood upright, balancing carefully on the slippery, unstable perch. What I saw made me grasp my rifle tighter, for there, a mere thirty yards away, above the feathery tops of the tall, swaying reeds, with their curled tips pointing in my direction, nostrils wide flared, was a line of rigid trunks raised high in the air like a row of malignant, seeking periscopes; and their owners were advancing purposefully towards me.

I and my companions were in a hazardous position. In most directions the dense reeds reduced our visibility to a mere twenty paces. We were surrounded by water and a good thirty yards from the shore. Our slightest movement in the swamp could not fail to be heard by the elephants and would probably provoke an immediate charge – there was no mistaking the menace in their steady, remorseless advance. And to cap it all the sun had already dropped below the tops of the hills, signalling the near approach of the darkness that would soon engulf us with tropical suddenness.

My mind raced as I considered our predicament and our alternative courses of action, but before I had time to act the massive head of the leading elephant broke through the screen of reeds only twenty yards away. Instantly I threw up my rifle and fired. Then everything seemed to happen at once.

The recoil of the heavy rifle threw me off balance; my feet shot from under me on my slippery perch; and I toppled over backwards into three feet of murky water. As I fell, frantically trying to save my rifle, I saw the elephant throw up its head and collapse in its tracks.

I scrambled hurriedly to my feet, clawing a tangle of mud and weed from my face and hair, and stared anxiously in the direction of the remaining elephants. The raised trunks had disappeared, but there were still sounds of stealthy but purposeful movement through the papyrus. Although I could hear the elephants I could no longer see them, and I was not certain whether they were still advancing or not. Altogether, with the light rapidly fading, it was an eerie sensation!

It was possible that the sound of my shooting and the death of four of their number had begun to frighten the herd, a state of mind that I was anxious to encourage. So, to press home my imagined advantage, I seized my ·416 from Firipo – who had caught it with one hand as I fell – and quickly but carefully I fired three rapid shots into selected points in the reeds. I aimed not at the hidden elephants, with the attendant risk of unnecessary wounding, but close to the place where I could hear them moving. The result was, to say the least of it, unexpected.

The three quick shots were greeted with a series of savage, blood-chilling screams, followed by a gargantuan turmoil of splashing water and tearing reeds. Then four elephants plunged out of the swamp and rushed up the hillside. Whether they were misled by the rolling echoes of my shots I know not, but there was no mistaking their aggressive intent. Without stopping they charged around in wide circles, ripping up grass and bushes, all the time screaming and trumpeting in frenetic rage. It was an alarming sight.

Those four elephants could well have been the four cows who had rescued the wounded bull, but by this time the light had faded too much for me to see. However, there was no longer any doubt as to our immediate course of action. Under cover of the bedlam, ourselves somewhat shaken and unnerved by what had occurred, we waded rapidly ashore. The moment we reached dry land, we hurried away, down-wind, into the gathering darkness, leaving the elephants in full possession of the field of battle. But even when we had left them far behind we could still hear their savage screams fading into the night.

*

The following day, soon after dawn, we returned to the scene of our previous night's encounter. With us we brought a party of villagers, armed with axes, *pangas* and knives; their task was to cut out the tusks and carve up the meat, while we ourselves tried to find out what had happened to the herd. It did not take us long to unravel the signs.

A pair of vultures was circling high in the sky; a third had already settled on the body of one of the elephants lying in the swamp; it was squatting there gloomily, glaring morosely at the dead bull's inch thick hide. Apart from the birds there was no sign of life.

The hillside was littered with broken trees and torn bushes, surrounded by large areas of flattened grass and gouged, red earth. It was clear that after our departure the herd had gone berserk, the elephants venting their rage on the man-tainted ground in their vain search for a hated enemy. It was also clear that as their rage cooled it had been replaced by a rapidly growing uneasiness, which had finally turned to fear. Ultimately the elephants must have panicked for, leading away from the devastated area, there was a clear track of a fast travelling herd; a well-beaten trail covered with loose droppings that told their own tale. Leaving the villagers behind to start removing the tusks of the dead beasts, we followed the trail at a brisk walk for over an hour; then we turned back. From the signs it was obvious that the elephants, driven by fear, were still travelling hard, hurrying back to the peace and tranquillity of the Katonga valley, far from the haunts of their hated enemy, man. Our task was accomplished. We headed for home.

*

On the way through Mityana I dropped in to see the Mukwenda. Wide-eyed he listened to my story. He was obviously delighted, but at the end he shook his head wisely and said – 'I warned you, Major Kinloch! These elephants are savage, *very* savage. And I thank you for what you have done.'

I then called at the hospital to see the injured Mganda Game Guard. He was sitting up in bed, his right arm in a plaster cast, his chest heavily strapped with layers of bandages. He looked remarkably cheerful; Joseph Katete was a tough character. I asked him what had happened to him.

'I found the elephants in some long grass near a shamba, Bwana,' he said speaking in Kiswahili. 'I shot one bull and then a cow charged me. I tried to reload my rifle, but when I opened the bolt all the spare cartridges jumped out of the magazine and fell to the ground. The elephant caught me with her trunk and threw me into a tree. After that I can't remember anything until I woke up here in hospital.'

When we reached Entebbe, I was as near exhaustion as I have ever been. It was late, and I was hot, tired, thirsty, unshaven, and filthy. All I wanted was a long, cold drink, a bath, a shave, and several hours sleep in a comfortable bed.

Passing the local shops I decided to drop into a store to stock up with some bottles of ready-cooled beer. As I entered, I was confronted by the wife of one of Entebbe's most senior civil servants. I greeted her politely, then stepped aside to allow her to pass. For a moment or two she stared at me in growing astonishment, her gaze travelling slowly up and down my disreputable, mud-caked figure, on her face a look of thinly disguised and ever-growing disgust. Finally, with an imperious jerk of her chin, and a curt acknowledgement, she swept out of the door, leaving me feeling like a plough-boy who had entered the drawing room of a dowager duchess, not only unasked and unannounced but without even bothering to wipe his dirty boots!

The next day I reported to the Chief Game Warden in his office and gave him the full details of the safari. 'I was pretty tired and dirty when I got back yesterday evening,' I said, 'and as it was late I didn't think you would want to be bothered in your house.'

'Quite right, Bruce,' Charles Pitman smiled. 'As a matter of fact, I heard last night that you had returned. One of our local gossips dropped in on us and told us that she had met you in the shops. I was beginning to wonder why she had called when she said that she was surprised to see that my officers did not shave on safari!' His eyes twinkled. 'She then added that she thought it set a *very* bad example to the local people!'

'Don't worry,' the Chief Game Warden grinned sympathetically, noting my obvious embarrassment, 'that's Entebbe for you; it's the civil servants' Mecca. Until recently, the only European living here who was not a civil servant was the bank manager!'

*

So ended my first elephant hunt in Uganda. In many ways it was the most interesting and most arduous elephant hunt I have ever experienced. I have described it at length and in detail since it clearly illustrates certain important facts of which the general public is blissfully unaware, particularly in an era during which it has become fashionable to regard all wild animals as being beyond reproach, and to condemn any man who lifts his hand against them.

Wild animals, especially the large, dangerous species, existing peacefully in national game parks or reserves are one thing; the same animals when they encroach on man's living space are another. The responsibility for dealing with them then falls squarely on the shoulders of the game departments, and it is a task which is often both difficult and dangerous. Moreover, what had been an exciting hunt for me was almost a routine duty for the African game guards and the game wardens whose job it is to train them. Month after month they are faced with problems of a similar nature and, if they are not having to deal with crop-raiding elephants and buffalo, they are often involved with cattle-killing or man-eating lions and aggressive, armed poachers.

Every year, in Africa, numbers of game guards, and sometimes game wardens also, are killed or seriously injured in the course of carrying out these duties, of which the general public is ignorant. Occasionally, but not often, the public hears about the tragedies. Usually there is little more than a brief paragraph in an annual report – 'The Chief Game Warden regrets to have to record the death, in the course of duty, of Game Guard . . .'

*

There is a postscript to this story and an important one. It arises from the fact that the Game Guard who was attacked and nearly killed by a cow elephant near Lake Wamala, would probably have escaped injury had his rifle not failed him at a critical moment.

The standard weapon of the Uganda Game Department has been, for years, the ·404 magazine rifle. It fires a 400 grain solid or soft-nosed bullet at a muzzle velocity of 2,125 feet per second, giving a muzzle energy of 4,010 foot-pounds. With these ballistics, and a magazine holding four spare rounds, it is a suitable rifle for all dangerous game, and when properly made by a conscientious gunsmith it is a sound and reliable weapon. Nearly all the Uganda game guards were issued with ·404's, with a sprinkling of other bores among the game wardens and for special tasks. And until the war these sturdy rifles, purchased from old British gunmakers of repute, gave yeoman service. It was after the war that the trouble started.

The source of the trouble was twofold. First of all there was the problem of obtaining supplies of the very strong and reliable

German military Mauser long bolt action, on which the British gun and rifle trade had long relied for their powerful, large-bore magazine rifles. Secondly, after the war, certain new firms with no previous experience of building and – more important – of finishing and regulating powerful magazine rifles intended for use against dangerous game, entered this very specialised field. The effects of this situation were sufficiently serious to merit a lengthy comment in the Uganda Game and Fisheries Annual Report for the year 1950. In that report, under the heading 'Post-War Rifles', I wrote as follows:

Since the recent world war British rifle-makers have found it almost impossible to obtain supplies of the Mauser bolt action on which to build up their sporting rifles. A number have attempted to adapt other types of actions made in the First World War, but this Department has found these actions to be most unreliable in the field.

There have been several cases of strikers and extractors breaking at critical moments, and some have developed the bad habit of the magazine base plate flying open on a shot being fired and emptying all spare rounds on to the ground. This can be most embarrassing when in the middle of a herd of elephant or buffalo.

Others have the fickle habit of suddenly and unexpectedly hurling all the rounds from the magazine into the air, like a jack-in-the-box, when the hunter is trying to reload his rifle in a hurry while in a tight corner.

The Mauser action is one of the best made and strongest in the world, and most suitable for powerful magazine rifles. However, it seems extraordinary that British gunsmiths, who have an international reputation as both gun and rifle makers, should for years have been forced to rely almost entirely on supplies of a foreign made bolt action.

In 1951 I went on home leave to England. Before my departure from Uganda I made advance arrangements to meet the Sales Manager of a firm which had supplied the Game Department with many of the offending rifles. Complete with bowler hat, brief-case, and a dark, tailored suit, the Sales Manager met me at the railway station and whisked me off in a taxi to his firm's main workshops. He was polite but hostile and, as I entered, the eyes of the veteran craftsmen at the work benches were cold and unfriendly. 'We don't understand your complaints,' said the Sales Manager, with icy sarcasm. 'All our rifles are tested individually on the range before being exported. Perhaps you would be good enough to demonstrate to us what your troubles are?'

For a moment I hesitated, a sinking feeling in my stomach. I knew how difficult it was to make the rifles perform their treacherous acts to order. I swallowed and breathed a silent prayer. Then . . . 'Certainly!' I said, with forced brightness. 'Give me a rifle and some ammunition and I'll show you.'

'Help yourself,' responded the Sales Manager, with an airy wave of his hand towards a rack full of brand new ·404 rifles, at the same time presenting me with a single ·404 cartridge.

Immediately light dawned. The answer to the mystery had suddenly flashed in my mind like a divine inspiration. 'I need four more rounds, please,' I said.

The Sales Manager looked surprised but handed me a packet of cartridges without further comment.

I selected a rifle at random, opened its bolt, pressed four cartridges into its magazine, and forced the bolt home again to feed a fifth round into its chamber from off the top of the rest. Then, with a quick twist of my right hand and wrist, I jerked open the bolt to extract the fifth round from the chamber. The extraction was perfect, but what followed was not according to the book of rules. There was a rattle like the noise of a rusty alarm clock and the four spare cartridges leapt out of the top of the magazine to fall with a clatter to the oil-stained floor, whence they rolled slowly under the benches, their brass cases glistening in the harsh glare of the electric lights.

For several seconds no one spoke, but work at the benches had ceased abruptly. The grizzled craftsmen were staring at me in undisguised surprise. At last the Sales Manager stirred uneasily. His Adam's apple bobbed convulsively as he swallowed hard. 'I . . . I see!' he stammered hesitantly.

'May I try another one on the range?' I queried confidently, taking a second rifle from the rack as I spoke.

The Sales Manager nodded miserably and we walked in silence to the short, sand-bagged testing range. There I charged the magazine as before, loaded the rifle, and fired a quick shot at the target. Immediately there was a metallic clang as the magazine base plate flew open and with an almost musical tinkle the four spare cartridges cascaded to the ground.

I turned to the Sales Manager. 'You've been testing these

rifles with single rounds, haven't you?' I said. He hesitated, then nodded dumbly, pale in the face.

'Well, in future I suggest you test them the way they are used in the field, with full magazines, as I've just done. Otherwise you're going to have more men's blood on your hands.'

I twisted on my heel and walked to the taxi. When I reached it I turned to the Sales Manager again. 'By the way,' I said, 'I'm afraid your firm will get no more orders from the Uganda Game Department.' And they never did.

CHAPTER 7

The Ivory Trade

Soon after my return from Lake Wamala, I had discovered, in Kampala, a particularly blatant and well-established ivory racket, involving a large number of elephant licence holders and some of the less scrupulous ivory dealers, in that busy, bustling town which is the commercial capital of Uganda.

With the help of certain well-known poachers, and the connivance of some of the local ivory dealers, the offending licencees – many of whom had never shot anything more dangerous than a guinea fowl in their lives, while a few did not even possess a rifle – had conceived a delightfully safe and simple way of making money.

Having first bought the ivory from a poacher, at a cut price of four or five shillings per pound weight, the licencee – valid elephant hunting permit in hand – would present the tusks at the nearest district commissioner's office for stamping and registration, as the law required. With this simple formality satisfactorily completed, the licencee would then sell the illegal tusks to an ivory dealer for slightly less than the ruling legal market price. Since the latter was seldom lower than fifteen shillings per pound, and sometimes as high as twenty, these 'armchair' elephant hunters stood to make an easy profit of ten to fifteen shillings on every pound weight of illegal ivory that they bought and sold.

With a good average pair of tusks weighing some fifty pounds apiece, and an elephant licence costing as little as one to three hundred shillings as their only overhead, these legally licensed elephant hunters could thus make from seven to fourteen hundred shillings, or more, net profit on every elephant licence they held. Furthermore, since any 'approved' person was permitted to purchase a total of three elephant licences annually, costing one, two and three hundred shillings each respectively, an unscrupulous licencee could, in this manner, with no physical danger or exertion on his own part, make a handsome net profit of one hundred, two hundred, or even, with a little luck, as much as three hundred pounds a year – tax free!

The risk of getting caught was minimal. As a rule it only arose when the ivory was being registered in the relevant district commissioner's office, or if the tusks were examined by an expert while they lay in the ivory dealer's store awaiting the issue of an export permit by the Game Department; but even at these two vital check points, the effects of the war and its aftermath had reduced the risk of discovery to a minimum.

In the halcyon days before the Second World War, a time of comparative tranquillity, most district commissioners were very experienced officers of long service and proven wisdom. Unhindered by the ever mounting, post-war volume of paper work, they travelled far and often, and largely on foot. The majority of them were keen naturalists and hunters, and there was little that went on in their feudal domains that they did not hear about. Their sources of information were many and varied, and news of such an important event as the shooting of an elephant invariably reached their ears with surprising speed and accuracy.

After the war the tempo of political and economic development accelerated rapidly throughout Africa. District commissioners became more and more office bound, and a new breed of young district officer began to arrive in ever increasing numbers. Their background was essentially urban rather than rural, and they had little knowledge of, or even interest in, anything to do with wild things or wild places. To be fair to them most of them were intelligent, receptive and willing to learn, and the great majority soon became staunch and useful allies of the game departments, but in the course of their learning they inevitably made many mistakes as far as wildlife was concerned, not least when it came to registering ivory.

Only the keenest and most game-minded of the post-war district commissioners could still find the time to deal personally with such matters as game licences, ivory and connected formalities. Most of them were forced to delegate these routine duties to one or other of their district officers. As often as not this would be a lad who was yet to see an elephant outside a zoo. To him ivory was ivory whatever its condition. Be they fresh and malleable, or old and brittle, he accepted any tusks produced before him, together with the owner's statement of their origin, without query. And with their illicit ivory legally stamped, and the false statements on their licences formally passed and registered, the guileful poacher and the 'armchair' hunter would go gleefully on their way to the ivory dealer with the most elastic conscience.

Depending on the locality of its origin, elephant ivory ranges in colour from a smooth, dead white, through a soft, warm cream, to a beautiful rose peach and sometimes a deep yellow. All tusks vary in this manner but in one important respect they are all the same – the *initial* colour and texture of their butts.

The butt of the tusk is the hollow portion that is encased in the skull of the living elephant. The tusks are, in fact, the elephant's incisor teeth, and like all teeth the hollow butt contains the nerve. What few laymen realise however, is that often a good third or more of the total length of an elephant's tusks rests within its head; and it is from examining this portion of a tusk that an expert can tell if it is fresh or not.

When the tusks are first removed from the skull of a dead elephant, the thin walls of the hollow butts are moist and slightly flexible. However, once out of the head, and after the long, fibrous nerve has been removed, a tusk soon starts to dry out. In fact, in as little as a week or so, depending on the temperature and degree of humidity of the surrounding atmosphere, a large tusk can lose several pounds in weight from loss of moisture.

As time passes the thin walls of the butt become progressively drier and more brittle. All ivory tends to grow yellow with age, and with really old tusks the colour of the rough surface of the butt portion gradually assumes the same shade as the smooth, hard, outer layer of the main portion of the tusk. These are the signs that enable an expert to judge the approximate age of any given elephant tusk. Moreover, even a comparative novice can soon learn enough to recognise the obvious differences between really fresh ivory and tusks which have been stored for a long time.

During the two years that I had served in Kenya, I had seen and handled scores of tusks of varying ages; fresh ones from elephants I had myself shot on crop protection; others taken from poachers and ivory smugglers; and the great store of many hundreds of tusks, of all vintages, from Kenya, Uganda and the Congo, that accumulated in the Government Ivory Room in Mombasa for the twice yearly ivory auctions. So, by the time I reached Uganda, not only could I tell at a glance if an elephant tusk was fresh or not, but I had learnt a lot about both the legal and illegal sides of the age-old ivory trade. It was a subject that fascinated me, and when old Mr Lobo, the veteran Goanese Head Clerk of the Uganda Game Department, placed a bundle of used elephant licences and unsigned forms on my desk, I studied the papers with interest.

'What are these, Mr Lobo?'

'Ivory export permits, sir. Either Captain Pitman or yourself must sign them.'

'Have the tusks been inspected?'

The old Goan hesitated. With his bald head, thin, wrinkled neck, sallow complexion, and faded, hazel eyes staring unblinkingly through the thick lenses of his spectacles, he reminded me of an aged tortoise.

'Sir?' he queried, looking blank, one hand cupping his deaf right ear.

'Has anyone from the Game Department examined these tusks?' I repeated raising my voice.

Mr Lobo's appearance belied him. Small, slight and frail as he seemed, he was, in fact, wiry and tough with a temper that made him the terror of the Entebbe Goan community. He had a charming wife, half his age, a number of strapping sons, and a pretty little daughter of six. He thrived on a diet of rank, black cheroots and cheap, raw brandy. The pungent smoke of his cheroots effectively drove all mosquitoes from the darkest recesses of his gloomy office, and regularly sent the African clerks into paroxysms of uncontrolled coughing. The brandy gave him an added zest for life and sharpened the edge of his often caustic tongue. All in all, he was a strong character and, during the war, when the Chief Game Warden had been engaged in sterner duties, the old Goan had run the Head Office of the Game Department virtually single-handed. He had long since learnt to take a severely practical view of the Department's responsibilities, and he coughed deprecatingly before answering my innocent query.

'The ivory is in Kampala, sir, with the ivory dealers.'

'Yes, I know that, but isn't it normally inspected before these export permits are issued?'

Mr Lobo looked at me pityingly, like a mother humouring an idiot child.

'Occasionally, sir. But not very often nowadays. Since the war started we haven't had the staff or the time to make special trips to Kampala to visit the ivory dealers. It's over twenty miles from here, you know, sir,' he observed, glancing at me severely over the rim of his spectacles. 'And these elephant licences *have* been signed by the District Commissioners,' he added acidly.

I was not to be put off. 'Thank you, Mr Lobo,' I said. 'However, I would prefer to ask the Chief Game Warden about this before I sign these export permits blind.'

Charles Pitman agreed with me. 'Of course the ivory should be inspected, Bruce, but until you arrived we didn't have the staff or the time to do regular, thorough checks. This is an excellent opportunity to start a clean up.'

*

The ivory dealers in Kampala were all Indians. They were traders and general merchants handling a wide variety of commodities in addition to ivory. Most of them had close relatives in a similar line of business in Mombasa, through which port all ivory from Kenya, Uganda and the eastern Congo was exported, legally or illegally.

The trade in ivory is one of the oldest known to man, and over the centuries an intricate network of collectors, handlers, transporters and craftsmen has steadily developed. Wrapped tightly around with ancient tradition, taboos and national customs, this age-old spider's web is highly organised. From the living elephant in the heart of the African bush, right through to the heavy bangles on the arm of the dusky, blushing bride in southern India, or to the skilled ivory carvers of Japan, China and Hong Kong, the well-forged chain has stood the test of time and change, the antiquity of its origins being vividly described in Masefield's famous lines:

> Quinquireme of Nineveh from distant Ophir
> Rowing home to haven in sunny Palestine,
> With a cargo of ivory, . . .*

The introduction of game laws, at the turn of the century, blocked some of the easier and more obvious channels of supply, but they did not stop the ivory trade altogether, nor were they intended to. Instead, since the demand continued to exceed the legal supply, the poaching and smuggling of ivory became in itself a specialised branch of the ivory trade.

I had had some experience of this illegal trade on the Kenya coast. There, the tusks of elephants killed with poisoned arrows were first cut up into sections and then hidden in sacks of charcoal, or in the false bottoms that had been cunningly built into the bodies of ancient, battered lorries. Then, on a quiet, moonless night, the lorries would be driven to some lonely cove for the ivory to be swiftly and silently loaded on to a waiting lateen-sailed dhow. With the engines of the lorries and the quiet orders of the *nahoda*† muffled and drowned by the rumbling roar of the surf on the reef, the job would soon be completed. The dhow would then slip quietly away into the night, heading for Zanzibar, the great clearing house for illegal ivory, while a lorry loaded with bags of charcoal would drive innocently on to Mombasa.

Occasionally, we managed to arrest a lorry carrying a cache of poached ivory, or intercept a dhow loaded with illicit tusks, but for every one we caught in Kenya a hundred slipped through our fingers. In Uganda it was different. It was a long haul from

* John Masefield (1878–1967), 'Cargoes'.
† Arab ship's captain.

Kampala to Mombasa, so long in fact that to try to smuggle ivory on lorries from Uganda to the coast was both too risky and uneconomic. So, for the Uganda end of the ivory trail, other methods had to be employed by the gentlemen who operated on the fringe of the law.

When I drove to Kampala, I had no idea what local ivory rackets there might be. Ten minutes after I walked into the first ivory dealer's shop I had found out.

The shop owner greeted me politely. His ancestors had been Gujeratis, but like so many of his kind in Africa, he himself had never been closer to Asia than the western shores of the Indian Ocean. Small; sallow of face, with lank, well-oiled hair; smelling strongly of a pungent mixture of garlic, sweat and cheap scent; and with his paunchy, round-shouldered figure dressed in a crumpled, grey linen suit and a grimy white shirt with no collar; all in all he was singularly unattractive, a poor and degenerate example of a still proud and industrious people.

'I'm from the Game Department,' I said. The merchant's face split into a sickly smile, his lips parting to show a row of uneven teeth stained red from the habitual chewing of betel nut.

'You are the new Game Warden, isn't it?' he grinned. It was more of a statement than a question; news travels fast in the shadow world outside the law.

I nodded, placing a sheaf of papers on the counter in front of him. 'You have applied for export permits for six pairs of elephant tusks. Here are the elephant licences and your covering letter. I would like to see the ivory, if I may please?'

He stared at me calculatingly, his eyes taking on a wary look. 'They are in my go-down, sir. My brother, he has the keys.'

'Where is your brother?'

He shrugged his shoulders. 'I do not know, sir. He is doing business somewhere.'

'Will he be back soon?'

'That I cannot say, sir.'

'All right,' I said. 'I've plenty of time, I can wait.' I sat down on a rickety, wooden chair and glanced round the shop. In one corner was a familiar looking shape covered by some old sacks. I went across and pulled them away. Underneath were three pairs of large tusks, not one of them less than sixty pounds in weight.

'What are these?'

The shopkeeper looked uncomfortable. 'Ah yes, sir. They are some tusks. My brother must have forgotten to lock them in the store, sir.'

I examined the tusks carefully. The registration numbers and weights stamped on them tallied with three of the elephant licences that I had brought with me. One of the pairs was obviously fresh; the butts of the other two pairs were dry and brittle, one being yellow with age. According to the statements recorded on the licences, all three of the licencees concerned claimed to have obtained their tusks from elephants they had shot less than a month before; but with two of the pairs that I was examining the condition of the tusks clearly showed these statements to be false. Moreover, in the case of the pair of very yellow tusks, there was no doubt whatever that they could not even have been obtained within the period of the validity of the licence, let alone within the preceding month. In fact, they were so weathered and worn that they could not have been less than eighteen months to two years old.

I turned to the shopkeeper. 'Have you paid for these tusks?'

'Ah yes, *of course*, sir. I'm an honest man. I *always* pay on receipt.'

'How long have you been dealing in ivory?'

The merchant's sunken chest swelled visibly. 'Many years, sir. My family are ivory dealers since my grandfather, sir.' he replied proudly.

I looked at him steadily. 'Then you know that these tusks are old?'

The dealer went ashen. His mouth fell open but no sound came from it. I picked up my papers and looked at him again before moving to the door.

'Take care of those tusks,' I said. 'The police will be coming to collect them as evidence.'

At the door I turned. 'By the way,' I said, 'I suggest that in future you wait until the Game Department has inspected the ivory before you pay for it. I think those tusks are illegal. If that's proved in court they'll be confiscated – automatically. That's the law.'

I nodded pleasantly and stepped out into the glaring sunlight of the busy street.

*

At two o'clock that afternoon I walked into the CID branch of the Uganda Police Headquarters in Kampala. By then I had visited three more ivory dealers in the town and my haul of illegal ivory cases had risen to seven. I introduced myself to the English Superintendent of Police and explained my mission.

'There's no doubt at all about these tusks,' I said. 'They're all old ivory; some of it very old. Even the freshest of these tusks couldn't have been obtained legally.'

The Superintendent was a big, broad-shouldered man with a sun-tanned face, determined chin and shrewd blue eyes. Above the left breast-pocket of his tunic were two rows of brightly coloured medal ribbons. I could see that he had served in several widespread theatres of the Second World War as well as in the Colonial Police. He had the air of the seasoned, experienced policeman who has seen so much of the seamier and more sordid side of life that there is little left to surprise or ruffle him. Moreover, he had obviously long ago learnt the value of caution before initiating police action. He looked at me appraisingly.

'How are you so certain?' he asked quietly.

I laid the elephant hunting licences on the desk in front of him. 'Have a look at these permits. Every single one of these so-called hunters only bought their licences a few days before they took their tusks to be registered. The longest gap is ten days; and they've all made statements to the district commissioner concerned saying that they had shot their elephants within the authorised time.'

'So?'

'Well, it's just not possible. Even the freshest of those pairs of tusks is at least two months old, while the oldest of these licences was only issued three weeks ago.'

'How can you tell the ivory's old?'

'I'm a game warden,' I said, slightly nettled. 'It's my job to know about ivory.'

The Superintendent looked at me again. His face was expressionless but there was an amused glint in his eyes. Like most senior police officers he was quite willing to be helpful, but he had too many serious cases of murder and robbery on his hands to be bothered with trivial offences and weak evidence.

'What's so important about all this?'

'It's a growing racket,' I replied. 'More and more people are taking out elephant licences merely to provide an easy legal market for the poacher. We're not worried about our total elephant population, but we *are* concerned about the drain on our large tuskers. We're losing far too many old bulls, particularly from the game reserves. It'll only need a few successful prosecutions and one or two heavy fines to put a stop to this particular blatant racket.'

'Who do you want to prosecute, the ivory dealers?'

'No,' I said. 'It's the licence holders who ought to be prosecuted. We can charge each of them with having been in illegal possession of ivory, for having sold ivory illegally, and for making a false statement. If we get any convictions the ivory automatically becomes government property and is confiscated. The total result will be that the licence holders will get fined – heavily I hope! – and under the game laws they will then also automatically be banned from taking out further licences for three years. The ivory dealers will lose the tusks they bought and that will cost *them* about two thousand shillings or more a pair. So they'll be very careful, in future, what sort of ivory they buy; and all this will block the poachers' easy market!'

The Superintendent grinned, 'You've thought it all out haven't you? But what evidence have you got? How can you prove the tusks are illegal?'

'Simple!' I replied. '*Professional* evidence. I'll get up in court and give my opinion, as a professional game warden, that the ivory is older than the licencees claim! All I want you to do is to charge these people, collect the tusks as evidence, and get one of your officers to prosecute in court.'

The policeman's brow furrowed. 'Sounds a bit chancy – but it *might* work.' He paused for a moment, then – 'OK!' he said, 'I'll give it a try. But I hope you have a sympathetic magistrate. And the best of luck to you, you may need it!'

*

The first six cases went without a hitch. The licence holders – two Asians and four Africans – were either too surprised or too self-confident to put up any effective defence. My professional evidence was accepted; and the accused, despite their protestations of innocence, were all convicted and heavily fined. I had been careful to brief the prosecuting officer – a keen young policeman – as to the amount of money each of the accused had already received from the sale of his illegal tusks. The prosecutor, in his turn, went to equal pains to make these facts quite clear to the magistrate. And the magistrate, in imposing the fines, in each case doubled the sum of money involved with a ten per cent bonus thrown in for luck.

The six cases were spread over three separate days. When sentence was finally passed, six, very shaken ex-licence holders left the court, followed by four, very angry ivory dealers vociferously demanding the return of their money. The police prosecutor stared at the ivory merchants and grinned. 'They've got a hope!' he said. 'It'll at least cost them a civil case each; lawyers' fees and the lot. This ivory's going to end up worth more than its weight in gold!' As he spoke, a government lorry drove up and, before the anguished eyes of the quarrelling group, two uniformed game guards loaded the confiscated tusks for removal to the Game Department's ivory store. The sight itself was salutary. 'That's really rubbing salt into the wound!' grinned the police prosecutor.

The seventh case was delayed. The accused was a Saza Chief, a wealthy land and cattle owner in his own right. He was a powerful, arrogant man, contemptuous of the game laws, who had been in trouble with the Game Department before. As a result he had been astute enough to employ a European advocate, at whose request the magistrate allowed an adjournment to enable the defence to assemble its witnesses.

When the case was finally heard, I have seldom listened to so many blatant lies told in a court room in a single morning. But before the defence produced its string of well-primed witnesses, I was in the dock myself as the chief prosecution witness; and what I suspected would happen did so.

After I had given my evidence about finding the ivory in the dealer's shop and my professional opinion as to its condition and age, the defence advocate rose to his feet to cross-examine me. He was a large, fat man with an ingratiating manner. 'May I ask you for how long you have had any experience of assessing the age of elephant ivory, Major Kinloch?' he asked in a silky voice.

'Two years,' I replied slowly.

The advocate stared at me in well-feigned astonishment.

'Could you repeat that, please, Major Kinloch? I thought you said *two* years. Surely I was mistaken?'

'No,' I answered defiantly. 'I did say two years.'

The defence lawyer rolled his eyes to the ceiling and spreading his hands in a gesture of mock resignation he turned to the magistrate.

'I ask you, Your Honour. With all due respect to Major Kinloch's ability, and without in any way wishing to question his conscientiousness and integrity, surely *no one* can be regarded as an *expert* on ivory after only *two* years experience?'

Behind his thick, horn-rimmed spectacles the magistrate's eyes twinkled. He looked from the advocate, to me, to the police prosecutor, and back to the advocate – whom he knew of old. At last he spoke. 'I suppose it's all a matter of degree and opportunity,' he said mildly. 'Perhaps the prosecution has other evidence to support Major Kinloch's opinion?'

The police prosecutor jumped to his feet. 'We have, Your Honour. I would like to call Mr Patel as our next witness.'

Mr Patel had been my trump card. I had not wanted to use him if I could possibly avoid it, since his evidence was likely to make him most unpopular with his fellows among the tight clique of Uganda Asian ivory dealers. He was short, tubby and normally jovial, and he had always been a good friend and ally of the Game Department. After some persuasion, he had reluctantly agreed to give professional evidence, if his help was really needed. In the first six cases his support was not required, but in the seventh it almost certainly was, and now he was looking worried. As a police prosecution witness he was right out of his element.

In the witness box Mr Patel rallied and proved his sterling worth. In a firm, confident voice he confirmed my assessment of the age of the tusks that the accused had sold. And when the prosecuting officer asked him to tell the court how long he had been dealing in ivory, he replied proudly, 'Nearly forty years, sir.' For a moment there was a hushed silence in the court. Then the police prosecutor cleared his throat ostentatiously and said, 'That closes the case for the prosecution, Your Honour.' And with a quick, harassed look round the court room, Mr Patel hurriedly left the witness box.

The defence advocate had declined to cross-examine Mr Patel – which, in the circumstances, didn't surprise me. Instead he produced his own, well-drilled troop of alleged eye-witnesses. Gleaned from the ranks of the Chief's most loyal subjects, they were herded together at the back of the court room; there they sat in a long, ragged row like a lot of moulting cock-sparrows eargerly waiting for a hand-out of bread-crumbs.

Once in the witness box these cheerful, uninhibited country folk really came to life. With much miming they proceeded vividly to describe and to demonstrate how, with their own eyes, they had seen the Saza Chief shoot the elephant in question. The average African peasant is a born actor and orator, and given the slightest encouragement he will dramatise a story to such an extent that it will become quite unrecognisable from the original version. In this case the defence witnesses obviously realised that it was very much in their own interest to make sure that their Chief was not convicted. There might be satisfactory rewards if they succeeded. They would certainly feel the iron hand of feudal retribution if they failed. So, the court was entertained by a vivid charade of crouching, leaping men, whispering and shouting as their story unfurled, and all ending with a realistic interpretation of the dying groans of the slaughtered elephant and the triumphant yell of the victorious Chief.

As a pantomime it was magnificent, but as a defence case it was a spectacular failure. Each witness tried to outdo the performance of the one before, each in his turn adding some extra embellishment, or a fancied variation of his own, to the previously agreed theme. One lean, grizzled old man so far forgot himself as to describe graphically how the Chief had actually killed the elephant with a single, powerful thrust from his razor-edged spear, instead of with three shots from a rather worn ·404 rifle. In demonstrating the follow through of the dramatic, fatal thrust, the sprightly old fellow was so carried away by his story that he forgot to let go of his imaginary spear; still clinging grimly to its invisible shaft, he dived headlong out of the open door of the witness box to land with a thud at the feet of the astonished advocate.

I looked at the magistrate. He had laid down his pen; his face was buried in his hands; and his shoulders were shaking. The only person who stayed impassive to the end was the large, corpulent Saza Chief. Throughout the proceedings his round, fat face remained as inscrutable as most of the traditional graven images of Buddha. The questions put to him he answered with curt monosyllables and the occasional shake or nod of his head. For the rest of the time he sat motionless, heavy-bellied and ox-like, only his eyes betraying any sign of emotion; deep set, cruel and snake-like, from time to time they narrowed and flickered as one or other of his followers deviated from the story he had been instructed to tell. On each occasion I was sorry for the man concerned, but when the case ended I felt nothing but elation at the result; the Chief himself was convicted and fined heavily, and later also had his firearms licence revoked and his rifle impounded by the police for the duration of the automatic three-year hunting ban – a severe blow to his grossly inflated ego.

*

These successful prosecutions marked the beginning of a pro-longed campaign to clean up the ivory trade. Although they shook the more unscrupulous ivory dealers of Kampala, it was like cutting off one tentacle of a giant octopus. Nevertheless, it was one of the longest and most favoured arms of an organisation that had previously moved openly and unhindered, to and fro between Mombasa and Kampala. A number of other tentacles still remained, operating in secret, while the powerful main body of this cancerous organisation, established for centuries along the full length of the East African coast, continued to dominate both the legal and illegal sides of the ancient ivory trade.

A couple of years later, when I obtained more staff, I was able further to tighten the grip of the Game Department. With an expanded and re-organised team it was possible to introduce closer and more careful checks on the activities of both ivory dealers and licence holders – to good effect.

One measure that I introduced, after I became Chief Game Warden, was a test that all applicants for hunting licences were required to pass. This test consisted of a simple but thorough examination on the aspirant's knowledge of the game laws and of the vital shots on dangerous animals, followed by a practical check of his ability to handle a rifle and shoot with it accurately.

When this measure was first proposed it was greeted with howls of protest. The idea was an innovation in Africa and as its instigator abuse was showered on my head. My reply was that a rifle is far more of a lethal weapon than a motor vehicle. Therefore, if it was considered necessary, in the public interest, for people to pass a strict test before they were permitted to hold a driving licence and use a car, then it was even more important that they should prove their knowledge and ability before being let loose with a high-powered rifle to hunt dangerous game.

As I pointed out at the time, a bullet from a modern, high-velocity rifle can kill a man a mile away. I also stressed that it is only too easy for a nervous, incompetent novice to wound and lose dangerous animals such as elephant and buffalo, rhino and hippo, leopard and lion. Quite apart from the humanitarian aspect, these animals themselves then become a very real danger to the general public. In fact, during my years as a game warden, I have known many innocent and unsuspecting passers-by, and also members of my own staff, to be killed or seriously injured by animals previously wounded and callously abandoned by poachers or incompetent and cowardly amateur hunters.

But the new measure had a secondary, yet almost as important, object. It was also aimed at thinning out the ranks of 'armchair' hunters – the people who bought illegal ivory from poachers, or 'lent' their rifles to others whom they hired to do their hunting for them.

The early days of these tests brought some surprising results. One of the most 'successful' elephant hunters of Uganda's Western Province – a man who for years had obtained his full, annual legal quota of big tuskers – when tested by a game warden in Fort Portal, was found to be quite incapable of even loading his own heavy magazine rifle, a ·404 bore with the normal, standard Mauser bolt action!

In yet another case fate stepped in and retribution was swift and final. A former licence holder, who had failed the Game Department's new test, appealed to a busy and indulgent district commissioner. The applicant complained that the shooting test was both unjust and too hard, and in a moment of weakness his appeal was allowed. The next day he went out hunting and wounded an elephant, whereupon the enraged beast turned and charged him. His tracker dived into a bush and escaped, but the hunter was too slow. His last minute, panic shot missed altogether and the elephant caught him in its trunk. What was left of his body was eventually found by his friends and relatives.

*

Contrary to a widely held belief, elephants in a large part of Africa – and particularly in East Africa – are in no danger of extermination. In fact, in many areas there are now far too many of these great beasts and in their own interests alone their numbers have to be controlled.

Ivory is the most important by-product of elephant control and as long as there are elephants in Africa the ivory trade will continue as it has done for thousands of years. There is no evil in the legitimate trade in ivory from such organised management operations. The danger lies in the killing of excessive numbers of the larger tuskers by poachers or inadequately supervised licence holders. It is this selective killing of the finest mature breeding material that inevitably leads in the end to the production of steadily increasing numbers of degenerate specimens, the final result being elephant population with poor ivory and often a high proportion of completely tuskless animals.

Food, environment, and vital trace elements in the soil, are undoubtedly all factors which have an important effect on the production of big, quick growing, high quality ivory, but it is equally certain that heredity plays a no less important part.

From the point of view of the healthy continuation of the species, there is no harm in the killing of very old bulls, well past their prime, and it is amongst these patriarchs that the very heaviest ivory is usually found. However, the proportion of these mighty tuskers to the overall elephant population is very small, and the average licence holder or poacher is therefore well content with the often fine tusks carried by the best specimens of mature bulls in their breeding prime. It is here that the danger to the species lies, which is why it is so important to protect this particular section of the elephant population from excessive exploitation – legal or illegal. When considered in this context, the few but successful prosecutions in Kampala at the end of 1949, the ivory cases that surprised the hunters and dealers alike, take on a new significance.

137

CHAPTER 8

Westward Ho!

IF you had glanced at a game map of Uganda at any time during
the past forty years, one thing would have stuck out like a sore
thumb – the fact that, until 1958, all Uganda's main game
reserves, sanctuaries, and latterly national parks also, were
concentrated in a long, tenuous belt stretching the whole length
of the country's western regions, from the Sudan border in the
north to the boundaries of the Congo and Rwanda in the south.
From this fact you would have been justified in assuming that
most, if not all, of Uganda's wildlife problems and resources
were to be found in the west, and, to a very large extent, you
would have been right. What the map would not have shown you,
however, is that the west of Uganda has also long been notable
as the final home of the country's few pioneer European settlers,
that rugged band of indomitable spirits whose exploits and esca-
pades have added a vivid chapter to the chequered history of
this fascinating country.

Around the turn of the century and the years that followed,
the west of Uganda, like the western frontier of America, was a
land of quarrelling tribes and tough European adventurers
seeking their fortunes. There was gold and there were vast herds of
buffalo, as well as other game. But above all there were elephant,
mighty herds of great, grey monsters bearing the gleaming ivory

for which there was an apparently insatiable market across the oceans.

It was the elephants, or rather the valuable ivory they carried, which drew most of the European adventurers to western Uganda in the early years of the twentieth century. But when professional ivory hunting became no longer legally profitable or illegally feasible, many of them turned their hand to prospecting, coupled with buffalo hunting – and a little poaching on the side – to help out the larder and ease the exchequer.

A number of these colourful characters eventually came to a violent or tragic end. Some were killed by elephant, others by buffalo; others again died a lonely death in the bush from black-water fever, while a few reached the end of their tether and blew out their brains over a bottle of raw spirit. Of the survivors, and there were not over-many, a small band finally settled themselves in the lush country that nestles in the shadow of the towering Ruwenzori Range; there, at the end of their travels, they attempted to make an honest living from growing coffee and later tea. Of this small remnant, a few were recruited as the first game rangers of the Uganda Game Department, elephant control then becoming their primary official duty just as before hunting for ivory had been their livelihood.

I arrived in Uganda the year after Captain R. J. D. Salmon, M.V.O., M.C., retired. 'Samaki,' as he was better known – after the Kiswahili word for fish – had been, of all the old-time game rangers, the greatest elephant hunter, not only because he was a brilliant shot but because, so it was said, he could think like the elephants he hunted and thus anticipate their reactions under any set of circumstances.

'Samaki,' who had operated mainly in Uganda's Western Province during his service with the Game Department, had been succeeded by Bill Pridham, a tough, humorous, adventurous and immensely likeable character, who had served his apprentice-ship as a hunter with several of the old-timers. Thus, at the age of thirty-six, Bill was a valuable link with a previous era, a bridge between the old and the new. He was the first of the Uganda game wardens whom I was to meet, but before that notable event occurred I was destined to have my first encounter with that redoubtable animal *Syncerus caffer*, the African buffalo.

No one has yet attempted to make a census of Uganda's

total buffalo population for the simple reason that it would be an impossible task. Although more dependent on water than the elephant – since it must drink daily even if it has to travel many miles to do so – the buffalo is just as adaptable and generally tougher and more resilient, besides being a far quicker breeder. In Uganda the buffalo is virtually ubiquitous, being found wherever there is adequate water and grazing; this means practically the whole country, with conditions of terrain varying from hot, low-lying, swampy valleys filled with dense stands of tall, tangled grass, through semi-arid thorn-scrub savannah dotted with widely-spaced water-holes, to high, cold mountain forest where the grassy glades and tinkling streams are chilled by frosty nights and the clinging tendrils of descending cloud.

Built like a small tank, a big bull buffalo is a formidable animal. Standing over five feet at the shoulder, squarely made, heavily muscled, his head protected by the iron hard bosses of his mighty, sweeping horns, and weighing nearly three-quarters of a ton, he can be a dangerous adversary. Normally shy and retiring, buffalo are blessed with good sight, hearing and scenting powers, but cursed with a suspicious but uncontrollable curiosity. They are not usually aggressive, unless sick or injured, but a cow with a calf is not to be trusted, while the temper of old bulls is sometimes uncertain. All in all they are probably the most dangerous of beasts to take liberties with, and if wounded they become the most vicious, aggressive, determined and revengeful of enemies.

Captain F. C. Selous, the doyen of all Africa's great hunter-naturalists and the model for Rider Haggard's famous fictional character Allan Quartermain, once summed up the opinion of most hunter-naturalists of his era: 'With regard to character and temperament, I consider the buffalo the pluckiest, and, when wounded, the most savage and cunning of all game considered "dangerous".'*

To this day, few knowledgeable people would disagree with his view. For me, while the elephant inspires feelings of awe and affection, the buffalo arouses a sense of wholesome respect bordering on fear. I have had some narrow escapes with buffalo, and on three occasions I have been charged quite unprovoked by crotchety old bulls, but when I went to Uganda in 1949, I had yet to see my first buffalo in the wild. This omission was very

* R. Lydekker *The Game Animals of Africa*.

soon to be rectified in a way that was eventful enough to set the seal on my respect for the buffalo from the beginning.

*

In the last week of January 1950, I was on safari, camped on the forward slope of a gently rising ridge overlooking the Katonga river, in the northwest corner of Masaka District, at a point close to where the districts of Masaka, Mubende, Toro and Ankole meet. This was the heart of some of Uganda's best buffalo country; rolling, grassy hills dotted with clumps of thorn scrub, and broad valley bottoms covered with patches of open bush interspersed with areas of open grass and occasional groves of large shady trees; some of the valleys were filled by papyrus swamps draining northwards into the Katonga. Everywhere there was an abundance of good grazing, ample water, shade from the sun, and protective cover. No buffalo could wish for more.

I had left Entebbe three days earlier, on the start of an extended tour of inspection of Uganda's Western Province, my first thorough look at some of the main wildlife areas of Uganda. Charles Pitman had briefed me carefully and had also given me several general and one or two specific objectives. 'I have always tried to tour each of the four provinces at least once during the course of the year,' he had said. 'And this time I would like you to do it. As far as game problems are concerned the Western Province is, in many ways, the most important of the four; it accounts for well over half of the Game Department's elephant and buffalo control work, and the majority of our main game reserves and sanctuaries are situated within its boundaries. It's for these reasons that all three of our game wardens, and the majority of our game guards also, are, at present, stationed in the Western Province.

'As you know, there are four districts in the Western Province,' Charles Pitman had reminded me. 'Bunyoro in the north, Toro and Ankole in the centre, and Kigezi in the south. Of our game wardens Bill Pridham is at present based at Kichwamba, on the border between Toro and Ankole. Mike Holmes, who has just completed his training, is at Fort Portal, the Toro District headquarters. The third of our wardens, John Mills, is based at Hoima, the district headquarters for Bunyoro. For this safari I think you should concentrate on Ankole and Toro, where we have a lot of problems. I would like you to spend some time in

Masaka – that's one of the western districts of Buganda Province, bordering on Ankole – on the way. The Senior Assistant Resident* in Masaka has written to complain about buffalo damaging shambas in the north of the district, near the Katonga. He says there are far too many buffalo there, and I think it would be a good thing if you could look into the matter on the ground. Apparently one of our game guards, Joseph Kapere, has just had a brush with a buffalo somewhere in that area. I don't think he has been badly hurt but his rifle has been broken.' Then, with a slow smile, Charles Pitman concluded, 'You might like to try your hand at dealing with them. It will be good experience for you and you can look into the poaching situation at the same time.'

The problem of buffalo control calls for some explanation. In a country like Uganda, much of which provides optimum habitat conditions for buffalo, it is a problem that is in most ways similar to that of elephant control. It has one special and particularly serious aspect however, the danger of disease, a danger which is enhanced in Uganda by the size of the country's buffalo population.

If I was asked to make an estimate, I should say that there were, and probably still are, at least a hundred thousand buffalo in Uganda. I doubt that there are fewer; there could well be many more. Bearing in mind that so much of the terrain is ideal 'buffalo country', I certainly do not think it is too much to claim that Uganda has at least four times as many buffalo as elephant.

When persistently and heavily hunted, elephant are inclined to abandon a given area – at least temporarily; not so the buffalo. This astute and determined animal, provided there is adequate cover, is just as likely to change its habits and become nocturnal, seeking the protection of the densest cover to rest by day and only emerging to graze at night. After dark the buffalo has little to fear from legitimate hunting methods. A few are taken by lion, but apart from man the only other factor which can effectively control buffalo numbers is the undesirable one of disease.

With any gregarious animal species disease is often the by-product of over-population and 'yarding' – the habit of remaining in the same general area, in large numbers, for a prolonged period of time. When this happens, not only does the habitat

* In the special case of Buganda Province, District Commissioners were called Assistant Residents.

suffer from excessive grazing or browsing, but a disease lying dormant but simmering may break out into a dangerous epizootic through the lowered resistance of the animals concerned. As Dr Frank Fraser Darling – one of the world's leading ecologists and one of the most eminent of living conservationists – has often pointed out, for this reason alone some disturbance is good for closely gregarious animals.

In the case of the buffalo the disease problem is aggravated by the fact that not only is this prolific animal extremely susceptible to rinderpest – unlike the elephant – but when infected it travels great distances in a very short time. In this manner the killer disease is spread far and wide, and at great speed, infecting many other species as well. Eland, bush-pig, warthog and all members of the bushbuck family are also particularly susceptible to rinderpest, and so, of course, are domestic cattle, while few ungulates are entirely immune. Thus the appearance of a rinderpest epizootic is dreaded by game wardens, farmers and veterinarians alike.

These few facts alone are more than sufficient to underline the importance of controlling the numbers of the more prolific animal species, such as the buffalo.

Elephant are frequently addicted to shamba raiding; buffalo much less so. Nevertheless, when they do decide to enter cultivation, buffalo can do considerable damage to standing crops, if only by the trampling of their sledgehammer hooves. Because of this, and in view of the importance of controlling their numbers as a measure to inhibit the outbreak and spread of disease, complaints of shamba raiding by buffalo were, as often as not, accepted at their face value by the Uganda Game Department. Even though it was sometimes transparently obvious that the complaint had been instigated by an irresistible desire for a feast of free meat, in turn inspired by the mere appearance of a herd of buffalo anywhere near the shambas in question, in all areas where buffalo were normally abundant, the game warden or game guard concerned would usually try to shoot one or two of these beasts if there really were any in the close vicinity of cultivation.

*

Joseph Kapere was one of the more senior of the Department's game guards. I had picked him up on my way through Masaka

township, where I had called at the district headquarters to see
the Senior Assistant Resident, John Wild – a most able man with a
quiet sense of humour who was to become a great ally and personal friend.

Game Guard Joseph Kapere had been waiting for me – a
small, tough, wiry little figure, brown and wrinkled like a ripe
walnut, his age indicated by the pepper and salt effect of his close
cropped skull. With apparent unconcern he had shown me a
massive bruise and extensive grazing on his left thigh where the
buffalo had struck him, and his khaki tunic ripped from waist to
collar by its vicious, hooking horns as it had tossed him into a bush.
In fact, he had been far more concerned about his ·404 magazine
rifle. The stock had been cracked and the foresight knocked off,
which had made it difficult for him to finish the animal, he said.
The little man's quiet confidence and lack of heroics impressed
me from the start. I had taken an instant liking to him, and my feelings were enhanced by the loving care with which he handled
the brand new rifle that I had brought for him from Entebbe.

Subsequently, we spent three days searching for the elusive
buffalo herds in the region of the Katonga. Their tracks were so
numerous that they looked like the trails of droves of cattle on a
well-stocked ranch, but the buffalo had all seemed to be favouring
the sanctuary of the swamp.

Every time we found buffalo tracks leading in or out of the
broad, reed-filled course of the Katonga, I had an uneasy sensation in the pit of my stomach, for I couldn't help remembering
the grim details of a report that had arrived at the Game Department office just before I had left Entebbe. It had come from
the District Commissioner of West Nile. 'A most unusual casualty
has just occurred,' the District Commissioner had written. 'A
Madi speared a buffalo which went off into a muddy swamp.
The hunter went after it and came on the buffalo which charged
him; neither was able to move very fast on account of the mud
which was up to the hunter's knees and the buffalo's belly. While
retreating before the enraged animal the African fell on his back,
whereupon the buffalo reached out and bit the man in the lower
abdomen removing his genitalia. The unfortunate Madi later
died in hospital.'

The District Commissioner's final, sardonic comment had stuck
in my mind. 'This is a curious reversal of the common practice

amongst certain tribes,' the District Commissioner had written. 'I refer to their custom of devouring the testes of buffaloes in order to increase their own virility!'

On our fourth day on the Katonga our luck changed. With me in camp, besides Joseph Kapere and Firipo, my gun-bearer, I had my safari cook, Sadi, and a local guide – a Muhima who knew every inch of the country, but was more interested in the lions that preyed on his long-horned Ankole cattle than in shamba raiding buffalo. I had also brought my dog Bhalu, a black Labrador retriever, whom I somewhat optimistically hoped to turn into a buffalo hunting dog, despite the fact that he was too fat and out of condition.

Before dawn on the fourth day we set out from camp. Joseph Kapere and the Muhima, with his long, broad-bladed spear, led the way, ranging ahead to look for fresh buffalo tracks. Firipo, carrying my heavy rifle, trailed behind me. At my heels, and soon panting from the unaccustomed exertion, ambled Bhalu. I was carrying my light ·275 Rigby, mainly in case of a chance to collect a pig or a small buck for some much needed camp meat towards the end of the day.

Turning to the pages of my safari diary. Under the heading 'Wednesday, the 25th of January – the Day of the Buffalo!' the scrawled words, faded and blurred with the passage of time, read:

About 7.30 a.m., sun well up and getting warmer, almost trod on a three foot puff adder which struck at Bhalu but luckily missed. Dog moved surprisingly fast despite his corpulence, but snake probably still rather sluggish after cool night. The Muhima killed the snake, removing its head with one swift spear thrust. Remembered old African superstition that a snake crossing one's path ahead at the beginning of a hunt is an auspicious omen – better still if the snake is killed! In fact, soon after this incident we found fresh tracks of a small buffalo herd that appeared to be moving away from the river.

Started tracking about 8.30 a.m. and followed the herd over the hills, getting very hot. At 11.00 a.m., still following tracks, met a party of Bahima bringing in meat from a cow which had been killed by a lion during the night. The kill had occurred a few miles further west near the Ankole border – a region notorious for cattle-killers and man-eaters according to Kapere and my Muhima guide. Noted for further investigation.

About 11.30 a.m. we almost caught up with the herd of buffalo, catching a brief glimpse of them in open bush. They were about thirty strong and galloped off when we were some one hundred and fifty yards away. The wind was in our favour, they could not have seen us, and we were moving very quietly. However, the dog was panting like an asthmatic steam engine from the heat and unaccustomed exercise. This strange noise was probably more than enough to alarm the buffalo! We stood and watched them disappear over a hill about a quarter of a mile ahead and then followed up hard.

Reaching the crest we saw the herd at the bottom of a valley, clustering in some patches of bush and big trees, some six hundred yards away.

How well I recall that scene even now, over twenty years later. The members of the herd were moving slowly, in and out of the bush, grazing quietly. Through my binoculars I could see that most of them were cows, but several were big, heavy-bodied bulls with massive, sweeping horns. At the time it seemed almost a crime to disturb them, but this feeling may have been influenced by the nervous flutter in my stomach. Steeling myself, I remembered my orders and the torn and trampled crops I had seen in the shambas a few miles away; slowly my feelings changed and very soon the excitement of the old primaeval hunting instinct gained control. Rising to my feet, I took my double ·470 from Firipo, ordering him to remain where he was with Bhalu and the Muhima guide, and signalled to Joseph Kapere to follow me.

Slowly and carefully, with the light breeze blowing in our faces, Kapere and I worked our way quietly down into the valley. Using every bit of cover, we got nearer and nearer to the herd until a mere thirty yards separated us from the nearest beast – a young and alert cow who seemed to be staring curiously at the bush behind which we were sheltering, her head raised and her moist, black nose thrust forward in the unmistakable stance of a suspicious buffalo. It was time for action.

An old bull, his head lowered and the ends of his massive, low-curved horns sweeping the tips of the short grass on which he was grazing, moved ponderously into the open about forty yards away. I wanted to see how Joseph Kapere could shoot, particularly after his recent near escape, so I whispered in his ear that he should take the unsuspecting bull. With a grin, the old Game Guard slowly raised his ·404 to his shoulder and started to ease himself round the bush for a clear shot.

146

All of a sudden I noticed that something was wrong. One minute there had been a scene of quiet, peaceful tranquillity; the next second every animal in sight was alert and watchful. The young cow had turned slightly and was now staring fixedly at a point behind us and to our right. Even the old bull had raised his massive head and was gazing intently in the same direction. For several, long-drawn seconds everything was still. The breeze had dropped, and, half-way round the bush, Joseph Kapere, the old and seasoned hunter, had frozen like a statue, his rifle still held loosely at his shoulder. Then, with an explosive snort, the cow tossed her head, whirled on her heels like a polo pony, and galloped into the bush, followed closely by the rest of the herd in a thundering, close-packed mass, their passage marked by a slowly rising cloud of soft, grey dust.

For a moment I was stunned; then, as I rose slowly to my feet, surprised, bewildered and acutely disappointed, a slight movement caught the corner of my eye – over to my right, not more than thirty paces away, a crouching figure was creeping stealthily forward behind a dense patch of low bush; clasped in one lean, brown hand was a long, broad-bladed spear; it was our Muhima guide.

'What the . . .!' I exploded in a flash of rage and chagrin. The Muhima stood up, a self-conscious smile hovering on his lips like that of an embarrassed child caught in the act of sneaking into the larder.

'What the *hell* do you think you're doing?' I shouted, in my fury forgetting to speak in Kiswahili – which the Muhima would probably not have understood in any case, although whatever language I had used he could hardly have failed to sense the meaning from the tone of my voice. He didn't answer for the simple reason that he did not have time to do so; but I discovered later, from Firipo, that this man had left him saying he wanted to urinate, although the truth was that he had been unable to resist the temptation to follow the hunt.

In response to my shout the Muhima slowly parted his lips as if to reply, but no words came. Instead his jaw dropped, his mouth gaped and a look of horror gradually spread across his face, his eyes bulging with terrified disbelief as he stared at the dense patch of bush behind which he had been sheltering. Suddenly there was an explosive snort, a crash of broken branches, and, with an earth shaking rumble of hooves, a great, black shape launched itself out of the tangled undergrowth, straight for the Muhima who seemed rooted to the ground.

Everything happened so fast and unexpectedly that I was taken completely by surprise. One second the lean Muhima was standing, transfixed with fear, as erect and rigid as a telegraph pole; split seconds later he was sailing through the air like a broken doll, arms and legs flung wide, his spear glinting in the sunlight as it followed his writhing body into a thorn bush in a slow graceful curve; over the spot where he had been standing, its head still raised in the follow-through of the toss, thundered an enormous buffalo bull.

Before I could even think my heavy, double-barrelled rifle was at my shoulder, and as the great bull turned to renew the attack I fired. The solid 500 grain bullet smashing into its right shoulder caused the buffalo to stumble but, quick as a cat, it recovered, changed direction, and came straight for me.

Close on my left I heard the roar of Joseph Kapere's rifle and I saw the dust fly from the buffalo's grey, mud-caked hide where the ·404 bullet had struck high on its back. The animal neither flinched nor faltered; without even a break in its stride it thundered on towards me, its black, scarred nose thrust menacirgly forward, the low, curving sweep of its massive, gnarled horns protecting the points of its powerful shoulders. Having only one shot remaining in my rifle, and no time to reload, I held my fire until the buffalo rounded the bush behind which I had been crouching; the instant it did so the bead of my foresight swung on to the centre of the great bull's heavily muscled chest and, almost automatically, I pressed the trigger of the left barrel.

What happened next is still a confused blur in my mind. I remember the leaping barrels, the roar of the shot, and a sensation like the smashing blow of a violent rugby tackle as I hurled myself to one side. Then, as I slowly got to my knees, still clutching my now empty rifle, there was a rending crash in the bushes behind me, followed by an earth-shaking thud, a long-drawn, moaning bellow and finally silence. A few moments later, still dazed and bewildered, I felt a firm hand under my arm. 'Amikwisha kufa – it is dead, Bwana,' the steady voice of the old game guard sounded reassuringly in my ear as Joseph Kapere helped me to my feet.

'How's the Muhima?' I asked, staring anxiously at the lanky figure of the herdsman, who was standing a few yards away, bent awkwardly over backwards, apparently trying to examine his now naked buttocks.

'He's all right, Bwana,' grinned Kapere, 'except for the thorns in his backside. Serves him right,' he added severely. 'He shouldn't have disobeyed orders.'

Both the Muhima and I had been lucky. He had made a frantic leap at the last moment and the buffalo's hooking horns had done little more than add momentum to his parabolic dive into the thorn bush. I myself had merely been caught a glancing blow as I jumped aside and had suffered no more damage than a few painful bruises. The buffalo, on the other hand, had paid the full penalty for his savage, and entirely unprovoked attack – but the reason for it puzzled me.

Whistling up Firipo and the dog, and helped by the limping, grumbling Muhima, we cleared the bush around the dead body of the buffalo and examined the carcass carefully. It proved to be an old and massive bull, just past his prime. He measured sixty-one inches at the shoulder and his horns, the tips of which were worn and splintered, spanned forty-two inches. Apart from the wounds caused by the bullets that Kapere and I had fired there was no sign of injury, nor were there any indications of sickness. Even when the body had been finally skinned and dismembered we could find no physical reason to account for the old bull's vicious and spontaneous charge.

Thinking things over at the time, I came to the conclusion that the old bull must have been lying down asleep in the bush until disturbed by the stampede of the herd and my shout at the Muhima. Following this train of thought, he could have awakened suddenly to see the tall, threatening figure of the Muhima – with his long, gleaming spear – standing almost on top of him. With most potentially dangerous species of animals, attack is often the preferred means of defence when surprised or caught at a disadvantage, and the old buffalo's immediate reaction had probably been to charge his traditional enemy. Whether my deductions were right or not, there had been no mistaking the savagery and determination of the old bull's attack. In fact, it is so firmly implanted in my memory that I have often thought of it since, particularly on the frequent occasions when, as a game warden,

I have had cause to warn well-meaning but inexperienced animal lovers that most wild animals are, at some time or another, potentially dangerous.

So ended my first and unforgettable encounter with the African buffalo. All that was left was the long, weary trek back to camp. My bruised leg gave me some trouble, but Bhalu, with his dense Labrador coat and his excess fat, was in a far worse state than I was. He was so out of condition that the miles of scrambling over the rolling hills in the burning heat proved almost too much for him. In the end I had to revive him at frequent intervals by pouring water into his mouth from my water-bottle, and in the final stages Firipo and I had virtually to carry him into camp. There, I came to the sad conclusion that, good as he was with game birds, he was unlikely ever to make the grade as a 'buffalo dog'!

The one bright spot of the journey was when we called at the village whose shambas had been damaged by the buffalo herd. There were scenes of wild excitement when the news of the old bull's death became known, and in a few minutes a long, straggling line of men, women and children, bearing knives, axes and baskets, to carry the meat, had set off over the hills, back-tracking our trail like a pack of eager bloodhounds.

By the camp fire that night, as we roasted great slabs of raw meat over the glowing embers, spitting them on the tips of our hunting knives, Joseph Kapere, the veteran game guard, regaled me with tales of his past encounters with savage buffalo. In the years that followed I was to hear many such stories from all quarters of Uganda, and every year, among the game guards, there were more casualties from buffalo than from any other animal. Sometimes, in fact more often than not, the initial fault was that of man, for the ubiquitous buffalo, with its massive load of juicy meat, has always been the main target of the callous poacher in Uganda. Slightly wounded by a poacher's careless rifle shot, smarting from a charge of buck-shot under its thick hide, or suffering agonies from a broken wire snare deeply embedded in the flesh of its neck or a leg, the always potentially aggressive buffalo then becomes a very dangerous customer indeed.

The humane destruction of such inevitably savage and vindictive animals was thus a routine and frequent task for the

Author's camp overlooking the Katonga River swamp

Uganda kob, Queen Elizabeth National Park

Game Department launch on patrol in Lake George Game Reserve

The author gaffing a Nile perch below the Murchison Falls

African game guards, many of whom, time and again, proved themselves to be men of the greatest courage, determination and endurance. One of these sterling characters later became my gun-bearer; his name was Nehemia Adjedra and, although what I am about to recount happened some four years after my own first buffalo hunt, I am telling the story here to emphasise what I have said above in regard to the fine qualities of most of the Game Department's game guards and the dangers they so frequently have to face.

In my official annual report for 1955, I included the following extract from the report of the Game Warden in charge of Bunyoro District – 'In May, 1955, Recruit Game Guard Nehemia Adjedra was attacked by a wounded buffalo, and fired three shots into it as it came for him. He failed to stop it in time, and was picked up on its horns by his trousers. He held on to the horns and was struggling to free himself, when the buffalo tried to toss him. A horn pierced his abdomen, fortunately without also piercing the gut, and he then got himself free. The buffalo was speared by a party of men who were following to get meat.

'The Game Guard walked some miles back to his house, holding his insides in with his hands. Later he was brought to Masindi hospital, and was operated on by the doctor. He brought his rifle back with him, and cleaned it while waiting for the ambulance. He is now completely recovered and back on duty!'

*

Two days after leaving the Katonga I arrived in Kichwamba, which is the headquarters of the Saza of Bunyaruguru, one of the counties of the District of Ankole; it is a small straggling village of mud-walled houses and thatch-roofed huts surrounded by banana shambas, sited in hilly, broken country resulting from massive and comparatively recent geological movements and volcanic action. In the deep, steep-sided valleys are a number of small, dark crater lakes, while the rolling slopes of the mountains are a green mosaic of open grassland interspersed with patches of tall tropical forest. The valley bottoms are filled with a dense tangle of high grass, low bush and further patches of towering rain forest, the whole forming a perfect sanctuary for elephant and buffalo, giant forest-hog and bushpig, bushbuck, duiker, and a variety of birds and monkeys besides many lesser mammals, as well as the sleek, darkly coated leopards that prey on all but the larger species.

The village ends abruptly at the edge of the escarpment that overlooks the western branch of the Great Rift Valley, the gigantic geological fault that stretches all the way from Syria, in the Middle East, thence via the Red Sea trough, Ethiopia, and Lake Rudolf in Kenya, right on down to the southern end of Lake Malawi. Its western branch extends in an arc through the great Uganda lakes of Albert, George and Edward, on through Lake Kivu in the Congo, and then down the four hundred mile length of Lake Tanganyika, finally rejoining the eastern branch of the Rift at Lake Malawi. But it is in Uganda that the Western Rift Valley is at its most dramatic, and nowhere more so than in the region below Kichwamba, where the blue-green waters of Lakes George and Edward – linked by the Kazinga Channel – sprawl lazily across the broad, grassy plains – teeming with great herds of game – that stretch, far and wide, under the brooding, sixteen thousand foot massif of the Ruwenzori Range, the awe-inspiring, snow-capped Mountains of the Moon.

The first thing that struck me, when I reached Kichwamba, was the siting of three isolated and widely spaced buildings perched high in commanding positions right on the lip of the escarpment. On the right was a small, white, thatch-roofed cottage. In the centre was a low, sprawling building strongly built of grey stone. On the left was a new, red-roofed bungalow of modern design. All three of these very different buildings had one thing in common – a share of one of the most magnificent views to be found anywhere in Uganda.

The cottage was occupied by an ex-Provincial Commissioner, by the name of Temple-Perkins, a keen naturalist, author*, and renowned elephant hunter, who, though a New Zealander by birth, on his retirement had been unable to tear himself away from the country of the elephants he loved so much. A tall man, with a deep, booming voice, and known affectionately to his friends as 'Purple-Tompkins', he was one of Uganda's great 'characters', and in the autumn of his years he perched quietly in his hunter's eyrie, the hunter turned watcher, happily studying the great herds and the mighty tuskers which had lured him to this colourful land in his more active days.

* E. A. Temple-Perkins *Kingdom of the Elephant.*

The low, stone building in the centre was a hostelry for travellers, a simple but attractive wayside inn which gloried in the name of the 'Kichwamba Hotel'. Unpretentious it may have been, but it provided a warm welcome and creature comforts for all who passed that way, as well as forming a focal point and gathering place for many assorted and widely scattered lovers of the wild.

The new bungalow on the left – at that time temporarily occupied by Bill Pridham – had been specially built for the Game and Fisheries Department as a home and base for a fisheries officer, an important part of the Government's post-war development plans, for between them Lake George and the Uganda waters of Lake Edward form one of the richest freshwater fisheries in the world. Even in those early days Uganda's small eastern portion of the 830 square miles of Lake Edward was producing some two thousand tons of fish per year, while from the tiny, shallow Lake George – a natural fish pond only eight square miles in area and nowhere more than eight feet deep – came the fantastic annual total of nearly three thousand tons of tasty, edible fish, mainly the carp-like *Tilapia nilotica*, locally known as *ngege*. The secret was a combination of shallow water, almost unlimited sunshine, and vast amounts of natural fertiliser provided by the enormous concentration of hippopotomi. These great, water-loving animals, of which there were later found to be some fifteen thousand in the region, not only literally manure the water with their dung, but plough up the bottom muds with their churning feet to release enormous quantities of vital nutrient salts into the shallow, sun-warmed water. The result is a prodigious growth of phyto-plankton, the microscopic algae – or aquatic vegetable matter – on which the numerous *ngege* wax and grow fat.

The Uganda shores of Lake Edward, and the northern and western shores of Lake George, were protected by two connecting game reserves, in all more than a thousand square miles of grassland, bush and forest containing many species of large, spectacular mammals as well as the ubiquitous hippo. Within the boundaries of these reserves there were often as many as two thousand elephants at one time, and even larger numbers of buffalo and various species of antelope. Of the latter the handsome Uganda kob – very like a stocky version of the unrelated but better known impala – was the commonest, while on the short grass plains

155

at the southern end of the Lake Edward Game Reserve, vast herds of the striking chestnut and rich plum coloured topi abounded.

But perhaps the most eye-catching of all the antelope in the Game Reserves of Lake George and Lake Edward were the great Defassa waterbuck, with their shaggy, brown coats and sharply contrasting white rumps. The males in particular, with their long, sweeping horns, regal bearing and imperious, mien, have always reminded me forcibly of the red deer stags on the high hills of my native Scotland. In fact, the waterbuck of the Lake Edward region of the Western Rift Valley have the longest horns of all the local races of this handsome African species, the world record of nearly forty inches having been obtained from this locality. Moreover, near Lake Edward I have myself seen, at various times, a number of magnificent waterbuck males the length of whose horns must have exceeded the official record by a handsome margin.

Last but not least were the now famous tree-climbing lions of the Lake Edward plains, the often present but seldom seen leopards, the giant forest-hogs that lurked in the riverine bush, the ubiquitous and comical wart-hogs, and water birds in their legions. So much and more was there in this scenically beautiful area, in describing which it is impossible to avoid the liberal use of superlatives, that it is small wonder that for twenty-five years it had remained the apple of the Game Department's eye. In fact, it was the heart of a region in which the Department had long concentrated much of its resources and efforts, sadly limited though the former had always been.

I shall never forget my first sight of this wonderful wildlife area, when I strolled to the lip of the escarpment in front of the Kichwamba Hotel and found myself looking down on the game filled plains far below. The landscape was peppered with tiny red, brown and black dots that were kob and waterbuck and buffalo, while almost every tree seemed to shelter an elephant or two – some solitary old bulls, their long, white tusks gleaming as they dozed in the shade; others restless, family groups of cows and calves shifting in and out of cover, never still for long. But, despite my penchant for elephants, I think it was the buffalo of these two game reserves that always impressed me most.

Great herds of these buffalo, hundreds strong, roamed the lakeside plains, while old bachelor bulls, singly or in small groups

Waterbuck, pursued by wild dog, takes refuge in the
Kazinga Channel, Uganda

Hippos in Lake Edward

of two or three or more, usually remained in chosen areas, often for days and weeks at a time. During the heat of the day these old buffalo bulls rested beneath the upward thrusting branches of some of the many grotesque looking *Euphorbia candelabrum* trees that graced the landscape. Lying in the shade, peacefully and sleepily chewing the cud, apparently as tame as domestic cattle, these battle-scarred old warriors would normally allow a vehicle to approach to within a few yards of them without even bothering to look up. I have said 'normally' advisedly, since it was one of these gnarled patriarchs who was responsible for one of three unprovoked attacks I have experienced from buffalo. It happened nearly thirteen years after I first visited the Lake George and Lake Edward Game Reserves, and over eleven years after we had converted the area into the now world famous Queen Elizabeth National Park.

On that occasion I was being taken on a tour of inspection by Frank Poppleton, the Senior Park Warden at the time, who was driving me around the Park in a Land-Rover station waggon. Near the north bank of the Kazinga Channel we spotted three old buffalo bulls. They were right in the open, grazing quietly on a grassy area which the hippo had already cropped almost as close as a well-kept lawn. As we drove up they raised their heads to stand and stare in the curious way that buffaloes have, and they continued to do so for some time after we drew quietly to a halt some thirty yards away from them.

The buffalo were on my side of the Land-Rover and for a few minutes we studied each other with mutual interest. Then two of them, their curiosity satisfied, turned away and wandered slowly off, leaving their companion still staring fixedly in our direction. He was old and scarred and it suddenly occurred to me that there was something rather belligerent about the baleful glare that he was projecting in our direction. The same thought must have struck Frank Poppleton for, leaning across me to get a clearer view, he said – 'That's an ugly looking old bastard!'

Scarcely were the words out of Frank Poppleton's mouth when, without any warning, the old bull launched himself at the Land-Rover in a fast canter. There was no time to restart the engine and I watched, fascinated, what was an unique, head-on view of a charging buffalo – unique because I was able to study it in detail from a position of comparative safety. With his nose thrust forward and his horns laid well back over his massive shoulders, the old bull thundered towards us with all the menace of an advancing tank. I studied him through the view-finder of my reflex camera, and when he was ten yards away I snapped a photograph of a buffalo in full charge. Then I lowered the camera – gripping it tightly – and braced myself for the shock of impact.

What happened next is etched as clearly in my mind as if it had occurred yesterday. I can see it almost like the frames of a slow motion film. When the buffalo reached the side of the Land-Rover I was still looking out of the window. At the last split-second, still in full stride, he suddenly dropped his head and hooked with his massive horns, like a boxer swinging a left-hand punch. There was a rending crash, the Land-Rover lifted on its wheels, and the buffalo dropped to his knees. For a moment nothing moved. Then the old bull got slowly to his feet and wandered unsteadily away, weaving from side to side like a drunken man. In the side of the Land-Rover, just below where I was sitting, was a long ragged gash. Frank Poppleton stared at the retreating buffalo in astonishment. Slowly a look of anger replaced the expression of pained surprise on the Warden's face. 'Hell, of all the ungrateful bastards!' he said with feeling.

However, this incident happened a long time after my first visit to this wonderful game area and my first meeting with Bill Pridham in the little bungalow perched watchfully on the top of the Kichwamba escarpment, immediately overlooking what was then the northern part of the Lake Edward Game Reserve.

*

As I drove up to the back door of the bungalow, the sun was disappearing behind the distant snow peaks of the Ruwenzori. A tall, athletic figure, clad in a faded bush-jacket and old khaki trousers, came to greet me. A lean, brown face, weather-beaten and mobile, surmounted by a shock of black hair, broke into a welcoming grin. 'Come in,' said Bill Pridham. 'You're just in time for a drink!'

Happily, there are very few persons whom I dislike on sight. Conversely, there are not many characters to whom I take an *immediate* liking, but Bill Pridham was one of these. In fact, he was one of those rare individuals who is almost universally popular

Buffalo in head-on charge just before hitting author's Land Rover

with people of all races and at all levels of society, and I don't think I have ever heard anyone ever speak ill of him – a rare thing for a game warden who does his job properly! He had a weakness for helping lame dogs, and many a soul in trouble has had cause to be grateful not only for Bill's kindly nature, but for the fact that he had been through the mill himself in his younger days and had not forgotten what it was like to be up against adversity.

William Ocock Pridham – he was very proud of his bizarre second name – was always an interesting and amusing person to be with. Invariably hospitable, he had a ready wit and was an amusing raconteur, added to which he had had a varied and colourful career, a combination that made him a delightful companion at any time and particularly on safari. Bit by bit, as I listened to his anecdotes and got to know him better, I pieced together the story of his life. He had started by learning farming in England, but found the life alien to his adventurous spirit. He had then tried for a short service commission in the Royal Air Force but, as he said himself, that august body had soon decided that their supply of flying machines could not keep pace with the demand caused by the *élan* of his landing techniques. So, they parted company with feelings of regret on one side and profound relief on the other, and Bill next sought his fortune in Africa, where his wandering footsteps led him to Uganda in 1932, when he was not quite twenty. There he became a professional elephant and buffalo hunter in Toro District, apprenticing himself to one of the old pioneers by the name of 'Red' Vivers, who also taught Bill the art of prospecting for alluvial gold in the streams that flowed through the dense rain forests of Toro and Western Ankole.

During the war Bill Pridham joined the 'Recces' – the popular name for the so-called East African 'Armoured Car' Regiment – a wild band of East African hunters and pioneer settlers who, in light trucks and armed with nothing more than rifles, grenades and machine-guns, played havoc with the Italian forces by their daring hit and run raids in the arid thorn bush, desert country along the Kenya-Somaliland border. Ending up in Abyssinia, at the close of hostilities, with a commission in the Somaliland Scouts, Bill eventually returned to his old way of life in Uganda, finally joining the Game Department in 1946, initially with the specific task of checking fish poaching on Lake George, for which he was paid the princely salary of thirty pounds a month. However, by the time I met him, over four years later, he had assumed the mantle of the famous 'Samaki' Salmon, and was the Game Warden responsible for the Toro, Ankole and Kigezi Districts of western Uganda.

That first evening at Kichwamba was an amusing one, for Bill soon launched himself into a series of racy anecdotes of which, as often as not, he himself was the butt. The bungalow was virtually bare of furniture and in the fading light we sat in folding canvas camp chairs, drawn up on the edge of the wide verandah, staring across at the shadowy outline of the distant mountains and the pale glimmer of the far-away lakes. An up-turned beer crate did service as a table and we drank our whisky and water out of deep enamel mugs. 'I'm only camping out here,' Bill had explained with a half-apologetic grin, but I had a shrewd suspicion that both the fancy trappings and the normal amenities of modern civilisation merely irked him and that he really preferred to live in conditions of some austerity.

'I had an embarrassing time not long ago,' Bill Pridham went on, as he topped up the whisky in my mug with water from a canvas *chagul**. 'I had a message from the retiring District Commissioner of Ankole that he was on a farewell tour and was calling to see me, with the District Superintendent of Police, in two days' time. I didn't worry too much until, on the morning of the day they were due to arrive, I got another message saying that they intended to stay the night. It was then that I realised that I had no crockery or cutlery and the only food I had left was a few strips of dried buffalo meat, half a sack of potatoes and some rather tired onions. Luckily my old friend the Kitunzi – the Saza Chief of Bunyaruguru – came to my rescue. He produced a couple of scrawny chickens and a wooden box full of assorted crockery, cutlery, and several unbreakable tumblers.

'My next problem was drink. I was right out of whisky and beer, and funds were low or I would have stocked up from the pub next door. Then I remembered that I had some *waragi* in my safari chop box, a reserve supply for emergencies. Have you ever tried waragi?' he asked, raising a quizzical eyebrow.

* Canvas waterbag, used on safari, for keeping water cool by evaporation.

I shook my head. 'Never,' I replied. 'It's distilled from green bananas isn't it?'

'That's right, it's a raw spirit. Properly made it's quite drinkable though it's got a kick to it like Irish potheen. Mostly it's real firewater and in any case it's highly illegal to either make it or have it. But I thought if I put it in empty gin bottles, and laced it well with orange squash, they mightn't notice the difference!'

'What happened?' I asked.

'I got my first shock when my cook laid the table,' Bill answered slowly. 'It was only then that I noticed that most of the plates were marked 'Imperial Hotel, Kampala' and half the knives, forks and spoons were stamped 'East African Railways and Harbours!' There was nothing I could do about it, so I poured myself a stiff drink and waited for them to come.

'They finally arrived, pretty late, full of apologies. They'd been celebrating his retirement at the pub, the DC said. Anyway, they refused a drink and we got stuck into the curried chicken. That relieved my mind a bit because I reckoned the curry would help to blunt the taste of the waragi, if they had any after supper, and that's what did happen. In fact, the policeman said it was damned good gin and asked me what brand it was – so I showed him the label on the bottle! Luckily, they were pretty merry and they didn't even notice the names on the plates and the spoons.

'After supper they said that they wanted to see if their prisoner was all right before going to bed. I asked them who the prisoner was, and it shook me a bit when the Superintendent told me he was very pleased with himself as he had at last managed to arrest a man he had been after for months, a man who had been operating a very profitable waragi still. Finally, we all went outside and the Superintendent shone his torch inside the back of the police van. It was then I nearly had a heart attack. In the torchlight, wrapped in a blanket and blinking like an owl, was a very familiar figure.' He paused again. 'It was my own waragi supplier!'

For me, the next three days spent on safari with Bill Pridham in the Game Reserves of Lake George and Lake Edward – an area the size of the English county of Dorset – were not only a delight but an eye-opener, a revelation of what the best of the old type game wardens managed to achieve in the face of apparently impossible odds and almost insurmountable difficulties. Short of funds, starved of equipment, and with a mere handful of game guards and scouts to help them both protect and control the wild animals in individual regions often more than half the size of Scotland, they regularly accomplished near miracles, through ingenuity, determination and sheer hard work. In fact, I frequently had to remind myself that this spectacular area was only a relatively small portion of Bill's far-flung parish, for the game in it was as numerous, as varied, and as tame as the inmates of a well-stocked zoo.

Wherever we drove across the grassy, lake-side plains, in Bill's battered Bedford truck, the kob and waterbuck merely watched us in mild surprise; the old buffalo bulls regarded us morosely; and the hippo, lying drowsily in the mud wallows like great, fat slugs, scarcely bothered to open a sleepy eye. Only the wart-hogs, suspicious as always, trotted briskly away, their tails as erect as the jack-staff of a ship.

Near the fishing village of Katwe, between the glittering salt pans of the craters and the blue waters of Lake Edward, there was an area much favoured by elephants. At all hours of the day family groups and single bulls paraded sedately before us, browsing quietly on the clumps of low bush that dotted the whole country from the lower slopes of the Ruwenzori to the shore-line of the lakes. But around midday was a special time; it was then that a small, well-known herd of elephants came down from the mountains to drink in the shallows of Lake Edward. Every day, at this hour, as regular as clockwork, this herd crossed the road by the fishing village; it was known as the 'Katwe Circus'.

Close to Katwe village the Game Department had erected notices by the roadside saying 'Elephants have right of way'; and it was a common sight to see a group of cyclists, or a lorry or two, obeying this terse instruction, patiently queuing while the elephant herd assembled at the roadside, on the outskirts of the village, prior to crossing in a sedate procession, led by an elderly cow. The villagers were salt gatherers and fisherfolk. The elephants were browsers and grazers. Each group, the simple peasants and the giant mammals, went their separate ways, neither interfering with the other's way of life. It was a perfect example of how, under certain conditions, man and wild beast

'The Road Builders'

Near the Congo border 'The Katwe Circus' crosses the road to Lake Edward

can live without conflict in close proximity, the two sharing an environment in a spirit of mutual respect and tolerance – when kept under the watchful eye of an alert game department!

Like most of his kind Bill achieved such results as these by almost continuous patrolling, by carefully training and closely supervising his game guards and scouts, and by maintaining a well-organised network of reliable informers. In this manner he kept the poachers on the hop, for he was nearly always on safari and they never knew when or where in the bush he would turn up next. In addition, sooner or later, his spies put him on the trail of the illegal ivory dealers and those in the towns and villages who dabbled in the smuggling of rhino horn, the illicit sale of leopard skins, and the unauthorised disposal of game meat in commercial quantities. With the staff and means at their disposal it was impossible for game wardens like Bill Pridham to prevent all poaching completely, but it was sufficient if they were able to keep it within reasonable limits.

Bill Pridham was one of those game wardens who virtually lived in the bush, a nomadic existence with a tent as his real home. Even when he later got married – to everyone's surprise – his habits changed little. He *had* a house, not far from the Toro District headquarters of Fort Portal at the northern end of the Ruwenzori Range, but for him it was hardly more than a base to which he returned at the end of each month to re-fit and re-organise. He also had an office – of sorts – an old thatch-roofed *rondavel* in the Fort Portal boma, a dark and odoriferous building filled with piles of confiscated game skins, wire snares, occasional elephant tusks, and a large, old fashioned desk fitted with a deep, wide drawer labelled 'Hell'.

Bill was allergic to paper work and civil service procedures irked him. When he returned from safari it was his habit to sort his accumulated official mail into two piles. The smaller of the two consisted mainly of those letters that could be answered with a few chosen words or a simple 'Yes' or 'No'. The larger pile comprised all documents, forms, circulars or queries that Bill considered to be sheer red tape or too difficult and time consuming for a normal game warden to answer; these were stuffed into the drawer labelled 'Hell'. Periodically, when 'Hell' became so full of papers that it would no longer shut, the whole contents were tipped on to a large bonfire outside the office. Bill was a firm believer in the old axiom that, if left long enough, all correspondence will answer itself.

By the time Bill Pridham and I finally left the Game Reserves of Lake Edward and Lake George, and turned our faces towards Fort Portal, I had come to at least one unshakable conclusion – that these two game reserves were a wildlife photographer's paradise. In my haversack I had half a dozen rolls of exposed film, scores of good pictures of elephant and buffalo, hippo and lion, a fine male waterbuck standing deep in the Kazinga Channel – seeking refuge from a pack of wild dogs – and topi and kob in their hundreds. That was only some twenty years ago, yet, at that time, big game photography was still in its infancy and good photographs of the more dramatic animal species invariably excited comment. In fact, many of the photographs taken on that early safari of mine were used to publicise the attractions of Uganda. Today, hundreds of pictures as good or better are taken by countless excited, camera-snapping tourists! When we reached Fort Portal's straggling, bustling township, Bill Pridham rightly insisted on introducing me to as many of the district's European settlers as possible; they were an interesting and colourful group. The first one – Leslie Graham – we had met on our way to Fort Portal, at the tiny village of Muhokya, not far from Lake George, where he was operating a simple lime works.

We arrived at Muhokya at midday, and Leslie Graham, wearing as always a battered pith helmet, welcomed us hospitably on the steps of his white-washed bungalow. 'Come in, come in!' he greeted us cheerfully. 'I've plenty of beer, but there's nothing to eat in the house.' Bill Pridham, ever resourceful, rose to the occasion. 'I can fix that,' he said, rummaging in the toolbox of his Bedford truck, from the depths of which he eventually produced a dark, leathery object covered in grease and streaked with engine oil. 'What's that?' asked Leslie Graham, peering doubtfully at the mysterious offering in Bill's hands which was already attracting the attention of a cluster of interested flies. 'Buffalo tongue,' replied Bill proudly. 'Oh! It's all right,' he added in a slightly injured tone. 'I only shot it last week and it's been sun dried.'

In Fort Portal itself we headed straight for a flourishing general store run by an astute and cheerful Goan called Braganza, for at the rear of his shop he operated a popular bar that had long been the accepted gathering place for all the local planters. 'You'll meet everyone here,' Bill Pridham announced confidently, as we entered the dark interior to welcoming shouts of 'Hullo, O'cock!' and 'Have a drink, Bill?' It was not long before the significance of the bar's nickname, 'The Glue Pot', dawned on me, for I soon realised that we would have difficulty in extricating ourselves at all, let alone in a fit state to drive on. 'Haven't you heard of a "Toro tea-planter's breakfast"?' Bill Pridham asked with a grin, noticing the bewildered expression on my face as we stood at the bar. 'No? Well, it's a cup of tea, three aspirins, and a vomit! Anyway, don't worry, they're a good crowd of chaps and they do a lot to help the Game Department. Most of them have been fine hunters in their time. I'll introduce you; we'll have a quick beer; and then we'll push on to meet Mike Holmes on the Semliki.'

There followed a bewildering series of friendly, rugged faces, hearty hand-shakes, and jocular introductions by Bill Pridham, all attended by firm refusals of countless generous offers of liquid hospitality. At last we again found ourselves outside on the pavement, blinking our eyes in the bright sunshine. 'Do you remember the last two chaps I introduced to you, the Busby brothers?' Bill enquired, as we climbed into his truck. I nodded. 'I don't suppose you noticed that one of them has a peg-leg? As a matter of fact he used to be a keen elephant hunter. He got over his handicap by riding up to the elephant on the back of a donkey. It worked very well, so he tells me, until one day, when he was hunting in West Nile District, he came unexpectedly on a herd of shaggy-haired female waterbuck. Apparently his donkey, an amorous male, took a fancy to them and gave chase. Busby's story is that he managed to hang on like grim death to start with, but he was finally thrown when the donkey caught up with one of the does and tried to mount her! You needn't believe it but that's a classic "Glue Pot" story for you.'

We were due to call on the District Commissioner, but even before we got out of the truck we could hear voices raised in anger echoing loudly somewhere within the building. The noise seemed to come from behind a door over which there was a notice saying 'District Officer', and the altercation appeared to be distinctly one sided. Suddenly the door was flung open and out stamped a small, wiry little man, dressed in a very worn khaki shirt and shorts, an old pith helmet, and a pair of gym shoes. As he emerged he shouted over his shoulder, 'You're nothing but a sewer rat, a *sewer* rat!'

Slamming the door behind him, he stamped off, muttering to himself. But after a few paces he halted abruptly, turned, retraced his steps, and flung the door open again. 'I apologise!' he shouted, his voice quavering with emotion. 'I take back what I said. I made a mistake. Sewer rats have their uses and *you* haven't!' Then, with a final triumphant and contemptuous flourish the small, wizened figure, still shaking with rage, banged the door firmly shut, dusted his hands together ostentatiously and with jaw jutting pugnaciously and his pith helmet at a defiant angle, marched jauntily away.

I was filled with awe and admiration. 'Who on earth was that?' I asked in astonishment. Bill Pridham grinned. 'One of Toro's most fiery settlers!' he said.

That evening we joined Bill's understudy, Mike Holmes, in his camp on the flat, grassy plains of the Toro Game Reserve in the broad valley of the Semliki River. To the south of us towered the northern peaks of the Ruwenzori. Across the Semliki, to the west, the dark mass of the Ituri Forest – home of pygmies and the rare okapi – sprawled in a dense, dark green carpet over the hills of the Congo. On every side of us, as far as the eye could see, the chestnut coloured forms of Uganda kob dotted the landscape. In the river hippos grunted, while high overhead white-headed fish eagles wheeled and soared filling the air with their yelping, laughing cries.

As night fell the occasional roar of a lion echoed across the rolling plains. 'They're after the cattle at Rwebisengo again,' Mike said quietly, and Bill Pridham nodded silently as he threw a fresh log on the camp fire. From nearby, in a clump of thorn scrub, came the deep sawing of a hunting leopard and in the tall rushes by the river an elephant trumpeted loudly. Slowly the fire died down to a deep, red glow and we rolled into our sleeping bags under the velvety, star-studded canopy of an African night.

Two days later I was back in Entebbe, my mind full of memories of forested, snow-capped mountains, and broad, blue lakes surrounded by wide, grassy plains teeming with herds of game.

But strongest of all was the strangely stirring recollection of a tough, ragged little figure, angrily defying the ponderous, slowly grinding wheels of modern bureaucracy, a memory that will always remain with me as being vividly symbolic of Uganda's 'Pioneer West'.

Uganda kob

PART THREE

Pioneering Days

*

Shoe-Bill (or Whale-headed Stork)

CHAPTER 9

Lest We Forget

THE month of August 1950 was a landmark in the history of wild-life conservation in Uganda, for, during that month, Captain Charles Pitman finally departed on leave pending retirement after more than twenty-five years as Chief Game Warden of the Uganda Protectorate.

Captain Pitman was one of a rare species, a distinguished professional soldier turned game warden, a man with the analytical mind of a born scientist coupled with the disciplined, practical outlook and administrative ability of the best type of trained army officer, and the knowledge and keenness of the experienced hunter-naturalist. These attributes had stood him in good stead over a long period of time during which the preservation of large numbers of potentially destructive wild animals, in the midst of Uganda's predominantly agricultural economy, could be justified on little more than moral and aesthetic grounds alone.

174

From the beginning Charles Pitman had realised that in order to preserve any quantity at all of Uganda's then teeming wildlife, in the face of an exploding human population and the remorseless spread of cultivated land, his primary object must be to prevent the large game animals from becoming a nuisance and thereby unpopular with the general public. At the same time he had to prove to a hard-headed and parsimonious, central government, during many years of severe financial austerity, that the Game Department was not an expensive luxury, an annual drain on the country's strictly limited exchequer, but an essential service that paid for itself from such revenue earners as the sale of hunting licences and the ivory of elephants shot on control. Over the years the achievement of these vital basic aims of necessity coloured his policy, and after more than a quarter of a century he himself had become as much an institution as the small but efficient game control oragnisation he had created.

Charles Pitman would be the last person to claim that, during the twenty-five years he had been at the helm, the achievements of the Game Department had been perfect. As in most fields of human endeavour the conservation of large game animals in modern times is essentially a matter of compromise, the finding of a workable balance between what is required to preserve substantial populations of often destructive and sometimes dangerous wild animals, and what is necessary to satisfy legitimate but conflicting human needs for land. However, the level of his success, both as an economic juggler and as a game warden, can best be judged by the fact that, when he retired, Uganda's elephant population alone, despite a quarter of a century of intensive control measures, was still as large as it was on the day the Game Department had been created. Moreover, although by the time Charles Pitman retired the amount of country freely available to wildlife in the Protectorate had inevitably been sadly reduced, he left behind him in Uganda a pattern of game reserves and sanctuaries covering an area of nearly five thousand square miles, over three thousand square miles of which were strict and – during the period of his stewardship – comparatively invulnerable game reserves.

These are some of the facts about the work of the Uganda Game Department that deserve to be better known. Charles Pitman himself retired with an international reputation as a herpetologist, ornithologist, and the author of three books* and a number of scientific papers. What is less well-known is that during the years 1931 to 1932, he was seconded for special duty to undertake a wildlife survey of Northern Rhodesia. The result – *A Report on a Fauna Survey of Northern Rhodesia* – was published in two volumes and formed the basis of the game conservation policy of that country, now known as Zambia.

Unless one accepts the artificial, Hollywood version as being the type specimen, there is no such animal as a 'typical game warden'. They come in all shapes, sizes and characters – tall and short, fat and thin, flamboyant and retiring. In Charles Pitman's case he had a lively sense of humour, but in contrast he was meticulous in his habits and tall, lean and somewhat austere in appearance, factors which made him look far more like a studious university don than the popular conception of a game warden. This impression was heightened by his habit of always wearing a sober lounge suit, except when on tour. Even on safari he invariably donned an immaculate, well-ironed khaki bush-jacket and shorts and a spotlessly clean pith helmet, unlike the majority of game wardens of those days who considered it *de rigueur* and traditional always to be dressed as untidily and as scruffily as possible.

Each game warden had his own special eccentricity of dress, which he clung to jealously as a mark of his individual personality, for the game wardens of that period were individuals to a man. But it was in the matter of hats that the old-time game wardens really excelled themselves, seeking, like women, to outdo each other in the outrageousness of their head gear. The older and more decrepit the hat, the better. Ionides – the 'Snake Man' – for instance, had a hat that was little more than a tattered cone of grime encrusted felt. He claimed it had magic properties and brought him luck, but worn like a candle snuffer – half obscuring his satyr-shaped features – it made him look like a bucolic pixie and it was so impregnated with vintage sweat that, if the wind was in the right quarter, a sensitive nose could detect his arrival almost before he hove into sight.

Bill Pridham had a similar hat, but still with a vestige of a brim, which was capable of striking terror in the heart of the beholder.

---

* *A Game Warden Among His Charges*, 1931; *A Guide to the Snakes of Uganda*, 1938; *A Game Warden Takes Stock*, 1942.

176

Mike Holmes once told me, with awe, of the day that Bill and he came on a group of giant forest-hogs at a water-hole in Toro. The fearsome looking animals were clustered protectingly round an injured companion, and, when the two game wardens approached, the massive pigs adopted a threatening attitude. Shouting only made the beasts more aggressive and one old boar prepared to charge. Not wishing to be forced to shoot in self-defence, Bill Pridham flung his hat at the animals, whereupon the injured one appeared miraculously to recover and the whole group fled snorting in panic. As Mike Holmes said later, with feeling, anyone who had had the misfortune to see Bill's hat would not be the least surprised at the effect it had on the hogs!

For years I myself had a treasured hat of this nature, about which I was very superstitious. It was as full of holes as the top of a pepper pot, a reminder of the day it had saved me from serious injury – a day in British Columbia when an over enthusiastic gunner had mistaken my hat for a partridge. Alas, years later in Africa it fell overboard from a launch on Lake Albert, and my companions averred that it had been swallowed by the crocodile whose rigid corpse we found on the beach the following day!

It saddens me somewhat that those colourful times of sartorial eccentricity have now almost vanished. The game wardens of today can seldom get away with dressing like tramps as their predecessors did. The few African wardens who have attempted to carry on the tradition have been forced to abandon it hurriedly; on one occasion irate African villagers siezed them, tied them up, and handed them over to the police as undesirable vagrants; their explanations and protests fell on deaf ears – no one but a crazy *Mzungu** would dress like a hobo unless he really was one, the villagers said.

So, in many ways Charles Pitman was ahead of his time, but he will be remembered best as a distinguished naturalist, a world authority on snakes and birds. Not long ago his work for ornithology was recognised by a rare and coveted award – the Gold Union Medal of the British Ornithological Union. It is ironic to think that nowadays, if he had his career all over again, he would almost certainly be considered unfit to fill the post of Chief Game Warden, for the simple reason that, like many of his kind, he had

* European, or white man.

177

no university degree in natural science nor any formal training in that scientific discipline.

Charles Pitman's departure marked the end of an era. In Uganda's game world he was the first and the last of the old brigade. He was a member of a generation and a school brought up to eschew personal publicity and despise ostentation, an attitude typified by the manner of his going.

I have never ceased to marvel at the way in which an elephant can just disappear suddenly and without a sound. One moment an old bull will be there, a massive, grey-brown hulk of giant bone, muscle and gently flapping ears, dominating the landscape. The next second, almost at the flick of an eyelid, he will have faded from sight, vanishing as noiselessly and as unobtrusively as a shadow before a dancing sunbeam. For hours he may have been standing quietly in a carefully chosen spot, just dozing or sleepily plucking a succulent bunch of leaves or a juicy tuft of fresh green grass. Then something will click in his brain . . . An unseen message borne on an eddy of wind? A change of light heralding the approach of dusk? A sudden awareness of thirst roused by the far-away scream of a herd at a distant water-hole? A sixth sense of danger? Who can tell the reason? Whatever the cause, at some given moment he will suddenly decide to move, fading smoothly and quietly into the surrounding grass or bush like some great, grey ghost, leaving in his wake an impressive sense of emptiness.

Captain Pitman's final departure from Uganda reminded me strongly of this vanishing trick of an old bull elephant. For a quarter of a century his powerful presence had dominated the wildlife scene of the Uganda Protectorate, while his reputation as a naturalist had spread far and wide. But when the time for his departure arrived – a time of his own choosing – he left the country as quietly and as unobtrusively as possible. He preferred it that way, he said and, with sincere regret, the members of the Game and Fisheries Department honoured his wishes.

'The war changed nearly everything out here, Bruce,' Charles Pitman said to me as we shook hands on Kampala railway station on the day he left. 'Things are going to be very different from now on. It's time for a "new broom",' he remarked, looking at me with a twinkle in his eye. 'And the best of luck to you!'

For the first six months between my first Western Province

safari and Charles Pitman's retirement, I had concentrated, at his suggestion, on getting to know the remainder of the country, and the field staff and the problems of the Department, as thoroughly as I could in the time available. I had sailed the wide, blue waters of Lake Albert with 'Bart' Bartholomew, the scion of the well-known Scottish map making family of that name. I had penetrated the swampy wilderness of Lake Kyoga with Don Rhodes, the Department's other newly-joined fisheries officer. I had explored the great elephant country of the Bunyoro-Gulu Game Reserve – later to become famous as the Murchison Falls National Park – with that region's game warden, John Mills, the dread of every poacher in the area. And I had accompanied Mike Holmes to the Northern Province, there to establish him in Gulu as the first game warden ever to be permanently based in the home country of the Acholi. There were still some vital areas that I had yet to visit – such as the important game regions located in the remote Districts of West Nile and Karamoja – but, by the time I replaced Charles Pitman in the Chief Game Warden's uncomfortable saddle, I had gained sufficient knowledge of Uganda to form a sound appreciation of the country's wildlife problems.

One fact seemed to shine out as clear and as bright as a beacon light – the greatest threat to Uganda's wildlife no longer lay in the problem of poaching but in the ambitious schemes of the post-war development planners. Common or garden poaching, with all its modern refinements, could not be ignored – but even more serious and more insidious dangers were hidden in the often grandiose land-use development projects that sprouted from the ashes of the Second World War. At the best these projects took no account of the effect on wildlife of their despoilation of the natural environment; at the worst they deliberately set out to destroy all major species of wild animals in the areas concerned. The official conscience was salved by an over-simplified policy summarised in a trite dogma which blandly stated that *When the interests of man and wild animals conflict the interests of man shall prevail.* Few people outside the Game Department seemed able to detect the fallacy on which this policy was based: that the problem was never a question of a conflict between the interests of wild animals and man but between rival interests of man himself. But then to appreciate the truth of this argument it was necessary to concede that wildlife itself was a valuable natural resource, a revolutionary thought at that particular time and a concept yet to be widely accepted.

In existing circumstances what needed to be done? What were the priorities? What were the difficulties to be overcome? How were our objects to be achieved? First and foremost if wildlife was to be preserved indefinitely in reasonable numbers, but in the right places, we had to gain the active support, and not merely the passive acquiescence, of the majority of the local people for sensible and necessary conservation measures, as well as obtaining adequate staff to implement the latter. This was obvious for generally unpopular restrictions and legislation could not be enforced either in the short or the long term, and we knew that a future elected government would inevitably rescind them. Secondly, to achieve the necessary public support we had to ensure that the Game Department's crop-protection service was as near as possible beyond reproach – Charles Pitman's long established policy – since we could not hope to convince the African population that game is a valuable economic asset unless we first showed them that it need not become a major nuisance to anyone if properly managed. The African is essentially a realist, and if we could demonstrate to him both the actual and potential economic value of Uagnda's wildlife resources, and appeal to his budding national pride by revealing the great prestige value of his country's unique and beautiful game areas, as being the envy of the western world, we would be a long way towards achieving our goal.

But before we tackled the general public we had to convert the central government! The first hurdle was a not unusual one – lack of the necessary finance. The Game and Fisheries Department had long been one of the major sufferers from this scarcity of funds; it was the 'Cinderella' of the government departments, and its annual 'slice' of the budget 'cake' had always been the smallest. As a result, by 1950, the policy, establishment and work of the Game and Fisheries Department had remained virtually unchanged for many years. From its inception the Department had had to fight against a widely held view that its mere existence was a 'luxury'.

In consequence, for a quarter of a century, the emphasis on the game side had been almost entirely on the control of elephant and buffalo. There were no national parks and the game reserves – despite their magnificence as wildlife areas – were policed by a mere handful of game scouts, while the majority of the game guards, whose job was purely 'control', were perforce supervised by the Provincial Administration for there were only three game wardens to cover the entire 94,000 square miles of the Protectorate.

Uganda's freshwater fisheries were officially regarded as being of some value – mainly as a comparatively small local source of protein food – and therefore requiring minor care and attention; but despite not inconsiderable landings of a wide variety of fish from the country's fourteen thousand square miles of lakes, rivers and swamps, fisheries were not generally considered to be of any great consequence, with the notable exception of those of Lakes George and Edward. The responsibility for fisheries management had been tagged on to the Game Department in 1933, as a matter of convenience, but it was not until 1949 that the title of the Department was changed to 'Game and Fisheries'! There were then only two fisheries officers for the whole Protectorate, with a small force of fish guards, and there was no separate Ordinance to facilitate the management of the fishing industry. Furthermore, there were few facilities on the lakes – for example there were no motor-powered African fishing boats, and many of the nets in use were still being hand-braided from sewing cotton or the threads laboriously extracted from old motor tyres.

In 1950 the Game Department's equipment was limited, primitive or non-existent. We did have good rifles and camp equipment, but there was no departmental transport of any kind, no launches other than a few old harbour craft belonging to the Public Works Department, no fishing gear, and few funds for travelling. In fact, officers were often required to travel by local bus – where these existed! On Lake Kyoga, Don Rhodes, the Department's first fully qualified fisheries officer, even had to resort to hiring a dug-out canoe, and his wife and his African cook helped him with the setting of experimental nets and long lines.

The headquarters office, with what can only be described as a skeleton staff, was housed in two dark, antiquated and gloomy rooms, with one equally gloomy, ancient and bat-infested store, all tucked away at the rear of a rambling, old-fashioned building that was mainly occupied by the Forestry Department and the

Entebbe Magistrate's Court. There were also few office facilities in the field, where nearly all administrative and clerical work had to be carried out from the officers' private houses. However, there were so few letters that there were no official typewriters in the field; or is it truer to say that there were so few letters because there were no typewriters? Perhaps this was a blessing in disguise, that in this instance the 'good old days' really *were* the 'good old days'!

That was how it was in 1950. These were the problems with which I was faced. The small, austerely simple organisation, which had served its purpose well enough for so many unhurried years, had become an anachronism almost overnight. Post-war threats and pressures demanded something bigger and better, no matter what the cost – or so I thought. I was soon to learn that the satraps of Uganda's Civil Service machine did not automatically share this view! That 'the old order changeth, yielding place to new',* was a natural development they accepted with reluctance.

I should have been warned by what Charles Pitman had said in his last official annual report, which was for the year 1949 – the year that the word 'Fisheries' was added to the title of the Uganda Game Department. 'This is the first occasion since the establishment of the Department in 1925 that expenditure has exceeded revenue,' he wrote, 'but it must be realised that from 1933 onwards the Fisheries Section of the Department, which is non-revenue producing, has been steadily expanding. In 1949 the cost of the Fisheries staff . . . and their relevant activities, has deprived the Department of showing the customary excess of revenue over expenditure. This revenue is derived from the sale of Game and Special licences and from the proceeds of the sales of ivory, rhinoceros horns, and hippopotamus teeth.'

The nature and somewhat apologetic tone of Charles Pitman's remarks are misleading when viewed in the light of the popular opinions of the present day. They are certainly liable to be misinterpreted by the average reader, who may well take Pitman's comments to indicate that for twenty-five years the chief aim and object of the Uganda Game Department had been to destroy enough elephants and issue sufficient hunting licences to pay for its own up-keep, regardless of the effect on the country's wildlife

* Alfred, Lord Tennyson *Idylls of the King*, 1859.

resources. Such an erroneous interpretation would be both damaging and unfair to the reputation of an outstanding naturalist and conscientious game warden. The truth is that, although, over the years, the Department's essential activities had regularly produced more than enough annual direct revenue to cover its normal running costs, this fact had been largely fortuitous. However, Charles Pitman's remarks do clearly reveal that throughout the long period of his stewardship, financially speaking he had been forced always to fight on the defensive. From the beginning he had been compelled, by the hard, blue pencils of hawk-eyed, stone-hearted treasury officials, to pinch, scrape and save in order to show an annual profit without, at the same time, crippling the effectiveness of the Game Department as a wildlife conservation organisation.

Time-honoured concepts and long established policies die hard and when the demands of moral principles clash with the rigid dictates of economic necessity, the winner is seldom in doubt! In fact, I soon found that my first and biggest task was to persuade the government's financial experts not only that Uganda's wildlife was a true natural resource that had to be actively managed if it was to survive and flourish, but also that its economic value was not confined to the sale of elephant ivory and hunting licences alone. Eventually, I was convinced that the key to my problem lay in the magic word 'Tourism' – the still embryonic industry which had then only just begun to blossom in East Africa from the post-war boom in international air travel.

Under present day conditions – particularly in the 'big game' countries of the world – sound wildlife conservation depends on three basic essentials. First of all there has to be adequate scientific knowledge on which all official management policies and planning must be based. Next, there has to be adequate legislation not only to enable these management plans properly to be implemented but also to control public utilisation of the wildlife resources. Finally, there has to be adequate staff both to implement the management plans and to enforce the necessary controlling legislation. In Uganda in 1950, there were none of these things for the simple reason that government thinking on wildlife matters had not kept pace with the speed of human development in other fields.

Uganda was not alone in this malaise. For years the main

183

game areas of East and Central Africa had been protected as much as anything by their remoteness from major concentrations of human populations, coupled with the poorness of internal communications. Where game management problems had been officially recognised as such, it had usually been a question of protecting humans from wild animals rather than the reverse. In fact it is surprising how many people, at that time, fondly believed that all that was necessary to conserve game was to pass a few laws, make some fancy regulations, draw a few sweeping circles on a map and call them game reserves or national parks, and even arm the local people so that they could protect themselves and their crops from the depredations of wild animals. That legal restrictions, without adequate staff to enforce them, merely penalised the law-abiding citizen and turned a good many game reserves into 'poachers' paradises', never seemed to occur to those who controlled the purse strings. 'Paper preservation' – to coin a phrase – may have salved the conscience of the highest government authority but it did not protect the game.

Who was to blame? The answer is probably 'No one!' Some have criticised the Colonial Office, the London bastion of Great Britain's now defunct 'Colonial Empire', which housed an expert technical adviser for each separate form of land-use and natural resource in the colonies. For instance, there was an 'Agricultural Adviser', a 'Veterinary Adviser', a 'Forestry Adviser', and so on. After the Second World War, they even appointed a 'Colonial Fisheries Adviser', but there was never an official adviser on colonial wildlife matters, although the indefatiagble Keith Caldwell, in his retirement, did much to fill the gap in a strictly honorary, totally unpaid capacity. The reason, I think, was simply a question of economics. Proper wildlife conservation costs money and most of the countries where wild animals still existed in significant quantities during the colonial era were as poor as the proverbial church mouse; too poor, in fact, to contribute substantial sums for an emotional cause that offered no obvious economic return. Who else was to pay? The long suffering British tax-payer? His burden was heavy enough already, too heavy to expect him to shell out for yet another purely aesthetic project; while in those days international interest and financial aid for wildlife conservation were yet to be properly organised.

The whole picture altered when the conservation of wildlife in Africa ceased to be merely a moral problem and became the chief *raison d'être* of a tourist industry with a really massive economic potential.

When I became Chief Game Warden of Uganda, the value of wildlife as Africa's key attraction for the tourist became my chief sales line on the game side. With fisheries my task was easier; their economic potential was more obvious and Don Rhodes was a pillar of strength. A hard-headed, clear thinking and determined Yorkshireman, with a flair for figures, he could prove almost anything with an endless flow of irrefutable statistics that he produced, like a magician, from some apparently bottomless source. The combined assault had the desired effect. The outer defences of the Secretariat were soon breached and, one by one, the various inner strong points of deeply entrenched resistance were overcome. Like all wars of attrition it was a slow process. Success was progressive and, although it took time and we had our full share of reverses, we gained virtually all our objectives in the end. I say 'we' deliberately, for as the Game and Fisheries Department expanded, its ideas and achievements depended more and more on a team approach.

People joined the Game and Fisheries Department not for financial reward – which was small – nor for the chances of advancement – which were virtually non-existent – but for their interest in wildlife and the relative freedom of the life that it offered. Formality was kept to a minimum, everyone's ideas were given a fair hearing, and the whole concern was based on a 'family' concept of mutual trust and co-operation. Our overall aim was to create a department that really was capable of both conserving and making optimum economic use of Uganda's wildlife and fisheries resources, in the face of post-war conditions and pressures, and to establish sound management plans for the protection and controlled utilisation of these resources. This may sound like starry-eyed idealism but, on balance, the policy and the system worked well. In fact, it was the only feasible way to manage and get the best out of such a widely scattered bunch of dedicated and determined individualists. Inevitably, we had our fair share of internal 'family' quarrels and I remember one game warden, who had been transferred to Karamoja, complaining bitterly about the quality of the game guards he had

185

inherited from his predecessor. 'Never mind, John,' I wrote to him consolingly, reminding him of an old saying. 'One man's swans are another man's geese!' His reply was explosive. 'Geese!' he wrote bitterly. 'Geese! You should see this lot. They're not geese, they're *vultures*!'

Ionides – The 'snake-man'

CHAPTER 10

Poaching, the age-old Problem

ONE sunny day in September 1950, I climbed aboard an old
Sunderland flying-boat at Port Bell near Kampala. The great
engines roared, the silvery hull vibrated, and with the port-
holes lashed with frothing spray we churned our way across the
sparkling waters of Lake Victoria until, suddenly, we were airborne. Then, like some giant migrating pelican, we flew sedately
south heading for the mighty Zambezi river.

It was the last flight of the old and dying BOAC flying-boat
service, the service – appropriately a child of the former British
Imperial Airways – that was almost Victorian in its slow and
stately luxury, its calm and unhurried progress across the vast,
bush-covered wastes of Africa. Ploughing majestically through
the rolling seas of billowing white cumulus, like some gleaming
galleon of the skies, high above the brown, game-filled plains,
the green jungle-covered hills, the occasional silver streak that
marked a river or lake, we stopped only for a brief rest on the
broad, blue bosom of Lake Nyasa*, before finally settling quietly,

* Now Lake Malawi.

like a homing goose, on a placid backwater of the Zambezi, a mile or two upstream of the roaring cauldron of the Victoria Falls. And there I stayed, in sybaritic comfort, at the luxurious Victoria Falls Hotel, as Uganda's delegate to the East and Central African Fauna Conference, a gathering of wildlife experts and enthusiasts from all parts of Africa and beyond.

For the greater part of a week we talked and exchanged ideas and told of our experiences, discussed our problems, argued our pet theories. In between, we toured the famous Wankie Game Reserve, and, whenever I could steal a spare moment, I sneaked off with my spinning rod to cast a glittering spoon for the savagely fighting tiger fish that swarm in the swirling waters of the great Zambezi river. Looking back I often think with deep nostalgia of the simplicity, the happy comradeship of the wildlife world of those early post-war years.

I remember, in particular, how obsessed we all were with the age-old problem of poaching, the illegal killing of game in a multitude of ingenious, hard-to-combat ways, the reason, in fact, why game keepers and game wardens came to be created in the first place, some hundreds of years ago. It was a far cry from the days of feudal England when Robin Hood, with his long yew bow and his goose-feathered shafts, had literally risked his neck to poach one of the king's deer in some sun-dappled glade in Sherwood Forest. Over the centuries the penalties for such offences had become less savage, but the reasons for their being classified as crimes had increased rather than diminished. Moreover, with the decrease in wildlife and the increase in humans, such crimes had long since ceased to be merely an infringement of a royal prerogative, while the taste for venison had not been lost by the common man.

Poaching is a time-honoured term, yet, like so many terms in general use, remarkably few people who employ it really understand its true meaning and the breadth of its implications. Basically, poaching is a crime against man-made laws rather than morality, for man is naturally a predatory, omnivorous animal who has included meat in his diet for many thousands of years. The Oxford Dictionary defines poaching as to 'take game or fish illegally or trespass for this purpose', and, as a crime, it first developed very much as a western concept, though Moses had already referred to it in Deuteronomy: 'If a bird's nest chance to be before thee in the way in any tree, or on the ground, whether they be young ones, or eggs, and the dam sitting upon the young, or upon the eggs, thou shalt not take the dam with the young.'*

Laws on poaching often appear to be contradictory if not discriminatory. What is a poaching offence in one country, or even part of a country, may be a legitimate action in another, depending on a complexity of factors varying from local laws governing the ownership of land, to traditional customs that restrict or prohibit the killing of certain species of wild animals or control an age-old, communal hunting pattern. Thus, when I first went to Uganda, I discovered, to my surprise, that 'tribal hunting' – the unlicensed hunting of such beasts as buffalo, hartebeest and many species of smaller antelope by organised groups of men using spears, nets and dogs – was legal and author- ised for certain Northern Province tribes such as the Acholi, but that similar hunting was classified as 'poaching' if indulged in by the native inhabitants of most of the rest of Uganda. 'It's according to native law and custom,' I was told airily by a very senior Provincial Commissioner when I enquired the reason. 'The Acholi have a strong hunting tradition and their hunts are controlled by a strict code of time-honoured tribal rules,' he concluded with lofty finality. No one could explain to me why the equally strict tribal 'taboos', which forbade various clans of the Baganda and Batoro, for instance, from killing or eating certain 'totem' species of animals, were not also officially regarded in the same hallowed light, but being new at the time I thought it wiser not to press the point!

Like most game wardens I have often felt a sneaking sympathy, a certain fellow feeling, for the small-time poacher. I have never been able to condemn the tribesman who has speared a bush- buck to feed his hungry family, or the peasant who has set a trap at the edge of his shamba to catch a plump guinea-fowl. Nor can I feel any animosity towards the young 'have not', driven by a natural and irresistible urge, an inherited instinct, yet hedged in by legal restrictions and lack of the necessary hard cash, who resorts to a little mild 'poaching' to quench his craving to smell the wood smoke of a camp fire, to sleep in the bush under the stars, to *be* a hunter at last and not just dream of it. As a lad, I was often in the same predicament myself and I know what

* Deuteronomy, Ch. 22, v. 6.

it feels like. Many is the pheasant, mallard and rabbit I have hidden in a hedgerow, to be retrieved after dark, while I limped home awkwardly with a folding shotgun down one leg of my trousers. And I think I became a better game warden for it! But large scale, commercial poaching, poaching for fat profits, is invariably a greedy, material thing, a dangerous evil, a very different matter.

In the early 1950s, poaching in Uganda covered a broad spectrum of methods, the cruellest and most indefensible of which was the wire snare. What later came to be widely known as 'The Wire Snare Menace', the modern development of an ancient method of capturing game – the simple noose trap – was, and unfortunately still is, one of the most serious threats to the survival of wildlife wherever wild animals still exist in Africa. The wire snare is cheap, easy to make, easy to carry, easy to set, easy to hide, and can be left unattended until the coast, for the poacher, is clear. In the meantime, a trapped animal may have undergone hours, even days, of unspeakable torture often leading to an agonising death.

Although I was conscious of the problem almost from the beginning, it was not until the Game Department had expanded, and we had double the number of game wardens and nearly treble the number of game guards in the field, that the true extent of the wire snare menace in Uganda became apparent. In one of my early annual reports I wrote: 'The wire snare menace continues to spread. It remains both the major threat to the Protectorate's wildlife resources and the one most difficult to combat.' And for year after year I found myself repeating this statement, almost verbatim, with monotonous regularity. However, it was very soon after I had returned from the Fauna Conference at the Victoria Falls that my eyes were first really opened to the dangers of this evil poaching method.

I was on a foot patrol with John Mills, who, at that time, was the Game Warden in charge of a vast region stretching from the Mubende District of Buganda to the Acholi District of Northern Province, and including the whole of the area of fine game country now enclosed in the Murchison Falls National Park – then the Bunyoro-Gulu Game Reserve. We were walking across the northern flats of Lake Albert, from Baker's Camp on the Nile to Kisenyi in the Bugungu area, when we discovered four poachers' huts

Uganda kob cruelly snared

Rhino caught in foot-snare

Snares and traps collected during *one* routine patrol

cunningly hidden in the bush. Although the cooking fires were still smouldering the huts were deserted, the owners probably having fled at our approach. A quick search revealed ten wire snares in the huts, together with one foot trap and four hippo spears complete with ropes and floats. Under a lean-to, close to some meat-smoking racks, we discovered the skins of ten adult kob, twenty-two juvenile kob, one hartebeest, two bushbuck and two duiker, and the tails of fourteen hippo.

A few miles further on, not far from the lake shore, we came across a small cluster of mud-walled huts. Even by African bush standards one could hardly have called it a village, particularly as there were no obvious shambas in the vicinity and even the inevitable goats were missing. Admittedly there was one very ragged fishing net hanging up to dry, and a battered dug-out canoe was hauled up in the reeds, but the huts had no obvious reason for being there. The mystery however, was soon solved by John Mills.

As we scouted curiously around among the small, thatched dwellings I heard him shout: 'Look at this, Bruce!' I walked over to where he was standing by one of the huts, in the doorway of which an old man was sitting. 'Jambo Bwana!' the old fellow greeted me cheerfully, and went on happily with his work. I stared fascinated. At his feet were three old lorry tyres from the cores of which he was busily extracting lengths of wire. By his side was a tidy pile of neatly made snares. A rapid check of his hut revealed twelve more wire snares, two gin traps, and a pile of game meat. Later – after John Mills' investigations had disclosed that the old man, with the help of an assistant, had worked up quite a considerable trade in wire snares and game meat – he was prosecuted in the local African Court. The astonishing thing was that the old man himself was a leper, terribly mutilated by the disease; he was, in fact, totally blind!

I had sympathy for the old leper in his terrible affliction, and I admired his fortitude in the face of such adversity, but no knowledgeable person could have condoned his nefarious trade either then or now. And as time passed, and our investigations into the poaching problem gathered momentum, my official reports to the Uganda Government became increasingly forboding. The year after my encounter with the leper, I wrote, in gloomy tones: 'The use of wire cable snares has reached such proportions, and is so widespread throughout the Protectorate, that it can be regarded as one of the greatest menaces to game conservation at the present time. Cable of varying sizes, capable of catching anything from a buffalo to a dik-dik, can be bought for a few shillings from almost any country duka, where it is stocked for no other evident purpose, or obtained for nothing from the pieces of discarded cable left lying around by various construction units.

'These snares are unutterably cruel,' I emphasised, 'particularly as the poacher does not visit them regularly. An animal, if held, will either die a slow death from terror, thirst and strangulation as it strains against the wire noose around its neck, or, if caught elsewhere, is doomed to a slower death – provided it is not eaten alive by hyaenas, or the poacher does not return in time to end its suffering with a spear.

'In many cases, especially if the animal caught is a large one, it tears the snare from its fastening or drags away the log to which it is anchored. The wretched beast may then wander for days, or weeks, suffering agonies with the wire noose biting deep into its neck, head or a limb, until the flesh putrefies and becomes maggot ridden, and death, or loss or hideous malformation of a limb results. There have been cases recently of elephants being found dead, with the ends of their trunks missing or practically severed, while a large percentage of buffalo and rhino shot during recent operations by the Tsetse Control Department have had wire snares on various parts of their bodies.

'Apart from the cruelty involved, animals such as buffalo, elephant, rhino and the carnivores, become a very serious danger to human beings when in this condition. They will charge on sight or scent, without warning, and death or serious injury to an innocent passer-by may result. There has been a steadily increasing number of cases of this nature – mainly due to snared buffalo but some from elephant – which have caused deaths and injuries among the general public, while even armed and experienced game guards have had frequent narrow escapes.

'The man who sets a wire snare,' I concluded, 'can therefore only be looked upon as a major public enemy, to be dealt with accordingly with the utmost severity.'

A typical example of the terrible death that snared animals frequently suffer was reported to me by a European prospector in

Ankole District. For five days he had heard elephant screaming in the forest about half a mile from his house, he said. He had thought the noise was being made by an elephant herd, but when prospecting in the area some time later he discovered the cause of the trumpeting – a dead cow elephant caught by a fore-foot in a wire cable snare, all vegetation around her pulled up and eaten, and, nearby, a small stream of water which the tortured animal had been just unable to reach.

In the majority of instances snared elephants were caught by their trunks, usually as a result of their mode of feeding. When feeling about in the bush for a tuft of grass or a juicy branch, an elephant would put its trunk through the loop of the snare without noticing the wire. Then, as its trunk curled up to transfer the food to its mouth, the noose would tighten – and that would be that. Sometimes elephants would be caught in a similar manner when investigating a strange object – the snare – victims of their innate curiosity. But, however it happened, almost invariably the result would be terrible injury, frequently the amputation of part of the trunk and, more often than not, an agonising death. Surprisingly enough a few did manage to survive this dreadful mutilation and, before long, in some areas of Uganda, the distressing sight of an elephant with only half a trunk ceased to be uncommon. Such animals managed to eke out a precarious existence by feeding and drinking direct with their mouths, occasionally kneeling awkwardly to do so, but usually browsing off bushes and grass at head height and wading deep into lakes and rivers until the water flowed into their gullets.

But buffalo were certainly one of the greatest sufferers from the heavy wire cable snares. I remember one particularly pitiful case that I saw near Alero, in the west of Acholi District, when I was on safari with my old friend and colleauge 'Robbie' Robson, one of the best game wardens Uganda has ever had. 'Robbie' – or Captain K. B. Robson to give him his full name and rank – was then in charge of Uganda's Northern Range, an area covering the whole of the fine game country of Acholi District – the home of Uganda's great hunting tribe of that name – and also the District of Lango. Unfortunately, snaring was rife in Acholi and Robbie had become almost hardened to the grim sight of snared animals. Nevertheless, even he was shocked at what we saw on this occasion, when we followed a mounting scent of rotting

The author studying breeding herd, North Karamoja

Elephant, with trunk amputated by snare, drinking in the Kazinga Channel

flesh, and the guide sign of vultures circling slowly overhead, which together led us into the heart of a dense clump of bush.

Pushing through the thick cover, while more vultures flapped clumsily out of the sheltering trees, we came to a small clearing and there before us lay the remains of what had once been a magnificent buffalo bull. All the signs were clear to read. The mighty animal had evidently walked into a heavy wire cable snare, but the great sweep of his horns had prevented the noose from slipping over his head. Jerking his head away, the noose had slipped down and pulled tight around his muzzle – the harder the buffalo had pulled, the tighter the noose had become. At last he had set off at a run, dragging behind him the heavy log to which the wire cable was attached. After a while, the log had caught against a substantial tree, firmly anchoring him. The frantic beast had then started to circle, plunging and straining against the long wire, until a large area had been flattened and ploughed into a quagmire by his wildly thrashing hooves. As he had run round the tree, so the cable had shortened until, after what must have been a long time, he had finished up with his muzzle hard against the bole of the tree – and there he had stuck, until he died slowly of thirst. The wire had bitten through his nostril cartilage so that he had been able to continue to breathe to the last, and the noose was so firmly embedded that we had to chop it out with an axe.

Not far from the scene of the tragedy, we found signs of the same thing having happened to another buffalo. There was a similar trampled area around a tree, but on this occasion the tortured animal had managed to break free – taking the wire noose with him. We attempted to follow the injured beast but the tracks were too old. We finally lost them in a patch of dense bush, which we vacated with considerable relief for the buffalo would not have been a nice customer to meet at close quarters!

During this safari, Robbie told me how one of his game guards had found himself in a very nasty situation after discovering a dead baby elephant which had been slowly strangled by a wire noose. Coming upon a blood spoor, the game guard had followed it up until he discovered the still fresh carcass in the bush. Unknown to him the herd was still in the near vicinity, and the first intimation he had of this was when he was savagely charged by a cow elephant – probably the mother. He shot her when she was almost on top of him, and then discovered that he was surrounded by elephants. The great beasts were all in a very ugly mood, so much so that the game guard was forced to shoot another four before he could get himself clear.

The following month an elephant had to be destroyed at Anaka, in western Acholi, as it was seen to have a wire noose buried deep in its trunk. In the same area a dead baby elephant was discovered with one fore-foot caught in a heavy wire cable snare, from which it had been unable to escape. And in the same month, but a little further to the north, a game guard was forced to shoot an elephant which wandered into the market place at Atiak. The terminal six inches of the wretched animal's sensitive trunk had been torn off – yet again by a wire snare.

I could continue to quote endless cases of elephant and buffalo, quite apart from lesser animals, that members of the Game Department – including myself – found dead or dying in horrible circumstances, all of them victims of the diabolical and deadly wire snare. But it would be merely a sickening series of horror stories, a catalogue of cruelties. The extent of the wire snare menace during those years can better be judged by the number of wire snares found by members of the Game Department during routine patrols. The record was reached when one game guard patrol, operating in the Rigbo area of West Nile District, picked up one hundred and eight wire snares in *one day*!

Almost equally alarming numbers of wire snares were regularly recovered from many other parts of Uganda; while in Toro District, when the Kilembe Copper Mines' electricity power-lines were erected, local poachers even began helping themselves to the galvanised iron earth-wires to turn into snares. These thefts constituted more than just a game hazard, they also exposed the power-lines to damage by lightning and the poachers themselves to death through electrocution, yet my warnings to the Government fell very largely on deaf ears. 'There is a grave danger of too complacent and defeatist an attitude being taken to the wire snare menace,' I wrote. 'In fact, there is a serious risk that the present state of affairs may become generally accepted as an unavoidable evil for which there is no solution, and which, like the poor, will be always with us. The general viewpoint appears to be that the problem is too difficult and therefore nothing much can be done about it. If the loathsome cruelty to the beasts concerned and the real physical danger to the public from tortured dangerous animals are both properly appreciated, then it will be realised that something *must* be done.'

True, it was an extremely difficult problem to solve. There was no easy, rapid answer. The soundest and most enduring solution quite clearly lay mainly in reducing the chief incentive to poach, the hunger for meat, and in educating the great mass of the public to understand and accept the fact that to conserve wildlife could be just as much in their interests as the husbandry of their cattle and their donkeys, their sheep and their goats. But this would inevitably be a slow and lengthy process. The short term answer – obvious but relatively expensive – was to have sufficient Game Department staff to police the main game areas really properly and thus make poaching, even with wire snares, too risky a proposition to be worth the candle.

But perhaps the greatest obstacle was the pessimism of most of those in high authority, which sprang from their deeply ingrained belief that when Uganda was granted independence game reserves would be abolished and all large game animals would be slaughtered. The Game Department never shared this view, probably because its work in the field brought it into much closer contact with the African people than the bulk of post-war expatriate government officials were able to achieve. A game warden sitting beside a camp fire in the bush at night, discussing local matters with his gun-bearer, a village guide, and perhaps a senior game guard or two, inevitably learnt a great deal more about the true feelings and inner thoughts of these Africans than a harassed, paper-ridden district officer, rushing hurriedly from one organised *baraza** to the next in an official Land-Rover, could possibly hope to.

That some intelligent and responsible sections of African opinion were becoming alive to the dangers of the poaching problem during the later part of this period, was clearly indicated by the contents of a letter that I received from Robbie Robson, who was still in charge of Uganda's Northern Range at the time. Robbie – who was regarded with both affection and respect by the local people and understood them a great deal better than most Europeans did at that period – wrote to tell me that he had been asked, at a moment's notice, to address a meeting of all the

* Official gathering.

Acholi chiefs on the subject of tribal hunting and game problems. He went on to say that during the subsequent discussion the following incident occurred, and I quote his words verbatim:

One of the older chiefs got up and asked me what was causing the shortage of game. After explaining the increase of human population, cultivation and subsequent loss of game areas and game, I put poaching by different methods, over-shooting of licences, and tribal hunting, as top of the bill.

He replied, was it not a fact that wire snares were probably the most destructive, as he and the other chiefs had always thought so. I agreed. He then asked, what was I doing about it, as it was well on the increase? I asked him in return, what *he* would do about it, and he immediately replied that he would forbid the sale of wire in the shops. I countered that we could not do that as some people might have a legitimate reason for buying it. At that there was a roar of derisive laughter, with the question – 'Who would have a legitimate reason for buying it?' If anybody really wanted it, it would be the chiefs, and he personally couldn't care if he never saw any wire again. Anyway, he went on, if some people really needed wire, it would be a very small quantity and why could it not be obtained on a district commissioner's permit, at least that would give some measure of control? I asked if that might not cause hardship in some cases, to which the reply was an emphatic negative. I then quickly asked the meeting, in general, if everyone supported this view, at which a great number of hands went up, and there was a growl of agreement.

Although the wire snare was and is the single greatest poaching evil throughout the length and breadth of Africa, each country seemed to have its own special problem method in addition. In Kenya I think it was probably the poisoned arrows of the Waliangulu elephant hunters of the Nyika. In Tanganyika it was certainly the ubiquitous muzzle-loader, a relic of the great Arab slave and ivory collecting days. In Uganda it was the home-made gun and the stolen, unlicensed rifle.

The Province of Buganda was the centre for Uganda's trade in illegal firearms and in particular the centre for the manufacture of home-made shotguns. The firing mechanisms for these latter 'Heath Robinson' weapons were frequently most ingenious, but equally often they were highly dangerous. The barrels were made from all sorts and conditions of metal tubing, the favourite being old bicycle frames. On one occasion, when there was an amnesty for illegal arms, the owners of a number of these very unsafe home-made weapons tried to get them properly licensed. They were surprised and indignant when it was pointed out that the original serial numbers stamped on the bicycle frame tubes, from which the barrels of these dangerous weapons had been made, did not constitute sufficient cause for them to be registered as authorised weapons! However, when I first arrived in Uganda the biggest headache was undoubtedly the number of illegal ·303 service rifles in circulation.

For a long time the source of these ·303 service rifles was a complete mystery. A few could have been weapons stolen from or lost by the armed forces during the Second World War; but the supply was too constant for that to be the full answer, since as soon as one was recovered another seemed to appear like magic to take its place.

John Mills was particularly good at tracking down these illegal rifles. In fact, anti-poaching in any form was his particular forte and he had built up a formidable network of agents and secret informers who kept him supplied with information of often surprising variety and detail. Sitting, large and impassive, at the centre of his 'spider's web', he always reminded me of a character in a novel on international espionage, the impression being heightened by the unruffled politeness of his manner.

For a long time the problem of illegal ·303 rifles dragged on until, on the 20th of July 1950, the brutal murder of a game guard brought matters to a head. On that day Game Guard Erinayo Muno was hunting buffalo in the Siba Forest near the Waki river in Bunyoro. He had five porters with him. In the heart of the forest, about four miles from the nearest road, they came on a small thatched hut around which the vegetation had been cleared and cotton planted. As they passed the hut a man ran out carrying a locally made shotgun and shouted at the porters to go away. Erinayo Muno, who was new to the district and didn't know the hut owner, asked him why he was shouting at his porters – whereupon the man turned round and shot him stone dead with a blast of buckshot in the head.

The porters, who recognised the murderer as a man called Mulisi Alideki, a notorious poacher for whom the Game Department had long been searching, immediately fled. The poacher fired two more shots to frighten them and then dragged Erinayo

201

Muno's body into the hut to which he set fire. And by the time the police had arrived on the scene, some hours later, Mulisi Alideki had completely disappeared taking his shotgun and the Game Guard's ·404 rifle with him.

Mulisi Alideki, who had been hunting elephant and buffalo with an illegal ·303 rifle for a very long time prior to the murder, had been caught by another game guard in the Budongo Forest in Bunyoro earlier in the year. He had been found with an elephant he had just shot and after a fight the game guard and his porter had secured the rifle but Mulisi Alideki had escaped. All efforts to trace him had failed but two months later he was again hunting in the area, with another illegal ·303 rifle, after issuing an ultimatum that he would shoot any government servant who came near him. The murder of Game Guard Erinayo Muno proved that his threat was no idle one.

Immediately after the murder, I gave orders that all game guards and game scouts in Bunyoro District were to be called off all other duties for a month to assist the police in the hunt for Mulisi Alideki, but without success. For two years he remained at large living by his rifle and his wits. That he was able to escape justice for so long was due to the fact that he was helped, fed and hidden by local people whom he either intimidated or bribed by supplying them with game meat. During the early months of 1952, however, as a result of the sustained efforts of a number of departments, public opinion began to turn against him and information as to his movements began to trickle in. Eventually, on the night of the 4th of July 1952, he was arrested near Kabwoya in Bunyoro.

Mulisi Alideki's final capture was dramatic. A reliable informer, who brought in the news that the murderer would be attending a beer drinking party near Kabwoya that night, was given a 'Mickey Finn' to slip into Mulisi's drink at a suitable moment. This he did, and late that night he crept back to a pre-arranged rendezvous to report that the murderer was lying in the bush, near the road, sleeping off the effects of the beer and the drug. The waiting patrol then set off.

The patrol was an oddly assorted party. Led by the District Superintendent of Police, it consisted of an African Sub-Inspector and some askaris and game guards, accompanied by the District Commissioner of Bunyoro, the Agricultural Officer, the Medical

Officer and the Fisheries Officer. The latter four officers – all ex-rugby players – insisted that their presence was essential in case there was a fight. No one knew how many people might try to help the murderer, they pointed out firmly.

In the event the patrol found Mulisi Alideki on his own, asleep in the bush under a mosquito net. By his side was a rifle, fully loaded and cocked. Cloaked by darkness they quietly surrounded the murderer's sleeping, white-shrouded form, then silently fell on him like a rugger scrum. Mulisi fought with the savage ferocity of a cornered leopard – neither the beer nor the drug had had much effect on him, or else the effect had had time to wear off – but the odds were literally too heavy for him. Handcuffed and trussed like a chicken for the oven, he was taken to the nearby road to await the arrival of a police van and thence to jail.

Mulisi Alideki was later tried, sentenced to death and – uttering diabolical threats to the bitter end – finally hanged. Strange to relate he was once a game guard, and a very fine elephant hunter, who went to the bad and was eventually convicted of ivory offences and dismissed. In fact, the whole grim story was an interesting reversal of the old axiom that poachers make the best game keepers. During a short and inglorious reign of terror, Mulisi Alideki became the doyen of Uganda's poachers, a sort of evil Robin Hood whose example encouraged a number of other armed poachers to issue threats that they would kill any government servant who interfered with them. At his demise the Game Department breathed a sigh of heartfelt relief, but long before that John Mills had solved the mystery of the source of the illegal ·303 rifles.

One day, some six months after the murder of Game Guard Erinayo Muno, John Mills walked into my office in Entebbe. 'I've got some information you won't believe,' he said. 'It's about those illegal ·303 rifles.'

'What about them?'

'I've discovered where they are coming from.'

'Where?' I asked.

John Mills glanced behind him to check that my office door was closed.

'You won't believe this. From the central armoury of the Uganda Police in Kampala!' he announced triumphantly.

'What?' I gasped. 'That's *impossible!*'

The central armoury, with its great steel doors, was securely barred, locked and guarded in the heart of the old fort in Kampala. It held many hundreds of ·303 service rifles, pistols, and the spare parts for such weapons, the entire small arms reserve for the whole of the Uganda Police Force. To steal weapons from the armoury without a pitched battle with the armed police guard would have been impossible. The only feasible alternative theory was that it was an 'inside' job involving some person or persons employed in the armoury itself. But even this idea did not seem to hold water, for all the weapons in the armoury were checked and counted at regular intervals by an independent board of survey, quite apart from the routine inspections made by senior police officers, and missing rifles would soon have been noticed.

I stared at John Mills with growing concern. Had he taken leave of his senses?

'I know you think I'm round the bend,' his voice cut in. 'But I'm absolutely convinced that my information is reliable. I don't yet know how the rifles are being removed from the armoury, or by whom, but I'm quite certain that is where they are coming from.'

I had sufficient faith in John Mills' ability to send his report immediately, under secret cover, to Police Headquarters in Kampala. As we both expected it was laughed to scorn. 'If there were any rifles missing why had no board of survey ever noticed the fact?' we were asked in reply. In fact, the Police took exception to the report, which they regarded as little better than an irresponsible joke on the part of the Game Department, and relations became strained in consequence. Then, a few weeks later, an event occurred which altered the whole picture. It was the big annual board of survey that all government departments have to suffer.

Despite themselves the Police were secretly a little worried by the Game Department's alarming but mystifying report, so they asked the members of the annual board of survey to take particular care in checking the numbers of firearms on ledger charge in the armoury. And this the survey board proceeded to do, most meticulously and in the time-honoured manner, which was as follows.

The rifles – almost entirely that old fashioned but reliable model of British service rifle the ·303 bore Short Magazine Lee

Enfield Mark III – were propped upright in single rows in open racks along the walls of the armoury, or in blocks of similar racks stacked, honeycomb fashion, in the centre of the floor. In the case of the former the whole rifle could be seen and checked with ease, but of the weapons in the centre of the blocks of racks only their metal nose-caps were visible in normal circumstances. Nevertheless, this was quite naturally regarded as being fully adequate visual proof for conventional counting purposes, since the rifle racks were heavy and required considerable effort to shift.

On this occasion, however, a member of the board, after examining some of the rifles lined up along the walls, stepped backwards into the central block of racks sending the outer row of rifles flying. Embarrassed, he stopped to pick up the fallen weapons, then stopped aghast as his eyes fell on the middle rows of rifles that now stood naked and revealed. Slowly he counted. One, two, three, a dozen, a score or more were not rifles at all but dummies – broomsticks with the regulation metal nose-cap stuck on the end to fool anyone trying to count the numbers! The rifles themselves had long since vanished, far into the bush, each of them sold to an eager poacher for a fat sum.

Police investigations led to the arrest of an Asian armourer – a Sikh – and his African assistant. The pair had worked up a very profitable trade in stolen ·303 rifles, which they smuggled out of the armoury leaving dummies in their place; a simple scheme and almost foolproof – until fate stepped in and took a hand. The two men were finally awarded heavy jail sentences and the regular supply of rifles to poachers ceased abruptly.

Slowly but surely, one by one, the stolen rifles were tracked down by the Game Department and the Police working hand in glove. Eventually all but a few were recovered and some of the latter were known to have been destroyed in hunting accidents. The final result was greatly improved co-operation between the Police and the Game Department, for the whole affair had markedly increased the respect of the former for the latter.

And so one major poaching problem in Uganda was solved. But, as long as the great game reserves and national parks of Africa are surrounded by growing populations of under privileged, meat hungry people – people who scratch a marginal existence from the soil, who are frequently starved of protein, and whose subsistence crops are often devastated by drought or pestilence or the depredations of wild animals – then there will continue to be a poaching problem in some shape, form or degree.

Fortunately, poaching, like war, despite its many evils and horrors, often has its lighter side, and whenever I think of Uganda's poaching problems, I cannot help recalling a bizarre incident involving home-made guns, which occurred in Toro District – part of Bill Pridham's far-flung range.

During one of his anti-poaching forays in the Semliki Valley, Bill Pridham discovered a home-made shotgun in a hut, the owner of which appeared to have escaped into the surrounding bush just before Bill and his game guards arrived on the scene. Two months later, when I was on safari in the area, Bill and I decided to launch another raid on the same hut with the help of the police. However, despite all our attempts at secrecy and caution there was again no sign of the owner when we entered the hut although, after a very thorough search, we found a second home-made shotgun hidden in the thatch of the roof.

It was a hot day and one of the African police constables, weary from his exertions, his feet aching in his heavy boots, decided to have a rest before we continued on our patrol. In one corner of the hut was a rough string bed on top of which was a crudely made, but bulky and inviting looking mattress; and with a cavernous yawn the weary constable stretched himself luxuriously on the vacant bed. His relief was short-lived. Scarcely had he relaxed than his sleepy features were transformed by a look of incredulous horror and surprise, and with a startled yell he leapt to his feet. . . . Inside the mattress was the missing poacher!

CHAPTER 11

Kidepo—'Valley of the Elephants'—I

Hunters, we are told, develop a curious
affection for the quarry they needs must stalk,
an emotion born of the understanding that comes
from age-long observations of its nature and its
way of life.

PAUL GAULTIER
(*The Scallop at the Table*, 1957)

IN March 1951, I realised a youthful ambition, for in that month
and year I penetrated to the remotest region of one of the still
truly wild and unspoilt areas of Africa – Karamoja. But it was
more than just the irresistible lure of wild places that drew me
there, for Karamoja had long meant one thing to me above all
else – ELEPHANT!

I think that most of the old-time game wardens had a special
'totem' animal, one particular species their interest in which
amounted almost to an obsession, a fixation so strong that their
names became permanently linked with the animal concerned.
Thus the late Philip Teare, who chose the massive head of a bull

207

buffalo as the symbol and badge of the Tanganyika Game Department, was renowned as a 'buffalo man'. In more recent times George Adamson, of 'Elsa' the lioness fame, has become world famous as Kenya's premier 'lion man'. And I myself have frequently been referred to in my own presence as being – like a good many game wardens – an 'elephant man'.

Elephants fascinate me, they always have. For as long as I can remember, and that dates back to my earliest childhood days in the dense, northern Indian forests of the ancient Siwalik Hills and in the jungles of the great Terai at the foot of the mighty Himalayan Range, elephants have been my favourite animals. In the wilds of the African bush I can watch them happily for hours as they pursue their purposeful wanderings, while I have few more nostalgic memories than those of 'gooming' quietly through the beautiful, park-like, sal forests, in the United Provinces of the old 'Imperial India', on the back of a well-trained pad elephant, searching for tiger, sambar and lesser game, in the crisp, sunny air of a cold weather dawn. The noiseless, measured tread of the majestic animal, and a vantage point nearly ten feet above the ground, had unchallengeable advantages over the modern, low-slung, clattering, four-wheel drive safari car, while for the true lover of the wild there can be no comparison between the two.

Even in the confused jungle war in Burma, I had had cause to be grateful to the elephant or, to be precise, to two well-trained timber-working elephants supplied by that famous forest man, 'Elephant Bill' Williams. Without the aid of these two patient leviathans, which carried most of our rapidly dwindling medical supplies and our few remaining boxes of ammunition, what was left of my war-torn, malaria-ridden Gurkha battalion in 1942, would have had an even harder time struggling over the rugged, jungle-covered mountains that divide the swirling waters of the great Chindwin River from the wide plains of Manipur and the rolling hills of Assam. However, it was not until I went to Africa, soon after the close of that bloody jungle war, that my interest in elephants developed into a near obsession.

I was raised on a heady diet of tales of the great explorers and hunters of Asia and Africa, and two books in particular influenced my youthful thoughts. The first of these was my grandfather's book, with the imposing Victorian title of *Large*

Game Shooting in Thibet, the Himalayas, Northern and Central India.
Later, a second book took pride of place in my affections; it was
The Wanderings of an Elephant Hunter by Captain W. D. M. Bell,
better known as 'Karamoja' Bell, a Scot, born near Edinburgh in
1880, who became one of the greatest elephant hunters of all
time.

In recent years Bell's memory has been reviled and his reputation denigrated by ignorant sentimentalists who know little
if anything about elephant and nothing at all of either Bell the
man or the wild and savage conditions under which he hunted.
True he killed well over a thousand elephants – mostly large bulls
– during the course of his dramatic career as a professional ivory
hunter, but it must always be remembered that this apparently
stupendous total was spread over a period of nearly a quarter
of a century and in widely scattered regions of Africa where law
and order were conspicuous by their absence, while elephants
abounded. In fair comparison, it is worthy of note that the Uganda
Game Department alone, ever since its inception, has been forced
to shoot nearly a thousand elephants *per year* – sometimes more –
merely to keep the numbers of these lovable but destructive great
beasts under reasonable control; moreover the average annual
total for the Tanganyika Game Department has long been nearer
the three thousand mark!

The scene of many of Bell's most incredible adventures, the
country in which his name became a legend even during the
earliest of his elephant hunting days, was Karamoja – to this
day a 'never never' land, a harsh region of wild enchantment. In
its whole area Karamoja is so unlike any other part of Africa that
it is impossible to talk about it intelligibly without first describing
it in some detail. For a start it lies in the north-eastern corner of
Uganda and it has a total area of some twelve thousand square
miles – a little larger than Beligum or one and a half times the
size of the Principality of Wales – extending from the foothills
of the tremendous fourteen thousand foot massif of Mount Elgon
in the south, northwards all the way to the Sudan border. On
the east it marches with the semi-desert Turkana country of
Kenya's Northern Frontier Province, from which it is separated
by a rugged, mountainous escarpment, while on its western
flank lie the Uganda districts of Acholi and Teso.

An arid country, sparsely populated by still backward, semi-nomadic tribes, Karamoja differs very markedly from the rest of Uganda, not only in its scenery and its people, but in its fauna and flora also, for it lies astride the watershed between the Nile and Lake Rudolf – the strip of land which forms the natural dividing line between the fauna of Uganda and that of the dry regions of northern Kenya.

The flattish country of southern and central Karamoja, much of it fine game country typical of many of the drier parts of East Africa, is studded here and there with the crumbling ruins of long dead volcanoes towering high above the surrounding plains; Mount Kadam (or Debasien), its magnificent red battlements rising sheer from its forested lower slopes to its ten thousand foot summit; the cloud-capped peaks of Moroto Mountain, at whose western foot lies the small settlement of the same name which is the administrative headquarters of the District. To the west is Napak, much eroded, but still recognisable as the remains of a once mighty volcanic cone, whilst the southern horizon is dominated by the sprawling mass of Mount Elgon whence flows the Turkwell river – the scene of some of Bell's earliest adventures with elephant – which wanders quietly across the arid wastes of Turkana before emptying itself in the far-away basin of lonely Lake Rudolf.

Northwards, as one nears the Sudan border, in the country of a tribe known as the Dodoth, the character of the landscape alters, becoming more broken and undulating. There are ranges of attractively wooded hills and broad, park-like valleys where elephant, buffalo, lion and great herds of plains game still roam much as they did when Bell penetrated this distant corner of Africa, more than sixty-five years ago – the first white man ever to do so. This is the region in which Bell performed the most incredible of his elephant hunting exploits and this was the remote country that I determined to visit as soon as I knew that I was going to Uganda.

For nearly two years I had to suppress my burning ambition; other more urgent tasks occupied my time and it was not until late in 1950, that a threat to the fine game areas of north Karamoja began to develop, a threat that not only demanded my urgent attention but gave me a valid excuse to explore this remote region for myself. The problem can be summed up in five words – cattle versus the tsetse fly.

The inhabitants of Karamoja are mainly Nilo-Hamites, a group of tribes loosely known as the 'Karamojong Cluster' – which also includes the Turkana across the eastern border – all of whom are closely allied to the Masai and Nandi of Kenya. They are a primitive but colourful people, most of whom live a semi-nomadic existence guarding and tending their herds of cattle and other domestic stock. Of a warlike and lawless nature, they are constantly engaged in raids and counter-raids with their neighbours in an effort to acquire more cattle. In fact, cattle dominate every aspect of life in Karamoja; wives are bought with them, battles are fought over them, blood money and fines are paid with them, and they provide the blood and milk on which the people mainly rely for their food.

The great cattle herds of the Karamojong are also the source of considerable headaches to the Uganda Government, since, not only are they the direct cause of much bloodshed, but their ever increasing numbers have resulted in steady deterioration of much of the land through overgrazing. Over the years a variety of official de-stocking schemes have been tried with varying, but usually limited, degrees of success and the really only effective controlling factor has been the presence of the *nagana* carrying tsetse fly – in the few regions of Karamoja where this tough and resilient insect has occurred. And one of these regions is the great game country that lies in the far north, starting in the wilds of Dodoth and sprawling across the wide Kidepo Valley into the little known Didinga country of the southern Sudan.

Northern Dodoth has long been a no-man's-land, a vast gladiatorial arena where, over the years, with almost monotonous regularity, warring tribes have clashed and skirmished and ruthless raiders have swooped down like wolf packs from the hills to murder and pillage the weak and the unwary. Here the warriors of the Dodoth have battled with Didinga invaders from the wide plains of the southern Sudan, while from beyond the towering escarpment to the east the fierce *moran* of the Turkana and the Merile have pounced with merciless ferocity on remote *manyattas* to blood their spears and rifles on luckless human bodies, to rustle what stock they could from dry-season cattle camps, and – on the side – to hunt elephant for their ivory and rhino for their horn. And, when the coast has been clear, the ever-watchful Napore and Mening have descended from their mountain fastness of the Nangeya Range, brooding darkly on the western flank, to stage their seasonal tribal hunts, surrounding the teeming herds of game with an ever-tightening circle of gleaming, razor-sharp spears to take their annual toll.

For hundreds, perhaps thousands of years – no one really knows how long – this scenically beautiful, game-rich region of rolling acacia savannah, merging with areas of dry thorn-scrub that lead down to wide sand rivers edged with groves of tall borassus palms, has been devoid of permanent human inhabitants – apart from the Teutho, a tiny tribe of a few hundred shy, wandering honey hunters. The reason has been the presence of that tough, savagely biting tsetse fly *Glossina morsitans sub-morsitans*, the arch-enemy of the nomadic, warlike pastoral tribes, one or other of which would otherwise have occupied this rich grazing country with their swarming herds of hungry cattle.

In the eyes of the Game Department this situation had its advantages. For years the fierce, internecine, inter-tribal skirmishing, coupled with the powerful deterrent of the tsetse fly, had protected the great game herds of northern Dodoth almost as effectively as the presence of a strong Game Department force would have done. But all good things are liable to come to an end, and in the year 1950, the elders of the Dodoth complained bitterly to the District Commissioner of Karamoja that the tsetse fly were advancing southwards, like an invading army, into their cattle country. The District Commissioner informed the Secretariat in Entebbe, and the Secretariat immediately alerted the Department of Tsetse Control which responded with alacrity; ever eager for fresh fields to conquer, it immediately despatched its officers to reconnoitre the area and establish a permanent camp as a base for future operations. From the wildlife conservation point of view, almost overnight the situation in northern Dodoth had changed from one of comparative tranquillity to a state fraught with the gravest possible danger. For twenty years it had been widely accepted that the panacea for the tsetse fly threat was to destroy all the large game mammals which – so it was then believed – formed the sole food supply of this blood-sucking insect.

As a result, in the interests of the cattle industry, the larger game animals were virtually exterminated in extensive regions of Buganda, and other parts of the Uganda Protectorate, by the hunters of the Tsetse Control Department. Small wonder, therefore, that I was horrified when I learnt that Dodoth, the elephant country of my dreams, had become yet another target for their ghoulish attentions.

It is sad to recall that, only a few years later, as a result of the discovery of a technique for positively identifying the blood meals of tsetse flies – a fool-proof method developed by that brilliant scientist Dr Bernard Weitz of the Lister Institute in London – it was conclusively shown that much of this game destruction was unnecessary. Weitz's technique revealed that although they have distinct preferences tsetse flies can and do subsist on the blood of a very wide range of animal species, including birds, and that even in rich game country the so-called game animals are often not only not the only source of food of tsetse flies but sometimes not even their primary one!

What I wrote in my official Annual Report for the Game Department for 1960 – ten years after the Tsetse Control Department's threat to the game of north Karamoja had developed – therefore makes interesting, though ironic reading in retrospect:

Recent figures for the analysis of the blood meals of tsetse fly (*Glossina morsitans submorsitans*) caught in northern Uganda (Karamoja and Acholi) are of considerable interest to those concerned with wildlife conservation, indicating as they do the species on which tsetse fly rely mainly for their food in this area. Of 311 meals which were analysed it was found that ruminants had provided 51% of the feeds, primates (including man) 18%, pigs 11%, other mammals (including elephant, rhino, dogs and cats) 14% and birds 8%. The species providing the highest number of feeds was *man* with 13.5%; the second was buffalo with 11%, then warthog with 7%, followed by hartebeest and rhinoceros with 6% each. It seems remarkable that man should top the list, considering that most of the area is comparatively thinly populated. In Karamoja birds provide a considerably higher proportion of the food of tsetse fly than in Acholi, the percentage in Karamoja being 10%, and that in Acholi being less than 2%.

If only these scientific facts had been fully available in 1950, how many magnificent animals might have been saved from needless slaughter in Uganda. On the other hand, without the sudden and unexpected threat that arose in 1950, perhaps what was finally achieved to conserve the spectacular wildlife of north Karamoja – indeed of Karamoja as a whole – might have been long delayed through lack of the necessary sense of urgency, even to the extent of never coming to pass at all.

Properly to understand the wildlife situation in Karamoja in 1950, it must be realised that during the whole period of the Uganda Game Department's existence up to that time, a full twenty-five years, there had never been even a junior game guard, let alone a game warden, permanently stationed in Karamoja – or even visiting that District, other than casually or on rare occasions. The official view had always been that because of the remoteness of the region, the largely pastoral nature of its inhabitants, and the fact that it was by law a 'closed district' – entry into which was forbidden to strangers and non-officials alike, except by special permit – and finally, but by no means least, because there were no serious elephant control cum crop protection problems in the District, the wildlife of Karamoja could well be safely left to look after itself without the help of the Game Department. Surely, a more damning indictment of the short-sightedness of the old colonial government attitude to the value of wildlife would be hard to find!

*

With conscious self-control, I postponed my safari to Dodoth until the month of March, 1951. I knew that the Tsetse Control Department was still busy with its camp building and fly surveys – essential preliminaries to any plan of operations – and I also knew that to get a true picture of the wildlife potential of the area I had to visit it at the height of the dry season, the time when the great game herds would be most concentrated and easy to observe. In the north the rains usually broke early in April, after which the game quickly scattered to the fresh grazing around numerous, newly-filled water-holes and much of the country soon became impassable to ordinary vehicles.

In those days the now ubiquitous four-wheel drive Land-Rover, or similar safari car, was yet to make its debut in East Africa, and in the Uganda Game Department the one and a half ton Bedford truck, with a locally built wooden box-body, was the *de rigueur* safari vehicle for all discerning game wardens. It was a tough, reliable vehicle and a useful load carrier, but lacking four-wheel drive it was often defeated by the loose, shifting surface of wide sand rivers and unexpected patches of greasy, black-cotton soil – both of which involved much heaving, sweating, digging, cutting of branches and a continuous stream of oaths and profanity, before the vehicle could be rescued. And even when firm ground was finally reached one was, as likely as not, in the same unenviable position as a shipwrecked mariner isolated on a lonely coral atoll surrounded by a treacherous sea. So, in Uganda, the timing of safaris into largely unknown country had to be judged to a nicety, in so far as the advent of the rains was concerned.

I chose Gulu in Acholi District as the jumping off place for my Dodoth safari. This meant entering Dodoth from the southwest after rounding the southern end of the Nangeya Range, the fifty mile long massif that separates the northern areas of Acholi and Karamoja Districts. I was anxious to see the Acholi side of the Nangeya Range, and I had decided that it was most important that I should make the safari a combined one with Mike Holmes, who was then based in Gulu. He was the nearest game warden I had to north Karamoja and, as such, he would have to keep a close eye on the situation there until better arrangements could be made.

Gulu is the headquarters of both the Acholi District and the Northern Province of Uganda. Usually dry and dusty and frequently extremely hot, it is not the most salubrious of government stations. Since the introduction of better communications and some modern amenities people have learnt to get used to it, and even develop a strange affection for it, but it is not so long since Gulu was regarded as being something of a punishment station. Before the Second World War, a district commissioner posted to Gulu for more than one tour of duty usually felt like a Russian commissar who has been banished to Outer Siberia.

Mike and I planned to lose as little time as possible getting away from Gulu. I arrived there from Entebbe on the 1st of March, and we packed all my safari kit and his into Mike's Bedford truck ready for an early start the following morning. The day was rounded off with a pleasant evening at the bungalow of the District Commissioner, a New Zealander named Peter Allen, and his wife Joan, old friends of mine and staunch allies of the Game Department. In fact, most of the district commissioners in Uganda were very wildlife conscious, and those that later went on to exalted positions in the rarified atmosphere of the

Secretariat were frequently valuable unseen allies to us in our battles with the hostile minority. Peter Allen was no exception for he had a good brain and a pleasing personality – assets which gave him a meteoric rise in the Administrative Service at a time when the Game and Fisheries Department needed all the friends at court that it could muster.

The next night Mike and I were bivouacked in the bush below the 7,600 foot peak of Rom, at the southern end of the Nangeya Range. We had not got as far as we had hoped as our departure from Gulu had been delayed by the disappearance of my gun-bearer, Firipo. At dawn, when the truck was ready to go, there had been no sign of him and both Mike's cook and his own gun-bearer had blandly disclaimed all knowledge of Firipo's where-abouts. 'If he's not here by nine o'clock we'll leave without him,' I had said in cold fury. Hardly had I spoken when a bat-tered bicycle weaved unsteadily round the corner of the bungalow. The rider, a strange Acholi, was very much the worse for wear. His clothes had been torn and streaked with dirt. His face and legs had been cut, scratched and covered with blood. His pas-senger, clinging precariously to the groaning carrier, was in a worse state than he was. They finally crashed into the front of Mike's truck and ended in a heap on the ground with the bicycle's twisted frame on top of them. Both were as drunk as lords. The passenger was Firipo. It took us half an hour to sober him up by holding his head under a gushing cold water tap, after which Mike's cook and gun-bearer chucked him bodily into the most uncomfortable place in the back of the truck.

It was the only time that I had ever known Firipo to get drunk. After we reached our camp site that evening, he apologised to me humbly, but with great dignity, for his lapse and I did no more about it. At least he had managed to get back to me some-how and all the time he served me as a gun-bearer he was never drunk on duty again.

When we sat by the camp fire under the stars that night, the conversation inevitably turned to the tsetse problem in Dodoth and our plans for the safari ahead.

'I met Fazal Haq in Gulu last week,' said Mike, his stocky, fair-haired figure silhouetted against the flickering flames as he knelt to poke the embers into a blaze. 'He's got a permanent camp in northern Dodoth, about twenty miles from the Sudan border, on the slopes of a hill called Lomej, and he was in Gulu buying stores. He asked me to tell you he thinks that, with a bit of luck, they can fix a tsetse consolidation line far enough south to save most of the best game country. He also gave me news of elephant,' continued Mike, eyeing me with a sly grin. 'Said he thought you might be interested! Apparently, he spent some time in these hills last month and he says he's been making a careful study of elephant movements in Karamoja during the last year or so.'

I sat up sharply in my camp chair. I had been beginning to get drowsy, now I was wide awake. Fazal Haq, born in what is now Pakistan, was a good friend of mine and one of my best Honorary Game Wardens. He was not only a skilled and fearless hunter but a fine and observant field naturalist. He was also one of the most valued field officers of the Department of Tsetse Control! As such, in him the Game Depatrment had a staunch ally in what was often, unfortunately, 'the enemy camp'.

Mike handed me a sheet of rather soiled paper smelling strongly of petrol and oily cotton waste. 'Here are some notes Fazal asked me to give you.' Switching on my big torch I studied the grimy sheet of paper with quickening interest. Despite the grease marks and oil stains the neat handwriting was still decipherable. It was headed 'Some Observations on Elephant Movements in Karamoja,' and the text was as follows:

There are at times large numbers of elephant in Karamoja, very few of which are permanent residents of the district; seasonal movements bring them in from Acholi and the Sudan.

During the early part of the year the elephant live largely in the hills and mountain country in the north; in February they start moving down into the valleys and by March there are virtually no elephant left in the hills. The main movements in this area appear to be governed by the ripening of the fruit of the borassus palm. In a year when there is a good crop of borassus nuts, large herds of elephant concentrate at night in the groves of borassus palms that line the sand rivers, there to feast on the nuts during the hours of darkness and dig for fresh water in the dry river beds. At first light they leave the palm groves to spend the daylight hours in the acacia country, six to seven miles from the rivers, returning again when darkness falls.

Another attraction for the elephant in this area is the desert date – *Balanites aegyptiaca* – also called the soap nut, which usually starts to ripen in February.

217

As soon as the rains break in April, the elephant start on a southward movement, travelling right down to Napono and the Labwor Hills. Sometimes a few get as far south as the great marsh of Longorokippi, where they have been reported in May, and in recent years they have even reached Lake Salisbury in eastern Teso, as they used to in the old days. At the end of the rains, about October/November, the elephant return to the hills and a large number leave Karamoja altogether.

Thoughtfully, I turned the paper over. On the reverse side of the foolscap sheet were a few more lines of writing.

Dear Major, I thought these notes might interest you. There were several large herds of elephant in the northern hills last month and I saw some big bulls high up on Lonyili. I think they have now moved down into the Kidepo as the locals say there are a lot of borassus palms there and it is a good year for the fruit, but I have not had a chance to get that far north myself yet. Hope to see you at Lomej. Yours, Fazal Haq.

I opened my map and studied it. Lonyili was marked as a 7,613 foot peak at the northern end of the Nangeya Range, right on the Sudan border. From it the Kidepo Valley lay some twenty miles to the north east. In between was another broad valley, that of the Narus, the main tributary of the Kidepo. I could see that once we arrived in Dodoth, we would still have some sixty miles of rough, trackless country to traverse if we ourselves hoped to reach the Kidepo. The next morning we entered Karamoja.

As we crossed the border I felt as if I had stepped back a hundreds years in time. It was not just the battered notice at the road side warning all travellers that Karamoja was a 'closed district'. There was something else, some hidden barrier, and as we crossed the invisible demarcation line the atmosphere seemed suddenly to change. I had noticed the same sensation previously when I had entered Karamoja from the south to visit Moroto. There was an added harshness, a natural wildness about the surrounding country. This time the feeling was enhanced by the sight, on the rough track ahead of us, of a tall athletic figure, naked except for a length of thin black cloth – slung carelessly from one shoulder – that streamed behind him as he loped along, his lean, dust-covered legs moving rhythmically in tireless, mile-eating strides. From his head-dress proudly sprouted a tall, white

218

ostrich plume, and in his right hand he carried a long, slim spear with a slender, leaf-shaped blade.

The lonely traveller greeted us courteously as we halted alongside of him, shifting his spear to his left hand and raising his right in a sign of peace. We studied each other with mutual interest. On the back of his head was a sort of ornate skull cap of grey clay mixed with hair, with a small forward extension whence sprouted the tall ostrich plume. In a hole in his lower lip was a heavy plug of ivory. From the lobes of his ears large, shiny white metal earrings hung pendulously; and around his neck were coiled yard upon yard of brilliant red and yellow beads threaded on wire and giraffe tail hair. For the rest he was stark naked except for a broad ivory bangle on his left wrist and the thin black cloak that hung down his back. His jet black skin shone with a purple sheen and his manhood was not only magnificent but swung free and obvious for all to see. I, for one, gazed at this colourful sight in undisguised admiration. Here was my first view of a true Karamojong warrior and I felt drab and inadequate beside him.

Firipo was the first to recover. In a dialect I did not understand, he shot a stream of questions at the dignified figure by the roadside. The only words I could distinguish were *etom* – the Karamojong for elephant – and *Karenga*, the name of the Napore village the track to which we were seeking.

Leaning nonchalantly on his long spear, the tall warrior answered briefly, almost curtly, pausing frequently to spit in the dust and point to the north with forward jerks of his chin so emphatic that they caused his ostrich plume to bob wildly and his ivory-studded lower lip to fly open as if in surprise. Finally, when we offered him a lift, he stared long and doubtfully at our dirty, over-loaded truck, and then politely but firmly refused, indicating gravely that he really preferred to walk.

The track we followed to Karenga was little more than a foot-path hugging the lower slopes of the eastern side of the Nangeya Range. We reached the village by mid-morning and found it dirty and untidy, and its people sullen and suspicious. The reason for their attitude was not apparent but I have never really liked or trusted the Napore – and with some cause.

The Napore, as a tribe, have a reputation as 'Borgias', their knowledge of vegetable poisons being extensive, and I once had a game guard who was the victim of their attentions. There had been some *fitina* – feuding – in our camp at Opotipot, on the Nangeya Range, involving an Acholi game guard and two Napore porters. One evening the game guard was missing and, after a long search, we eventually found him lying, in dense bush, on the hillside, about a hundred yards below the camp. He was semi-conscious and at regular intervals his back would arch and his lips would be drawn back from clenched teeth as his body went into violent muscular spasms. It was clear that he had been poisoned, but we had no idea what kind of poison it could have been and we were a hundred miles or more from the nearest doctor, much of it over rough, bush tracks.

We carried him into the camp, covered him with blankets, and considered the situation. Suddenly, Elizabeth – who was with me on that safari – had an idea. With her she had some tablets of pethidine – a powerful muscle relaxant, two tablets of which, at fifty milligrams each, are a strong dose. It was literally a case of kill or cure, so we crushed up four tablets and managed to get the semi-conscious game guard to swallow them with the aid of some sips of warm tea. Within two hours he was sleeping like a babe, quiet and relaxed, and the next morning he was his normal, cheerful self. But the two Napore porters had disappeared during the night.

This was long after my first visit to Dodoth, but I had been warned, from the beginning, about the Napore and I was not really sorry when the villagers of Karenga would not co-operate with Mike and me, and stubbornly refused to provide us with either guides or information.

Instead, we found a couple of cheerful Dodoth who had been returning south to Kaabong, after doing some work for Fazal Haq, but seemed delighted at the chance of a free ride back north, with pay and food thrown in! Despite their helpful advice however – or rather because of it – we suffered a hazardous, spring-testing, body-jolting drive across the grain of a section of very broken country. The trouble was that the two Dodoth had greater faith in the hill climbing capabilities of a normal Bedford truck than even the makers of this worthy vehicle themselves! Nevertheless, by following elephant trails – elephants being the best natural road surveyors in the world – coupled with a certain amount of judicious tree felling and rock moving, we managed to reach the upper part of the Narus Valley by dusk and, in gathering darkness, pitched camp below a tall, granite kopje.

I was awakened by the slanting rays of the early morning sun streaming into my tent and the sound of lions roaring close by. The air was fresh and still cool. Rolling off my camp bed, I pulled on a pair of shorts and gym shoes, gulped down a mugful of hot, sweet tea, and climbed slowly to the top of the rocky kopje that towered above our camp like the battlements of an ancient, weathered castle.

Reaching the summit I sat down and studied the landscape. Below me, on all sides, stretched a wide expanse of park-like country, dotted with herds of game. To the west loomed the long, dark line of the Nangeya Range. To the east the near horizon was dominated by the unmistakable 6,500 foot peak of Lomej with, behind it, the awesome, brooding massif of Morungole, cloud-capped and menacing, towering over nine thousand feet into the azure sky. Far away to the north, hazy blue in the distance, I could discern the outline of the Didinga Hills, deep in the Sudan.

Using my binoculars I examined the game herds below me. Among the stands of tall acacias were scattered large, mixed herds of the ever restless, boldly striped Burchell's zebra; heavy, dewlap-swinging eland, the old bulls slate grey and massive; and the clown-like, chestnut coloured Jackson's hartebeest with their long, lugubrious faces. Here and there, browsing among the high branches of the thorn trees, were groups of the five-horned Rothschild's giraffe, some of the males having hides the colour of dark chocolate. Far in the distance I could just discern a slowly moving, densely packed mass of buffalo; and in one open glade I spotted a herd of twenty roan, their large, tufted, donkey-like ears and their striking, gaily painted faces – quite apart from their size and proud, almost arrogant, gait – making these regal looking antelope unmistakable at a glance.

The open grassland was dotted with black and grey blobs. Closer inspection with my binoculars revealed these to be ostriches. With their flouncing feathers, their scrawny necks topped with bulging heavily-lashed eyes, and their long, bony legs ending in naked, flesh-pink thighs, they reminded me of a troupe of ageing ballet dancers. In striking contrast, frisking among these ungainly birds in gay abandon, were the dainty, fawn-coloured shapes of numerous, fairy-like oribi, perhaps the most ethereal of all the antelopes. I have never seen so many before or since. Very nearly as abundant were the Bohor reedbuck; they seemed to be everywhere in groups of up to a dozen. And among this varied miscellany of game, short-sighted and even shorter tempered, puffed a massive rhino heading ponderously across the plains for some distant water-hole.

All the time I watched, the lions were roaring, their deep, resonant grunts echoing from the rocky face of the kopje as if it were a giant sounding board. Search as I might I could not locate the source of the noise until, suddenly, far below me, I saw a herd of zebra scatter, their high-pitched, yelping alarm calls carrying on the still air like the sound of a pack of hounds in full cry. And into the glade they had vacated strolled a tawny feline shape, steely muscles rippling under its glistening yellow hide, its every movement indicative of power and arrogance; it was a magnificent, black-maned lion, the long, dark hairs of his great, shaggy mane carrying not only well back behind his shoulders but deep on his belly also. In the centre of the glade he halted and looked slowly round. With my powerful binoculars I found myself staring straight into his deep, amber-coloured eyes. The expression in them gave me a strange sensation. I felt as if I was an eavesdropper, a trespasser in some royal preserve. And as I watched his mouth half-opened, his belly contracted, and from deep in his throat came a series of rumbling roars. '*Hii nchi ya nani? Hii nchi ya nani?* YANGO! *Yango! Yango!*' is the Swahili interpretation of the call. '*Whose* country is this? *Whose* country is this? MINE! It is *mine!* It is mine!' in ever diminishing volume, ending in a series of coughing, deep bellied grunts. 'Do you know I believe you're right!' I said to myself softly as I watched the royal figure disappear among the trees, followed closely by his harem of four sleek young lionesses and three gambolling cubs.

As I lowered my binoculars and slid down the rock, a movement in a tall acacia caught my eye. Glancing up, I saw a young leopard stretched at his ease on a high, overhanging branch; the white tip of his long tail hanging free and twitching as he stared at me had attracted my attention. For a moment our eyes met, unafraid. Then, his ears flattened on his head, his lips drew savagely back from his sharp, white fangs in a silent, hissing snarl, and in a flash he was gone in one graceful bound.

Leopard in a thorn tree

I sat down and glanced at the sky. Overhead, in ever-widening circles, soared a striking, broad-winged, stubby-tailed, black and white bird, its crimson, fiercely hooked beak and its bright orange legs and cruel talons contrasting vividly with the pallor of its belly and the blue of sky. Its outstretched wings hardly moved as it swayed and banked on the shifting air currents, its direction delicately controlled by the feathers at its wing-tips, wide-stretched like the parted fingers of an extended hand. It was a bateleur eagle, aptly named by some long forgotten Frenchman after *bateleur* – in the argot of France the slang term for a tight-rope walker – an acrobat gracefully walking the single strand with outstretched, balancing arms, hands and fingers tense and strained. Whatever the origin of his name, to me the bateleur eagle, savage but colourful, fierce but free, soaring where he will on the wings of the wind, is truly symbolic of the very spirit of the African bush.

While I watched this handsome eagle, sailing effortlessly and gracefully over the tall thorn trees and the wide grassy plains, a revelation came to me. As if in a vision, slowly but with in-creasing strength, it began to dawn on me that here at last I was in the true, unspoilt wilds of Africa. There was nothing artificial or man made about this broad expanse of game filled country. It was not a national park. It was not a game reserve. It was not a private estate owned by some rich land baron. It was not even one of the many forms of officially demarcated area in which hunting is restricted. And yet here were great herds of many species of game, cautious but not terrified of man; game to be watched and even to be shot at if there was real need of food in the camp. The lions and the leopards could spare the odd eland or hartebeest and a reedbuck or two; there was enough and to spare for all. With mounting excitement I began to under-stand that here was what, in my heart of hearts, I had long been searching for. My safari was, in part, a pilgrimage in the pioneer-ing footsteps of my boyhood hero, 'Karamoja' Bell, and I had not been disappointed. This was what the country must have been like even in his day. The realisation was enough and com-plete. There and then I swore an oath that this was one area which I would endeavour to keep in its truly natural state, free from artificial interference, for as long as I possibly could.

When I got back to camp the sun was high in the sky and Mike was looking worried. I had broken all the rules by wandering off on my own, without a rifle and without telling anyone where I was going. 'I was beginning to think you had got bushed,' he said reprovingly. 'Anyway, I've got something to show you.' He pointed to a broad swathe cutting through the grass a few yards from the camp. It was the track of an elephant herd heading purposefully north towards the Kidepo. Some of the foot prints were enormous. As silently as ghosts they had passed during the night while we slept.

*

Mike halted the Bedford at the foot of a long, rocky ridge that barred our passage like some giant breakwater. Four days had passed since we had entered Dodoth, days which had been fully occupied in getting the truck through to Fazal Haq's camp at Lomej and studying the tsetse problem with him on the ground. The hidden hand of some celestial cynic must have guided the Tsetse Control Department in its choice of Lomej as its advance field headquarters for, in the tongue of the Karamojong, 'Lomej' means literally 'the place of hunting'! In any case, for me the days had been a time of mounting impatience dominated by my desire to reach the Kidepo. Now, at last, we were in striking distance. Mike pulled out his map and pointed with a stubby forefinger. 'I reckon we're about here,' he said. 'If so, we should be able to look down into the Kidepo from the top of this ridge.'

With suppressed excitement we climbed the steeply slanting slope of rock, our approach heralded by the staccato alarm calls of numerous hyrax – the coney of the Bible – which darted like giant guinea pigs into the deep crevices that seamed the hillside. Just before I reached the top I hesitated. We were now right in the heart of the land that 'Karamoja' Bell describes so vividly in his books, the country to which he gives the name of 'Dodose'. Not far to the north east of where we were at that moment was Moru Akipi – the 'Mountain of Water' – Bell's ivory El Dorado that he called 'Murua Akipi', the lonely hill whence he saw the surrounding plains dotted with the dark shapes of scores of elephants, all of them mighty bulls carrying heavy ivory. What was I myself about to see? I had waited so long for this moment that I dreaded an anti-climax, a disappointment. So, as I reached the top of the ridge, I deliberately shut my eyes, groped around for a convenient rock, and sat carefully down. Then, slowly and cautiously I opened my eyes and studied the scene before me.

The background was dominated by the towering cone of Lotuke, the 9,170 foot peak at the southern extremity of the Didinga Hills, at the foot of which were mile upon mile of the arid plains of the southern Sudan. The foreground was a wide expanse of dry, yellow grassland, ending in a belt of tangled thorn scrub – *acacia sayal* – that shone like dull silver in the shimmering heat waves of the afternoon sun. In the middle distance, running from east to west, was a long, winding, double line of borassus palms, disappearing into the distance like the avenue of some stately, ancestral home. Between the palms, twisting like the coils of a slowly writhing snake, stretched a broad sand river – the Kidepo!

The scene was magnificent. I stared at it in wonder, awed by its wild majesty. But something, the key factor, seemed to be missing. Then slowly and with measured tread, as if in slow motion, out of the thorn belt appeared a series of great, grey shapes – one, two, three, a group of seven and four more – fourteen in all. The creamy white of heavy ivory gleamed in the sunshine. They were elephants, every one a massive bull, but the last in line was a giant towering a good foot above the rest. I released my pent up breath in a long, deep sigh of relief and satisfaction. My boyhood dream was unfolding before my eyes, but the act was not yet over, the real drama was still to come.

The elephants wandered slowly into the open grassland far below us, moving purposefully onwards, grazing leisurely as they went, pulling up large tufts with their trunks and halting occasionally to beat the roots on an extended foreleg to remove the clinging soil, before stuffing the now clean grass into their cavernous, steadily chewing mouths. It was an almost idyllic scene, majestic yet peaceful, but in a flash it changed. One moment the elephants were a scattered, contentedly feeding herd; a few seconds later they were a tightly packed mass fleeing panic stricken in our direction, their passage marked by the mounting cloud of fine grey dust churned up by their pounding feet. And as they drew closer we could see, hot on their trail, loping rapidly along like a pair of eager hounds, two tall, black, naked figures, the sunlight glinting on the razor sharp blades of their long, metal shafted spears.

'Karamojong!' exclaimed Mike, his binoculars glued to his eyes. 'Spear blooding!' For a time I was hypnotised, fascinated. Here in front of me were being re-enacted, in flesh and blood, scenes immortalised in *The Wanderings of an Elephant Hunter*. Bell's own sketches in his African classic were coming to life before my eyes. And as I watched, uncertain what to do, the elephants blundered down into a dry river bed and the two Karamojong sprinted forward to narrow the gap.

The giant bull was the last to reach the steep bank of the small sand river. For a long moment he hesitated at the edge and in those few seconds the Karamojong closed in and hurled their spears into his massive body. Shaking his head and waving his trunk the old bull turned on them, but the men dodged nimbly out of his way and the badly injured beast swung round again to rejoin the herd, blood oozing steadily from two, deep wounds in his side.

The Karamojong recovered their spears, which had fallen out, and continued the chase which then passed directly below the ridge on which Mike and I were sitting. By that time the hunters were again very close behind the elephants and one caught up with another bull into which he hurled his spear. The blade flashed in the sunlight, buried itself in the animal's flank, and hung there momentarily before falling to the ground. The elephant turned on the spearman and charged screaming at him, whereat he beat a hasty retreat but not before the enraged beast had sprayed him with water from its trunk.

By now the whole herd appeared completely demoralised and the two injured bulls were squirting water from their trunks over their sides and backs as they ran; obviously the spear wounds were paining them.

Up to that moment, the whole action had taken place with such speed that both Mike and I had been too astounded and bemused to interfere. It was an amazing sight and it was not till later, when I had had time to think, that I began to wonder at the facility with which the stampeding elephants had been able, as they ran, to thrust their trunks deep into their gullets to draw up liquid – presumably from their stomachs. Fazal Haq had told us of having seen an almost identical sight, only a short time previously, when he and a fellow field officer of the Tsetse Control Department had observed a pair of Jie warriors hunting elephant with spears. I had found parts of his story hard to believe and now the action was being repeated for my benefit!

Suddenly and simultaneously it dawned on us that we must do something. With angry shouts Mike and I leapt to our feet and raced down the hillside brandishing our rifles, our gun-bearers pounding behind us. The two Karamojong jerked to a halt, gaping at our lumbering approach in open mouthed astonishment. Then, in a flash, they had gone. One moment they were there, tall, ebony figures, motionless as statues; the next second they had disappeared, diving down a convenient donga with the speed and agility of the hyrax in the rocks above. By the time we arrived at the spot there was no trace of them and once again the landscape had donned its deceptive cloak of majestic calm. Of the elephants the only signs were a far-away dust cloud rapidly disappearing into the distance and a trail of fresh blood on the grass.

I turned to my companion. 'Mike,' I said grimly. 'That big bull is badly hurt. We can't just leave him. We'll have to try to follow him up.'

Mike Holmes nodded. 'I reckon the herd's heading for the Kidepo,' he replied. 'They'll want to drink soon. I think it'll be quicker for us to bring the truck round the end of this ridge and cut their tracks nearer the river. So saying he shouldered his rifle and led the way back to the Bedford. A quarter of an hour later we were bouncing across the grassy plains, aiming diagonally for the long line of tall borassus palms that loomed like sentinels in the middle distance, marking the course of the river.

Within half a mile of the palm trees we crossed the tracks of the herd. We turned and followed the freshly beaten trail until we were faced with a tangled mass of secondary growth that flourished under the protective umbrella of the borassus palms and the occasional spreading tamarind. Jumping out of the truck, and keeping to the fresh elephant tracks, we pushed our way through the prickly barrier until we burst forth into the open again. At our feet was a low bank. In front of us was a broad stretch of sand, nearly a hundred yards wide, curling gently away on either side until it disappeared from sight. The surface of the sand was pock-marked with dozens of small craters; dug by elephants in search of pure water, they looked like the aftermath of an intensive mortar barrage. Below the opposite bank was a dark and sinister

Kidepo, valley of the elephants

Lokidul, water-hole in the Kidepo

looking pool of water, murky and covered with patches of green, slimy weed. The whole area was so littered with elephant droppings, old and new, that it resembled a midden. We were at a bend in a mighty sand river. We had reached the Kidepo at last.

Clearly imprinted in the sand before us were the tracks of the herd we had been following. Pausing only long enough to drink hastily at one or other of the small, water-filled craters in the river bed, they had circled the odoriferous pool and disappeared through the fringing bush beyond. Grains of sand were still gently trickling down the steep sides of some of the small water holes. We had missed the herd by moments.

Mike and I looked at each other uneasily. The border was somewhere very close, that we knew; but where? We turned to one of our Dodoth guides, using Firipo as an interpreter.

'What's the name of this water-hole?' I asked, indicating the murky, spring-fed pool.

'Lokidul,' replied the Karamojong.

My feelings of unease increased. I had heard of Lokidul. It was claimed by both the Dodoth of Uganda and the Didinga of the Sudan. Over the years much blood had been spilt in disputes for its ownership. It was not the safest place to linger. In any case the injured bull had gone on and I felt duty bound to follow him up even if he had entered what, on the maps, was the Sudan.

Then I caught sight of Mike Holmes's face. Suddenly he was deathly pale; his forehead was beaded with sweat; and his eyes were glazed and staring.

Something was very, very wrong.

*

It took us half an hour to set up a temporary camp in the shade of the spreading branches of a large tamarind. I chose a site about fifty yards from the river bank and some two hundred yards down wind from Lokidul. I wanted to be out of the main stream of traffic, as it were, to avoid disturbing the animals visiting the water-hole – and I also wanted to be hidden from any curious, and very likely hostile, human eyes that might pass that way. Lokidul was notorious as a transit spot for gangs of often heavily armed raiders – Didinga, Merile and Turkana – entering this no man's land from the Sudan, Kenya's Northern Frontier, and even from the borders of Ethiopia. There was no point in asking for trouble and in this sort of country it paid to be constantly on one's guard.

Mike Holmes was shivering with ague and his temperature was soaring. Having dosed him heavily with anti-malaria drugs, I rolled him in a pile of blankets and left him on his camp bed in the shelter of the tamarind, while I escorted one of the Dodoth to collect water from Lokidul. The Karamojong refused to go without an armed guard and his fears were not unfounded.

When we were within forty yards of the spring, the Karamojong – who was walking a few paces ahead of me with an empty four gallon kerosene tin on his head – crouched so suddenly that the tin seemed to rise in the air of its own volition. He caught it deftly before it hit the ground and then pointed a shaking hand at a thorn bush only ten yards away. My eye was drawn by a faint movement and gradually the scene took shape. There, in the shade of the bush, lying on her back with all four legs in the air, fast asleep, was a large lioness. Beside her were three tiny cubs, one of which had just awakened and was looking at us with a mixture of interest and alarm. Beyond, and only just visible, was the recumbent form of another full grown lioness or lion. Our silent approach on the soft sand had very nearly led us into an extremely nasty situation. A lioness with young cubs, surprised at such close quarters, would undoubtedly have attacked without hesitation. Slowly and quietly we backed away, my rifle at the ready, watched with drowsy curiosity by the one wakeful cub. And after a wide detour we collected water from one of the more distant of the pools which the elephant had dug.

A few minutes later I again set off after the elephant herd, accompanied by Firipo and the second of our Dodoth guides, leaving Mike in a deep sleep and the camp guarded by his gun-bearer, his cook and the other Dodoth. Firipo was carrying my faithful old double barrel ·470 and the Karamojong strode along happily with my ·416 Rigby over his left shoulder and his long, slim spear in his right hand. I glanced anxiously at the sun; it was getting very low in the sky. There was no time to lose.

Luckily the trail was easy to follow for there was no mistaking the tracks of the big bull. The forefoot of a really large bull elephant will measure eighteen to twenty inches or so in diameter, very occasionally more. I took out my coiled steel pocket-tape and stretched it across a print of the big bull's forefoot clearly etched in the sand. It measured just over twenty-two inches!

Having crossed the Kidepo at Lokidul the herd had immediately swung eastwards, much to my relief for, wherever the border actually was at that point, at least they were heading back towards Uganda. Our luck held. After covering a little over two miles, almost at a trot, across open grassland interspersed with patches of dry thorn-scrub, we reached a belt of tall acacia. And there, in front of us, in a small clearing, was a cluster of massive grey shapes. They were so still that for a moment I thought they might be a clump of rocks. The slanting rays of the evening sun shining obliquely through the trees were casting strange, misleading shadows. But a glance through my binoculars settled it. As I watched a massive trunk was raised slowly and quietly to read the wind, and then lowered just as gently. The rest of the herd remained as motionless as the rocks for which I had mistaken them.

Two things seemed certain. First, the herd was obviously trying to avoid detection; and second, the old bull must surely be very sick indeed or the herd would have travelled much further from the river before lying-up in the bush. My task was to try to discover how badly injured the big elephant was and then to decide whether or not he should be put out of his misery. I, took my double rifle from Firipo, checked that it was loaded, and signalled to him to take the ·416 from the Dodoth. Then after carefully testing the wind direction with my ash bag, we advanced slowly and cautiously towards the herd.

Forty yards from the elephants we halted behind a thin screen of acacias. I studied the herd carefully through my binoculars. They were in a tight huddle, the big bull in the middle. Only the top of his back was visible, but that was a good foot higher than any of the other elephants in the herd – and they were all big bulls. I reckoned that he stood an easy eleven foot six at the shoulder, but I couldn't see or judge anything else because of the tight, protective screen of elephants that surrounded him. Then, suddenly, the two bulls nearest to me moved a few feet to one side to feed on a projecting branch, and through the gap I got a clear view of the injured giant.

One look was enough. His head drooped. His ears hung limp like the sails of a becalmed ship. The end of his trunk, encrusted with dried blood, rested curled on the ground. In his side were two gaping spear wounds from which a pinkish froth still bubbled. There was no doubt that his lungs were injured and it appeared as if he might collapse at any moment. Left with no choice I moved in.

At the crash of the heavy rifle the old bull just crumpled until his eighty pound tusks prevented him from dropping any further. For the merest fraction of time all was still – then the rest of the herd came for me in a silent, vicious rush. Poor devils, they had had enough and I didn't blame them, but I had to act, and act fast, to save my own skin. I was in the open. There was no cover near. All I could do was to shoot straight and hope for the best.

When the leading bull was a dozen paces from me – a matter of a couple of seconds – I fired my second barrel. The frontal brain shot on a charging elephant is not easy, but the bull's legs gave under him and he rolled over like a shot rabbit not ten yards from me. What followed was so fantastic that it will ever be imprinted in my mind as one of my most vivid memories of the African bush. The three elephants charging immediately on the heels of the leading bull tripped over his fallen body and crashed to the ground, rolling over with their massive legs thrashing wildly in the air until the whole scene was hidden in a vast cloud of dense red dust.

There was no time to reload and seizing my ·416 from Firipo I prepared to repel the next attack. But, as the screen of reddish dust slowly cleared, to my intense relief I saw the rest of the herd, now completely demoralised, thundering off through the thorn scrub heading into the blood red orb of the setting sun.

We made our way slowly back to the Kidepo as the crimson evening glow turned to the pure silver of bright moonlight. Mike's cook had hung a hurricane lamp high in a tree to guide us in, and as we entered the firelit circle of the camp we could hear the pig-like squeals of rhino and the angry screams of elephant competing for the water-holes at Lokidul just below us. Mike was still asleep and I rolled into bed with the night wind rustling in the fan-like leaves of the borassus palms.

CHAPTER 12

Kidepo—'Valley of the Elephants'—II

IN the pale pink light of a semi-desert dawn, the water-hole of Lokidul had the sordid appearance of the morning after a giant mammalian bacchinalia. Pitted and pock-marked with hundreds of footprints of all types and sizes, the surface of the sand looked like a badly rumpled bed sheet. Litter was everywhere. Instead of cigar butts and cigarette ends there were the massive bolas of elephant droppings; the dry, scattered dung of rhino; the cow-like pats of buffalo; and the daintier trade-marks of the antelope species. Broken palm fronds replaced the discarded cocktail sticks of a human sundowner party; and instead of olive stones the sand was covered with the half-chewed remains of the fibrous, orange coloured borassus fruit. Last but not least, criss-crossing everything like a sinister over-print, there were the deeply etched pug marks of a pride of lions.

Having circled the water-hole to make sure that there were no fresh human footprints, other than our own, Firipo and I returned to the temporary camp in the cool shade of the spreading tamarind.

Rothschild's giraffe in North Karamoja, with Mount Lotuke behind

Black rhino, Karamoja

By the time we got back there was already warmth in the sun and Mike Holmes was awake. His fever had left him, but he was pale and weak and in no fit state to travel; so I took the Bedford truck and drove Firipo and one of the Dodoth out to the scene of our previous evening's encounter with the speared elephants. Over two hundred pounds worth of ivory was lying there and it had to be recovered.

As we bumped across the open plains our passage was marked by a swirling cloud of dense, grey dust, a cloud which turned to brick red the moment we left the dark soil of the grasslands to enter some of the murram patches in the thorn belts. Ahead of us, like a squadron of spotter planes, circled an ever-tightening spiral of vultures, culminating in a few dark specks so high in the sky as to be almost invisible to the naked eye. Leaning forward from his seat in the back to stare fixedly through the windscreen, the Dodoth watched the circling birds uneasily, his gaze darting swiftly from them to the distant massif of Lotuke. He muttered something under his breath.

'What's wrong?' I asked Firipo, who was sitting next to me.

'This man says he's worried about the Didinga, Effendi,' my gun-bearer replied solemnly. 'They will see the birds and read the meaning. The Didinga say this is *their* country,' he concluded simply but with emphasis.

My scornful comment died before it was born. One look at the two dark faces beside me was enough; they were deadly serious. We drove on in a silence broken only by the crackle of crushed grass and snapping thorn twigs and the tortured groans of the Bedford's battered body, until, at last, we re-entered a familiar clearing. There, in front of us, lay two shapeless grey mounds, already covered with a shifting, squabbling flock of vultures. Occasional gleams of white between the scrabbling birds revealed that the ivory was still intact.

We wasted no time. In a few moments the head skin of the first elephant had been sliced away and the Dodoth was hacking fiercely at the bony casing that holds the tusks of an elephant in a vice-like grip. He was using a razor sharp, long handled axe, with a slender, tapering head the shape of a Red Indian toma-hawk, and in his expert hands long slivers of bone were soon flying fast. But even in the hands of experts the cutting out of elephant tusks is a protracted and wearisome task calling for both care and energy. So, I decided to leave Firipo and the Dodoth to it, spend the day in camp catching up with such delayed chores as the writing of my safari diary, and return to collect the two men and the ivory in the evening. My only worry was their uneasiness about the Didinga, but Firipo finally set my mind at rest on that score.

'Leave me the *banduki ndogo*' – my ·275 Rigby – 'and we'll be all right, Effendi,' he said stoutly, and I drove away with my doubts suppressed if not eliminated.

*

Late in the afternoon Mike Holmes sat up sharply in his camp bed, listening intently. 'Did you hear that?' he queried after a moment's pause.

'Hear what?' I asked.

'I'm almost certain I heard a rifle shot, far in the distance,' Mike replied.

I called to the cook to stop clattering his pots and pans and for several minutes we all listened intently, but apart from the rustling of the breeze in the palm fronds and the sudden angry scream of an elephant deep in the thorn belt, all was quiet.

'You probably imagined it,' I said to Mike. 'Or else you were dreaming. Could be the malaria.'

'Maybe, but I don't think so. I think you should take Rafael with you when you go back this evening.' To placate him I agreed and after a mug of hot tea I set off again in the Bedford with Mike's gun-bearer sitting beside me, hugging my ·416 between his knees.

We drove to the edge of the clearing where I halted the truck and surveyed the scene. The remains of the two elephants were still there, much distorted, heavily white-washed with vulture droppings, headless and with their tusks missing. A few gorged vultures flapped heavily away at our approach, but apart from the birds the clearing was deserted. With my binoculars I studied the trees around the edge, half expecting to see Firipo and the Dodoth waiting for us in the shade, but to no avail.

We walked across to the carcases examining the ground carefully as we went. Suddenly Rafael exclaimed and pointed. Immediately in the vicinity of the dead elephants the dusty surface of the ground had been churned up by the feet of countless, squabbling vultures; but leading away from the bodies, heading in the direction of the Sudan, were several lines of human footprints. At least half-a-dozen men must have passed that way and the marks were fresh. Of Firipo, the Dodoth and the ivory there was no sign.

Slowly and carefully we circled the clearing searching for further tracks, calling and whistling as we went. We kept this up until the evening sun touched the tops of the thorn trees, when I fired a series of signal shots. Finally, as the moon climbed into the sky, we gave up the search and drove back to camp in gloomy silence. Our one remaining hope was that the missing men – somehow and for some unknown reason – had made their own way back to camp by a circuitous route, but our hopes were dashed before we even dismounted from the truck. The anxious, questioning faces of Mike, his cook and the second Dodoth, all of whom had heard my shots, were enough to give us the answer. Firipo, the other Dodoth and the ivory had vanished as completely and mysteriously as if they had been whisked away on a magic carpet. The only clue was the sinister line of human footprints heading into the heart of the southern Sudan.

That night we packed up camp, damped down the fire and took it in turns to remain on guard while the others slept fitfully on the ground, wrapped in a single blanket or a sleeping bag. During my spell of sentry duty the moon was well up and three separate herds of elephant came to drink at Lokidul. Sitting at the edge of the low bank of the Kidepo, my rifle across my knees, I could see the dark outline of their massive forms silhouetted against the pallid background of the river bed; and I could hear the familiar scraping, crunching sounds which revealed that they were digging for water below the surface of the loose sand. The only other noise was the quiet gurgle as they sucked the clean water up into their trunks, followed by the cascading rush – like someone filling a cistern with a large bucket – as they emptied the contents of their trunks down their cavernous gullets into their great, tank-like stomachs. They must have sensed our presence for they made no other sound, coming and going as silently as ghosts, the big bulls departing with as much as fifty gallons in their stomachs – enough to keep them going for two or three days if need be and depending on what they ate.

In the greyness of first light we also stole quietly away, leaving

Lokidul looking strangely deserted and forlorn, and we arrived at the now putrid elephant carcases just as the first vultures, the wind hissing through their wing feathers, began to descend like dive-bombers from the sky. I looked slowly around, my heart sinking lower as I did so. There was still no sign of Firipo and the Dodoth. I had half-expected, half-hoped that we would find them by the dead elephants at dawn. The disappointment was bitter and the problem now appeared really serious. Two men, plus a rifle and over two hundred pounds worth of ivory, had disappeared as completely as if the earth had opened and swallowed them up. Then Rafael gave an excited shout and following his pointing finger I saw two forlorn looking figures climb slowly out of a nearby donga. The one in the lead carrying a rifle – my rifle – was Firipo; the other, limping badly, was the Dodoth.

As they came closer I saw that Firipo's khaki uniform was soiled and badly torn, while his companion had a dirty, blood-stained rag wrapped round his left foot. 'Jambo, Effendi,' said Firipo.

'Well!' I said, feeling the irrational mixture of anger and relief of a parent who has just recovered a straying child. 'And *where* have *you* been may I ask?' Then my heart softened as I realised that Firipo was in an advanced state of exhaustion. He was swaying on his feet and his eyes had the unseeing stare of a sleep walker.

'Sit down, Firipo,' I said. 'And drink this,' I added, handing him a mug of hot, sweetened tea from my Thermos flask, liberally laced with whisky.

For a long time Firipo sat on the ground with his head bent, gratefully sipping the hot, sweet liquid, while Mike handed another mugful to the Dodoth who unwrapped the rag from his left foot to reveal a deep, ugly gash still oozing blood.

'Tell us what happened, Firipo,' I said gently when I felt that he had recovered sufficiently to talk.

'Effendi,' he replied quietly. 'It was the Didinga as we had feared. The Dodoth and I worked fast after you left us, so fast that we had the tusks out soon after the sun had reached its highest point in the sky. The Dodoth was nervous; he kept saying the Didinga would come; so we took the tusks and buried them deep in the sand of the river bed over there.' He paused and pointed with his chin towards the donga from which they had just emerged.

'Then we returned and sat in the shade of the trees to await your arrival.' He paused again before continuing thoughtfully.

'Late in the afternoon six men appeared from the north, all carrying spears. They were Didinga and at first they greeted us as friends. Then they said that this was the Sudan and they wanted to know who had killed the elephants and taken the ivory. I told them that I was a game guard from Uganda, as they could see from my uniform, and that I also wanted to know the answer to these questions. At this they got angry and threatened us with spears, saying that I was a liar and demanding to be told where I had hidden the tusks.

'Suddenly one man siezed the barrel of my rifle and tried to take it from me. A fight started and I hit him with the rifle-butt. He fell to the ground and I then saw that the Dodoth was struggling with a second man who managed to stab a spear into his foot. At that point I fired a shot into the ground in front of the rest of the Didinga who were rushing at me with their spears. Then the whole group broke and fled, shouting over their shoulders that they would return with more men and guns to kill us and take the tusks.

'The Dodoth and I were frightened as we were not sure when you would arrive. We thought the Didinga might return before you did, so we covered our tracks carefully and crept away to the south to hide in some dense thorn scrub a mile or more away. We heard your shots at dusk but we were too far from you and we thought the Didinga might be between us. So we slept the night in a dry river bed. We were tired, cold and thirsty because we could find no water, even by digging, and early this morning we returned here as we were sure that you would come again to look for us. The tusks are safe, Effendi,' he added. 'They are buried over there in the river bed and I saw, this morning, that no one has disturbed the place. But we must hurry, Effendi. The Didinga will surely be here soon,' he concluded anxiously.

Half an hour later we were bouncing southwards, the springs of the Bedford groaning under the additional weight of two pairs of massive tusks of the short, thick Sudan variety. We were heading for a rocky ridge, a vantage point from which to spy for any signs of pursuit. The thorn scrub at its foot was dense and as we parked the truck in a clearing we disturbed a pair of black rhino which peered at us in short-sighted disbelief before crashing off through the bush in alarm, puffing and snorting like two runaway steam engines.

Clambering over the loose boulders, Mike and I and our two gun-bearers soon reached the top of the ridge and looked back. Dominating the whole stretch of country to the north, the tall mass of Lotuke loomed dark and menacing. In the middle distance the place where the dead elephants lay was still marked by circling vultures. It was the foreground that rivetted my attention. Advancing across the open plain, some four hundred yards distant, was a loosely grouped party of about thirty, near-naked tribesmen moving at a brisk jog-trot along the wheel tracks of our Bedford. Through my binoculars I could see that they were all armed with spears. Three of them, dressed in ragged khaki shirts, were also carrying some sort of firearms. We were not left in doubt of their intentions for long.

The advancing party spotted us almost as soon as we saw them. With triumphant shouts they split into three groups and started what was clearly intended to be an encircling movement. Two of the khaki-clad figures halted however, and a second or two later there was a whip-like crack, a shower of splintered rock, and the high-pitched whine of a ricochet as a rifle bullet struck the boulders just below us, followed almost immediately by another which came uncomfortably close.

'They're shooting at us!' roared Mike, his voice a mixture of astonishment and fury as we dived for cover. 'What a bloody nerve!'

'How did you guess?' I replied. I had not been shot at deliberately since the war in Burma and I did not intend to remain entirely on the receiving end. Aiming carefully and firing steadily I emptied my magazine. The roar of the powerful rifle reverberated from the rocks and I watched with satisfaction as the heavy bullets kicked up great fountains of dust at the feet of the advancing Didinga. Their yells of triumph turned to cries of alarm and the tribesmen scattered in panic, racing like startled rabbits for the nearest cover.

'Tell them if they come any closer we'll shoot at *them*, not their feet,' I growled at Firipo; and when the echoes of my gun-bearer's voice had faded, I turned to Mike. 'Time to go,' I said urgently and the four of us scrambled hurriedly down the hill to the Bedford. Late that afternoon we reached our old camp site in the valley of the Narus and bivouacked for the night at the foot of the same, towering granite kopje as before.

Prior to rolling into our sleeping bags that night we sat around the camp fire talking over the events of the previous three days. The reality of the Kidepo had exceeded my expectations and matched both the tales of Bell and my boyhood dreams. Our clash with the Didinga had been an added excitement, but not one I would care to experience as a regular practice. To be heavily outnumbered and attacked by well armed tribesmen in remote and virtually unknown country, with no hope of help or reinforcements, is too much like 'Russian roulette' for anyone's peace of mind.

Mike Holmes had the last word. 'You know,' he mused, staring into the glowing embers of the fire. 'I don't know that I can entirely blame the Didinga. For years they've suffered from the imposition of a totally artificial boundary that no one can recognise on the ground; and, unlike our tribes on this side of the border, I think they've always been allowed to hunt a number of elephant as a tribal right. I believe they *really* felt that we had stolen their ivory!' He paused for a moment before continuing thoughtfully. 'One thing puzzles me – those men who shot at us. Who were they? The Merile and Turkana raiders have rifles but I didn't think there were many firearms among the Didinga. *Were* they Didinga? If not, who were they?' He shook his head doubtfully and I remained silent. It was a question that bothers me still.

We went to sleep to the deep, bass chorus of lions roaring in the Narus, their resonant grunts echoing on the cool night breeze. Four days later I was back in the semi-suburbia of Entebbe, the Kidepo already a colourful dream.

Of the last ten miles of my drive to Entebbe I can recall little. My head felt like a pumpkin; there seemed to be a pneumatic drill hammering at the base of my skull; and I had increasing difficulty in focussing my eyes on the road. Elizabeth and Bydie were in England, and my arrival at my bungalow was a confused blur of anxious, welcoming, dark faces and myself rolling thankfully, in my dusty, sweat-soaked safari clothes, on to a familiar bed; and then merciful oblivion. The next thing I remember was waking up in a strange, white-walled room with the government doctor sitting beside me. I felt as weak as a kitten and there was a foul taste in my mouth.

I tried to sit up but the effort was too much for me and I fell back on the pillows.

'Where am I, Doc?'

'Entebbe hospital. You've been delirious for three days.' He grinned at my look of alarm. 'Don't worry. It's only malaria, but you've had a pretty bad go. I've been pumping you full of quinine injections and you'll be o.k. now. But take it easy, you had us all worried for a time!'

Two days later I received a buff coloured envelope with OHMS printed on it. Inside, issued on command of the highest government authority, was an official reprimand for failing to take adequate anti-malaria precautions. 'I am instructed to remind you that Government Officers are not paid to get ill,' it concluded with a bite.

I read the letter twice, carefully, thinking as I did so of the anopheles mosquitoes – the vicious carriers of malaria – that swarmed in so many of the areas of Uganda in which a game warden had to do his job. I thought also of the times when a game warden was forced to sit-up at night, waiting for shamba raiding elephants or hippo, or the stealthy approach of a man-eating lion, while swarms of determined mosquitoes whined hungrily about his ears. Under these conditions to use a protective net was impossible, while insect repellants were often ineffective and the prophylactic drugs of those days were far from infallible.

For a few moments I was filled with mounting anger and resentment at the apparent injustice. Then I remembered Charles Pitman's warning words about certain government officials' lack of understanding as to the working conditions of the Game Department. Slowly I lit a match and put it to the corner of the paper, watching it burn until my fingers singed and the ashes fell to the floor. 'There,' I thought to myself sardonically. 'There goes *my* good conduct medal!'

When I came out of hospital, I had only a little more than a month in hand before I was due for home leave, but I was determined to get the north Karamoja tsetse control question firmly settled prior to my departure. Luckily, the Tsetse Control Department was co-operative and we came to an amicable agreement on a workable and mutually acceptable tsetse consolidation line, to the north of which the vegetation and the game would be left undisturbed. The boundary ran from Lomej, on the east, in a shallow, S-shaped curve to Opotipot – 'the place of heavy and continuous rain' – on the lower slopes of the Nangeya Range to the west. To the north of this line, right up to the Sudan border and including the valleys of the Narus and the Kidepo – in all some five hundred square miles of the finest game country of Dodoth – the Government agreed to preserve as a natural 'wilderness area'. I was well satisfied.

*

The London bound flight arrived from Nairobi on time. On board was a friend of mine from Kenya. 'There's a man on this plane you must meet,' he said firmly. 'He's a sisal planter who is retiring to England. His name is Ralph Medcalfe. I'll introduce you.' And he led me across the lounge to where a burly, middle-aged man, with a cheerful, sun-tanned face, was sitting reading the *East African Standard*.

'Bruce Kinloch; Ralph Medcalfe. I'm sure you'll have a lot in common,' he added with a smile. 'Medcalfe is a nephew of "Karamoja" Bell!'

On our flight Medcalfe – himself a hunter of some prowess – told me much about the background and early career of his famous uncle, Captain Walter Dalrymple Maitland Bell, M.C.

Hunting and sailing were the ruling passions of 'Karamoja' Bell's life and he became a master of each of these crafts. Bell himself wrote that his earliest recollection of his boyhood was of his sole and insatiable ambition to hunt. First he wanted to be a bison hunter in America, but after reading Roualeyn Gordon Cumming's book on Africa he determined to become an elephant hunter, and in due course an elephant hunter he became, one of the greatest of them all.

In his teens Bell travelled round the world as an apprentice in a windjammer, and for several years he lived in New Zealand, doing odd jobs after working his passage there. In 1897, still in his late teens, he landed in Mombasa and was employed as a lion killer by the new Kenya-Uganda railway, whose construction gangs were being much troubled by man-eaters at that time.* He then left Africa to take part in the gold rush on the Yukon,

* Lt-Col. J. H. Patterson *The Man-Eaters of Tsavo*.

finding little gold but making a living by shooting game to supply Dawson City with meat. This was followed by the South African War, in which he served with the Canadian Mounted Rifles, was taken prisoner, but managed to escape. Finally, in 1902, he returned to British East Africa to become a professional elephant hunter for close on twenty-five years, interrupted only by the First World War, when he served with the Royal Flying Corps and was awarded the Military Cross and a bar, and was five times mentioned in despatches.

It was in the Karamoja region – from which I myself had just returned – that Bell's amazing exploits finally earned him the world-famous nickname of 'Karamoja'. Still one of the wilder and more sparsely inhabited areas of Africa, in Bell's time Karamoja was a savage land, unexplored and uncontrolled; and torn by inter-tribal strife, armed raids and blood-shed of a scale unknown in the present era. But in those days it also abounded with elephants carrying magnificent ivory, the bait which lured Bell to this unknown country. He was the first white man to be seen by many of the Karamojong and other tribes in whose country he hunted alone for a number of years, and to whom, as a result of his exploits, he became an almost legendary character.

I asked Medcalfe his opinion as to the reasons for his uncle's outstanding success as a professional ivory hunter. He answered without hesitation. 'First,' he said, 'Walter Bell was incredibly fit, tough and utterly fearless. That enabled him to penetrate country which few other hunters dared to approach. Secondly, he was a brilliant marksman, an artist with a rifle, and he knew the anatomy of the elephant so thoroughly that he could instinctively place a killing shot from any angle, his favourite being the brain shot which, as you know, causes instantaneous and painless death. He also carried his rifle everywhere until it became almost a part of him. That, on top of his marksmanship, enabled him to use a light, small bore weapon instead of the massive and tiring special, heavy rifles that most hunters have always been forced to use on elephant. Lastly, he really understood elephants; he had an intimate knowledge of their habits and characteristics.'

Ralph Medcalfe paused for a moment before continuing. 'You know,' he said quietly. 'A lot of people nowadays, most of them cranks or 'arm-chair' preservationists, are fond of condemning my uncle as a bloodthirsty killer. That is not true. He worked hard and often risked his life for nearly every elephant he shot. Somebody – I can't recall who – once wrote that, like all truly great hunters, 'Karamoja' Bell genuinely loved and was fascinated by his quarry, an apparent paradox not generally understood.'

'I can understand that,' I said. 'I have always liked what Negley Farson wrote about Bell in his preface to *Karamoja Safari*. He described him as being that not too frequent combination of professional killer and artist-adventurer and I liked his final conclusion even better – "A man must have something of the poet in him to become a great hunter".'

Medcalfe nodded and for a time we sat in silence. Then – 'What happened to your uncle when he gave up elephant hunting?' I asked.

'He retired to his home in Scotland. Then he concentrated on his second passion in life, sailing; ocean racing to be exact. He had a beautiful yacht called *Trenchemer* which he kept on the Clyde. He won several notable races with her and was second in the Fastnet Race in 1934.'

I hesitated for a moment. 'When did he die?' I asked finally.

Ralph Medcalfe stared at me in surprise, then roared with laughter. 'Die!' he said. 'Walter Bell's not dead! He's still hale and hearty and living at his old home near Garve in Ross-shire. If you're going up to Scotland I know that he would be more than delighted to see a kindred spirit, particularly with your recent news of his old hunting grounds in Karamoja.'

I wrote to Bell as soon as I joined Elizabeth and Bydie at our home leave base, a historic, 161 ton yacht named *Amphitrite*, an old schooner – owned by my father-in-law* – then moored in the Salcombe estuary in South Devon; she had been a famous ocean racer herself in her time and I thought it might rouse Bell's interest even further if I mentioned her as well as the subject of Karamoja and elephant hunting.

Bell's response was prompt and warm. 'Delighted to see the three of you when you come up to Scotland,' he replied. 'I am keenly looking forward to hearing up-to-date news of Karamoja!'

Three months later my wife, my daughter and I, booked in at the Garve Hotel, close to the Blackwater River, famous for its

* Colonel W. F. Charter, M.C., a retired Indian Army colonel with a Second Mate's ticket in sail, who is a 'Cape Horner' as well. Like Bell, he served his apprenticeship in square-rigged ships.

salmon. Most of the hotel's patrons appeared to be dedicated anglers, and while I signed the hotel register, large men in well-worn tweeds and strange, shapeless hats adorned with rows of small, exotic feathers, their powerful legs encased in thigh-length, rubber waders, strode purposefully across the lobby.

As I turned to look for the telephone, a glass-fronted show case on the wall caught my eye. To my surprise it was full of harness trappings which, instead of the traditional brass, had been most beautifully carved from ivory. The handsome, white-haired proprietress, Miss Mackenzie, smiled with pleasure at my interested enquiry. 'Aye, they're bonnie enough, they were carved by my grandfather,' she replied proudly in her soft Highland accent. 'He was head coachman to a laird in these parts. The laird was a famous hunter, a wild, braw man with a great, red beard almost down to his sporran. They do say he always hunted in a kilt and a bonnet even in Africa. And one year he brought home some great elephant tusks. He gave one to my grandfather, who was so proud of it that from the ivory he made these ornaments for the harness of his beloved horses.'

Something clicked in my mind. 'Would the name of this laird have been Roualeyn Gordon Cumming?' I asked. Miss Mackenzie stared at me in astonishment. 'And how did ye know that?' she gasped. It was my turn to smile. 'Your description of him,' I said. 'It reminded me of a picture I once saw in an old book!'

Despite myself I could not suppress a glow of youthful excitement. This was the same Roualeyn Gordon Cumming whose books had inspired Bell to become an elephant hunter. The trail was getting warm! I asked my last question. 'Captain Bell?' replied Miss Mackenzie. 'Aye, we know the Captain well. He was a famous hunter too.' She looked at me curiously. 'You wouldn't be a hunter yourself, by chance?' I could not help smiling again. 'Of a sort, I suppose!' I said. 'Now, may I please use your telephone?'

The next afternoon I drove Elizabeth and Bydie up to Corrie-moillie, a large, stone-built house standing in a typical Highland setting of wild, heather-clad slopes. I discovered later that the estate itself covered some one thousand acres – small by Highland standards, but strategically situated between two vast deer forests. Bell had chosen his place of retirement with typical shrewdness and foresight, and the eye of the born poacher!

247

Hunting would be in his blood until he died and in the autumn of his days, when the call became too strong to resist, he could still stalk the great red stags that wandered across his property from one sprawling deer forest to the next – sometimes to the fury of the powerful land barons on his flanks. There was something of the modern Robin Hood about Bell, for he and his wife had started a thriving cottage industry among the local crofters – an industry based on the making of articles from deer skins and antlers – while he himself could well have been the model for John Buchan's immortal 'John Macnab'.

The front door of Corriemoillie was opened by an elderly, white-haired man of soldierly bearing, great charm of manner and remarkably blue eyes. 'How very nice of you to come all this way to see us,' he said rather shyly, as he led the way into a rather old-fashioned drawing-room where a slender, sweet-faced woman was seated behind a round, oak table groaning with cakes, scones, strawberry and blaeberry jam and a gigantic silver teapot. 'We thought perhaps some of you might be hungry,' said Katie Bell gently, giving our six year old daughter a conspiratory smile.

It was not long before we were poring over maps, reliving Bell's travels in Uganda and comparing my own recent experiences with his memories of the same areas half a century earlier. Our call ended with an invitation to stay at Corriemoillie for several days and then join the Bells at the Royal Show in Aberdeen, a typically hospitable offer that we accepted gladly.

The time passed all too quickly for, reticent as he was about his accomplishments, Bell was intensely interesting when persuaded to talk about his travels and his hobbies. Rifles, particularly high velocity small bores, fascinated him and he had made a close study of them, becoming a ballistics expert consulted by several British gun firms. He told me that he regularly exchanged information with his friends and opposite numbers in the United States – notably the famous Colonel Townsend Whelen – and that they often posted to each other, for testing and comment, such things as some newly designed and specially constructed bullet, or the latest design in rifle sights.

Bell's gun-room contained a variety of weapons – including the last of the historic ·275 Rigby Mausers with which he had achieved such fantastic successes as a professional elephant hunter. He also showed me a take-down model ·318 in a special light case, saying rather wistfully that he had planned to visit Uganda by air in 1939, for a last elephant hunt, but that the war had intervened, and that he now felt he was too old. He was then in his early seventies but still stalking red deer on the high tops.

Apart from his other accomplishments Bell had great artistic ability. I well remember his pictures dotted about the house, and one in particular sticks vividly in my memory. It hung at the top of the stairs at Corriemoillie and I stopped to study it every time I went up to bed. It was a study, in oils, of a pride of lions and a lone old bull elephant drinking on opposite sides of a water-hole in the moonlight. It captured every nuance of the brooding watchful atmosphere of night in the African bush and I have often wondered where and when Bell painted it. I shall always regret that I never got round to asking him.

Shortly before we left Corriemoillie, Walter Bell said to me, in an unexpected burst of candour – 'You know, just before you first called, I suddenly wondered what sort of person you were expecting 'Karamoja' Bell to be; probably a tough, swashbuckling old ivory poacher; and I felt that you'd be surprised to be met by someone who looked like a retired country parson'. He was not far from the truth, for the last memory I have of 'Karamoja' Bell is of an elderly but very distinguished looking man in tweeds, leading by the hand our small, blonde daughter – to see the horses at the Royal Show in Aberdeen. He had just presented her with a beautiful model of a pony in Copenhagen china, a model to which he had carefully attached a label saying – 'Best Pony in Show.' I had stared in wonder, remembering the pattern of his life.

I said good-bye to 'Karamoja' Bell with regret, and sad to say for the last time. Although we corresponded regularly after my return to Uganda, nearly three years later he died peacefully at his home among the heather-clad hills, far from the wild bush country, the great herds of elephant, and the primitive tribes among whom his name became a legend which persists to this day.

*

There is a long drawn sequel to my own story of the Kidepo. In 1952, when Mike Holmes transferred to another wildlife post, he was succeeded as the Game Warden for the North by Captain

K. B. Robson. I took advantage of the change to move the headquarters of the Game Department's Northern Range from Gulu
to Kitgum in the north of Acholi District. As a base Kitgum suited
Robbie well, for it took him within easy striking distance of the
Nangeya Hills to the east and the shortest route to Dodoth and the
Kidepo Valley, which he visited as often as he could. By then the
Land-Rover had appeared on the scene, but Robbie – always an
individualist – had invested in an Israeli made Jeep. These four-
wheel drive vehicles reduced the problems of cross-country travel
to child's play and Robbie and I did several safaris together into
the Kidepo at various seasons, getting to know the area and its
problems better than anyone had been able to do before.

Robbie had a number of clashes with Didinga and Turkana
raiders, and although in each incident actual bloodshed was
narrowly averted, on several occasions this was only avoided
either by Robbie's own cool courage or by mere chance. Finally,
it became obvious that there had to be a strong Game Department
presence permanently established in Karamoja and, after a long
battle with the powers-that-be, I managed to get the necessary
authority and additional funds to base a game warden at the
District headquarters at Moroto, with a supporting force of game
guards just adequate enough to police the most important areas
of Karamoja District.

The man I chose for this important and challenging job was
Tony Henley, a hefty, Kenya-born lad in his middle twenties.
Tony was an old friend of mine. During 1948 and 1949 – when
he was a young Elephant Control Officer and I was helping the
Kenya Game Department – he and I had hunted shamba
raiding elephants together in the dense tropical bush of the Kenya
coast. As a result I knew, from personal experience, that he was
not only an exceptionally tough, competent and courageous
hunter, tracker and general 'bush-man', but also an outstanding
field naturalist. In 1950, he went back to professional hunting,
but applied to join me as one of my new game wardens when I
began to expand the Uganda Game Department in 1952. Having
just married an attractive blonde wife he wanted a rather more
settled existence than the colourful but gypsy life of a professional
hunter! I, for my part, was glad of the chance to recruit someone
of his calibre. And so, after a year involved mainly with elephant
control problems in western Uganda, Tony Henley went to

Moroto in November 1953, to open up the newly formed Karamoja Range.

Tony spent nearly three years in Karamoja; during this time
he concentrated much of his efforts in the north, where he built
a permanent base-camp at Opotipot at the eastern base of the
Nangeya Range, constructed a strategic network of rough patrol
tracks linking all the main game areas of Dodoth right down to the
main water-holes of Lokidul and Kananarok in the Kidepo
Valley, and established a tough, well-armed game guard force
which did much to discourage the previously bold and aggressive
Turkana and Merile raiders, as well as the inevitable Napore
and Mening poachers. His efforts were remarkably successful
and when he left Karamoja nearly three years later, not only
was the wildlife situation of the region well under control, but a
very great deal of valuable information had been accumulated
in regard to the species, numbers, breeding and seasonal movements of both the mammals and birds, for Tony Henley was also
a very keen and knowledgeable ornithologist. In fact he discovered
a new species of greywing francolin as well as the unusual mane-
less zebra, not hitherto recorded. However, by the time he departed from Karamoja, heavy storm clouds of political strife had
begun to mount rapidly along Uganda's northern border with
the Sudan, and these boded ill for the Kidepo.

Towards the end of 1955, just after the former Anglo-Egyptian
Sudan had achieved complete independence as a Republic, the
troops of the southern 'Equatorial Corps' of the crack Sudan
Defence Force – Africans to a man and both Nilotic and Bantu
by race – mutinied against their northern Arab officers. It was a
case of the black Nilotic south, memories of the savage cruelties
of the slave trade still strong in their minds, fearing domination
by the largely Arabic Muslim north. The mutiny took place in
Torit, only fifty miles north of the Uganda border, and the bulk
of the mutineers, most of them men of the border tribes, their
pathetic radio appeals to Britain for support having fallen vainly
on embarrassed diplomatic ears, marched into Uganda in fully
disciplined companies, complete with their arms and equipment,
to seek political asylum. A handful of them however, also carrying
their weapons, faded quietly into the densely forested fastness of
the Imatong Mountains, a range of rugged hills rising to heights

of over ten thousand feet close to the Acholi border of Uganda, there to become bandits dedicated to fighting the northern Sudanese.

Living partly with the help of local people and partly by shooting and trapping game, this small bandit force soon became a very real thorn in the flesh of the new Sudanese administration. Led by a man called Latada, a strong character and a brilliant marksman, they attacked the northern troops and officials at frequent intervals. On one occasion Latada and his son, between them – so it is said – ambushed a motorised column of northern troops of the Sudan Defence Force and held it up for the greater part of a day. The story that reached my ears, via the 'bush telegraph', was that Latada shot the driver of the leading vehicle which crashed and blocked the road, and that Latada's son dealt with the rear vehicle in the same manner. The two of them then systematically picked off man after man who moved, until, some hours later, with their ammunition running low and the SDF machine-guns and mortars now scything the hillsides around them, they slipped silently away into the mountain forests.

Whatever the rights and wrongs of their cause it was difficult not to admire their courage and daring. But when they started poaching game – particularly elephant and giraffe – on the Uganda side of the border, I regarded their activities with far more jaundiced eyes and with rapidly increasing hostility. As far as I was concerned Latada was setting a bad example. Activities such as his, if seen to be successful, are very liable to be catching, and this soon proved to be the case.

Whenever we got any information, the Game Department hunted – or helped to hunt – Latada and his gang. On occasions Robbie Robson certainly got close to him, even finding the hot ashes of his recently abandoned camp fire, but neither Robbie nor any other member of the Game Department ever actually caught up with him. After several years Latada seemed to just disappear altogether and the rumour spread that he had been killed by a wounded buffalo. Whatever the truth of the matter the damage had been done. His activities had stirred up trouble along the border which continues to this day* and Tony Henley's

* By 1970 the bandits had expanded into a sizeable guerilla force, over eight thousand strong, calling themselves the 'Anyanya'; some informed sources put their numbers as high as twenty thousand – it is difficult to be sure.

successor in Karamoja, John Blower, was the first to experience its worst effects.

John Blower had been a Forest Officer in Tanganyika who had transferred to the Tanganyika Game Department in 1952. Later he had volunteered to fight the Mau Mau in Kenya, where he had commanded a small striking force and tracker team operating in the dense jungles of the Aberdares. He had then applied to join the Uganda Game Department in 1954. He was a large, powerfully built man, a strong walker and a keen mountaineer. An outstanding game warden he eventually succeeded me as Chief Game Warden of Uganda, and later became Chief Game Warden of Ethiopia.

Elephant poaching along the Kidepo and general border raiding both started to increase soon after John Blower's arrival in Karamoja; and in July and August of 1957 alone, armed Turkana raiders shot and killed seven Didinga and one Teutho near the foot of Mount Lotuke. Long before then, however, it had begun to dawn on me that my vow to preserve northern Dodoth as a natural, unspoilt 'wilderness area' could only be achieved by making it a properly policed game reserve. John Blower was keen on the idea and after many months of battling and arguing in Moroto and Entebbe, agreement was eventually reached with both the Karamoja District Council and the Central Government. And so, at last, on the 30th of June 1958, the 'Kidepo Game Reserve' came into being – some five hundred square miles of scenically dramatic country, a unique area teeming with game of many spectacular species, the first entirely new game reserve to be created in Uganda for twenty-eight years.

Despite the creation of this game reserve – which gave the Game Department complete legal powers to control and manage the area and prevent any unauthorised entry by humans or domestic stock – and the strengthening of the game guard force to police it, the border incidents continued. Ironically, the Sudan Defence Force, whom we had helped so often in their search for Latada, in their merciless hunt for ex-SDF mutineers were often the worst offenders.

On the 18th of October 1959, two game guards based at Opotipot Camp, William Warija and Talip Atia, were approached by a Mening who later turned out to be a spy. Following up his report that there were elephant poachers camped in the Kidepo, the two game guards, accompanied by their Karamojong porters, went to investigate. Close to Lokidul they walked into a Sudan Defence Force ambush and, despite the fact that they were wearing Game Department uniforms, the two game guards were shot down in cold blood with automatic fire. Only one of the Karamojong porters escaped to return to Opotipot with the news of the murder.

Eventually a police signal reached Moroto and John Blower immediately flew up to Opotipot to investigate. The plane, a Uganda Police Air-wing Piper 'Tri-Pacer', was piloted by an ex-war time RAF flier named Chris Treen, a big-bellied man with a walrus moustache and an infectious chuckle, who was also a skilful bush-pilot. With considerable courage they landed in chest high grass on a disused air-strip. John Blower told me later that it was like a reaping machine ploughing through a corn field at fifty miles an hour! He had added that they had tried not to think of the possible hidden ant-hills and game animals. At the time all that had mattered was that they had to get there.

After a long search they found the bodies of the two dead game guards in a shallow grave. The murdered men had been stripped of their uniforms and their rifles were missing. Before the affair was finally cleared up, compensation paid and the rifles returned, it developed into what very nearly became an international incident. The Sudan Defence Force's excuse was that the two game guards were believed to be ex-mutineers, wanted men with a price on their heads.

When I eventually departed from Uganda, in 1960, to take up the post of Chief Game Warden of Tanganyika, one of my deepest regrets was that I was leaving Karamoja – and particularly the Kidepo – behind me. However, I was, to some extent, consoled by the fact that I and my colleagues had done all that we personally could to make the magnificent game country of Karamoja as safe as any such areas can hope to be in this uncertain, mercurial world.*

* In addition to the Kidepo Game Reserve in north Karamoja, gazetted in June 1958, the Debasien Animal Sanctuary – an area of nearly 1,000 square miles – was created in south Karamoja in September 1958; while the whole of the remainder of Karamoja District was declared a Controlled Hunting Area in the following year. The Kidepo Game Reserve finally became a national park in 1962.

As I warned that I must, in the telling of the long drawn sequel to my early exploration of the Kidepo Valley, and of my meeting with that legendary character 'Karamoja' Bell, I have raced far ahead of my story of the rest of Uganda. Like many another lover of the wild, I have found that Karamoja – even thinking, talking or writing about it – is very liable to make one lose one's sense of both time and space. The region itself seems almost timeless; a country whose people have been by-passed, forgotten, preferring to squat in the shade of a thorn tree, content to watch their cattle placidly grazing while the rest of the world, like the Gadarene swine, rushes phrenetically on – to what? And so I must now go back on my tracks, back to the time when I was preparing to go to England on home leave after my first exciting experience in the north of Karamoja, the wildest part of a wild land, the Kidepo, which to me will always remain – 'The Valley of the Elephants'.

CHAPTER 13

National Parks—Genesis

So geographers, in Afric maps,
With savage pictures fill their gaps,
And o'er unhabitable downs
Place elephants for want of towns.

DEAN JONATHAN SWIFT
(*On Poetry*, 1733)

SHORTLY before I went on home leave in May 1951, a long out-standing wildlife conservation issue at last began to come to a head; it was the problem of national parks in Uganda – to be more accurate it was the lack of them.

The idea of national parks originated in the United States of America with the creation of the Yellowstone National Park in Wyoming, as long ago as 1872, the primary object then being to preserve that scenically magnificent area of country as an aesthetic playground for the American nation. However, the conception of national parks as a major, although not the only nor even necessarily the primary, wildlife conservation measure in Africa in general dates back to the London Convention of 1933, which I have mentioned before. Nevertheless, largely due to the disruption of the Second World War, the implementation of this idea was

256

slow in coming in the British controlled territories of East and Central Africa.

Even when I myself first sailed for Kenya at the end of 1947, in the length and breadth of the British colonial territories there was only one true national park, the tiny, forty-four square mile Nairobi National Park – pioneered by Archie Ritchie, and later Mervyn Cowie – which had been established in 1946. Not until 1948 did things come to a head. Some people opine that this was due to the 'Fauna Conference of East and Central African Territories' held in Nairobi in May 1947. But having myself seen how the central administrative organisation of most colonial governments finally reacts to resolutions emanating from conferences of this nature – after first passing such recommendations through a form of human mincing machine comprised of civil servants of varying ability, experience and bias – I have another and more intriguing theory, one that is based on information I obtained some years later from a famous game warden.

In June 1947, an old friend of mine, Major Ray Hewlett, was on home leave in England. Having served with the West Somerset Yeomanry and the Royal Flying Corps, from 1914 to 1918, in many active theatres of the First World War, Ray had gone to India with the Royal Air Force, and between 1919 and 1926 had fought with the Indian Army in the Second Afghan War and in a number of tribal insurrections on the North West Frontier. Always keen on wildlife and *shikar**, he then became a professional hunter in East Africa until 1933, when he joined the Tanganyika Game Department as a game warden. On the outbreak of hostilities in 1939, he joined the armed forces and served with the King's African Rifles and the RASC in the East African campaign on Kenya's Northern Frontier and in Italian and British Somaliland, Abyssinia and Eritrea until 1945, when he returned to the Tanganyika Game Department. In 1947, at last able to take some hard-earned and long overdue home leave, he made his way back to the place of his birth – Taunton in the county of Somerset.

Not long after his arrival in Somerset, Ray Hewlett was asked by his brother – a prominent Rotarian – to address a Rotary Club lunch at Taunton as the guest speaker. Ray was appalled at the suggestion. Like most game wardens the very idea of

* The Urdu word for hunting.

public speaking filled him with horror and trepidation. He could face a charging elephant, buffalo or lion without a qualm, but to stand up and talk to a massed audience, a sea of critical eyes and bored, condescending faces, was quite another matter. But his protestations were waved aside. 'I'm sorry,' said his brother. 'You've got to do it. It's all laid on.'

'What on earth can I talk about?' Ray asked desperately.

'That's easy,' replied his brother airily. 'Tell them about your job. Everyone's interested in a game warden from Africa. It'll give you a wonderful chance to disillusion them,' he concluded with a sardonic smile.

And so, on the dreaded day, with two stiff whiskies under his belt to boost his morale, Ray Hewlett stood up and talked. After a nervous start he sensed he had a sympathetic audience, a body of attentive listeners won over by his obvious sincerity and transparent honesty. Devoid of all guile, unused to the devious wiles of diplomacy, and forgetting that even as a game warden on leave he was still a colonial civil servant – and thus forbidden publicly to comment on, let alone criticise, official policies – he warmed to his theme, castigating the East African governments for their negative, even obstructive, attitudes to wildlife conservation. It was nothing but a scandal, he concluded, that although the Parc National Albert in the Congo and the Kruger National Park in South Africa had both been established for many years, there was only one single, tiny national park in the whole of East Africa – and that one had only just been created.

Ray Hewlett sat down amid loud applause, much to his satisfaction for he knew that Admiral Cunningham, Lord Lieutenant of the County, was present at the lunch, and he felt that it might do some good if the truth concerning the East African wildlife situation became known in influential circles. What he did not know, until afterwards, was that four newspaper reporters were also present and that the proceedings of the Rotary functions were always reported in full!

The speech got thorough press treatment in the national newspapers and the result was a stream of letters to the papers from such influential organisations as the Fauna Preservation Society*, the Zoological Society of London, the British Museum of Natural

* Then under its old title of the Society for the Preservation of the Wild Fauna of the Empire.

History, and many others, as well as from numbers of important individuals. No doubt the Colonial Office was also approached direct by the same influential bodies and persons, for on his return to Tanganyika from leave, Ray Hewlett was asked, by the Chief Secretary in Dar es Salaam, to explain his statements.

Despite his reprimand, politely but firmly Ray Hewlett stuck to his guns, refusing to retract what he had said. Finally, in January 1948, the Secretary of State for the Colonies wrote to the Governors of Tanganyika, Kenya and Uganda asking them to state their past, present and future game policies! Later the same year, the then Governor of Uganda, Sir John Hathorn Hall, instructed his Chief Secretary to set up a committee whose terms of reference were – 'To consider and make recommendations concerning the institution in Uganda of a National Park or Parks, including their location, extent, constitution, control and management'.

Ray Hewlett would be the last person to claim that his speech alone was responsible for altering the official attitude to wildlife conservation throughout East Africa. For instance, long before Ray went on home leave in 1947, that versatile, gifted and imaginative character, Dr Barton Worthington*, had included in the Uganda Protectorate's first, post-World War Two, 'Development Plan', a sum of £16,600 for the proposed development of national parks during the decennium of the Plan. Having known Barton Worthington for over twenty years, I now have little doubt that he – a particularly astute and experienced man – deliberately inserted this comparatively insignificant amount (confident that it would not be spotted as the thin end of a then not very popular wedge) in an attempt to break the long deadlock and get something moving. Nevertheless, no further positive action to establish national parks in Uganda was taken until the setting up of the Uganda National Parks Committee in December 1948. The timing is significant and I, for one, would not be at all surprised if pressure from the Colonial Office did not have something to do with it. In those days British governments were still often highly sensitive to public criticism and Ray Hewlett's

* Leader of most of the earlier scientific expeditions to the East African lakes, followed by a varied and distinguished career leading to his appointment, in 1965, as the first Scientific Director of the newly created 'International Biological Programme'.

innocent speech the year before had certainly sparked off enough of that!

I am glad to say that Ray himself eventually received a well deserved reward. At the end of 1950 he was transferred to become the first Warden of the new, legally constituted, Serengeti National Park. He pioneered the development of the Serengeti, including the Ngorongoro Crater, and for six happy years he was king of this wildlife paradise. Then, suddenly, like so many game department pioneers before and since, he found himself unwanted by a new régime with radical ideas which did not appreciate his particular talents.

But this is looking some time ahead and, as far as I myself was concerned, when I went to Uganda in late 1949, there were still no national parks in that country and the Uganda National Parks Committee was still engaged in studying the matter in what, to me in my youth and enthusiasm, appeared to be an unnecessarily stately and ponderous manner. However, there was no doubt that the Committee was being thorough, perhaps too thorough for it asked so many and varied people for their opinions that the members found themselves surrounded by a forest of problems – some real, many exaggerated, a number purely imaginary. As a result, the Committee's final report – when at last it did appear in print at the end of 1950 – was, in my humble opinion, like a damp squib. It started off with a fizz and a roar but ended with a feeble splutter. To me it was a great disappointment.

It was some time before I first had an official sight of the report. When I did so I went to see a senior officer in the Secretariat to complain about the obvious weaknesses contained in a number of the Committee's observations and recommendations. I soon found that I had chosen the wrong man. Peering over the tops of his glasses, he regarded me condescendingly with what appeared to be ill-feigned surprise.

'But I was under the impression that the Game Department was not in favour of national parks,' he remarked in a tone of pompous superiority.

I stared at him in astonishment. 'Where on earth did you get that idea from?' I demanded angrily.

He watched me almost gloatingly, like a cat with a captive mouse. When he answered his voice was a velvety purr as if he was savouring every word. 'Ah – I seem to recall we have it on record that in the opinion of the Game Department national parks are little more than a lip service to the preservation of wildlife!'

My denial was heated but I realised that for the moment I was blocked. However, I had learnt two things from my preliminary reconnaissance. First, that we were up against some fairly solid opposition in certain influential official quarters. And second, that it was all too easy for the Game Department's views to be misrepresented, either deliberately or accidentally, by their being misquoted or taken out of context. I later discovered that the Chief Game Warden had once said that to create national parks *without also giving them adequate funds and staff* would merely be paying lip service to wildlife conservation. This wise observation, by the time it had passed through a dozen official hands – sympathetic, disinterested or hostile – had become so distorted as to be almost unrecognisable.

Two busy months later I boarded the plane for London, leaving John Mills to hold the fort in my absence as Acting Chief Game Warden. In my briefcase was a copy of the 'Report of the Uganda National Parks Committee', attached to which was a formal letter from the Chief Secretary asking for my comments and recommendations. It was the opening I had been waiting for.

Three days after my arrival in England I was sitting in the deck-house of the schooner *Amphitrite*. All around me the sun sparkled on the rippling waters of the Salcombe estuary. A full cable's length away, on the port beam, the verdant green of a South Devon hillside rose sharply from the rocky shore until it suddenly merged with the gloomy canopy of Halwell Wood. An old grey heron was fishing in the shallows. The only sounds were the quiet lap of the rising tide against the weathered hull of the old ship and the occasional, plaintive mew of a passing herring-gull sailing effortlessly by with the on-shore breeze. Spread on the chart table before me was a map of Uganda and the report of the Uganda National Parks Committee. It was a perfect place to study such an important document quietly and dispassionately.

A detailed analysis of any official report is liable to provide reading as ponderous as the original document. For this reason alone I do not intend to attempt it here. Instead, I propose to confine my comments to both the good and the bad aspects of the 'Report of the Uganda National Parks Committee', as they appeared to me in May 1951, and in particular to some of the surprising – even astonishing – contradictions contained in the Committee's recommendations, conflicting observations which struck me forcibly at that time and remain an enigma to this day.

Starting with basic essentials, what, in fact, *is* a national park in the African context? The Committee advised that Uganda settle this question by accepting, for application in the Protectorate, the definition of a national park included in Article 2 of the London Convention of 1933, which reads as follows:

The expression 'national park' shall denote an area; (a) placed under public control, the boundaries of which shall not be altered or any portion be capable of alienation except by the competent legislative authority; (b) set aside for the propagation, protection and preservation of wild animal life and wild vegetation, and for the preservation of objects of aesthetic, geological, prehistoric, archaeological, or other scientific interest for the benefit, advantage and enjoyment of the general public; (c) in which the hunting, killing or capturing of fauna and the destruction or collection of flora is prohibited except by or under the direction or control of the park authorities.

In accordance with the above provisions facilities shall, so far as possible, be given to the general public for observing the fauna and flora in national parks.

This definition seemed reasonable enough to me, except that a small amendment to a single section of the existing Game Ordinance would have given to all Uganda's long established game reserves the same security of tenure as the Committee was envisaging for the proposed new national parks. In fact, I could not help thinking at the time that it would be a great deal simpler to strengthen the Game Department, both legally and financially, and let it get on with the job of developing the game reserves on national park lines!

In stating its case for the introduction of national parks to ensure the continued preservation of game in Uganda, the Committee had stuck rigidly to the aesthetic approach, quoting the now time-honoured dogma that it is man's duty to conserve wildlife for posterity.

On the other hand, in listing the considerations that it felt should govern the selection of suitable areas for national parks, the Committee observed that, in such areas, 'there should be few or no possibilities of agriculture', and 'there should be no mineral possibilities'. To my mind these were misleading and undesirable observations for it could hardly have been stated much more baldly that the Committee considered that, as a form of economic land-use, wildlife conservation came at the very bottom of the list; that national parks, and similar wildlife conservation projects, should only be established on land which could not be used for any other conceivable purpose.

In contrast, one of the Committee's observations cheered me; it stated that in a national park dedicated primarily to the pre-servation of game, the area must be large enough to allow for necessary migration. I was pleased that this important point had not merely been made but emphasised. I was equally pleased that the report listed most of Uganda's main wildlife regions as being suitable for conversion to national park status and that the regions mentioned included the important elephant country embodied in the game reserves in the vicinity of Lakes Edward and George, and also the great game reserve lying astride the Vic-toria Nile in the Districts of Bunyoro and Acholi.

But then came the shock. Concealed in a detailed appendix to the report, under the title 'Location, Extent and Description of Proposed Uganda National Parks', were the Committee's specific recommendations for the size of the four national parks it proposed. When I first discovered them I stared at these figures in disbelief. In the case of the two main wildlife parks, despite the emphasis it had placed on the importance of allowing adequate room for migration, the Committee had recommended areas so small as to be ridiculous. An elephant could have strolled from one end to the other of either of them in a matter of a few hours – and it would not have had to hurry to do it.

As I continued to stare at the figures in shocked surprise a dark bank of cloud swept across the face of the sun, the surface of the estuary became a leaden grey and a chill breeze lifted the papers on the chart table before me. The gloom seemed almost symbolic and I glanced up dully as a sudden whicker of wings and a patter of flat, webbed feet on the deck head announced the arrival of Baxter, the tame but domineering herring-gull who owned the old schooner. He waddled arrogantly into the deck-house, flapped clumsily on to the chart table and greeted me with a curt squawk. No doubt it was my imagination but with his head on one side he seemed to be glaring belligerently and contemptuously at the report on the table, his cold, yellow eyes even frostier than usual. Suddenly, with a fierce, yelping laugh he hunched his wings and fouled the papers before me with a powerful jet of strong smelling, white excrement. For a moment he gazed at his handiwork with what appeared to be a look of grim satisfaction; then, with another mocking laugh, he launched himself through the open door of the deck-house and sailed effortlessly away up the estuary. 'You have expressed my sentiments exactly,' I said under my breath, watching him disappear behind the dark mass of Halwell Wood, before I again turned my attention to the report with a resigned sigh and a hunk of cotton wool.

With the sobering threat of the world wide human population explosion plain for all to see, it should be obvious, even to the layman, that the primary object of the majority of national parks in Africa is to ensure the preservation of substantial numbers of wild animals – and particularly the large game species – *in perpetuity*. In this respect the *modern* concept of a national park is rightly held to be superior to the *old* concept of a game reserve – an area whose legal status was such that, in theory at least, it could be shrunk, or even abolished altogether, on a political whim, at the stroke of a government minister's pen. However, in turn, this also means that it is essential for any national *wildlife* park to be both large enough and its habitat varied enough to meet, at all seasons of the year, the full ecological requirements of the various animal species it is designed to protect.

For some strange reason, in making its final recommendations the Uganda National Parks Committee – a panel of experts with profound knowledge of the Protectorate and certainly weighted in favour of wildlife conservation – had apparently ignored the very simple and equally obvious basic principle which I have just outlined. And so, the Uganda National Parks Committee must go on permanent record not only as having recommended that less than ten per cent of the total area of Uganda's game reserves should be granted the greater security of national park status, but also as having proposed what can only be described as a self-defeating exercise. Had the Committee's proposals been implemented, the consequent national parks would have been so small that the fate of many of their wildlife populations would have for ever been dependent on the fortunes of the less secure game reserves surrounding them. Without the supporting game reserves, except for a few of the smaller, non-migratory species the wildlife populations of the proposed 'micro national parks' would have withered and died.

Like many thousands of wildlife enthusiasts before and since, the first national park I ever visited was Kenya's miniature, forty-four square miles, Nairobi National Park, a unique area which, to the casual observer, would appear to be a flourishing contradiction of all the opinions I have just expressed. Frequently have I heard people praise this 'micro national park' as a gem – and rightly so. But those who quote it as an example of the value, for conserving large animal species, of even a comparatively small area, are ignorant of the truth – the fact that many of the Park's animals need the supplementary habitat provided by those parts of the Athi and Kapiti Plains that lie within the adjoining, 455 square mile Kitengela Game Conservation Area and Ngong Reserve. For a number of species these Plains could well be regarded as the factory and store-house, with the Park providing the shop window in which the goods are displayed. Should the Kitengela Game Conservation Area ever be abolished the Nairobi National Park would atrophy like a ligatured limb cut off from its blood supply, shrivelling as surely as an autumn leaf deprived of sap. Moreover, despite its total *effective* ecological area of between five hundred and one thousand square miles, the Nairobi National Park has no elephants; these mighty animals need space to survive and during the 1950s my main interest and concern was the long term conservation of Uganda's great elephant herds.

'You say elephants need space, then what about the Addo Elephant Park?' That is a fair question, one I have often been asked when I have aired my views on elephant conservation. It is also a pertinent question for the Addo Elephant Park, which protects the last remnants of the great herds of elephant that once roamed freely in the dense Addo bush of the Sundays River Valley of South Africa's Eastern Cape Province, is a tiny national park covering an area of only twenty-six and a half square miles in all. Since 1931, when the Park was created, the elephants in it have increased from a mere handful, eleven strong, to their present total* of fifty-six animals, and when I saw them in 1967 they looked healthy enough. Nevertheless, these elephants live an entirely unnatural existence; from 1954 onwards they have been completely imprisoned by what must be the strongest and most expensive fence in the world and, although their diet is artificially supplemented with surplus oranges from the surrounding citrus farms, it is more than possible that these elephants will progressively degenerate as a race due to the lack of some essential trace element in their diet – some unknown item of feed which previously they obtained in their seasonal wanderings.

Since the Addo Park has been in existence for less than the full life span of a single elephant it is impossible to be dogmatic, but the evidence is there from other parts of Africa. For instance, I have a note of what Professor Irven Buss wrote to me in December 1962, after he and I had collected some soil samples from a high bank bordering a track leading down into the Ngorongoro Crater in northern Tanzania. The samples were dug from a point regularly visited by elephants, a place where these intelligent animals had gouged deep into the bank to excavate and eat the earth so obtained. 'The analyses of the soil samples I took with me show a very definite concentration of cobalt and manganese,' wrote Irven Buss, 'both of which are important to the elephant in his enzyme control. This might be pretty important, and cutting off migratory routes to such "licks" could be rather harmful to the elephants'.

In 1951, when I was faced with the difficult task of passing judgment on the recommendations of the Uganda National Parks Committee, a group of senior and highly respected officials, I lacked the benefit of such hindsight and I suffered from the additional handicaps of comparative youth and apparent inexperience. Moreover, at that time, a great deal less was known about the ecology of the African elephant than is the case today. Nevertheless, I found myself in strong disagreement with the Committee's proposals on several basic issues. In particular I was convinced that acceptance of the Committee's recommendations would, sooner or later, in the face of mounting human and economic pressures, lead to the abolition of the main game reserves, leaving the tiny national parks proposed by the Committee isolated and forlorn, their game populations effectively sealed off from much

* As at November 1970.

266

of their essential habitat. In fact, when I picked up my pen from the chart table of the old schooner on the 21st of May 1951, and prepared to draft the all important memorandum to the Chief Secretary of Uganda, I had no doubt in my own mind that if the Committee's recommendations were implemented as they stood the results would be disastrous.

Staring with unseeing eyes across the calm waters of the estuary, I found myself imagining great herds of elephant ploughing through acres of standing cotton, or sprawling banana plantations, as they made their stately way along their traditional migration routes between Lake Edward and the dense forests of Maramagambo, Kalinzu and Kibale, and the mountain jungles of the Ruwenzori. Further to the north, I could visualise even bigger herds trampling through fields of waving millet and maize as they headed purposefully to the Budongo and Zoka Forests, and the lush, rolling grassland to the east of the Albert Nile, from the sanctuary of their tiny national park around the Murchison Falls. The outcome would be inevitable – a bloody and internecine struggle culminating in the virtual death knell of the Uganda elephant. It was obvious that a critical point had been reached and that it was vital that my views on the creation of national parks in Uganda should be put to the Protectorate Government as clearly, convincingly and forcefully as possible – and without delay. Grasping my pen firmly, and with a weather eye open for the return of a bellicose herring-gull, I started to write.

A copy of my memorandum to the Chief Secretary is in front of me now. It is too long to repeat here in full, but for the sake of the story it is important that certain extracts from this document should now be recalled.

The Katwe and Murchison Falls regions, which would be the main national parks in Uganda, are beset with problems, I wrote. The Katwe region, to start with, is a magnificent area containing a good quantity of game which can be easily displayed to the public and with the added scenic attractions of Lakes Edward, George and the Kazinga Channel surrounded by fine hill country and backed by the beautiful 'Mountains of the Moon'. In addition it is well served by roads and hotels. However, it is my considered opinion that the size of the area the Committee has proposed as a national park is far too small to contain the large herds of elephant and buffalo which are its main attraction. These animals are great wanderers and cannot be kept on a 'postage stamp'. It must also be remembered that the whole of this region is threatened by proposals for extensive mineral and agricultural development and that it is likely that in the future game would be unable to wander outside the confines of any national park that was created there. If a national park is to be established in the region, then a much larger area must be set aside for it, even at the possible expense of some other development. Ideally, the area should extend to both sides of the Kazinga Channel and connect up with the Parc National Albert north-west of Katwe and also at the southern end of Lake Edward.

The Murchison Falls region, containing as it does the world famous Murchison Falls and quantities of game of a number of species, is a 'must' for a national park. Here again to make it worthwhile and workable in the future the area must not be stinted. Unfortunately the Acholi Council have declared themselves to be completely opposed to the whole idea although the area concerned is a sleeping sickness restricted one and there are no definite alternative proposals for its future development.

In the selection of areas for national parks, it should be borne in mind that the areas suggested, even though they may be extended, are almost minute in comparison with the area of the Protectorate as a whole. In this respect, it is to be hoped that African Local Governments will, in the future, become less parochially minded. Further, in view of the magnificent opportunities that the Murchison Falls and Katwe areas offer for the creation of national parks that will be a joy to the public and of very great economic value in connection with the tourist trade, it should be most seriously considered whether the creation of national parks in these two areas should not, to some extent at least, take priority over the agricultural and other considerations mentioned by the Committee as deserving of preference.

In concluding my memorandum – which also dealt with such matters as management, finance and the law – I reiterated the case for national parks which I had stated at the beginning:

Much opposition has been raised by one African Local Government at least to the creation of national parks in Uganda, and the words of His Majesty King George VI, quoted in paragraph 18 of the Report, cannot be too strongly stressed; they are repeated herewith – '*The wildlife of to-day is not ours to dispose of as we please – we hold it in trust for those who come after.*' The wildlife of Uganda is a national asset both from the economic and the cultural point of view, but it must be stated, quite bluntly, that the majority of African Local Governments are not yet at a sufficiently advanced stage of development to appreciate this. If they are permitted, at this stage, to prevent through ignorance the establishment of national parks, they will come to regret it in the future. By then, however, it will be too late, for game once it has gone cannot be replaced. It is vital therefore, that the Protectorate Government should now decide finally what it intends to do in regard to the creation of national parks in the light of the interests of the people of Uganda as a whole and of the future as well as the present.

The real sting I kept carefully for the tail. In my last sentence I stated loftily:

It may be mentioned, that if national parks are not created, Uganda will be flouting world opinion and will stand alone as the only territory in Africa still enriched by the presence of large quantities of big game that has not established national parks.

Coming from a government servant this final, pungent remark was what is referred to in the popular Westerns as 'fighting talk'! It was meant to be. In those days there were no effective international wildlife conservation pressure groups. The now justly famous World Wildlife Fund was not dreamed up for another decade, while the International Union for the Conservation of Nature and Natural Resources was in its very early infancy, a wide eyed, stumbling babe, born in the Forest of Fontainbleau in October 1948, still lacking power and influence. Something had to be done to jerk a reluctant and lethargic colonial officialdom into action, and if I didn't take the initiative who else would?

To the same end I had included the identical caustic comment in my departmental annual report for 1950, the draft of which I had passed to the Secretariat shortly before departing on leave. In so doing I was attempting to commit the worst crime in the civil servant's book – to criticise publicly the policies of the government by which he is employed. But then, like most game wardens, I have seldom been a good civil servant for, in the old days at least, to be an effective game warden and a righteous colonial civil servant at one and the same time was, as often as not, a contradiction in terms.

By a whimsical twist of fate – a pure misunderstanding – the offending paragraph escaped the blue pencils of the normally vigilant Secretariat censors, but when it was finally printed it was not missed by the searching eyes of a hawk-like press. Astonished but delighted they pounced on the newly published document, tearing at the juiciest portions like vultures on a lion kill. 'UGANDA FLOUTS WORLD OPINION', gloated the *Uganda Herald* in banner headlines, the thinly veiled sarcasm of its subsequent comments clearly indicating its almost sadistic pleasure at the inevitable discomfiture of various red faced Secretariat officials. 'It is unusual, to say the least,' the *Herald* observed with dry relish, 'for the head of a government department openly to criticise the government in an official document printed and published by the government.' The editor might well have added, for the inference was there, that his paper also found the situation most refreshing; so, if the truth be told, did a good many government servants – including a surprising number of officials in the Secretariat!

The newspaper comments certainly helped; they focussed on the problem the critical spotlight of public opinion and poured scorn on the bigoted opposition of certain African Local Governments at a most opportune time, for my annual report was not published for some eight months after my memorandum on national parks had reached the Chief Secretary in Entebbe. During those months the wheels of the government machine had at last begun to turn in a positive direction and with increasing speed, while the opposition of the African Local Governments had crystallised.

Back on the old schooner in South Devon, there was little more I could do for some time after sending my comments and recommendations to the Chief Secretary, but in Uganda John Mills was not allowing the grass to grow under his feet during my absence. He found a powerful and enthusiastic ally in the Secretariat in the person of Barrie Cartland*, the then Administrative Secretary – in effect the 'pivot' of the Uganda administration – an imaginative man with a receptive mind, newly arrived from the problems of West Africa. With typical astuteness Barrie arranged with Mervyn Cowie (then Director of Kenya National Parks) for the temporary loan of Ken Beaton, the Warden of the Nairobi National Park, to visit Uganda to advise the Protectorate Govern-

* Later to become Sir George Cartland C.M.G., Registrar of the University of Birmingham.

ment on the suitability of the areas that had been recommended as national parks.

K. de P. Beaton was a great character and a most able man, a former settler farmer and a keen naturalist who had done wonders in building up the tiny Nairobi National Park. But, at that time, if the truth be told, in the whole of East and Central Africa there was not one person who could honestly be described as an 'expert' on African national parks in general, for even the Kenya National Parks had only been in existence for the short period of five years and inevitably their knowledge and their problems were largely specialised and parochial. In Uganda the climate and habitat were entirely different, many of the larger mammal species were different, and the elephant control problem was certainly different. Ken Beaton, despite his many valuable attributes, was not a qualified scientist, he had no knowledge of Uganda, and never having served in any game department he had no experience of the problems of managing elephants *en masse* in a comparatively densely populated and predominantly agricultural country, such as Uganda. In fact, Ken was not an 'elephant man' although Uganda's primary wildlife management problem was then, as it always has been, the humane but sensible control of its great elephant herds, a large proportion of which were centred in and around the areas proposed as national parks.

In theory, therefore, it was something of a farce to expect Ken Beaton to comment and advise on recommendations based on the Uganda Game Department's combined knowledge and experience accumulated over twenty-five years. In practice however, following the principle that a prophet has no honour in his own country, Ken Beaton was a valuable part of a conjuring trick, a most effective rabbit to pull out of the hat to convince a public to whom he was truthfully introduced as the leading Warden of the Kenya National Parks. Ken, who was a great showman as well as a great charmer, played his part in the charade without faltering. After being taken on a conducted tour of all the proposed areas, he first of all expressed some doubts as to whether they would be large enough; then, after due deliberation, he pronounced his final judgment – that, due to the quality of the grazing in Uganda, the areas suggested in my memorandum were not only very suitable but had the potential of being turned into some of the finest national parks in Africa!

Although Ken Beaton's visit to Uganda took place while I was still on home leave, I also was not sitting back and letting the grass grow under my feet during this period. In late September, I had an interesting letter from Charles Pitman, then living in London. 'You will certainly know that Sir John Hall is retiring,' he wrote. 'But I have just heard the name of the man who has been chosen to succeed him as Governor of Uganda. It is to be Mr A. B. Cohen, O.B.E.*, at present Assistant Under-Secretary of State and head of the African Division at the Colonial Office. It might be worth your while to call on him before you return to Uganda.'

Until I met Andrew Benjamin Cohen, although I had taken the trouble to check on his already brilliant record, I had little idea what to expect. I had hoped to arrange an appointment well in advance but circumstances prevented it. Instead, I telephoned him at the Colonial Office on my arrival in London, explained who I was (one of the most junior of his future heads of department!), and asked if I might call on him that day. I had thought it would be of interest to him, I had added, to hear something of Uganda's wildlife conservation problems before he took up his new appointment. The reply I received was polite but to the point – certainly, as long as I did not mind repeated interruptions.

On entering Andrew Cohen's office I was confronted by a tall, heavily built, and unexpectedly youthful looking man, who rose from his chair and came round his desk to greet me courteously, but with a strange shyness of manner. His face was broad and rather pallid, its lack of colour accentuated by an unruly lock of straight, dark hair that fell repeatedly across his forehead. I wasted no time coming to the problem of establishing national parks in Uganda, and as we talked he paced the room like a caged lion, hardly ever glancing in my direction but shooting questions at me in rapid succession, scarcely waiting for me to answer one before firing another. He seemed to sense what I was going to say long before I had finished, sometimes even before I had started, and the whole impression he gave me was of enormous nervous energy backed by a razor sharp, analytical mind. It came almost as a shock when I recalled that this dynamic man was only forty-two – scarcely ten years older than myself.

From time to time, while we talked, harassed looking aides

* Later Sir Andrew Cohen, K.V.M.G., K.C.V.O., O.B.E.

272

hurried in with imposing looking documents for Andrew Cohen's attention. Scarcely checking in his stride, he would halt momentarily, glance at the document, scribble his signature or make a curt comment, and then continue his pacing, picking up our conversation at the precise point where he had broken it off. Suddenly he halted and stared at me hard. 'I believe in national parks,' he said. 'And I think that Uganda should have them. I will look into the matter directly I arrive.' It was the signal for me to leave and I departed deeply impressed; more impressed than I have been with any other colonial governor I have ever met, bar one. Before I saw him again he had been knighted.

*

Sir Andrew Cohen arrived in Entebbe by air in January 1952, and, after a brief respite to allow him to change into the bizarre fulldress uniform of a colonial governor, he was whisked away to Kampala to be sworn in publicly as Governor and Commander-in-Chief of the Uganda Protectorate.

I was one of a long line of local dignitaries and ill-assorted civil servants detailed to file past the new Governor and shake him by the hand. When he caught sight of me Sir Andrew's features suddenly brightened. I suppose I was one familiar face in an embarrassing sea of curious, staring eyes. He looked like a marooned mariner who has just spotted an approaching ship. 'Hullo, Kinloch!' he said, almost with a sigh of relief. 'We must have a talk about national parks.' Three days later I was summoned to Government House in Entebbe for that very purpose.

'We have made some progress with the local rulers since I last saw you, Sir Andrew,' I said as he paced up and down his top floor office. 'The Omukama of Toro seems to be much less hostile than he was to the prospect of a national park in the area of Lakes George and Edward, and the Omugabe of Ankole appears to have become reconciled to the idea that the park should extend into his kingdom. Frankly, our main trouble in that region now comes from the long-term land-use plans of the Agricultural Department. They say there is good cotton growing land around Lakes Edward and George and they are reluctant to agree to its being permanently absorbed in a national park. It's already in the game reserves and therefore uncultivated at the moment. Personally, I can't see that a few extra square miles of cotton are going to make all that difference to the future economy of Uganda, while a really viable national park in that area certainly could.'

Sir Andrew smiled but continued with his pacing. There was something rather wolf-like about his smile. 'I'm sure the Director of Agriculture will be co-operative,' he said blandly. 'I'll have a word with him. But what about the other area you mentioned to me in London, the one in the north?'

'Well, the Banyoro seem to be coming round a bit, thanks to the Omugabe, but the Acholi Council are still bitterly opposed to the whole project. The area has been completely uninhabited for over forty years – ever since the big sleeping sickness epidemic – but the Acholi believe that we are trying to take away their tribal land and deprive them of their traditional hunting rights. I haven't got much sympathy for them. More and more Acholi are setting wire snares whenever and wherever they can, and if that continues at the present rate there won't be a four-legged wild animal left in Acholi in another decade – apart from rats and elephants!'

Sir Andrew Cohen bared his teeth in another mirthless, wolf-like smile. 'I met Lord Willingdon* in London just before I left,' he said, staring out of the window towards the distant blue streak that was Lake Victoria. 'He invited me to meet Keith Caldwell and Mervyn Cowie to talk about national parks in Uganda. Cowie said that the Uganda National Parks Committee's recommendations had been hampered by the opposition of African Local Governments. It confirmed what you told me. Lord Willingdon urged me to use my influence to get something done, as the Fauna Preservation Society is concerned at Uganda's lack of action over establishing national parks. I told him he was preaching to the converted!' Sir Andrew turned and stared straight at me. 'I am convinced that Uganda must have national parks and I agree with you that if we have them at all they must be large enough to be worth while. If necessary, I intend to force this matter through the Legislative Council. I shall ask the Attorney General to go ahead with drafting appropriate legislation, for which he will need your advice. In the meantime I

* The Marquess of Willingdon, since 1946 the President of the very active Fauna Preservation Society – originally the Society for the Preservation of the Wild Fauna of the Empire – founded in 1903, whose Patron is Her Majesty Queen Elizabeth II.

want you to get these boundary questions settled as quickly as possible.'

'Certainly, Sir Andrew,' I replied brightly, as if he had said nothing in any way unusual, but I walked down the stairs in a daze, my mind a turmoil of conflicting emotions with elation overshadowed by astonishment. Here was a man of brilliant intellect, frequently casual of dress, often eccentric of habit, normally unpredictable of manner, loathing pomp and ceremony and reputed to have strong Left-wing leanings; in fact, a man who, in almost every way, could hardly have been more atypical of the popular image of the austere and dictatorial colonial governor. Yet, with my own ears, I had heard him say that he would *force* national parks through against any short-sighted local opposition – something that no previous governor, however firm, had been willing to attempt. 'Good for Cohen,' I thought to myself. 'I'm his man from now on!' And I never had cause to change my mind for, all the time he was Governor of Uganda and after, until his early death in 1968, Sir Andrew Cohen continued to demonstrate his keen interest in and support for wildlife conservation.

Two days after my first visit I was back in the Governor's office. This time both Barrie Cartland and Ralph Dreschfield, the Attorney General, were also present. Sir Andrew reiterated what he had said to me earlier and the green light for the go-ahead was given. For me it signalled the last phase of a comparatively friendly but none the less determined contest with the Department of Agriculture, to whom cotton was king and coffee the heir apparent. The main scene of our jousting was the area of country bordering on Lake Edward. The Agricultural Department was determined that this strip of land should be developed for growing cotton; I was equally determined that it should be kept undisturbed to allow free movement of elephant between Uganda and the Parc National Albert of the Belgian Congo, on both sides of Lake Edward, and also through to the Ruwenzori. To make certain of the regular elephant routes from Lake Edward up into the dense mountain rain forests to the north, I went – for the first time – to see Paul Chapman, an old Etonian who chose to live a lonely hermit's life in a remote mountain fastness high in the southern foot-hills of the Mountains of the Moon.

275

Paul Chapman, who was one of Uganda's legendary 'characters', was blessed with an inventive streak and a puckish sense of humour. He got on well with the local people, but since he was wary of more civilised visitors and did not encourage those who arrived unannounced, I took the precaution of sending a message ahead. The reply I received was a guarded welcome and as I drove slowly up into the foot-hills, along the rough, winding track locally known as 'Chapman's Road', I wondered what my reception would be. I was met by a sparely built man of indeterminate age dressed in an old boiler suit. His greeting was courteous but the eyes in the lean face were like those of a watchful animal. However, when I told him I had come to ask his advice about elephant movements into the hills he relaxed visibly and he was soon telling me all I wanted to know. But my testing time came at supper, for which we seated ourselves at a battered wooden table lit by a smoking hurricane lantern.

Paul Chapman himself brought in the main course, carrying it in a familiar looking vessel which he placed on the table with a dramatic flourish. I stared in amazement, first at the vessel and then at its contents. There in front of me, squatting blatantly on the table, was a round, white-enamelled container, dented and chipped, with a black metal handle and the letters UP stencilled in black on one side – a Uganda Protectorate, government issue, chamber pot! In the pot was a roast bird, its long neck, with head still attached, dangling limply over the side; it was Uganda's national emblem, a crowned crane – a fully protected species!

Looking up I saw that Paul Chapman was watching me covertly with mocking eyes. 'I hope you like roast crane?' he asked. 'I think it's excellent! Don't worry,' he went on. 'This one was eating my chicken food. I looked up the game laws and they say that I am entitled to kill protected species in defence of my property. They also stipulate that any animal so killed must be handed over to an officer of the Game Department; and so, here I am delivering it to the Chief Game Warden himself – what could be more appropriate?'

When finally I left Paul Chapman's mountain hideout, I had gleaned a great deal of valuable information about local elephant movements, and I learnt later that he took particular delight in pulling the legs of government officials. I was neither the first nor the last to be served roast crane in a chamber pot!

With Sir Andrew Cohen's firm support, effective opposition to national parks collapsed as rapidly as the defences of a defeated army, so much so that the final stages of the struggle were almost an anti-climax. The Department of Agriculture, with very nearly an audible sigh of resignation, reluctantly abandoned its long-term claims to virtually all of the potential cotton growing land in the areas of Lakes Edward and George. In return, I agreed, equally reluctantly on the surface, to the excision of a portion of the Game Reserve to the north of Lake George; secretly this apparent concession worried me little for the western extension of the Uganda Railway, linking Kampala with the new Kilembe copper mine in the Ruwenzori, had, by then, been planned and the surveyed alignment cut straight through this part of the Lake George Game Reserve. The line would have been an ugly embarrassment in a national park but I felt that it would form a useful northern boundary in an otherwise featureless stretch of flood plain! The end result was agreement for what I had all along proposed – a scenically dramatic national park taking in most of the land covered by the two adjoining Game Reserves of Lake Edward and Lake George and linking up with the Parc National Albert both to the north and south of Lake Edward.

Local resistance to a national park astride the Victoria Nile, with the Murchison Falls as its focal point, was also overcome. The Acholi, stubborn to the end, eventually gave in after being lectured to severely by the Provincial Commissioner, Rennie Bere; and the Banyoro were mollified by an agreement to excise small areas of the eastern and western portions of the Bunyoro section of the Bunyoro-Gulu Game Reserve. This meant that the way was clear for the creation, as I had hoped, of another scenically magnificent national park covering some of the finest elephant country in the whole of Uganda and containing most of the mightiest tuskers left in the Protectorate.

The climax came on the 3rd of April 1952, when the Legislative Council of the Uganda Protectorate, presided over by Sir Andrew Cohen, solemnly approved the National Parks Ordinance of Uganda, a law which authorised the Government to establish national parks to be run by a Board of Trustees appointed by the Governor. Less than four months later, when all the necessary boundary details had been finally agreed and settled, Uganda's first two national parks were officially gazetted. One, in the Lakes Edward and George area, which, with the gracious consent of Her Majesty the Queen and the genuine pleasure of the Rulers of the Kingdoms of Toro and Ankole, was named 'The Queen Elizabeth National Park', had a total area of 764 square miles – a little larger than the English counties of Buckinghamshire or Oxfordshire. The other, astride the Victoria Nile and named 'The Murchison Falls National Park', was nearly twice as big; it covered an area of 1,504 square miles – almost exactly the same size as the county of Hampshire and very nearly as large as Cumberland, Essex or Kent. The date was the 22nd of July 1952.

When I finally saw the official notices printed in black and white in the *Government Gazette*, it suddenly dawned on me that, for wildlife, at last the tide was beginning to turn. Two years later, when Her Majesty Queen Elizabeth II, accompanied by His Royal Highness Prince Philip, Duke of Edinburgh, paid a State Visit to Uganda, an official reception was held at the new Mweya Safari Lodge in the Queen Elizabeth National Park. It was an historic occasion, a milestone in the annals of wildlife conservation in Uganda, and among the guests of honour, who were presented to the Royal couple, was a slightly built man with quiet, humorous eyes set in an ascetic face; he was dressed, as usual, in a full-length boiler-suit, carefully laundered and pressed. As someone said to me at the time, a note of envious admiration in his voice, 'Only an old Etonian could carry it off!'

CHAPTER 14

The Turn of the Tide

THE creation of national parks in Uganda was a major breakthrough for wildlife conservation in the Protectorate, but it was
by no means the end of the Game Department's problems. In
fact, by the very nature of this key development, it brought with
it certain attendant stresses and strains of a type about which the
general public is seldom informed. Books about animals and the
work of game wardens tend to gloss over such problems, concentrating instead on the lighter and more glamorous aspects of the
subject. I am no iconoclast but I have often felt that this is an
unsatisfactory policy; that in the true interests of wildlife conservation, light should sometimes be shed behind the scenes to
reveal a few of the hidden difficulties that bring additional compli-
cations to wildlife conservation on the African continent. Therefore, before going further with my account of my personal experiences, I intend to outline and comment on the nature of some
of these shadowy problems, which have had and are continuing
to have an effect on the wildlife situation.

Personalities are bedevilling the cause of wildlife in East Africa! This penetrating observation was issued as a solemn warning at the 'Conference on Wildlife Management and Land Use' held in Nairobi as recently as July 1967. Its author, who insisted that his words be recorded for posterity, was an eminent East African plant ecologist and all-round naturalist – that quiet, brilliant and level-headed scientist and practical conservationist, Dr Phillip Glover, a man of international stature for whose opinions I have always had the greatest respect. Coming from a person normally as reserved and non-aggressive as he is, the statement really means something. In fact, it is my contention that the first signs of this corrosive malaise in East Africa coincided with the hiving-off of the newly created national park areas from the direct control of the game departments, two decades earlier.

I myself am a dedicated protagonist of national parks as such and I always have been – let there be no misunderstanding on this point. On the other hand I have always been equally antagonistic to the idea that national parks should be administered and managed virtually in isolation from other territorial wildlife conservation problems. The fact that the responsibility for the welfare of wildlife in Africa is now shared by a multiplicity of organisations, both official and demi-official as well as private, is in itself a major source of confusion to the general public. As I have so often observed, that there should be any difference between a 'Game Department' and a 'National Parks Department', and between a 'Game Reserve' and a 'National Park', is to most people a baffling mystery; to a steadily increasing number of informed persons it is also a matter for sober and sincere regret. I myself have always held strong views on this subject, views which have been strengthened, not weakened, by the passing of the years. Time and experience have revealed many of the drawbacks and dangers of any system of divided control of a largely nomadic, nationally owned, natural resource which does not recognise or respect artificial, man-made boundaries. For some strange reason, however, this is a topic which, hitherto, has nearly always been hurriedly hushed up when raised in general conversation outside the hallowed precincts of government offices, just as the universally important subject of sex was barred from Victorian drawing-rooms! Certainly, when wildlife is threatened, it is essential that all those who are sincerely interested in the welfare of wild animal life should sink their differences and present a united front, being ever mindful of the wise old maxim that 'a house divided against itself must fall'. The sad part is that with less division of responsibility for wildlife there would be fewer differences!

A number of countries in Africa have resisted the temptation to follow the once popular practice of separating the administration of national parks from overall wildlife management; others, after a trial period, have reverted to unified control and have been thankful for the change. It is my view that these decisions were right. The very nature of Africa's abundant wildlife, and the problems of its management – particularly in financially poor but developing countries – cry out for strong, centrally co-ordinated direction. The spectre of an intransigent government as the legendary ogre in the wildlife conservation fairy-tale is an out-of-date myth, a concept originally fostered by sincere idealists driven to desperation by the bigoted opposition of myopic officialdom. In the game-rich countries of Africa, this indictment is to a large extent a long dead horse, now flogged only by the ill-informed or those whose interests are not entirely altruistic, but it was founded on dangerous truth during the colonial era, when game was widely regarded as being of small economic value. With the conversion of African governments to whole-hearted belief in the new dogma that wildlife is one of Africa's most valuable, but hitherto most neglected, natural resources, the legend has become a canard.

Wherever the system of divided control of wild animal life has been tried, it has invariably led to clashes of interests and profitless conflict between those jointly charged with its care, although the severity of such disputes has fluctuated according to the personalities at the time. During the years that I was Chief Game Warden, first of Uganda and then Tanganyika, I had long and sometimes regrettably bitter personal experience of these harmful and fruitless conflicts. Some years later, when I became Chief Game Warden of a unified department in Malawi, the difference was striking and the relief profound. Many game wardens have suffered similarly, so much so that I sincerely believe that the question of the wisdom of any policy of divided responsibility for wildlife management is a subject which could well benefit from being thoroughly aired, particularly since it appears to have arisen from a misinterpretation of certain intentions behind the London Convention of 1933.

The wise and selfless men who drafted the London Convention

of 1933 were surprisingly short-sighted in some respects. When they proposed the creation of national parks under separate 'public control', they apparently envisaged neat, self-contained areas, wildlife Utopias in which the animals would always be happy to remain, enjoying idyllic lives blissfully free of human interference of any sort, and subject only to the gentle, natural controls of a kindly 'Mother Nature'. Experience has shown us how far off the mark they were. Sufficient free land areas big enough to sustain uncontrolled numbers of wide-ranging and destructive animals such as elephant, in the face of an exploding, land-hungry, human population, just were not and are not available. As time went on situations arose where large and expanding elephant herds used the national parks as sanctuaries from which to raid cultivation for miles around. This sometimes led to head-on clashes between the game departments, who were responsible for cultivation protection, and the national park authorities, for the latter were not only unwilling themselves to control elephant numbers* but reluctant even to permit game department staff to follow up injured elephants which had sought refuge in a national park.

The most farcical situation I have personally come across was when I was Chief Game Warden of Tanganyika. Many of the great wildebeest herds of the Serengeti dropped their calves in the area to the east which was under the control of the Ngorongoro Conservation Unit: they then trekked westwards right across the Serengeti Plains, following the rains and the grazing – during this time under the protection of the Tanganyika National Parks Trustees – until they emerged into the region of the River Grumeti, where they became the responsibility of the Game Department. Every year the pattern was the same and, although I was a member of, or represented on all three organisations, it was like having a herd of open range cattle owned, at different seasons, by three separate farmers, each with his own individual ideas as to how the herd should best be managed.

It is important to note that nowhere does the London Convention of 1933 discuss or recommend the form that the management and administration of national parks should take. However,

* Years later, after much soul searching, many national park authorities were forced to amend their former rigid protection policies and organise control of animal numbers within the boundaries of their parks.

twenty years later the 'Third International Conference for the Protection of the Fauna and Flora of Africa', held in Bukavu, the capital of the Belgian Congo's Kivu Province, in October 1953, reviewed the 1933 London Convention and recommended certain amendments to it. I was a member of the British delegation to the Bukavu Conference and one of the meeting's universally agreed and formally recorded proposals – 'Recommendation No 3' – on permanent record in an imposing, leather-bound volume, clearly and firmly states:

> d) that in each territory, the conservation and control of wild animals should be vested in a *single authority* adequately staffed and suitably equipped; . . .

However, by then, throughout East Africa, the various national park organisations were so well entrenched as separate, independent authorities that, to this day, this basic and vital recommendation – made by a large body of the most experienced and knowledgeable wildlife conservation experts and scientists from many parts of the world – has failed to come to pass in any country in East Africa, although Kenya is now considering it.

That no effort has been made to implement this wise proposal is, to my way of thinking, a sad but clear reflection on the true nature of man himself; that at heart he is still little more than a territorial animal primarily – even though sometimes subconsciously – concerned with protecting his own personal interests and status, for such a move would inevitably have involved a number of influential persons and bodies having either to take a rear seat, or surrender altogether their previous controlling powers. Furthermore, in my opinion, those who contend that national parks are safe from government interference, when established as a theoretically independent 'trust', are living in a 'fool's paradise'. Under such management national parks certainly enjoy a greater degree of administrative and financial flexibility and an enviable freedom from the frustrations of bureaucratic red tape, compared with government game departments; but since the national parks are still to a major extent dependent on substantial, annual financial subsidies from the governments concerned – who also appoint and discharge the members of the national parks' administering bodies, the Boards of Trustees – it is the governments who retain the ultimate power of control of policy, the 'iron hand' being carefully concealed in a somewhat ostentatious 'velvet glove'.

Both forms of administration I have mentioned above have their advantages and disadvantages; it is a matter of choice as to which is preferable in the circumstances existing in any given country. But it is my contention that, whatever form the administration of the wildlife resource in any African country may take, unified control as opposed to divided control should, without qualification, be the goal to be aimed at. Perhaps, the best answer is some sort of 'Wildlife Commission' with overall, country-wide powers, on the lines of the Forestry Commission of the United Kingdom. To be avoided at all costs is any system which leads to conflicting territorial claims and disputes over management policies, both of which can all too easily result in major personality clashes. I am not decrying the truly notable achievements of the national park authorities of East Africa; why should I when I myself was a National Parks Trustee in Uganda and Tanganyika for thirteen years! What I am saying is that even more could have been achieved, with greater speed and far less emotional conflict, had there been unified as opposed to divided control of the wildlife resource in the countries concerned; and, mark my words, the need for unified control, the power of a united front, is going to increase not decrease as time races on.

In support of my contentions I am able to quote a recent serious and most disturbing case. By the end of 1970, it was clear that the Uganda Government had decided to ride, rough-shod, over all valid objections to its gradiose plan to establish a hydro-electric scheme at the Murchison Falls, the heart of Uganda's most popular national park. Despite the fact that viable, if not cheaper and better alternative dam sites exist outside this famous national park, and that international experts had decried the economic necessity of the scheme, it seemed that political intransigence and expediency, boosted by false pride, had won the day. The Director of Uganda's National Parks, Francis Katete*, supported by his Board of Trustees, had fought a gallant battle against this commercial and political juggernaut, and international

* His untimely death in a car accident on the 9th of June 1970, robbed Africa of one of its most promising conservationists, a man who was universally liked and respected by people of all races.

pressure had been brought to bear – all to no avail. Finally, it appeared certain that shouting gangs of workmen would invade the Park; that the mighty roar of the Falls, the voice of the Nile for thousands of years, would be muted and replaced by the hammering crescendo of pneumatic drills; and that the giant plume of water, one of the true wonders of the world at which countless visitors have gazed in awe ever since this dramatic sight first held the eyes of the famous explorer Sir Samuel Baker, would be stilled for ever. Only a miracle could save it – and at the last minute this miracle came in the strange form of a military *coup d'état*. In January 1971, the Commander of the Uganda Army, General Idi Amin, overthrew the government of Dr Milton Obote, and the planned desecration of the Murchison Falls was cancelled by order of the new President.

So much for the imagined safety of national parks administered by Boards of Trustees. The sobering truth is that it has been the individual personalities, determined men with often conflicting views and characters, who have really influenced the course of wildlife conservation in Africa. This personality problem had become apparent long before I first submitted my own suggestions for national parks in Uganda, and I therefore proposed the creation of a unified 'Wildlife Service', incorporating both the old Game and Fisheries Department and the new National Parks. In this I so nearly succeeded that it was heart-breaking. The final official comment on record was the Chief Secretary's minute to the Governor. 'I think we should give the Chief Game Warden's proposals a trial,' he wrote. But at the last moment unknown but powerful influences intervened and Uganda meekly followed the then popular line of removing the management of national parks from the Game Department, while I found myself suspect of being a self-seeking empire builder!

Shortly before the Uganda National Parks Act became law, Barrie Cartland was summoned to the Governor's office to discuss various affairs of State. For him, as Administrative Secretary, it was a routine visit and the discussion was brief and businesslike, but when he turned to go Sir Andrew Cohen called him back.

'By the way, Cartland,' he said. 'This morning Dreschfield asked me whether he could be Chairman of the Uganda National

Parks Board of Trustees and I said he could. I thought you ought to know.'

'I remember I was bitterly disappointed at the time,' Barrie Cartland told me ruefully some years later. 'I knew I had half-hoped that I would get the appointment and subconsciously I think I had rather expected to be offered it after being involved so much in the early stages of the parks. But I was extremely busy as Administrative Secretary and I soon realised that to be an effective Chairman of the National Parks Trustees would have taken up a great deal more time than I, personally, could possibly have spared.'

'The law is a ass – a idiot,' so, with considerable truth, spoke Mr Bumble, the beadle in Dickens's *Oliver Twist*; far less frequently can the same be said of the law's exponents and certainly not of Uganda's Attorney General in 1952, Ralph Dreschfield, QC, a stocky, bald-headed, extrovert bachelor, with a shrewd legal brain. Ralph Dreschfield was a forceful character; determined, energetic and tough, but he also had a strong sentimental streak which made him the active champion of an assortment of charitable causes. The strange part of the whole affair was that, until he was asked to draft the Uganda National Parks Ordinance, Ralph Dreschfield had never shown any active interest in wild animals. In fact, the overruling passion in his life was sailing – he was Commodore of the Kazi Yacht Club on Lake Victoria – and if Barrie Cartland had arranged for anyone other than Ken Beaton to come to Uganda to advise on national parks, it is more than likely that he, Barrie Cartland, would have become the first Chairman of the Uagnda National Parks Board of Trustees and not Ralph Dreschfield. As it was, 'Fate', working in its usual devious ways, made quite certain how the die would be cast by ensuring that it was Ken Beaton and no one else whom Barrie Cartland should ask for!

The answer to the mystery was given to me by Ralph Dreschfield himself.

'Ken and I served together in the KAR* during the war,' he said. 'When he came to Uganda to advise, I asked him whether he would like the job of Director of Uganda National Parks. He said he would – provided I was made Chairman of the Board of Trustees! He was so enthusiastic when he was here that he got
* King's African Rifles.

me interested in the whole business.' And thus, as the Bible is fond of stating, *it came io pass*. A powerful triumvirate was formed consisting of Ken Beaton, Ralph Dreschfield and myself; a triumvirate which launched the Uganda National Parks and was, in effect, the executive body which kept them running during their formative years. In fact, the development of national parks, with all the attendant publicity to arouse the interest of the general public, is not unlike a theatrical production. Ken Beaton was cast in the combined roles of producer, stage manager and leading actor; Ralph Dreschfield was the sponsor and treasurer; and I myself – representing the Game and Fisheries Department – was the promoter, co-producer and local technical adviser, as well as being the backer who, with others, had campaigned to have most of the Uganda Game Department's finest wildlife areas converted to national park status.

From the start the triumvirate worked in an atmosphere of euphoria and enthusiasm engendered by a spirit of mutual trust and co-operation. This was due, in no small measure, to the fact that the Game and Fisheries Department, as a whole, extended itself to its utmost to ensure that the new venture was not merely successfully launched but safely navigated through the early shoalwaters of its inspired voyage. Credit was due to staff of all grades and Ken Beaton, ever generous, was not slow to appreciate and recognise this fact; it is all the more tragic therefore, that, in later years, the vital part played by the Game and Fisheries Department in the early days was forgotten and its continuing, active interest in national parks was often misinterpreted by suspicious but influential persons as a bid to regain complete control.

I took an immediate liking to Ken Beaton from the first time I met him. He was a powerfully built man of middle height, with dark hair, a small dark moustache, and humorous, twinkling eyes set in a round, rubicund face. Gifted in a number of ways, he was a keen observer which had made him a knowledgeable though untrained naturalist. His farming days had developed the practical side of his nature; his war years with the KAR had taught him leadership and the handling of men; he was blessed with a vivid imagination and a bubbling sense of humour, in addition to tremendous drive and energy, while his experience of the early formative years of the Kenya National Parks was an invaluable asset for Uganda.

One of the things I particularly liked about Ken Beaton was that he never put on side, he was always completely natural and was never too proud to ask for advice and help from anyone if he needed it. As the showman that any director of national parks must be to some extent, as part of his job, he was inevitably bathed in a good deal of publicity, but he never let it bother or influence him one way or the other. Unlike a number of other national parks directors and senior game wardens I have known in various parts of Africa, on his appointment he did not immediately assume the role and strike the pose of a crusading evangelist, a cross between a latter day St Francis of Assisi and a modern St John the Baptist with fire in his belly and a scourge in his hand. Such people have always been a real problem to practical conservationists. Being publicity-inclined, the poseurs are liable so to catch the eyes and imagination of the general public that they become the oracles of wildlife conservation overnight, no matter how limited their true knowledge and experience of the subject may be.

Publicity is like alcohol; taken in reasonable quantities it can be beneficial, a stimulant which can inspire creative effort; in excess it blunts and distorts the judgment and creates illusions of personal power and grandeur. I often think that the old time game wardens, true lovers of the wild, individualists and real solitaries who were in the job because it gave them the nearest thing to a natural way of life, must be turning in their graves at the publicity-orientated wildlife world of today.

Fortunately for Uganda and myself, Ken Beaton was alive to these dangers and problems and was as anxious as I was to avoid them arising in Uganda. Nevertheless, Ken was no plaster saint; on the contrary he was a most human, colourful personality who lived with panache, so much so that I often had the feeling that he was really a character who had been born out of his time. With his normal dress of a sleeveless leather jerkin worn over a brightly-hued shirt, and his trousers held up by a broad leather belt with a massive brass buckle – all worn with a swashbuckling air – it only needed a pair of sea boots, a headscarf, a gold ear-ring in his left ear and a cutlass and a flintlock pistol at his waist, to turn him into the traditional concept of an Elizabethan buccaneer! All in all, of the many national park directors I have known, few have matched up to Ken Beaton; most have been mere pallid shadows in comparison. A eulogy? Why not? How many people now remember the name of Ken Beaton, despite all he did for the National Parks of Kenya and Uganda?

But even Ken Beaton, despite his stature as a leader, could not have achieved what he did in Uganda without the help of his two most able lieutenants, John Mills and Mike Holmes, with their intimate knowledge of the country and the people. I have already described the valuable part played by John Mills during the campaign to establish national parks in Uganda, but the subsequent roles of both himself and Mike Holmes were equally important – they were the first wardens in charge of the Murchison Falls and Queen Elizabeth National Parks respectively.

One of the earliest tasks that had faced the 'executive triumvirate' of the National Parks had been the selection of the two senior Park Wardens. From the beginning both John Mills and Mike Holmes had expressed their keenness to join the National Parks. I had supported this proposal strongly for two reasons. First, John Mills knew the Murchison area like the back of his hand, while Mike Holmes had a sound knowledge of the region around Lakes Edward and George. Secondly, not only were they both very capable game wardens, but their transfer from the Game Department to National Parks would, I had been certain, do much to ensure the closest and most amicable working link between the Game Department and the new National Parks organisation; if there was not to be a unified 'Wildlife Service', this would, I had felt, be the next best thing. Fortunately, both Ken Beaton and Ralph Dreschfield had agreed with me.

My faith in the effectiveness of the proposed team had proved to be justified, for within less than two years the development of the two parks was far advanced. Efficient ranger forces had been recruited and trained; a comprehensive system of motorable tracks had been constructed, many of them through difficult country, as well as an air-strip in each park to take Dakota-sized aircraft; specially designed game-viewing launches were in operation on the waterways; a picturesque, log cabin type Safari Lodge, constructed of local makindu palms and papyrus thatching, had been built on the Mweya Peninsula with beautiful views over Lake Edward, the Kazinga Channel and the Ruwenzori; and the building of another Safari Lodge had also been started at a strategic site on the north bank of the Victoria Nile, some ten miles down-stream from the Murchison Falls. All this was no mean achievement within the time and with the resources available.

From the very start it had been agreed that Ken Beaton should concentrate his own initial efforts in the Queen Elizabeth National Park, where he would be based. This had left John Mills rather on his own in the Murchison and Ken Beaton had asked me whether I would be willing to take a 'special interest' in that park and help John Mills as much as I could. Willing? I had been delighted! Not only was John Mills an old friend and colleague of mine, but of the two parks the Murchison Falls National Park was, and still is, my favourite, for it is an area which holds two special attractions for me – giant elephants and giant fish!

Until now, in telling the story of my life and memories as a game warden, I have scarcely mentioned the subject of fish, a form of animal life which constitutes an important, though usually less dramatic and less glamorous, part of the complete wildlife scene. This is a serious omission for Uganda is a country exceptionally well endowed with great lakes like inland seas, mighty rivers and extensive areas of permanent swamps. All of these waters contain a rich variety of edible fish, a number of which also provide good sport for the angler, and by the time I arrived in Uganda in 1949, the development and management of these productive fisheries had long been one of the major responsibilities of the Uganda Game and Fisheries Department. Furthermore, to understand properly the importance of these fisheries in the overall wildlife conservation context of Uganda, it must be appreciated that most of Uganda's main fisheries regions coincide with the majority of that country's more important game areas and particularly its main elephant areas. As a result, the fisheries and game staff of Uganda's combined Department of Game and Fisheries have always worked in the closest co-operation, continually helping each other out in a variety of ways ranging from the prevention of both game and fish poaching to the control of shamba raiding elephants.

In my capacity as head of the Department of Game and Fisheries, I had an overall official responsibility for the development and management of Uganda's fisheries. In effect, however, I

Crocodiles below Murchison Falls, Victoria Nile

Herds of topi near Lake Edward

could safely delegate virtually all of the responsibility for the commercial fisheries to my exceptionally able Chief Fisheries Officer, Don Rhodes, and his capable henchmen. Nevertheless, like the majority of game wardens I have always been a keen angler and, in consequence, the development of Uganda's sport fishing amenities was a matter in which I always made a point of playing a very active part. It was for this reason that I was particularly interested in the Murchison Falls National Park, for not only does the region surrounding the famous Falls still contain some of the biggest tuskers left in Africa, but also, deep in the swirling, tropical waters of the Nile, there swims a giant species of perch, one of the mightiest freshwater fish in the world. *Lates niloticus*, the Nile perch, the 'Fish God of the Nile', was worshipped and mummified by the ancient Egyptians and grows to a staggering size; the largest I have heard of was caught in a seine-net at the southern end of Lake Albert in 1960, my last year as Chief Game Warden of Uganda – it weighed 363 pounds! Among the great family of freshwater fishes only the mighty arapaima of the Amazon can challenge piscine giants of such dimensions.

The Nile perch occurs in many of the rivers and lakes of tropical Africa, but for thousands of years the Murchison Falls have presented an impassable barrier to its passage into the upper waters of the Nile and Lake Victoria. Was there an accumulation of these giants in the deep, swirling pools below the Falls and if so were there any record breakers among them? Or were there few if any of these great fish so far up the Nile? No one seemed to know the answer to these questions and, search as I might, I could find no record of anyone ever having attempted to fish at this remote and inaccessible spot. It was a mystery that intrigued me and as a dedicated angler it was one that I had long been determined to solve. The development of the Murchison Falls National Park eventually gave me the opportunity that I needed.

Early on the morning of the 23rd of February 1953 – according to my fishing diary – having travelled up from Lake Albert in the Game and Fisheries Department's launch, Tony Henley and I stepped ashore on the south bank of the Victoria Nile at a point called Fajao, some two miles downstream of the Murchison Falls. Fajao is the limit of normal launch navigation; upstream of that point the broad, yellow bosom of the Nile, flanked by the dark, beetling cliffs of an ever narrowing gorge, is broken up by a series of small, densely wooded islets and jagged rocky outcrops around which the powerful, foam-flecked current swirls and eddies, becoming increasingly turbulent the closer the Falls are approached. Tony Henley, who had succeeded John Mills as Game Warden in charge of Bunyoro District, was as keen an angler as I was and, with our long spinning rods dancing over our shoulders and eager anticipation in our hearts, he and I, trailed by our gun-bearers, made our way briskly along the south bank of the river, following a well-beaten elephant path that led, by the easiest route, deep into the heart of the gorge, heading purposefully for the distant, muted roar of the Falls.

Forty minutes later, still bearing our rods over our shoulders like crusaders' lances, Tony and I clambered carefully through tangled scrub along the crest of a rocky, knife-edged ridge that jutted out at right angles into the river. At the end of the ridge we paused and gazed around in awe, for towering above us on three sides were tall, jungle-covered cliffs that reached high up into the sky, while the cliff on our right looked like a human shoulder that had been slashed to the bone by a savage blow from some giant battle-axe. Through this deep, narrow cut – less than twenty foot wide – plunged the full force of the entire River Nile, arching out in a great plume of thousands of tons of foaming white water, like a mammoth, low pressure fire hose, to crash on the glistening black rocks one hundred and forty feet below with a continuous and deafening roar that echoed and re-echoed from the towering cliffs.

Tony turned to me, his eyes glistening with excitement, and said something. Drowned by the thunder of the Falls the words were whipped away on the spray-laden breeze, but following his pointing finger as it swept back and forth I gathered the inference of what he had said. Below us, swirling and eddying in a multitude of pools and runs, its water clear, peat-coloured, flecked with tumbling white wavelets, the Nile looked like a gigantic Norwegian salmon river – at least it did until I glanced down-stream to where, far in the distance, three large bull elephants were drinking purposefully in a shallow backwater close to a school of lazing hippo, while here and there, scattered motionless on the rocks, were the sinister shapes of basking crocodiles. It was then that it really dawned on me that the dramatic scene at which I was gazing in silent awe was unique, brooking no comparison. With a conscious thrill I remembered that this remote stretch of the mighty Nile, in the many thousands of years of its life, had never seen the flash of a twisting spoon or the gleam of a wobbling plug-bait; in other words it was an angler's rarely achieved dream – virgin fishing water! Not only had it never before been fished by any angler, but no one was even certain what species and numbers of fish, if any, swam beneath its turbulent surface. The watchful, waiting crocodiles alone knew the answer to this latter question and there was no means of getting them to break their inscrutable silence.

With a professional eye I scanned the river below me seeking for swirls and eddies, surface signs that signalled the hidden rocks beneath, current breakers which form the favourite lies of any lurking predatory fish. Choosing my site with care, I scrambled down to the water's edge and checked my tackle item by item. As befitting such an historic occasion I was using a truly international range of equipment. My spinning rod was a nine foot, tubular fibre-glass, double-handed 'Heddon' made in the USA. My reel was a large, salt-water fixed-spool model, the French 'Mitchell-Mer'. My line – purchased from Hardy Brothers of Pall Mall – was twenty-five pound breaking strain nylon monofilament of English manufacture, as was the twenty-pound breaking strain 'Elasticum' wire from which I had prepared my homemade trace. The last and most important item of my tackle was the lure, which I had selected with special care; it was a four and one quarter inch plug-bait called the 'Pikie Minnow'. A product of the American 'Creek-Chub Bait Company', and available in a wide range of colours, types and sizes, the 'Pikie Minnow' had proved irresistible to Nile perch when I had first introduced it on Lake Albert. The colour known as 'Natural Pikie' – a tasteful combination of bronze heavily barred with dark brown – had proved to be the most generally effective on the Lake, particularly the smaller model which attracted Nile perch of all sizes. It was therefore a small 'Natural Pikie' that I chose for this historic angling debut at the Murchison Falls.

I said a short prayer, spat on the plug for luck, braced my shoulders and, with a smooth, steady swing, cast the lure far out into the main stream of the Nile. Landing with a small splash, the plug was immediately caught in the powerful current which, with the side pull of the line, swung it shorewards in a wide,

Elephants parade through Paraa Camp, Murchison Falls
National Park

Elephants wading in the Nile

wriggling curve. For the next few moments as I reeled in I was tense with expectancy, but I finally lifted the dripping bait from the water at my feet without having detected any sign of a fish.

Shifting my stance slightly to the edge of a rocky ledge, below which there was a strong back eddy into a deep pool, I cast for the second time. Again the performance was repeated as before; but, just as I was about to lift the plug from the water at my feet, there was a swirl and a savage tug, my rod whipped into a straining, quivering arc and my line screamed out into the main current. Something, I knew not what, had obviously followed the wobbling bait right into the shallows to seize this apparently easy meal of an 'injured fish' before returning, at full speed, to its chosen lair in the main stream.

With mounting excitement and my line vibrating and humming like a taut violin string, I worked my way down-stream bringing to bear as much side pressure as I dared. The response was almost instantaneous; the line arched to the surface and out of the water, in a flurry of foam, shaking its head in frustrated fury at the gaudy plug-bait which rattled in its gaping jaws, there leapt one of the most magnificent looking fish I have ever seen; its shimmering silvery body had the purplish tinge of a fresh-run spring salmon and its eyes shone with a strange, fiery glow. In the powerful current the fight was fierce and prolonged, but the hooks held and twenty minutes and almost as many leaps later the big gaff went home. At my feet, in all its gleaming finery, its bulging, translucent eyes shining with an eerie, golden glow as if a fire was burning deep in its head, there lay the 'Fish God of the Nile'. The needle of the spring balance steadied at forty-three pounds and an age-old fishing mystery had been solved at last.

The rest of my tale of this fishing discovery is an angling story the details of which must wait another day. Suffice it to say here that long before noon Tony Henley and I had caught all the perch that he and I and our gun-bearers could possibly carry; and we remembered that it was a long haul back to the launch and on to the hungry mouths at John Mills's camp at Paraa on the north bank! In fact, it was almost a relief when I saw my third – and last – plug-bait disappear down-stream in the gaping mouth of a monster perch, a fish that finally thrashed on the surface like a harpooned whale and snapped my line like a thread of cotton. How big this fish was I would hesitate to guess, but the largest Nile perch landed below the Murchison Falls to-date was caught by John Savidge – then Warden of the Murchison Falls National Park – seven years later. His record perch took him over two and a half hours to land and weighed 160 pounds. Having studied photographs of this magnificent fish I am still left with the typical, nagging, fisherman's thought that the perch I lost on that first, pioneering day could well have been even larger!

But the Nile perch saga does not end there. In fact, the first test fishing below the Murchison Falls was only the beginning of a carefully planned experiment, the final object of which was to stock Nile perch in the upper waters of the Nile. Perhaps *re-stock* might be a more accurate term to use, since the fossil remains of Nile perch have been found in Miocene deposits on an island in the Kavirondo Gulf of Lake Victoria. Certainly, the fisheries experts of the Uganda Game and Fisheries Department were able to show that there was overwhelming evidence of the value of Nile perch, not only as a sporting and tourist amenity but as an important factor in maintaining the productivity of rich tropical fisheries. Despite this evidence however, in certain influential and conservative-minded quarters in Kenya and Tanganyika there was firm opposition to the idea. As a result, I had to wait until early in 1954, when the new Owen Falls Dam and hydro-electric scheme obliterated the Ripon Falls and effectively sealed off the fish fauna of Lake Victoria from the rest of the Nile system, before I could proceed further with my plan.

On the 24th of February 1954 – almost a year to the day after my first experimental fishing in the Murchison Falls National Park – I again visited the Murchison Falls, accompanied by Alec Anderson, then my Fisheries Officer for Lake Albert. He and I managed to catch only seven perch of easily transportable size, each being between one and two feet long. These small fish we placed in a zinc hip-bath which, with the aid of a team of Fish Guards, we carried laboriously up the steep, winding track that leads to the top of the Falls; there, with due ceremony, we launched them into the upper waters of the Nile – the first Nile perch ever to swim in those waters. But it was more of a token exercise than anything else; the proper stocking operation which I had planned started the following year. By that time I had had a special carrying tank made, designed to fit on a three-ton lorry, and John Stoneman, a keen, energetic and most able young Devonian, had taken over as Fisheries Officer on Lake Albert.

In September and October 1955, John Stoneman caught several hundred small Nile perch in a seine-net in Butiaba Bay on Lake Albert and successfully transported them across Uganda, in the new tank, to release them in the upper Nile below the Owen Falls Dam and at Masindi Port at the western end of Lake Kyoga, which is little more than a shallow valley drowned by the Nile. Further similar stockings were carried out in 1956 and 1957, in which Don Rhodes, Alec Anderson and Harry Simpson of the Fisheries Division of the Game and Fisheries Department also took part.

The results of these operations were, to say the least of it, spectacular! During the year 1955, when the first intensive stocking of Nile perch took place, the total commercial fish production from Lake Kyoga, which has a fishable area of 880 square miles, was only 4,500 tons; ten years later the weight of Nile perch alone caught in that lake was 4,374 tons. By 1966 the total fish production from Lake Kyoga had risen to 19,500 tons, of which 7,422 tons were Nile perch; 1967 saw the figures rise again to a total of 25,900 tons with Nile perch contributing 13,015 tons; in 1968 the figures were 32,580 tons and 17,725 tons respectively; and by the end of 1969, the last year for which I have official statistics to hand, the total catch had risen yet again to 48,945 tons with Nile perch providing 26,920 tons of the whole. In other words, in fourteen years, largely as a result of stocking with Nile perch, the commercial fish production from Lake Kyoga rose from 4,500 tons to nearly 49,000 tons – an increase of over 1,000%! And of this prodigious total the Nile perch now comprise more than 56% of the overall catch – a case of converting what the Americans call 'trash' fish (the smaller and less palatable fish which form the bulk of the Nile perch's food) into a readily catchable and marketable product.

It is not only the commercial fisheries that have benefited from this successful stocking programme. In recent years sport fishing for Nile perch in the Chobi Rapids near the new National Park Safari Lodge, several miles upstream of the Murchison Falls, has become a major attraction, while in the stretch of the Nile between the Owen Falls Dam and Lwampanga, angling for Nile perch has been organised on a commercial basis for tourists from Kampala. These waters now rival if not surpass the angling below the Murchison Falls and a fine perch of 170 pounds was taken at Lwampanga in 1966.

Should you care to ask for it at the Safari Lodge at Paraa – the headquarters of the Murchison Falls National Park – the Warden will show you the old angling record book; I started it when the Lodge was built and as far as I know it is still there. The old volume contains not only details of the earlier catches of Nile perch below the Falls, but a sketch map of the fishing water with every pool and run marked and named, as is traditional with the salmon rivers of my native Scotland. I chose the names with care – 'The Devil's Cauldron', 'Hippo Pool', 'The Expert's Pool', 'Small Chance', 'The Jack-pot', 'The Claw', 'Mputa Bay' and 'Fraser's Pool'. All these names had a reason or a story behind them, stories to be told another time, and all were scattered along the south bank of the Nile.

Due to steep, forbidding cliffs dropping almost sheer into the water on the north bank, there were few places on that side of the river where fishing was feasible. The two exceptions were 'Last Chance', a long run only approachable by an energetic angler with the attributes of a mountain goat; and a strange, still bay that cut back deep into the cliffs. At times, when the level of the Nile was very high, this bay received the overflow from the Falls in a small cataract of its own. The first time Ken Beaton saw the swirling pool, in his eye was the avaricious gleam of the old prospector.

'Could be a cool million in alluvial gold in there,' he said meditatively – and so 'The Cool Million' it became! But 'The Cool Million' may disappear and the great Nile perch with it, if the monstrous hydro-electric scheme ever comes to pass.

When the Murchison Falls National Park was created, those of us responsible had no idea that it would become Uganda's most popular park, yet in 1969 it had more than twice as many visitors as the Queen Elizabeth National Park – to be precise 37,666 as opposed to 18,719 – a steady trend over the years. At the same time we did not dream that, despite all precautions, in less than twenty years the very existence of the majestic Falls themselves, one of the wonders of the world and the heart of the

National Park, would be threatened by a politically motivated act of economic vandalism. Least of all did we realise that, long before even that danger arose, the Park would become so overrun with elephants that there would be a risk of these mighty beasts destroying their habitat and themselves with it.

The great rolling grasslands that lie in the broad bend between the Victoria and Albert Niles, extending northwards to the Sudan border and southwards, across the Victoria Nile, deep into the District of Bunyoro, have always been one of the strongholds of the African elephant. Both in numbers of animals and size of ivory the elephant herds of this region, in which over ninety per cent of their food is grass, can rival almost any other elephant area in Africa. Down on the Lake Albert flats I once counted a herd, or grouping of herds – an elephant 'aloe-eating convention' – over 1,200 strong. Such gatherings were not uncommon, while scattered throughout the region, much of which now lies within the Murchison Falls National Park, was a sprinkling of really mighty tuskers.

In course of time, as the Murchison Falls Park developed, these big tuskers became better known; and as familiarity with these ponderous, benevolent and usually placid old gentlemen increased so did concern for their welfare – for really big ivory takes a long time to grow. Inevitably, as individuals became recognised they were named for ease of reference and from sheer affection. There was one very ancient bull whom I christened the 'Patriarch'. His tusks were long and impressive, sweeping down almost to ground level before curving forwards and upwards again, and his skin hung in wrinkled folds on his bony frame like a wet sheet on a drying rack. He was very old and very slow, and it was my constant fear that one night he would wander vaguely across the boundary into someone's shamba and a waiting rifle. However, he normally patronised the Buliji area of the Park, close to the north bank of the Victoria Nile and far from the nearest cultivation, where he was escorted and guarded by an exceptionally alert young bull. The latter looked after the old bull so well that the 'Patriarch' eventually died from natural causes; we found his body in the bed of the River Tangi in 1958 and recovered his mighty tusks which weighed 158 pounds and 147 pounds.

Although I was worried at the steady decline in the number of

Returning to dry land

big tuskers in Uganda, I was not concerned at the total number of elephants in the country. In fact, one of the main tasks of the Game and Fisheries Department was – and always had been – to keep the numbers of these fascinating but destructive great beasts under proper control and prevent an elephant population explosion. Generally we were successful, but locally we were hampered by the National Parks policy of the early days, which was firmly opposed to any form of animal population control within the boundaries of the Parks. This very soon led to an unhealthy build-up of hippo in the Queen Elizabeth Park and of elephant in the Murchison Falls Park, from the sanctuary of which young bull herds in particular, regularly went on the rampage in the surrounding shambas.

'Almost all the genuine damage is done on "hit and run" raids by the National Park elephants,' I wrote in my Annual Report for 1953. 'This makes it very difficult to prevent damage, particularly as the elephants are normally back in the Park before the news that they are out reaches the nearest game guard. Apart from this, there is always a danger of a wounded beast getting away and becoming a menace to those ignorant people who look upon elephants as always being delightful, placid creatures who live on currant buns and carry children on their backs for free rides.'

Despite his sense of humour Ken Beaton did not like this oblique criticism of National Parks policy.

'How many elephant did you shoot in Bunyoro last year?' he demanded belligerently in my office, after he had read my report.

'Exactly two hundred, as a matter of fact, Ken,' I replied, surprised and nettled at his aggressive tone.

'I thought so,' he went on angrily. 'You're killing too many National Park elephants.'

It was my turn to be angry. 'How many elephants do you think you've got in the southern half of the Murchison?' I asked, struggling hard to curb my temper.

'There are only eight hundred elephant in that area south of the Nile,' Ken Beaton growled, growing red in the face. Then he brought his fist down with a crash on my desk. 'You'll go down in history as the man who destroyed all the elephants in Uganda,' he roared.

302

With an effort I controlled my voice. 'Nonsense, Ken,' I said as quietly as I could. 'I *know* there are at least two thousand elephant in that area.'

The truth was not revealed for another three years, when a long series of aerial game counts, probably the first scientific research project of its kind in Africa, provided the answer. Both Ken and I were wrong, but he was more wrong than I was. In the area under dispute, which covered some 1,500 square miles, the scientists* concerned discovered an average elephant population of nearly eight thousand animals, with the biggest count producing the astonishing figure of 12,321 elephants!

Sadly, Ken Beaton never learnt the truth, or else he knew it long before we did; it all depends on what you believe, for Ken became seriously ill in September 1954 and on the 22nd of October he was dead.

Ken Beaton's untimely death was a great loss for Uganda National Parks, for wildlife in Africa and for me. Little did I know it at the time, but Ken's passing also signalled the end of the honeymoon between the National Parks and the Game and Fisheries Department. Quietly and unobtrusively the tide had turned again.

* Dr Helmut Buechner and Dr William Longhurst, followed later by Dr Irven Buss – all of them American Professors of Wildlife Management – assisted as pilots by Game Warden Captain Richard Newton and National Parks Trustee Mr Chiels Margach.

CHAPTER 15

The Years Between

THE ten years following Ken Beaton's death covered a period of rapidly mounting and traumatic change in the East African political scene; they also constituted a decade of spectacular advancement in the sphere of wildlife conservation in East Africa, a sphere in which Uganda remained well in the van despite some internal discord. In fact, so much of interest, of excitement and of lasting importance happened during that period, that it demands separate and detailed treatment. The full story of those times must therefore await another day. All I intend to do here is to give a sketchy outline of the more important wildlife developments and problems during those years, sufficient to act as a bridge between the death of Ken Beaton and what, to me, was the climax, the 'Last Act', of nearly seventeen eventful years in East Africa. This climax I intend to describe in rather more detail, for personal reasons, since, as Sir William Gilbert so aptly wrote in *Ruddigore**,

> If you wish in this world to advance,
> Your merits you're bound to enhance,
> You must stir it and stump it,
> And blow your own trumpet,
> Or, trust me, you haven't a chance!

After Ken Beaton's death I served for a further six years in Uganda, making nearly eleven in all. Looking back on them, I realise that those six particular years were among the most interesting and most rewarding of my life as a game warden; but for me, at that time, they were often sadly marred by the friction that all too frequently developed between the Uganda National Parks Organisation and the Uganda Game and Fisheries Department. To avoid all mention of this damaging factor and thus pretend that all was well between the two wildlife organisations during those years would be both misleading and hypocritical, although fortunately the discord was seldom felt at field level. The park wardens – John Mills and Mike Holmes, followed by Frank Poppleton and John Savidge – were men who did a magnificent job; they kept well clear of the high-level disagreements and conflicts and remained on the best of terms with the game wardens of the Game Department. But, unfortunately, it was not the park wardens who dictated the National Parks' policy; that was the final responsibility of the Board of Trustees, a body in which the majority opinion was inclined to be influenced as much by sentiment as by practical considerations. In the ultimate it boiled down to a question of clashes of views aggravated by conflicting personalities, the same situation that has arisen in every country which has split the responsibility for the conservation of its wildlife. In fact, Uganda's experience was further proof of the fallibility and undesirability of the system of divided control.

Ken Beaton's successor, Rennie Bere, was an ex-Provincial Commissioner, a tall, craggy faced man who had served in the strictly feudal atmosphere of Uganda's old Administrative Service for many years. Rennie Bere, as I discovered after his appointment, had some very definite opinions on wildlife conservation. My difficulty was that my own and Rennie Bere's views on wildlife management matters were often diametrically opposed. In

* Gilbert and Sullivan's operetta, 1887.

this respect, my greatest shock was to discover that Rennie Bere held a completely contrary view to Ken Beaton and myself on one all important subject – the working relationship between the National Parks Organisation and its parent body, the Game and Fisheries Department.

Ken Beaton and I had agreed that it was essential for the National Parks and the Game Department not only to work in the closest liaison and co-operation, but to be seen to be doing so. In stark contrast, Rennie Bere's view was that the National Parks should be completely independent and that the general public should never associate them with the Game Department in any way. This view, which was based on the theory that the Game Department was heartily disliked by the general public for its enforcement of the game laws and that the National Parks would share this unpopularity if they were in any way associated, in the public eye, with the long established Game Department, was one I could never accept; in my opinion, which time has not changed, it just did not stand up to cold analysis.

To my mind it has always been illogical to expect either the simple peasant or the wily poacher to differentiate between a game department and a national parks organisation; in their eyes both these organisations exist simply to protect wild animals which they – the peasant and the poacher – dislike or covet or both. In fact, it has been my experience that a game department is often the less unpopular of the two among country folk, for it does at least provide substantial quantities of free meat, at regular intervals, from animals shot in protection of peasant shambas! However, whether Rennie Bere's view was right and mine was wrong, or vice versa, is for others to judge. All I can add in support of my own opinion is that, over the years, the separation of the two organisations has not led to any lessening of poaching pressure in national park areas, or of the intensity of effort required to contain it; in fact, the reverse has been the case!

Whatever the pros and cons of the matter, the new separationist policy of the Uganda National Parks had one particular result which distressed me. Neither John Mills nor Mike Holmes, both ex-Game Wardens and thus staunch Game Department supporters, were happy with the new policy. For a time they tried to adapt to it, but eventually they both resigned. Mike Holmes

306

emigrated to Canada where he was tragically killed in a car crash. John Mills returned to the fold of the Game Department as Game Warden in charge of the Southern Range – I was glad to have him back. In less than five years, with scant official appreciation for what they had achieved, the team which had pioneered the development of the Queen Elizabeth and Murchison Falls National Parks had broken up. The least I can do here is to place on record that it was largely due to Ken Beaton, John Mills and Mike Holmes that the development of Uganda's National Parks got off to a flying start.

While the National Parks were holding the centre of the stage for most of those years, with the help and active support of the Game and Fisheries Department, the latter was quietly forging ahead in the wings and behind the scenes. Fisheries development was spectacular – an increase in production from 10,000 tons landed in 1949 to 60,000 tons, worth £2½ million in 1959. Wildlife research, launched for the first time in strength with the aid of the American Fulbright Foundation, made notable strides. In place of the old, dark rooms at the back of the Forest Department, a brand new office and stores complex complete with garages, armourer's workshop, museum, library, aquaria and paddocks and cages for orphaned animals* was built on the shores of Lake Victoria at Entebbe. New and comprehensive wildlife and fisheries legislation was drafted and passed into law. And both the Game and Fisheries Divisions were reorganised and expanded.

For the symbol of the new Game and Fisheries Department badge – there had not been one before – I chose an elephant rampant, a shamba raider, as representing the Department's origins and one of the most important of its continuing tasks. The country I divided into six game 'ranges' – Northern, Southern, Western, Lake Albert, West Nile and Karamoja Ranges – each under a game warden with increased subordinate staff. Fisheries similarly were divided into three 'regions' – Lakes Edward and George, Lake Kyoga and Lake Albert Regions –

---

* See 'Orphans of the Wild' by Major Bruce G. Kinloch, M.C., in the *National Geographic*, November 1962, describing the author's conception and creation of Uganda's 'Animal Orphanage', an idea that has since been widely copied, notably at Nairobi in Kenya whose well publicised 'Animal Orphanage' is now far better known than the prototype in Uganda!

each under a fisheries officer and additional fish guards. Head-quarters staff were also strengthened to cope with the steadily expanding administrative burden, while specialist staff included a wildlife biologist, an armourer, a fisheries officer in charge of fish farming and a fisheries development officer.

The advent of the American scientists, provided by the Fulbright Commission, was a real 'shot in the arm' for wildlife research not only in Uganda but in East Africa as a whole. They were officially referred to as Fulbright 'Scholars', a most misleading term for each one of them, and there were five in all, was an expert in wildlife research and management, a leader in his own field in the USA. I applied for this 'Fulbright Aid' in January 1956, at which time there was little or no wildlife research under way in East Africa. The Tanganyika Game Department then had one wildlife biologist, Hugh Lamprey, a most able young man, who had been struggling along valiantly on his own since 1953; the Kenya Game Department had no research workers at all, nor had any of the East African National Park Organisations; and the Uganda Game Department's first wildlife biologist – Allan Brooks, a young Canadian who had previously worked in Tanganyika – did not take up his duties in Uganda until the end of March that year.

By good fortune, Dr Lee Talbot, then Staff Ecologist of the International Union for the Conservation of Nature and Natural Resources, arrived in Entebbe in February 1956. He was conducting a safari sponsored by Dr Russell Arundel, a Director of the American Committee for International Wildlife Protection and the American Wildlife Management Institute, to study the game situation in Uganda, with particular reference to the status of the white rhino and the mountain gorilla. Lee Talbot took an immediate interest in Uganda's wildlife research problems and offered to do what he could at the American end to push through my application for 'Fulbright Aid'. He was as good as his word; in fact, so successful was he that the normal procedure was shortened by months and the first three Fulbright scientists – Doctors George A. Petrides, Wendell G. Swank and Helmut K. Buechner – flew into Entebbe in October, almost before we were ready to receive them!

Hel Buechner remained initially for two years, concentrating mainly on the ecology of the Uganda kob as his primary project, with the study of various elephant problems in the Murchison Falls National Park and surrounding regions as his secondary task. His work on the Uganda kob in the Semliki Valley – which he later returned to complete – produced some fascinating results, in particular his observations on the territorial behaviour of the kob which received world wide acclaim and were commented upon at length in Robert Ardrey's brilliant book, *The Territorial Imperative**. His elephant project produced a great deal of interesting and useful initial information on elephant numbers and the effect they were having on their environment, work which provided an essential base from which his successor, Professor Irven Buss, also from Washington State University, was able to launch into detailed research on the elephant in Uganda. Like Hel Buechner, Irven Buss prolonged his field studies, returning again after Dr Horace Quick, the fifth Fulbright scientist, had stepped in to fill the gap for one year; and Irven Buss's important discoveries and conclusions have shed new light on the problems of elephant management and their logical solutions.

George Petrides, Professor of Wildlife Management at Michigan State University, and Dr Wendell Swank, Director of Research, Arizona Game and Fish Department, were landed with the task of investigating the most serious and most urgent problem – the apparent over-population of hippo in the Queen Elizabeth National Park and the effect that large concentrations of these great grazing animals were having both on the habitat and on other animal species in the Park. To the practised eyes of these experienced scientists the answers were almost immediately apparent, but they carried out a series of thorough tests and careful investigations before pronouncing their verdict to a full meeting of the Board of Trustees, a meeting which was held at the Mweya Safari Lodge in the Queen Elizabeth Park.

It was clear, the Americans said, that a hippo population explosion was in progress; this was obvious for all to see, since already there was a grossly inflated hippo population totalling some 14,000 animals in the Lakes Edward and George Region of Uganda alone. The cause, they believed, was the reduction in the previous steady poaching drain, the regular subsistence hunting which had probably been the main factor in controlling hippo

* Published by Collins, 1967.

numbers, until the extra protection provided by the creation of a national park in the area had tipped the balance in favour of the hippo – a theory which was supported by Bill Pridham who had known the area intimately for years. The result, they stated, was that the grass cover of the National Park was disappearing with alarming rapidity, and many species of grazing animals with it, while gulley and sheet erosion were spreading, like wildfire, where bare earth only remained; even the Safari Lodge itself was in danger of becoming an island in Lake Edward, they pointed out, for the grass had almost gone from the peninsula on which it stood; and where were the herds of kob, waterbuck and even elephant which used to graze around the Lodge?

What was their solution? The Trustees could let nature take its course if they wished, the Americans said. If they did this, inevitably there would be a hippo population crash eventually, through starvation, stress and disease; but in the meantime the Park and its other species could well be seriously damaged, possibly beyond normal recovery, while an outbreak of a deadly disease such as anthrax (endemic among hippo in the area) would become a threat to the lives of both humans and domestic stock. They therefore considered that the Uganda National Parks Trustees were faced with only two choices; action, involving artificial control, or inaction, with all its attendant serious and proven dangers. Both courses had their risks and unpalatable aspects, they warned, but whereas the effects of artificial control can be carefully watched, and the process halted at a moment's notice, man cannot halt the spread of disease amongst wild game or the destruction of vegetation by starving animals. Nature's inexorable law is 'the survival of the fittest'. But the victims of this grim law are not merely individual animals or plants; often whole populations of mixed species may disappear as a result of nature's enforcement of her ruthless dictum, and at the worst some species will become locally or entirely extinct. In their opinion therefore, the Americans declared, the Trustees should 'grasp the nettle' and reduce the hippo population by at least fifty per cent.

Many of the Trustees were shocked by this pronouncement made in the sacred precincts of a national park; to them it was like swearing in church. They had had drummed into them the dogma that all life in a national park is sacrosanct; that whatever happens man must never intervene for fear of disturbing 'the balance of nature', a glib phrase widely used by those who have little understanding of its true meaning, a phrase which, to the general public, conjures up a mental picture of 'Mother Nature' as a wise and kindly figure holding aloft a perfectly balanced pair of scales, like the historic symbol of justice that towers above the dome of London's Central Criminal Court, the famous Old Bailey. Although such a concept is entirely erroneous, the truth being that nature is in a continuous and remorseless state of flux, its so-called 'balance' being better likened to the slow, ponderous and uneven swing of an ill-balanced pendulum, the merciless process of evolution, it was still the idealistic image to which the majority of the Trustees faithfully clung.

The National Parks' Director, Rennie Bere, grimly declared that he believed that there would be a public outcry if the American scientists' recommendation should be implemented; that he considered that it would be the death-knell of the Park; that he would resign if it should be tried. I, on the other hand, agreed with the views of the scientists and disagreed with the fears of the Director. My opinions were based on the Game Department's many years of experience of properly organised game control and a number of the better qualified Trustees supported me. Faced with an embarrassing impasse, Ralph Dreschfield, as Chairman of Trustees, acted with the wisdom of Solomon. 'This is a situation without precedent,' he said, 'I suggest we circulate the details of our problem, together with the solution proposed by our American friends, to all the leading wildlife conservation organisations and experts throughout the world, seeking their candid opinion as to what we should do.'

The replies we received were enlightening. Almost without exception and with few qualifications they supported George Petrides's and Wendell Swank's proposal that we should shoot the excess hippo. Only a few national park organisations raised dissident voices, sticking rigidly to the tenet that no animal life in a national park must ever deliberately be destroyed. I admired their determination to stick to their principles although I firmly disagreed with their views.

In the event, at the request of the Director of Uganda National Parks, I arranged for the initial hippo reduction experiment to be carried out by Robin Fairrie, one of my Game Wardens, and his staff, under the overall supervision of Dr William Longhurst, Director of the Hopland Field Research Station in California, the Fulbright scientist who succeeded George Petrides and Wendell Swank. Himself a keen hunter, crack shot and brilliant bush pilot, Bill Longhurst saw to it that every possible scrap of scientific data and material was collected from the hippo carcases. The meat was sold cheaply to an eager, protein-hungry, local population, the proceeds going to help run the Park. Nothing was wasted and with suitable advance publicity there was not even a whisper of public criticism. The tourists continued to come; the animals in general remained as tame as ever; and the Director did not resign. Hippo cropping soon became a permanent feature of park management in Uganda and in two years the grass cover on the Mweya Peninsula, and in other seriously affected areas of the Queen Elizabeth National Park, was completely restored – and the kob, the waterbuck, the buffalo and the elephant returned with the grass.

The Uganda hippo cropping experiment was the first exercise in positive wildlife management in any national park on the African continent. Its importance lay not only in its success but because it dispelled a long cherished myth – the rigid belief, held by many sincere conservationists, that the only right and proper way to manage a game reserve or a national park in Africa is to guard it and its animals from any form of human interference.

Few tears need be shed for the hippo, whose sleepy, porcine appearance is misleading; quarrelsome and cantankerous in reality, it can be one of the most dangerous of African mammals, attacking both in the water and on dry land with little or no provocation. In Uganda human casualties from hippo were numerous and, at the end of the experiment, even the most soft-hearted of the doubting conservationists had to admit that, for this reason alone, seven thousand, well fed, contented hippo were preferable to double that number with their already short tempers honed to a razor's edge by overcrowding and starvation. Besides, no one wanted a national park much of which was rapidly becoming a vast hippo midden increasingly shunned by other species.

Thinking back and trying to summarise, I realise what a tremendous help to Uganda the American Fulbright scientists were. Men of wide experience and essentially practical, their quiet teachings, and their telling demonstrations of how wildlife management principles can best be applied, had an effect like the slow but steady opening of the flood gates of a dam. One by one the scales fell from official eyes and slowly but surely effective opposition to a number of my ideas and plans faded and disappeared. For instance, as early as 1952 I had drafted a completely new set of game laws designed to enable Uganda's wildlife resources properly to be managed, but my proposals had been blocked by influential persons in high places; sincere but misguided, until the arrival of the Fulbright scientists they had been prone to interpret any fresh wildlife management proposals as a sinister threat to the security and sanctity of Uganda's newly created national parks. In consequence, it was not until 1959 that my conservation legislation, the 'Game (Preservation and Control) Ordinance', was finally passed into law and a new era of practical wildlife management was born in Uganda.

The year 1959 was more than just the end of a decade in the wildlife world of East Africa; in each of the three territories it was noteworthy for widely differing reasons. In Uganda it was a triumphant year, for the passing of the new game laws removed the last obstacle to the launching of a variety of game management schemes that I had long had ready and waiting. In Kenya it was a sober year, for it saw the retirement from the post of Chief Game Warden of William Hale, the quiet man who had done much for that country's wildlife in a typically self-effacing way. For Tanganyika it was a year of tragedy. First, the headquarters of the Tanganyika Game Department was moved from its long established base at Tengeru, near Arusha, to the old slave port and capital city of Dar es Salaam; from the fine buildings of its traditional home in the invigorating, sunny climate of the great game country of the north, to a soulless row of dark, ramshackle offices in the steamy, enervating heat of the coast; it had been the protesting victim of what some call 'progress' – the introduction of a centralised government ministerial system designed to hasten Tanganyika's sprint towards independence. Then, with scarcely a pause, fate struck again; in September, while on safari at Morogoro, the Chief Game Warden, Gerry Swynnerton, died suddenly of heart failure at the early age of forty-nine. These two savage blows left the staff of the Tanganyika

Game guard carrying Nile perch at the Murchison Falls, heart of the National Park

The grave of Captain F.C. Selous, D.S.O.

Game Department leaderless and bewildered; for them it was a bitter end to a promising decade; for me it opened a door to fresh and challenging pastures.

*

The month of January, 1960, was a cross roads in my life. Within the space of a few days I received two vitally important letters; the first was the notification that I had been awarded a United Nations Fellowship in the field of Wildlife Management; the second was a formal letter from the Colonial Office offering me appointment, on transfer, to the vacant post of Chief Game Warden, Tanganyika. The trouble was that the two opportunities clashed.

The Fellowship – covering the costs of a four month tour of the USA and Canada, to study modern wildlife and fishery management techniques in the land which had made of them a true science – was a chance of a lifetime; it was also a signal honour for it was the first award of its kind ever made for the study of wildlife management. The Tanganyika offer was similarly a unique opportunity; it was not promotion for I was already a 'Chief Game Warden' and although it was a bigger job it carried no extra pay, but no one before had ever been Chief Game Warden of more than one African country and, with independence looming on the near horizon, such a chance to broaden my specialised experience might never occur again. On the other hand, did I really want to leave Uganda just when my cherished ideas and the labours of my colleagues and myself were really beginning to bear fruit? I had many sleepless nights before Bill Bell, a good friend of mine in the Secretariat and a valuable National Parks Trustee, helped me to make up my mind. 'It's all fixed,' he said. 'It has been officially agreed that you can, if you wish, postpone your Fellowship and take it from Tanganyika next year.'

I thought of the sprawling Mandated Territory of Tanganyika; four times the size of Uganda; as large as the whole of France, Germany and Belgium together; almost half as big again as Texas; probably the greatest game country in the world. I thought of the wide, rolling plains of the Serengeti – the famous, 5,000 square mile national park created by the Tanganyika Game Department – and of the awe-inspiring Ngorongoro

315

Crater, one of the wonders of the world. I thought particularly of the then little known Selous Game Reserve, 20,000 square miles of really wild country, steeped in history and now the largest remaining wildlife sanctuary on this earth; an area stretching from north of the River Rufiji way down through more than two hundred miles of harsh bushland, almost to the River Ruvuma and the border with Mozambique; an area named after the legendary hunter, naturalist and explorer, Captain Frederick Courteney Selous*, who lies buried in its heartland, the victim during the First World War of a German sniper. In fact, of all the specially preserved wildlife areas for which the Tanganyika Game Department was responsible at that time, the prospect of the Selous Game Reserve – wild, remote, unspoilt, and the home of a large proportion of Tanganyika's 350,000 elephants – attracted me most. Besides, I had been Chief Game Warden of Uganda for rising ten years and had I not always contended that this was quite long enough for any person to remain as head of the same department? Suddenly, my mind was made up.

* On the outbreak of World War One, although by then he was already sixty-three, Selous bullied the War Office until he was commissioned in the 25th Royal Fusiliers. It was not long before Selous was promoted to Captain and awarded the D.S.O, but on the morning of 4th January, 1917, this man of iron was killed, shot through the head as – in the face of withering machine-gun fire – he led his company in an attack on strongly defended German positions at Beho-Beho, Chogowali, near Kissaki; there his grave still lies, in the heart of the African bushland he loved so much.

PART FOUR

The Last Act

*

CHAPTER 16

The Grand Finale

WE reached Dar es Salaam on the 8th of August 1960; myself, my wife, my daughter, an old retainer, two Labrador dogs, a Ford pick-up truck, fifty-two crates of accumulated possessions, and a battered bicycle. It had been a long, tedious journey, first by steamer across Lake Victoria and then by train clattering slowly across the whole breadth of Tanganyika from west to east, but we had had a memorable send off from Entebbe, a mixture of sadness and hilarity.

Having bade a sad farewell to the animals in the 'Orphanage' – so well cared for by the Department's Armourer, Roy Miller – we had hurried down to Entebbe pier, vainly trying to block our ears against the despairing whistles of Toby, our favourite otter, and had scrambled aboard the good ship *Usoga*. Half an hour later we had sailed on a sea of alcohol and good wishes, but, for some strange reason, two of our best friends had been missing from the crowd and the finale had yet to come. As the *Usoga* had reached the mouth of the bay, two specks had appeared in the sky, circled and dived – Dick Newton, Game Warden Head-quarters, flying his own Auster, and Paul Elwell, Bill Pridham's brother-in-law, flying a De Havilland 'Rapide' belonging to

'Caspair', had proceeded first to 'buzz' the ship and then to 'bomb' it with roll after roll of coloured lavatory paper. Soon the sky had been criss-crossed with a slowly descending rainbow of fluttering, multi-hued streamers, until the masts, the bridge and the decks of the *Usoga* had taken on the appearance of a cross between a maypole and the day after a Mardi Gras carnival. Suddenly, the red, angry face of the Chief Engineer had appeared from the bowels of the ship. 'What the hell's goin' on up heir?' he had growled in a broad Glaswegian accent, fixing the Captain with a steely blue eye. The Captain had blushed scarlet; enthralled by the aircraft, he had completely forgotten to ring the 'all clear' on the engine room telegraph!

My first day in office in Dar es Salaam sobered me up with a jerk. As a result of the unpopular move from Tengeru the morale of many of the Game Department staff was low, ranging from resentment through depression to apathy, and I discovered, to my concern, that although Tanganyika's first, post-independence, three year development plan was in the course of preparation – and only a few days remained before the closing date for sub-missions – no proposals for any expansion and improvement of the Game Department had been prepared or submitted by the Ministry.

Perhaps even more significant, in the circumstances, was that, not long before, the Game Department had proposed that most of its finest game areas should be considered for re-classification as national parks, which, in turn, meant handing over full responsibility for their control to the National Parks Trustees.* At that time there was still only one national park in the whole of Tanganyika – the Serengeti, while the Game Department was responsible for all wildlife management matters throughout the remaining 357,000 square miles of the country, including over 70,000 square miles of game reserves and game controlled areas. Although the extension of the national park system was therefore obviously important and had my full support, the timing and circumstances of the Game Department's proposal were such that it bore the scent of abdication.

When I examined the Tanganyika Game Department's organisation, it immediately struck me that its main defect was

* The Chief Game Warden was an ex-officio member of the Tanganyika National Parks Board of Trustees.

321

that for a country the size of Tanganyika it was too centralised, with insufficient delegation of responsibility. It was also grossly under-staffed. The inevitable result was that some of the remoter game warden stations were very seldom visited by a senior officer and the game wardens concerned tended to regard themselves as 'forgotten men'. When the Department's headquarters was at Tengeru, one of the areas so affected was the Selous and south to the Ruvuma river. There, the late George Rushby, a famous game warden and elephant hunter, once had an arresting notice displayed in his dusty, ramshackle little office. In protest at what he felt was a particularly petty and officious headquarters reprimand for the manner in which he drafted official memoranda – on the infrequent occasions that he felt compelled to do so – he posted up in large letters, evenly spaced around the four walls of his office, a notice saying – 'IF YOU WANT TO BE . . . A GOOD ELEPHANT HUNTER . . . YOU MUST NOT FORGET . . . TO NUMBER YOUR PARAGRAPHS!'

George Rushby's action was amusing, but it was a bitter humour that revealed the dislike and mistrust of headquarters felt by many game wardens in the outposts at that time.

Burning the midnight oil, I managed, with the help of my patient deputy, Keith Thomas – an ex-paratroop gunner and qualified vet – to produce a comprehensive document; entitled 'A Review of the Wildlife Situation in Tanganyika in 1960', it contained detailed recommendations not only for doubling the size of the Game Department and its facilities over a period of three years, but also for reorganising the Department on the basis of four game 'regions' with their headquarters at Arusha, Morogoro, Tabora and Mwanza respectively. Each of these game regions was to be under the control of a 'Senior Game Warden' (a new rank) with considerable local autonomy but ultimately responsible to the Department's headquarters in Dar es Salaam.

In addition to the reorganisation and expansion, I included a plan for the creation of a training school, an establishment to produce men qualified to fill what I had long referred to as 'the missing middle ranks' – the massive rank gap between the game guards or game scouts on the lowest rungs of the ladder and the game rangers or game wardens at the top. This gap had always appeared to me to be a serious weakness in the organisation of all African game and national park departments. It was like having

Backbone of the service—a typical game scout of the Tanzania Game
Department, Joseph Petro of the Mbena tribe

an army with private soldiers at the bottom and commissioned officers at the summit, but no non-commissioned or warrant officer ranks in between – yet the latter have always been recognised as the 'backbone' of any disciplined force. In Uganda I had created the rank of 'Game Assistant'*, but suitable training had continued to be a problem and with independence and 'Africanisation' coming nearer, the advent of this new rank was not, in itself, enough. Hence the vital importance of starting a wildlife management training school, an institution which just did not exist anywhere in Africa at that period – and time was running out fast.

Most of my proposals for the development and reorganisation of the Game Department were approved with remarkably little pruning; and within eighteen months the four new game 'regions' were established with the four Senior Game Wardens appointed. The latter were Bill Dick, a steady and valuable old-timer, now retired; Bill Moore-Gilbert, ex-Indian Police and a particularly able game warden, later killed in an air crash; Peter Achard, one of the best, most dedicated and most likeable game wardens I have ever known, a man who worked himself literally almost to death and is now an invalid as a result; and Brian Nicholson, a tough, versatile, amusing character and outstanding hunter-naturalist who was a protégé of the great Ionides. Of the four only Brian Nicholson is still in Tanzania at the time I pen these words; he is in charge of a special wildlife development project for the area to which he and Ionides were drawn above all others – the Selous Game Reserve, a project the foundations of which he and I laid together. By then Keith Thomas had also left; a quiet, determined man, tough but courteous, he was missed by all.

Tony Mence, one of the Tanagnyika Game Department's most experienced game wardens, now became my deputy as Assistant Chief Game Warden. A strong, wiry, little Welshman with a degree in zoology, quiet, unflappable and a most efficient administrator, he was a tremendous asset. As an ex-Royal Marine Commando, with the swarthy good looks of a popular screen star, Tony had been pestered with requests for his services by the

* An ugly, clumsy title not of my choosing but one ordained by the Public Service Commission (P.S.C.) and the Establishments Division of the Secretariat, who, between them, decided such matters as titles and salary scales for the Civil Service.

American 'Paramount Film Corporation', a Hollywood company whose high-powered field unit, directed by Howard Hawkes, had descended like a whirlwind on the surprised inhabitants of Arusha late in 1960, to make on location, with the help and guidance of the Game Department, a dramatised game-catching film called *Hatari* – Swahili for 'danger'. Impressed by his appearance and his ability to ride a wild rhino with the carefree nonchalance of a bronco-busting cowboy, Paramount had wanted Tony to double for one of their highly paid stars – but neither his wife nor the Government had shared Paramount's enthusiasm for the idea.

Scarcely had the dust settled on the departure of the Hollywood galaxy – taking with it into orbit such celebrated personalities as John Wayne, Elsa Martinelli, Hardy Kruger and Red Buttons – than another event disturbed the lives of the bewildered, starstruck people of Arusha. This time it was a top level, international wildlife conference to be attended by leading scientists and wildlife conservation experts from all over the world.

The Arusha Conference* took place between the 5th and the 10th of September 1961. It became not only the launching pad of IUCN's 'African Special Project', but a turning point in the annals of African wildlife conservation. That Arusha was chosen as the venue, spotlighted its world-wide recognition as the centre of some of the richest and most varied wildlife areas in Africa.

The Conference was opened by Sir Richard Turnbull, K.C.M.G., the Governor of Tanganyika, a brilliant man with an infectious sense of humour, well known as a strong but humane administrator. During his opening speech he appealed for realism in the approach to wildlife conservation, quoting an earthy rhyme which he claimed to have learnt during his school days –

> East is East and West is West,
> Though this may not seem relevant,
> You all know how to milk a cow,
> But you can't muck about with an elephant.

---

* 'A Symposium on the Conservation of Nature and Natural Resources in Modern African States' sponsored by the Commission for Technical Co-operation in Africa South of the Sahara (C.C.T.A.) and the International Union for the Conservation of Nature and Natural Resources (I.U.C.N.), supported by the United Nations Educational Scientific and Cultural Organisation (U.N.E.S.C.O.) and the Food and Agricultural Organisation of

My own contribution to the Conference consisted of a paper on training entitled '*The Urgent Need for Formalised Training Facilities for Wildlife Management Personnel in the Africa of Today*'. I had written the paper, at the request of IUCN, after a discussion I had had with Monsieur Claude Cheysson, Secretary General of CCTA, in which he had expressed enthusiastic interest in the training school project that I had prepared for Tanganyika's 'Three Year Development Plan'. We had agreed that it would be an ideal regional project, if Kenya and Uganda approved, since the problem was clearly the same in all three territories. It was on this basis, therefore, that my paper was prepared, and what was probably the key paragraph in it was quoted by Sir Richard Turnbull in his address. 'May I read you,' he said, 'what Major Kinloch has to say in his paper – "It is clear that the time is long overdue for wildlife management to be regarded in Africa as a true branch of natural science comparable with forestry and agriculture. It has long been so treated on the North American continent; why not here? The foresters and agriculturists have always considered it necessary to have a high percentage of both scientifically and technically qualified officers; why should we continue to consider that those responsible for managing our wildlife resources are in a different category?" '

My detailed proposals and plans for a regional wildlife management training school, an establishment to be sited somewhere in the Arusha region, were finally discussed and universally approved by a special session of the Conference. At the same meeting, at the request of the delegates, Dr Jacques Verdier, Scientific Secretary of CSA, accepted the responsibility of approaching the American Agency for International Development (AID) for the financial assistance necessary for the project. Not unnaturally I was delighted at the outcome of my efforts, and when the 'Arusha Manifesto' – a clear declaration of the Tanganyika Government's unqualified support for wildlife conservation – was presented to the applauding delegates, my cup was full. It was a fitting conclusion to an outstandingly successful conference.

The Arusha Manifesto can justly be described as a beacon in

the United Nations (F.A.O.), and organised by I.U.C.N., C.S.A. (C.C.T.A.'s Scientific Council for Africa South of the Sahara), and the Tanganyika Game Department – representing the host government, Tanganyika.

the history of wildlife conservation in Africa. In this impressive declaration, Tanganyika, one of the finest game countries on the African Continent and the first of the British East and Central African Colonial Territories to become independent, came out solidly in support of wildlife conservation by making an official and most solemn pledge; drafted as a formal document of state, it was signed by the Prime Minister, Julius Nyerere, and two of his Ministers* responsible for wildlife. Kenya was swift to follow this example, and the pessimists – the dismal prophets of doom who had forecast the dissolution of the national parks and the game reserves and the massacre of the great herds of game, immediately the countries of East Africa became ruled by elected African governments – were forced to eat their words. When the time came the contrary was the case, the truth being that there was greater support, both moral and material, for wildlife conservation by the countries of East Africa *after* they became independent than was ever the case before. I had always been one of the optimists, but when, at the end of September 1961, Elizabeth and I flew to America on my United Nations Fellowship, things seemed to be going much better than even I had dared to hope.

*

For four glorious but hectic months Elizabeth and I toured Canada and the USA, thrilled by the wonders of those two great countries and overwhelmed by the never failing courtesy and warm hospitality of their vital peoples. On our return journey London seemed suddenly to have shrunk, like a gracious old lady who is feeling her age; and when we reached Dar es Salaam at the end of January, 1962, it took us some time to come down to earth.

*

During my absence from East Africa there had been important developments and significant changes. To begin with it was clear that Tanganyika was well set on the shortest possible road to becoming a republic. To further this end Julius Nyerere had resigned from the post of Prime Minister and had withdrawn,

* Chief Abdulla Fundikira, hereditary Paramount Chief of the Wanyamwezi and El Haj Tewa Saidi Tewa.

327

Arusha Conference 1961, four wildlife pioneers:
LEFT TO RIGHT: *Dr Hugh Lamprey,* Biologist, Tanzania Game
Department and first Principal, College of African Wildlife
Management, *Tony Mence,* Assistant Chief Game Warden,
Tanzania, later the second Principal of the College, *John Millard,*
Chairman, Executive Committee of the East African Wildlife
Society, *Major Bruce Kinloch,* Chief Game Warden, Tanzania and
founder of the College of African Wildlife Management

Arusha Conference 1961:
LEFT: *Professor Bernhard Grzimek,* Director of Frankfurt Zoo and
leading champion of East African Wildlife, RIGHT: *El Haj Tewa
Saidi Tewa,* Minister of Lands, Forests and Wildlife, Tanzania

ARUSHA MANIFESTO

The survival of our wildlife is a matter of grave concern to all of us in Africa. These wild creatures amid the wild places they inhabit are not only important as a source of wonder and inspiration but are an integral part of our natural resources and of our future livelihood and well-being.

In accepting the trusteeship of our wildlife we solemnly declare that we will do everything in our power to make sure that our children's grand-children will be able to enjoy this rich and precious inheritance.

The conservation of wildlife and wild places calls for specialist knowledge, trained manpower and money and we look to other nations to co-operate in this important task - the success or failure of which not only affects the Continent of Africa but the rest of the world as well.

Julius K. Nyerere.

7:9:61.

7. 9. 61

The 'Arusha Manifesto'—a historic document

like John the Baptist, into the wilderness. Although he did not say so publicly at the time, it was immediately obvious that his object in going into the highways and by-ways was to round up political strays; to rally the faithful of the Tanganyika African National Union – TANU, the ruling political party – behind him; and to return to power as the first, popularly elected President of the Republic of Tanganyika. In the interim, into Nyerere's shoes as Prime Minister had stepped a close friend and political ally of his, a tiny, bouncy, little man by the name of Rashidi Kawawa. For an ironic and little-known reason, this latter single factor was soon to have a profound effect on developments in the wildlife field.

Shortly after my return to Dar es Salaam, an advertisement appeared in the *Government Gazette* and the East African press calling for applications for vacancies in the post of Game Warden in the Tanganyika Game Department. The newly independent Tanganyika Government had agreed that we should continue to recruit suitably qualified Europeans, on short term contracts, until young Africans had been properly trained to take their places, it being clearly understood and accepted by all concerned that this would inevitably be a slow process. There were, at that time, a handful of academically qualified and physically suitable young Africans whom we were sending on four-year courses, at selected American universities, to study for degrees in Wildlife Management, while my training school project for the 'missing middle ranks' was still in the early stages of protracted financial negotiations with American AID. Into this carefully conceived dream world there dropped a bombshell which threatened to shatter my most cherished plans; taking the form of a letter to my Minister, Tewa Saidi Tewa, from the Prime Minister, Rashidi Kawawa, the contents of which I am unlikely ever to forget, it arrived on my desk with a request for my comments.

The text of the missive is graven on my mind to this day. 'Dear Minister,' it said. 'I have noted with great interest the advertisement for game warden vacancies. With my personal knowledge of this type of work, I consider that it is just the sort of post for young Africans with their experience of the bush. You are aware of the need to accelerate the Africanisation of posts in Government service, a policy which TANU has promised to the electorate. I consider, therefore, that we could select suitable

Standard 8* schoolboys, place them under a game warden, or possibly a senior game scout, for a year and then let them take over the game warden posts in the Game Department. I would appreciate your comments.' The signature revealed the letter's origins; it did not reveal the crucial fact, known to few people, that Rashidi Kawawa was a son of Mfaumi Ali, one of the finest senior game scouts who had ever served in the Tanganyika Game Department! Had this not been the case it is doubtful whether Rashidi Kawawa would even have noticed the advertisement; it is certain he would not have been moved to comment on it.

Mfaumi Ali, a grand old man and fine hunter who had worked for both Ionides and Brian Nicholson, had been killed while setting a trap-gun for a man-eating lion. If the accident had not occurred *after* Rashidi Kawawa had been conceived the history of the Game Department might have taken a different course. Alternatively, if the game warden vacancy advertisement had appeared *before* Julius Nyerere vacated the post of Prime Minister, it is also unlikely that Rashidi Kawawa would have been in a position to take formal notice of it and to act accordingly. As it was, the timing and circumstances were such that the hand of fate was clearly apparent. Overnight the son of a senior game scout had become the most powerful man in the country; a man whose brother, Saidi Kawawa, was still only a senior game scout, had suddenly been made Prime Minister of Tanganyika; as such his opinions and wishes could not lightly be brushed aside.

Without waiting a moment, I sat down and drafted a closely reasoned letter to my Minister, carefully listing the serious drawbacks and dangers of the Prime Minister's proposal and citing the horrors of the Congo as a sobering example of what can happen when discipline goes, training is forgotten, and armed men go on an extended rampage. I stressed that there were over six hundred, tough, well armed game scouts in the Tanganyika Game Department; a force which could terrorise the countryside if they got out of control. And what of the effect on Tanganyika's increasingly valuable tourism, an industry which was almost entirely dependent on proper care and management of the country's wildlife?

* Standard 8 was four grades *below* School Certificate level (which became 'O' levels) which was Standard 12.

A month later I received my Minister's reply. It consisted of four words at which I stared in growing disbelief. 'The Prime Minister insists,' they said; no more, no less, just that!

For a few moments I was stunned. 'So much for the Arusha Manifesto,' I thought to myself bitterly. Then suddenly I realised that I had been naive to expect the Prime Minister to retract his proposal for this could have been regarded in political circles as loss of face. Given time, and provided I played my cards with care, the Prime Minister's instruction might be suitably modified, but to achieve this I would have to provide some convincing alternative – and fast. If not, then the Game Department, with its proud traditions, would soon be in real trouble; and the National Parks would not be far behind. My training school project, the real answer to the problem, was still in the early stages of protracted negotiations with AID; it would be months before even the money might be voted, let alone building started and staff recruited. Something else had to be thought of in a hurry to fill the gap.

My first idea was to press again for the amalgamation of the Game Department and National Parks to form a unified wildlife service, a policy I had always strongly and openly advocated ever since my earliest days in Uganda. This move would not only have cut overheads by having one wildlife department headquarters instead of two, but would have made fuller use of available staff, thus enabling us to stall on further recruitment to senior posts until proper training facilities were ready and operating. Ironically, the motives behind my outspoken opinions had frequently been misrepresented by others as a personal bid for power. If amalgamation was to be achieved in a hurry, therefore, there was only one possible proposal I could make.

I went to see John Owen, Director of Tanganyika National Parks, whom I knew to be firmly opposed to any policy which might infringe on the complete independence of national parks. After explaining the problem in detail and emphasising the threat it posed to wildlife conservation in general, not merely to the Game Department, I presented my proposition. 'John,' I said, 'I suggest the time's come for the National Parks and the Game Department to get together and form a strong, unified "Wildlife Service"; and in case it'll persuade you and convince you that I'm being entirely sincere, I want to say that if you agree to this amalgamation I'll be willing to step down in your favour. You can take over the combined department. I'll just pull out.'

John Owen stared at me in surprise. I think he realised what a tremendous effort it had been for me to make the offer to step down, for there is scarcely a national park in the length and breadth of Africa that did not start life as a game reserve, or similar protected area, conceived and developed by the game department concerned, before being handed over to a newly created national parks organisation; and invariably the latter owe their existence to having been initiated by one of the old, traditional game departments. This was certainly the pattern in both Tanganyika and Uganda, where the national parks organisations had been granted special status and given only the choicest of the game departments' preserved wildlife areas to look after. When I went to Tanganyika in 1960, the Serengeti was the only national park; by the time I left, four and a half years later, there were five national parks*, all of which the Game Department had been largely instrumental in converting to national park status. In the circumstances, therefore, my offer to hand over control of the remainder of the Game Department's widespread responsibilities was a bitter and indigestible pill for me to swallow.

For a few moments John Owen was silent, thinking hard. Then he replied. 'I appreciate your offer very much, Bruce,' he said. 'But I feel I must refuse. I don't think it would benefit the National Parks to become involved with all the extensive and complicated wildlife management problems with which the Game Department has to deal throughout Tanganyika. The National Parks have their own problems, but at least they are clear-cut and concentrated and I think it's best to keep them that way.' Somehow I felt relieved. It would have been a sad day if the characteristic paratroop-red berets and glistening, brass, buffalo head badges of the Tanganyika Game Department were to disappear from the scene. However, there was still one other person to whom I felt I should present a similar proposal – Robert Sangster, Chief Conservator of Forests in Tanganyika. Robert was an ex-officio Trustee of the Tanganyika National Parks and,

* Serengeti, Lake Manyara, Ngurdoto Crater (now Arusha National Park), Ruaha (part of the great Rungwa Game Reserve) and Mikumi National Parks, all previously game reserves or game controlled areas developed and managed by the Game Department.

like many professional foresters, keenly interested in wildlife. Furthermore, in certain other parts of the world it is still the government forestry department which is responsible for wildlife conservation. Would an amalgamation of the Tanganyika Forestry and Game Departments be a possible answer? After all, we were already in the same Ministry. When I put the suggestion to him, Robert Sangster also thought hard about the idea before politely turning it down. His reasons were similar to John Owen's. He had enough problems on his plate already, he said regretfully.

The most immediate possible solutions having been tried and failed, there appeared to me to be only one answer left. I had to get a suitable 'crash' training programme under way as quickly as possible. This meant staff, equipment, funds and suitable buildings for a permanent base.

Wasting no time, I went straight to the Permanent Secretary of my Ministry and obtained authority to side-track the minimum necessary requirements from the projects already approved in the Game Department's three-year development plan. Then I sent an urgent circular letter to all Provincial Commissioners in Tanganyika, asking if they could offer me any empty buildings suitable for a training project, preferably in the Northern Province. One by one the answers trickled in, each more depressing than the last, and by the time I flew to Nairobi, at the end of March 1962, for urgent discussions on 'Africanisation' training problems with Dr Jacques Verdier and the Chief Game Wardens of Kenya and Uganda, it appeared that there were no suitable buildings available anywhere. The only bright spot in this otherwise depressing period, was the advent in the Kinloch menage of a young banded mongoose; 'Pipa', as he was called, soon proved to be a strong character who quickly dominated the household and his colourful life story was eventually published in my first book.*

The first sign that my luck was changing came at Arusha, on my return trip. On landing there I was met by Bill Dick, Senior Game Warden for the Northern Game Region, and he and I paid a courtesy call on the Acting Provincial Commissioner of the Northern Province, Tony Golding. With little hope I asked Tony

* *Sauce for the Mongoose* by Bruce Kinloch, first published by the Harvill Press, London 1964. New edition by Ashford Press Publishing 1988.

334

Golding again about possible buildings for my training project. He shook his head regretfully, but when I rose to leave he had a sudden thought. 'I've just remembered,' he said. 'There are some old school buildings on the lower slopes of Kilimanjaro in an area called Mweka, a few miles from Moshi. They were built by German farmers in the area, between the wars, as a school for their children. During the last war they were used as a nurses' training school, but they've been empty for some time and I believe they're now in need of a fair amount of repair. I don't suppose they would be of much use for your purpose, but you might like to inspect them.'

'I can't afford to pass up any chances,' I replied. 'Bill Dick and I'll drive down there straight away and have a look.'

Late that afternoon, Bill Dick's old Land-Rover clattered up the rough, winding road leading from Moshi to Mweka. Climbing steadily through mile after mile of coffee plantations of the Chagga country, we eventually passed between the old, stone pillars of what had once been an impressive entrance gate, on to a long-neglected drive. On our left was a small but adequate playing field, over which a number of scrawny chickens were fossicking industriously. On our right was a group of old but imposing and obviously very solid stone buildings; shabby they might be, with grimy stone-work, blistered paint and here and there a broken window, but it was the threadbare shabbiness of a well-made suit which has seen hard and worthy use – worn but not worn out. As we stared our excitement grew. Then, suddenly, the clouds behind the school rolled back like a curtain drawn by an unseen hand, and through the last filmy wisps, high in the sky, there thrust a great, towering, white-capped dome, pink-tinged and glistening in the dying rays of the evening sun – it was the snow-capped peak of Kibo; what the Masai call *Oldonyo Oibor*, 'the White Mountain', the tallest peak of Kilimanjaro; at nearly 20,000 feet, the highest mountain in Africa.

Slowly I turned to Bill Dick. 'We've found it at last, Bill,' I said quietly. 'This is the end of the search.'

The next day I was in Dar es Salaam and went straight to see the powers that be. 'The school is ideal for our purpose,' I said. 'Not only are the buildings suitable, although they need some repair, but the site itself could hardly be better. It's the centre of, or close to a number of major game areas of varying ecology, all

College of African Wildlife Management at Mweka near Moshi, Tanzania, with Kilimanjaro's Kibo Peak in the background

of which would be essential for field demonstrations and practical training. May we have it please?'

The man behind the desk smiled. 'Certainly!' he replied. I rocked back on my heels. He had not even bothered to glance at his files!

As soon as I could I returned to have a closer look at the school. Elizabeth accompanied me and we were joined by Oscar Charlton, the Game Warden from Tanga. Armed with chalk, tape-measures, pencils and paper, the three of us crawled about, on hands and knees, among the accumulated dust and cobwebs of years, planning and marking out such refinements as cubicles in place of former dormitories and staff quarters where none had ever existed. By the time we had finished, dirty and dishevelled, I reckoned that, with the liberal use of hardboard partitions, we could just about manage to adapt the existing buildings sufficiently to meet our major needs. The next problems to solve were money for basic running expenses, staff and equipment. I could drain off some of the Game Department's always slender resources, but very little without crippling it. Whom could I approach for financial help?

Fortunately, I did not have to think very hard. Two old friends immediately sprang to mind – Professor Bernhard Grzimek, Director of the Frankfurt Zoological Society; and Judge Russell Train, at that time a judge of the United States Tax Court by profession, but a dedicated hunter-conservationist by interest and inclination. Bernhard Grzimek, internationally known conservationist, author, television personality and hard fighting, philanthropic champion of wildlife in Africa, needs little introduction. Russell Train, on the other hand, despite his subsequent meteoric rise to power and fame in the wildlife conservation world,* was a comparative newcomer to such circles at that time. However, young and dynamic he had just been instrumental in forming the 'African Wildlife Leadership Foundation' – of which he was President – a body dedicated to the important cause of educating young Africans to appreciate and care for their great wildlife heritage, a body whose members I had been asked to

* In 1965 he became President of the Conservation Foundation; in 1968, Under Secretary for the Interior; and in January 1970, he was appointed Chairman of the newly formed, United States 'Council on Environmental Quality'.

address, only the year before, at a luncheon they had given in my honour in Washington, DC. I was soon to discover that my words, mainly on the urgent need for proper training, had not fallen on deaf ears.

I wrote to both Bernhard Grzimek and Russell Train, explaining the crisis in detail and saying that I needed £10,000 urgently, to get the training school launched and to keep it going until the hoped for American AID project materialised. In both cases their response was immediate. Bernhard Grzimek wrote from Germany to say that the Frankfurt Zoological Society had made an initial donation to the value of £2,000 and more would follow. Russell Train cabled from Washington saying that the 'African Wildlife Leadership Foundation' was sending $25,000 and to whom should it be paid?

To whom *should* the money be paid? This was a poser. If I allowed it to be swallowed up in the ever hungry maw of the Tanganyika Treasury, its regurgitation and effective use would be gagged by a tangled mass of red tape and civil service regulations. Such a prospect was so ominous that I immediately suppressed my never very active civil servant's conscience and sought a more workable alternative. Happily, in cases like this I had a well established standby in the East African Wildlife Society, that immensely valuable and effective organisation conceived and created in 1956 by the efforts of Noel Simon, one of those truly dedicated individuals who has done so much for wildlife conservation behind the scenes. The Society was always willing to act as banker for any worthy wildlife conservation project financed from private sources, and on this occasion again it readily came to my aid.

Later, I rode rough-shod through further civil service principles by authorising the opening of a private bank account in Moshi, in the name of the training school. In so doing I laid myself open to severe official censure – or worse – but there was really no alternative since somehow the school had to be enabled to pay its day-to-day expenses during the critical construction period. It was a risk I just had to take.

With buildings and basic running expenses assured, the next problem to be settled was the question of staff and particularly the instructional staff, for it was on the latter that the success or failure of the whole project would ultimately depend. Here I was fortunate in having several game wardens who were not only suitably qualified but – equally important – keen to try their hand at training. First I needed a good administrator, a game warden who could not only organise and supervise the day-to-day management of the school and its subordinate staff, but also instruct as well. For this post I chose David Anstey. As a general instructor in a wide variety of subjects from basic zoology to anti-poaching measures, I picked Gilbert Child, a versatile East African born game warden with a degree in zoology. Finally, I was left with the problem of selecting the key man – the head of the establishment.

I jotted down the attributes for which I was looking in the person to be selected as 'Principal' of my wildlife training school. The ideal incumbent had to be a firm disciplinarian but diplomatic, for it was important that he should both inspire confidence and command respect. He had to be a good organiser and an able administrator. His approach had to be scientific but strictly practical at the same time. He had to be both a scholar and an athlete, a good teacher, physically tough, ingenious, adaptable, and a good mixer with people of all races. Above all he had to have a more than normal interest in wildlife and considerable practical experience of the many thorny problems associated with its management. Where could I find such a paragon? There was one person in the Tanganyika Game Department who went a long way towards filling the bill. His name was Hugh Lamprey, he was thirty-four, and he was the Game Department's Biologist.

Not only had Hugh Lamprey an outstanding academic record, but he had served for two years as a gunner subaltern in Palestine and Egypt – valuable discipline training – before going to university. While an undergraduate at Oxford he had been a member of three university expeditions, including one to the Tehri-Garhwal region of the Central Himalayas in 1952, when he had taken part in the first ascent of the 21,560 foot Mount Gangotri III. He had graduated in 1952 with 2nd Class Honours in Zoology, and had then joined the Tanganyika Game Department as its one and only Research Biologist. From that time on he had been employed on a variety of tasks – including that of acting as a game warden – until finally he had managed to hide himself away in the Tarangire Game Reserve to complete his research work for a doctorate! Before he had finished his research he had learnt to fly, as a valuable aid to his work, and by the time I reached the stage of looking for a head for my wildlife management training school, Hugh had become not only a most competent pilot, but was back at Oxford in the final process of obtaining his degree as a Doctor of Philosophy.

I now had two problems: would Hugh Lamprey accept the offer of the post of Principal; and would the British Government be persuaded to pay the salaries of the school instructors if the officers concerned were seconded to the job? The people who could provide the answers were Hugh Lamprey and the Department of Technical Co-operation*, the successor to the old Colonial Office. Both were in England. Letter writing on the issue would be slow, tedious and very liable to lead to misunderstandings. Somehow I had to find the means to fly home and talk to those concerned. But where could I raise the money for my return air-fare to London? Suddenly I had an idea. I picked up my telephone and asked for a Nairobi number.

On the 11th of September 1962, I found myself somewhere high over north Africa, the focus of row upon row of frankly curious brown eyes set in a sea of dark, bewhiskered faces. I felt like Gulliver in Lilliput for most of my travelling companions were under two feet tall. I was aboard the weekly British United Airways 'animal freighter' aircraft flying between Nairobi and London, travelling officially as a 'monkey attendant'. The firms exporting the vervet monkeys – animals needed for such vital medical research purposes as the production of poliomyelitis vaccine – were required to provide one person to assist the steward on these journeys; and, through the courtesy and kindly help of Allan Lambert, Freight Manager of BUA, it had been arranged that, on this particular occasion, the Chief Game Warden of Tanganyika would travel aboard, not only to help the steward but also to experience and see for himself the conditions under which the monkeys were being transported. There had been some very vocal but often misguided public criticism of the export of monkeys for medical purposes at that time, and in particular of the handling and shipping arrangements involved in such export, so this gave me a chance to kill two birds with one stone –

* Later re-named the Ministry of Overseas Development (O.D.M.) and now the Overseas Development Administration (O.D.A.).

see officially how the monkeys fared; and get a free ride to London and back at the same time!

When I had boarded the aircraft at Nairobi I had been met by a cheerful cockney steward. Having greeted me like a long lost brother, he had led me courteously betweem closely packed rows of cages to a cramped canvas seat at the rear of the aircraft. 'Mind your 'ead on the corner of that there parrot's cage, sir,' he had said, malevolently eyeing a lemon-crested cockatoo and sucking a blood-stained thumb. 'It's sharp and 'is beak's a bloody sight sharper! – Think you'll be all right there, sir? Not exactly four star comfort, but I'll bring you come coffee and sandwiches once we're airborne.' So saying he had disappeared like a wraith up the narrow, murky alley-way leading to the bows of the aircraft, leaving me the centre of attention of several hundred excited and uninhibited primates, a few curious birds, several rather sad and bewildered looking dogs, and a couple of very bored cats.

By the time we were over the Sudan I had discovered that my responsibilities were not arduous. My chief duty appeared to be to keep out of the way. At the same time, I had to ensure that my fellow passengers were kept well supplied with water, and that the lashings which held the cages remained secure. At Khartoum and Malta I was let out for a run, escorted by a large and friendly Alsatian who seemed to enjoy the exercise as much as I did. When I arrived in London and reported favourably to the RSPCA on the care of animals in transit, I was feeling remarkably perky.

Hugh Lamprey was at the airport to meet me. The warmth of manner, the old world courtesy, the quiet confidence which, in turn, inspired confidence – all were there. I had written ahead to warn him that there was an urgent and important matter which I wanted to discuss, but I had thought it wiser not to mention what it was. Travelling in Hugh's car to London I explained the situation in detail. Later, over a pint of draught beer in one of my favourite pubs – The Red Lion tucked away in that ancient, narrow alley called Crown Passage, between St James's and Pall Mall – I put the final proposition to him. 'Hugh,' I said, 'I know you're a research man and that's where your heart really lies. But, to my mind, to get this training school running smoothly and on the right lines is the most urgent and important wildlife task in Africa today. I think you're the ideal person for the job.

Will you take it on? Wait – think hard before you answer. I must have a "willing horse", someone who is really keen on the idea, not just a friend who is tackling it from a sense of duty.'

For a few moments Hugh was silent, staring into his tankard; then he looked up and smiled. 'I'll be glad to take it on, Bruce,' he said.

The next day I called at the Department of Technical Co-operation, whose Permanent Secretary was my old friend and ally from Uganda days, Sir Andrew Cohen. I had not seen him for seven years, but, despite his tour of duty in the difficult and testing diplomatic post of Britain's Permanent Representative to the United Nations, I could detect little change. The same youthful energy, the same rather mirthless, almost wolf-like smile, both were still there. He greeted me warmly. 'What can I do for you, Bruce,' he asked. I told him the whole sad story. By this time I knew it off by heart, like the glib patter of a practised travelling salesman. What I was hoping, I said, was that the British Government would agree to meet the cost of the Principal and a Bursar who would also double as an instructor. Sir Andrew thought for a moment. 'How long are you in London for?' he asked eventually. 'About ten days,' I replied. 'I'm waiting for the return freighter flight.' 'Come and see me at the end of the week,' he said. 'I'll give you an answer then.'

Sir Andrew was as good as his word and I climbed aboard the return BUA freighter with a light heart. Not only had Hugh Lamprey's reaction cheered me, but my spirits were buoyed up by the knowledge that the Department of Technical Co-operation had agreed to meet the costs of the school's Principal and Bursar for a period of three years in the first instance.

Shortly after I returned to Dar es Salaam, I was able to give the school project the final push that really started it moving. Like a snowball it gathered size and momentum as it rolled and, by December 1962, the necessary building modifications were well advanced, repairs and renovations were in hand. David Anstey was firmly installed in what had been the matron's cottage at the school – with a nucleus of subordinate staff such as drivers, game guards and a clerk – and Hugh Lamprey and Gil Child had moved into houses in Moshi. Between us we had also worked out a provisional syllabus for a two-year course, a syllabus for which I had laid down the guide lines. It had to have a simple but sound scientific basis, and it had to cover all facets of a game warden's many-sided duties – from elephant control to office administration; from anti-poaching measures to the supervision of tourists and the safari hunting industry; from map reading to vehicle maintenance; from road building to court work and prosecuting under the game laws; from game population assessment to the capture, marking and translocation of animals; from the care and use of firearms to the collection and preparation of scientific specimens; and so on and so forth. Above all, I stressed, at least fifty and preferably seventy-five per cent of the training had to be practical work in the field; the rest could be lectures, demonstrations and instruction in the class room.

In January 1963 a climax was reached, for during that month a high level meeting was held in Moshi to make formal recommendations on the establishment of the training school. It was attended by the Chief Game Wardens and Directors of National Parks of Kenya, Uganda and Tanganyika; representatives from the East African Common Services Organisation and from the relevant ministries in the three East African countries; and also a Senior Game Warden from Northern Rhodesia. The Chairman was Dr A. C. Evans, who, by then, had succeeded Dr Jacques Verdier as Scientific Secretary of CCTA/CSA.

The proceedings were opened by the Regional Commissioner of Tanganyika's Northern Region, who said, 'This is a very special occasion. This meeting marks the beginning of the last phase of a project which is not only unique, but of far reaching importance. I refer to the creation in Africa of an institution to train Africans in the modern techniques of conserving wild animals as a natural resource.' . . . 'With these few words,' he concluded, after reviewing how the school had come to pass and thanking those benefactors who had made it possible, 'I wish you success in your deliberations, the results of which will be of long term importance to the economy of Africa.'

The Moshi meeting set the final, official seal on the training project, giving the school the security and respectability of formal recognition. A number of important practical administrative matters were thrashed out and decided, including the formation of a governing body, the details of courses, and the charges to be levied per student. A course fee of £400 per student per year, to be paid by the governments concerned, to provide the basis of the funds required for recurrent expenditure, was agreed as fair and reasonable, since the capital costs involved were already covered by substantial grants of both money and equipment received or promised from outside sources.

By the time the Moshi meeting was held, in addition to the actual school buildings and staff provided by the Tanganyika Government, the money sent by Russell Train's African Wildlife Leadership Foundation (later followed up by a further $16,000 for a laboratory) and by Bernhard Grzimek on behalf of the Frankfurt Zooloigcal Society, as well as the aid promised by the British Department of Technical Co-operation, further promises of firm assistance had been received from abroad. These included $50,000 from American AID (later increased to $95,000), while the West German Government made a most valuable contribution of Mercedes 'Unimog' four-wheel drive lorries and essential safari equipment and clothing, as well as the services of an additional instructor. To my delight the latter was Anno Hecker, a qualified German forester-game warden who had not only served with the Tanganyika Tsetse Control Department for several years, but had also been one of my honorary game wardens; and due to the television broadcast appeals of the indefatigable Professor Grzimek, the generous public of West Germany donated £4,500 towards the cost of a house for Anno Hecker. Later still the Ford Foundation offered $30,000 for recurrent expenditure and the Rockefeller Brothers Fund provided $36,000 for scholarships. In fact, in the course of a few months, an enterprise based on little more than inspiration, faith and hope, had become a well endowed project which had aroused widespread international interest and support.

The concluding actions of the Moshi meeting were to approve the draft syllabus which we had drawn up – with emphasis on the nearby Mkomazi Game Reserve as the main working area for basic field training – and to agree that the first, two year course would commence in June 1963. Finally, the meeting formally decided that the training school should be given the title of 'College of African Wildlife Management', with the authority to grant a Diploma of Wildlife Management to all students successfully completing the senior, two year course designed to produce men capable of filling game warden posts, and a Certificate of Wildlife Management in respect of the shorter, one year, middle-grade courses for game assistant ranks, which were planned for the future.

The first course started on the 24th of June 1963. The old buildings shone from their recent face lift and from the flagstaff proudly floated the college flag, emblazoned on it the symbol of a lion encircled with the words 'COLLEGE OF AFRICAN WILDLIFE – WE HOLD IT IN TRUST.' As if to mark the occasion the normal cloud blanket had lifted from Kilimanjaro, and the gleaming, sun-lit face of Kibo, the ice and snow of its glaciers sparkling like a birthday cake, looked down happily on the scene. And a novel scene it was, for parading on the sports field, awkward in their new uniforms, were twenty-three cadet wardens; one Arab the rest Africans; men of varying ages and education hailing from three different countries and five different organisations: the Game Departments of Tanganyika – ten, Kenya – seven, Uganda – three; the National Parks of Tanganyika – two, Uganda – one. Later they were joined by one African from the Forest Department of Nyasaland and a second from the Forest Department of the Cameroon Republic, making them twenty-five in all, from five different countries. They were the first non-Europeans to be trained as game wardens in Africa. Some were young, just out of school; others were men of long service. For the inexperienced a School Certificate pass had been the minimum educational qualification accepted for selection. In all cases a tough physical test had had to be passed. The oldest was one of the first two game assistants I appointed in Uganda, an ex-warrant officer of the King's African Rifles, an Acholi by the name of Daniel Otim. Our pleasure at meeting again was mutual.

From that day on, although my interest in it remained as keen as ever, my official connections with the management of the College virtually disappeared. In due course, the Tanganyika Government passed a special ordinance to establish the legal status of the College, which was followed by the formal appointment of its governing body. The latter included the names of a variety of persons; some venerable; a number resident overseas; a few who had been associated in some way with the creation of the College. My own name was not on the list!

Some years later still, after the College had been included in the United Nations Development Prorgamme, I listened to a

Students at the College of African Wildlife Management

The author congratulating one of the first graduates

United Nations official holding forth on the subject. To my surprise his version of how the College of African Wildlife Management came into being was a new one. It reminded me of the occasion when the State Opening of the British Parliament was first televised. To millions of viewers Her Majesty the Queen was shown reading the 'speech from the throne' – the miscellany of pious platitudes and grandiose promises which every government produces, at this time. One little girl – so I was told – after watching enthralled, turned excitedly to her father and said, 'Look Daddy, the Queen's reading a fairy story!'

The United Nations man was charming; it was not his fault that he had been fed only half the true facts. And so I told him the story I have repeated here.

January 1964 – six months after the start of the first Mweka course – was a dark month in the annals of East Africa. The horrors of the Zanzibar revolution, when the streets of that old Arab city ran red with blood, were followed by the army mutinies in Tanganyika, Kenya and Uganda. Like the shock waves of an earthquake the repercussions of the troubles rolled far and wide across the face of the land. The staff of the Game and National Park Departments of East Africa stood firm; they held their old, traditional loyalties and so, I was relieved to find, did the students at the College of African Wildlife Management. But the ominous thunder of revolution revealed the writing on the wall; the days of the European game warden in Black Africa are numbered, it said. The College at Mweka had been started only just in time.

In the quiet after the storm, the Tanganyika Government issued a courteous but definite edict. The process of Africanisation of the Civil Service must be accelerated, particularly in the higher posts. I just had time to complete the christening of my final brain-child – The Tanganyika Wildlife Development Company* – a government owned tourist safari company, designed to operate carefully controlled wilderness safaris in the 20,000 square miles of the Selous Game Reserve, under the watchful eye of Brian Nicholson. Then I packed my bags and, in August 1964, Elizabeth

* Now called Tanzania Wildlife Safaris, an idea which originated in Uganda with Uganda Wildlife Development Ltd., started by John Blower and Ernest Juer.

and I set out on our last, nostalgic tour of our old happy hunting grounds.

Late in September, we visited Mweka. The students were intelligent, interested and desperately keen; they were the game wardens of the very near future, and how my beloved elephants would fare under their control, only time would tell. As I watched the students being instructed, I thought of the old time game rangers and wardens they would be replacing. In my pocket was an almost visionary poem written while I was still in Uganda. Its author was T. R. H. Owen, C.B.E., a one time Governor of the Bahr el Ghazal Province of the Southern Sudan, a brilliant, human and generous man with a gift for writing what he humbly called 'doggerel', witty verse with which he was wont to lampoon any truly farcical situation. On his retirement from the Sudan, reluctant to leave Africa he had elected to fill a comparatively humble post as a 're-tread' – as he dryly called himself – in the headquarters of the Uganda Game and Fisheries Department. At one period, when we were receiving a spate of official requests, from exalted and influential overseas scientists, for obscure and complicated scientific specimens, requests blandly passed on by the Secretariat but which drove our game rangers and wardens to distraction, Richard Owen had come to our rescue and restored our sense of humour, with a delightful, but sadly prophetic poem which he dubbed 'The Triumph of Science'.

I sat down in the sunshine, on the steps of the College of African Wildlife Management and studied the poem again, for the hundredth time, to refresh my memory. As always it brought a smile to my face as I read –

Sam Scroggins was a naturalist and hunter from the nursery;
His maths were poor; his Latin weak; his grammar-studies cursory.
At three he was a graduate of field and forest lore,
And broke his father's windows with a catapult at four;
Could ride and shoot, – just sign his name, and loved a spice of danger;
Equipped in fact by Nature for the duties of a Ranger.
So when he grew to manhood and they offered him a billet
As a Ranger in Uganda, he was very glad to fill it.

He entered on his duties with efficiency and zeal;
Would face marauding lions with a nerve as true as steel;
Could deal with raiding elephants; could follow any track;
And Heaven help the poacher who felt Sam upon his back.

He lived in tents; he liked it tough; his beer was never iced,
And if the dukas hadn't gin then waragi sufficed.
His letters might be in arrear – his Guards were brisk and neat;
In fact he was 'The Ranger' as you might have said 'Compleat';
And everybody liked him, for depicted in his face
Was that hardy, horny kindness which transcendeth creed or race.

His prospects were unpromising; that didn't make him quail.
He liked the life, and didn't seem to bother with his Scale*.
Accountants, secretaries, clerks and all the inky crew
Were eligible for A1 (or anyway B2);
In the eyes of Mr Whats-his-name (the Establishments' Grand Cham)
Z7 was considered to be adequate for Sam.

But things are never static; Father Time is apt to canter;
Some dismal ancient poet has it '*Tempora mutantur*'.
The Warden told his Rangers (though it seemed a trifle tough)
The old bush-whacking qualities no longer were enough;
We must join the March of Progress, and he looked for some compliance
From subordinates in meeting the demands of Modern Science.

A letter followed presently – there wasn't long to wait –
From the USA containing application from a great
Demonstrator in Biology (God send he never tutor us!)
For a sample pregnant female Black Rhinoceros's uterus;
And Samuel, who when peevish was too honest, far, to mask it,
Read, shrugged, then tore it up and threw the fragments in the basket.

But short indeed his respite, for there followed an appeal
From a (Swiss) Monsieur le Professeur le Coq de Bogusville,
Requesting him to forward (here he grew a little flustered)
The tape-worm from the colon of *Neotis* (Denham's Bustard).
Sam wrote a rude epistle, and he hadn't much to say,
But he called the worthy professeur a Bustard with an A.

He had scarcely mailed his letter when again the postman came
With a large forbidding envelope addressed in Scroggins' name;
A letter from the Warden, in the which he could discern
A letter from the Minister, which forwarded in turn
A letter from the Governor, of slightly earlier date,
Conveying a direction from the Secretary of State

* For the uninitiated, salary scales in the Civil Service were graded by letters and numbers finally decided by the Establishments Division of the Secretariat and the Public Service Commission (P.S.C.).

To assist our politicians in a tricky situation
By acceding to a foreign scientific application –
A certain Dr Bunckheim, who was asking to be lent a
Hyaena (female)'s endotheliochorial placenta.
Sam scratched his head and spelled it out; he turned a little pale,
Then ground his teeth – his attitude was definitely ♂ (male);
At length he firmly gripped his pen, and moved by wrath primordial
Wrote a letter which was rather less than endotheliocordial.

And that was Scroggins' downfall; for alas there's no specific
To cure a brain which wallows in a bog unscientific.
They sacked him; and a firman came from out the P.S.C.
That Rangers must possess a University degree.

The post has been upgraded now, since applicants were few
And Bachelors of Science may aspire to enter Q:
And if they raise it to P3 we rather hope to get
Some Doctors of Divinity (we haven't hooked one yet).

By the time I had finished, my smile had assumed a wry
quality. Read at this time, the penultimate verse in particular,
was so near the hard truth as to be uncanny. I went inside and
watched the African students at work. By a weird coincidence one
was actually preparing a study skin from a greater bustard, and
doing it remarkably efficiently. I was tempted to ask him if he
had found any tape-worms in its colon! It dawned on me that I
was looking at the scientifically trained game wardens of the
future, that the brightest might go on to obtain a university
degree, and that not one of them was a European. In East Africa
the day of the old time game ranger and warden – those colourful,
tough and entertaining characters who achieved so much –
was fading; it was foolish to pretend anything else. Sadly and with
strangely mixed feelings I turned away; I was on the way out
myself.

A week later, Elizabeth and I sailed from Dar es Salaam in
a small, Holland-Afrika Lijn, cargo ship heading for England.
For as long as possible we remained on the upper deck of the
Oosterkerk, sadly watching the coast of East Africa fade slowly
in the distance. All too soon we could see no more than the waving
tops of the coconut palms which lined the coral-fringed shore.
At last even these disappeared beneath the horizon and quietly
we went below. For the time being I did not want to think about
the future.

350

CHAPTER 17

Lowering the Curtain

On the morning of the 18th of June 1965 I was reclining, relaxed but sad, in one of the comfortable window seats of a Fokker Friendship aircraft of East African Airways. After more than seventeen, eventful years, I was leaving East Africa – as far as I knew for good – and my mind was full of memories.

We had left Nairobi International Airport some time before and as we droned steadily south-eastwards at an altitude of twenty thousand feet, holding our course for Mombasa, Tanga, Zanzibar and Dar es Salaam, the ground below us was hidden by a thick, soft blanket of billowing, white cumulus that stretched in a rolling, unbroken carpet far away to the distant horizon.

Over the starboard wing-tip Kibo and Mawenzi, the twin, snow-capped peaks of Kilimanjaro, the mightiest mountain in Africa, awe-inspiring in their gleaming majesty, towered high above their encircling blanket of cloud like silent sentinels brooding watchfully on the Kenya-Tanzania border.

I glanced down through the sporadic gaps in the billowing

351

cumulus that swirled below the plane. Suddenly I realised that I was over familiar ground. Not far ahead lay the Taru Desert, part of a mighty expanse of thousands of square miles of dry thorn-scrub and tangled bush, stretching from the Tana River in the north almost to the very foot of the Kilimanjaro massif and the Taita Hills in the south. This was country that I had known well in my early days in Kenya; country in which I had hunted and slept under the stars, while the night breeze moaned softly through the tangled branches of the whistling-thorns with a noise like souls in torment; elephant country – some say the finest in Africa.

Virtually waterless for a large part of the year, this harsh land, the dreaded Nyika of the early explorers, holds a strange fascination for those who know it. During the rains the country is transformed. Almost overnight it dons a mantle of verdant green and numerous, shallow water-holes appear in the ochre-red earth. But with the advent of the dry season these rapidly disappear and the whole country again becomes desiccated under the burning rays of the equatorial sun. Much of the animal life of the region then concentrates on the great river that runs from west to east through the heart of the Nyika, bisecting the wild bushland with almost geometrical precision. Far away, towards the northern horizon, I could just make out an irregular line of darker green, the narrow belt of trees that marked the river's course.

The Galla, a nomadic cattle-people, Hamites from the north, named this river Galana – meaning literally *the* river – thus emphasising its importance to this arid land. The Galana is formed by the junction of the River Athi, which rises on the Yatta Plateau, far to the west, and the River Tsavo, which is born of volcanic springs that bubble from the ground more to the southwest, towards the foot-hills of Kilimanjaro. It then twists its way almost due eastwards, in snake-like coils, across the bush-covered wilderness, finally entering the Indian Ocean just north of Malindi, in my old hunting ground – the District of Kilifi, the land of the Giriama people who call the river the Sabaki.

This is a country steeped in the history of the early explorers, pioneers and slave traders. People like Ludwig Krapf and Johann Rebmann, the courageous German missionaries who were the first Europeans to venture into the unknown interior of the Nyika; Joseph Thomson, the intrepid Scot, who was the first white man to traverse both the Nyika and the land of the hostile Masai, to find the shortest route from the coast to Lake Victoria; Colonel Patterson, the British engineer who built the railway from Mombasa right through the Nyika and beyond, despite the ravages of man-eating lions; and 'Tippu Tib', the notorious Arab slave-trader who scoured the Nyika in his far-flung and rapacious search for slaves and ivory.

I thought of the Reverend Rebmann, the lonely man of God who, in April 1848, armed with nothing more lethal than his well-worn Bible and an old umbrella, and accompanied by only nine African porters, set out from the coast through the dense bush of the Nyika, to take his faith to a people called the Chagga. All he knew of the Chagga was that they were a tribe who lived in a mountainous country farther to the west, but on the 11th of May his courage was rewarded. On that day he saw what he, a devout and religious man, must first have thought to be a vision. Peering over the tops of the thorn trees his short-sighted eyes were greeted by an awe-inspiring spectacle – thirty miles away, high above the drifting clouds, was the summit of a mighty mountain, its dome-shaped peak glistening white in the sun; it was the snow-capped crown of Kilimanjaro, a sight no European had ever before seen.

Looking back through the windows of the aircraft, I could still see the gleaming, white-capped peak and I remembered the story of how poor Rebmann's triumph had been short-lived. No one in Europe would believe that there could possibly be snow on the Equator. The weakness of Rebmann's eyesight had been notorious and his discovery was laughed to scorn.

My thoughts then turned to Ludwig Krapf, the solitary missionary who, in 1849, traversed the Nyika and, on the 3rd of December, discovered another great snow-capped mountain farther to the north. The Kamba chief at Kitui told him that his people called it *kinyaa* – 'the shining thing'. Krapf was luckier than his compatriot Rebmann; his discovery was believed and Mount Kenya appeared on the maps of the world.

Studying my travelling companions it occurred to me how few people now know or care about this fascinating history and the epics of such pioneers as Joseph Thomson and Patterson, let alone the story of the East African Game Departments. Thomson who had proved that the warriors of the Masai – the arrogant and fanatical *moran* – were neither invincible nor unapproachable. Patterson, the determined and dedicated engineer who had built what had scathingly been referred to, in 1895, as 'The Lunatic Line'!

After a heated debate in the British Parliament, in which the wisdom of constructing the Uganda Railway – from Mombasa through the wilderness of the Nyika and on across the hostile wastes of Masailand to the shores of Lake Victoria – had been hotly contested, Henry Labouchère, the Editor of *Truth* had published the now famous couplet:

> What it will cost no words can express;
> What is its purpose no brain can suppose;
> Where it will start from no one can guess;
> Where it is going to nobody knows.
> What is the use of it none can conjecture;
> What it will carry there's none can define;
> And in spite of George Curzon's* superior lecture,
> It clearly is naught but a lunatic line.

Those were the days when elephant ivory was still Uganda's main and only really viable export, when Captain (later Lord) Lugard, of the Imperial British East Africa Company, had described Western Uganda, with its enormous herds of elephant, as being 'the ivory reserve of the world!' There are still vast herds of elephant in Western Uganda, but as I flew high above Kenya's Nyika, on that memorable June day some seventy years later, I was probably the only person aboard the aircraft who knew that over thirty thousand elephant roamed the wild bushland far below us; another vast ivory reserve, the home of some of the mightiest tuskers left in Africa, the region that produced the elephant with the heaviest tusks yet known to man – an old and almost legendary elephant who met his death in 1899.

During that year, the ivory hunters of the notorious slave trader, Hamed ben Muhammed ('Tippu Tib' – 'the man with the flickering eyelids'), were combing the bushland of the Nyika. Among them was an Arab named Senoussi, who came on the tracks of a gigantic bull. With the grim determination of the dedicated hunter, Senoussi set off in pursuit. Spurred on by the fascination of the giant footprints, for day after day he followed the elusive trail through the tangled bush, but always the great animal kept ahead. At last, after weeks of careful tracking, which

* George Curzon, Under Secretary for State for Foreign Affairs.

led him to the slopes of Mount Kilimanjaro itself, in the heart of the mountain forest the hunter caught up with his gigantic quarry. Scarcely believing his eyes, with trembling hands he raised his gun. The old muzzle-loader boomed and as the smoke dispersed in the jungle gloom the ancient elephant came to the end of his wanderings. His tusks were each nearly ten and a half feet long and over two feet in girth. While fresh they weighed 235 and 226 pounds. And so the mightiest elephant ever known in Africa came to his last resting place in the shadow of the mightiest mountain in Africa.

To me there is something symbolic in this story. I always think of it when I see Kilimanjaro. The tusks of this 'King of all Elephants' now lie in the British Museum of Natural History in London, a fitting resting place which they reached after much travelling and many vicissitudes. There I have often stared at them, fascinated and almost in disbelief that any living thing, even an elephant, could carry 461 pounds of ivory in its head, a weary burden indeed for an old and tired animal.

Some would deplore the manner of his death, but what was the alternative? Elephants, like men, are not immortal. Their life span is limited by their teeth. When these finally wear out, as they inevitably must, the elephant can no longer chew his food. He is then condemned to a slow death from starvation, hastened in the final stages by the ghoulish attacks of hyaenas and vultures. Nature's pattern is often a cruel one; death in the wild is seldom as quick and merciful as the death which results from the skilled hunter's carefully placed bullet. And it would have been a tragedy indeed if the gigantic tusks of this, the mightiest of all known elephants, had been lost for ever.

These huge tusks first found their way to Zanzibar and there, in 1900, they were sold to a New York dealer for the prodigious price of $5,000, a staggering thought when one equates this figure with the present value of money. They must have travelled, from Mombasa or Tanga, in one of 'Tippu Tib's' dhows, through the Pemba Channel, to the great ivory stores of the 'Island of Cloves'. I was dreaming of all this, and of the excitement the great tusks must have caused throughout their journey, when a voice at my elbow interrupted my reverie.

'Would you like the morning paper, Sir?' The voice was musical with only a faint trace of an accent. With a start I glanced up to find the stewardess standing beside me, holding a copy of the *East African Standard*, one of Africa's leading English language newspapers. Like the smartly dressed African business man across the aisle, she also was a Mkamba, a pretty, light-skinned girl trimly-clad in the neat, stone-coloured uniform of East African Airways.

'Thank you,' I replied, taking the politely proffered paper.

'You're welcome, Sir,' she said, with a strangely sweet smile, before undulating gracefully back up the aisle, under the appreciative gaze of my Mkamba travelling companion, who had rapidly removed his dark glasses the better to observe this titillating sight.

'The emancipation of Africa,' I reflected as I opened the *East African Standard* and there, in glaring headlines, as if to underline my thoughts, were the words 'NEW GENERATION TAKING OVER GAME CONTROL'.

With quickening interest I read on. The report that followed was a sympathetic and accurate account of an unique event. I skimmed through it and then gazed out of the aircraft, my thoughts following my eyes which wandered over the northern face of Kilimanjaro. Floating above the clouds in solitary grandeur, the glistening, snow-clad slopes of Kibo peak still seemed to dominate the horizon. Only the previous day I had been at Mweka, near Moshi in Tanzania, below the southern face of the great mountain, while I watched the same unique event about which I was now reading – the first graduation ceremony ever to be held at the newly created College of African Wildlife Management, in turn the first and only training establishment of its kind in Africa. In fact, if one comes to think of it, as yet there is probably nothing quite like it anywhere else in the world,* for, as I have already revealed in the tale of how it came into being, it is a very specialised institution – a school for African game wardens.

Almost reluctantly I studied the paper again. 'NEW GENERA-

* Since these words were written a new Wildlife Management Training School, modelled exactly on the College of African Wildlife Management at Mweka, has been established at Garoua in Cameroon. The new School, called École Formation de Spécialistes de la Faune Sauvage, is regional in concept, like the College at Mweka, and has been created for French-speaking Africans. It is being administered by the Food and Agricultural Organisation (F.A.O.), under the United Nations Development Programme.

TION TAKING OVER GAME CONTROL'. The words had an ominous finality about them and as I stared at this eye-catching headline it slowly dawned on me that it signalled, in general, the beginning of the end of a colourful era. Sadder still, for me personally, was the realisation that it also marked the culmination of what was likely to have been the most interesting and rewarding period of my life – seventeen eventful years in East and Central Africa, during fourteen of which I had been fortunate enough to be Chief Game Warden of first Uganda and then Tanganyika (now Tanzania).

Only a few months before, dislodged by the 'Wind of Change', I had sadly relinquished my post of Chief Game Warden, Tanganyika, handing over my responsibilities and good will to a young and earnest African. Returning slowly and reluctantly to England, I had wondered, unhappily, if this was to be the end of my life as a game warden in Africa; but a request from the Government of Bechuanaland* for British aid in the form of a wildlife adviser, on a short-term assignment, had offered me at least a temporary reprieve. For the first time in my life I found myself being referred to, openly and to my face, as a 'Wildlife Expert'. My chest swelled with pride at this flattering title, until Thane Riney, himself FAO's well-known wildlife expert in Rome, advised me, dryly, of the alternative definition of the term.

'X', he said with a sardonic smile, 'is the unknown quantity, while "spurt", of course, is merely a drip under pressure!'

Fate, working through the British Government, was unexpectedly benevolent. Routes and timings for my long flight to Bechuanaland proved sufficiently flexible to enable me to break my journey in East Africa, for long enough to visit Mweka, on the 17th of June, for a special reason. In England I had received a printed invitation card headed 'College of African Wildlife Management.' The invitation read: 'A short ceremony will take place on Thursday, 17th June, 1965, at 11.00 a.m., at the College, on the occasion of the Graduation of the students of the first Diploma Course in Wildlife Management. The Principal, Staff and Students request the pleasure of the company of Major B. G. Kinloch, M.C., at the Graduation Ceremony.'

Few people, other than myself, knew the full and true story of why and how this special training school came to be established,

* Now Botswana.

for the simple reason that, until now, the inside story has never been told. And it was because of my personal involvement in the creation of the school that I had wanted, above all, to see for myself the human products of the first two-year course ever to be held there. Having seen with my own eyes, and having formed my own conclusions, I was anxious to hear the impressions of others. The *East African Standard* report was the first public reaction. As the plane droned steadily on, high over the arid bushland of the Nyika, lulled by the muted hum of the engines, I read the paper again, slowly and thoughtfully.

Under its arresting headline the *East African Standard* went on to say:

Men with military backgrounds characterised the start of East Africa's national parks and game reserves. With few exceptions, the visionary early game wardens had seen active war service and bore military ranks.

They had the determination and dedication that put today's game departments and national parks on such a sound footing. But times change and things progress, the work of the ex-soldier is almost done. The time has come when a new generation of specialists, trained in game management and bushwork, takes over.

This is the purpose of the College of African Wildlife Management, an establishment at Mweka near Moshi in Tanzania, which is setting out to produce the modern game warden.

Here was food for speculation. Twenty years earlier this last announcement would have been greeted with widespread derision and disbelief for, in the Africa of those days, wild animals were not generally considered to have much intrinsic value.

Thinking back over my own experience, I remembered vividly the barren and stony ground in which for years the game departments had struggled doggedly to sow the early seeds of their basic conservation policies. In such a climate of opinion, the very idea of creating a special school to train men to manage wild animals scientifically would have been laughed to scorn.

But times change, as the *Standard* observed, and Africa's famous 'Wind of Change' hastened the appearance of a good many ideas and innovations that raised the status and the public image of Africa's incomparable wildlife resources. So, as it turned out, instead of critical opposition, widespread and welcoming interest was aroused when the same report in the columns of the *Standard* went on to announce:

Young men from all English-speaking countries of Africa are going to the College on two-year courses. The first graduates, nine from Tanzania, four each from Kenya and Uganda, and one from Cameroon, passed out yesterday when representatives from all three East African Governments, game departments and national parks were present.

In concluding its article the *East African Standard* quoted the words of the College's Principal, my old friend and colleague, Dr Hugh Lamprey, now one of Africa's leading wildlife biologists. Replying to his questioner, Hugh Lamprey had said:

This has been the first professional training of this kind made available in Africa – and it has been a great success . . . The next course is going to be a particularly interesting one as we shall be training men sent from the West African countries of Nigeria, the Cameroons and Sierra Leone, the Central African countries of Zambia and Malawi, and from Ethiopia in the north, besides students from the three East African countries of Kenya, Uganda and Tanzania.

Folding the newspaper I placed it carefully on the vacant seat beside me, the events of the previous day still clear in my mind. Watching the simple graduation ceremony under the inspiring, snow-capped dome of Kilimanjaro, the highest mountain in Africa, towering in symbolic majesty many thousands of feet above the College buildings had been a proud moment for me – but also a sobering one. The College had been my personal brain-child and it is not given to everyone to see their dreams materialise and their most cherished plans reach fruition during their lifetime. But my elation had been tempered with caution. One thing yet remained to be proved. One question still had to be answered. Unlike the game wardens they were destined to replace, many of these Africans were young and inexperienced men of very mixed backgrounds and upbringing. How would they perform in the bush when they had to face up alone to the multitude of varied problems and dangers that are the daily lot of the game warden in Africa? At the College, even during practical field exercises, these embryo African game wardens had worked with their fellow students and more often than not under the direction, or at least guidance, of a qualified and experienced instructor. In the bush they would be on their own – often literally so. More testing still they would be under the acutely critical eye of their less well-educated African subordinates. The latter were – and still are – mainly tough and experienced game scouts and guards, fine bushmen and hunters, but like all simple, unsophisticated people also conservative to a degree. These game scouts would be naturally suspicious of any major innovations such as the appearance of an inexperienced African game warden, however well trained, wielding all the authority of his traditionally European predecessors. How would these fledgling game wardens fare under such conditions?

The answer to the last question was all-important to the future of wildlife in Africa, but it could not safely be given before these keen young Africans had proved themselves in the critical testing period that was to follow their launching into the hard realities of the wildlife world. The answer, in fact, is only now becoming really apparent – long after the closing phases of this present story, which is chiefly concerned with the decade that followed hard on the heels of the Second World War, a period of East African history that is noteworthy as the beginning of an era of far-reaching and almost volcanic change in virtually every sphere. It is a story that I have therefore waited another five years to tell, but the compulsion to write it finally took positive shape when, drifting high above the clouds that cloaked the wild bushland far below, I studied the report in the *East African Standard* on the day after history had been made at the College of African Wildlife Management, in the shadow of the eternal snows of Kilimanjaro.

*

Those five additional years have now passed, and I am thankful that at last I am able to write, not merely with pride and a sense of relief, but also with honest conviction, that the overall results of the training at the College of African Wildlife Management, at Mweka, have exceeded most people's expectations. True, there have been some failures and the inevitable mistakes that accompany the launching of any new project that is radical, if not revolutionary in concept. It has certainly not all been plain sailing. There have been crises enough, numerous unexpected problems, and many a tense moment. But throughout, the attitude to the training programme has been kept flexible, with the emphasis heavily on the practical side; and as snags have developed and errors have become apparent, policies and plans have been modified to iron them out. In consequence, at the end of the first seven years of its life, it can justly be claimed that the results produced by the College of African Wildlife Management have fully vindicated the faith of the optimists and confounded the doubts of the pessimists.

Perhaps the most significant observation, made by a number of hard-headed and experienced European game wardens, is that the training at the College has given the new African game wardens not only the confidence that they so badly need to face the exacting and varied responsibilities ahead of them, but also a greater sense of purpose, a better understanding of what wildlife conservation really means, what it is all about – and this in addition to providing them with the basic scientific knowledge that the modern game warden *must* have, as well as a sound practical training in the wide range of duties involved in wildlife management under tropical African conditions today.

The credit for the ultimate success of this venture must go mainly to the instructors, and in particular to the original team consisting of Hugh Lamprey, Gil Child and David Anstey – all of the Tanganyika Game Department – and my old friend Anno Hecker, the trained Forester-Game Warden from the Federal Republic of Germany, who had previously been one of my Honorary Game Wardens in Tanganyika. They were the pioneers of the project; I was the architect and pilot. Between them they got the College under way in the face of often daunting obstacles, and they saw it through its teething troubles despite seemingly endless vicissitudes. The original idea, the whole conception of the College, was my own and I am unashamedly proud of this fact. The hard and sometimes strangely bizarre initial struggle to get the College actually launched was also my personal battle – and I am proud of that as well. But the successful exploitation of that early breakthrough of mine was largely due to the enthusiasm, the ingenuity, and the determination of the imaginative team of instructors whom I have mentioned above, my colleagues for whose unfailing loyalty and support I shall never cease to be grateful.

Since those early days the College has grown and developed

out of all recognition; in fact, long ago it achieved international status. It has now come under the wing of the United Nations Special Fund and it is sponsored by the Scientific and Research Committee of the Organisation for African Unity. The early benefactors, who made the project possible, together with the long list of later helpers who enabled it to expand, I have already mentioned in the previous chapter of this book; and the College is now attended by students of a dozen different countries in Africa. I have heard that applications for courses have even been received from Europe and America!

Instructors have come and gone. At the time of writing, of the old team only Gil Child is left, a pillar of strength as always. Hugh Lamprey, that dedicated biologist who led the instructors with such enthusiasm and competence in the pioneering days, has returned to his first love – research – in the important post of Director of the Serengeti Research Unit. It is now over four years since he was replaced as Principal of the College by Tony Mence, the ex-Royal Marine Commando and qualified zoologist, a most able wildlife administrator and game warden, whom, as I have already told, I was fortunate enough to have as my deputy when I was Chief Game Warden of Tanganyika.

David Anstey* was long ago recalled to a senior position in the Game Department of Tanzania, having served his term with credit. He was replaced by another ex-Tanganyika game warden, Brian Stronach, who has now retired to conserve the wildlife of the hills and boglands of his native Ireland after devoting several years of sterling service to the College. Anno Hecker has also gone, sadly missed by all; he is back in his beloved German forests among the red deer, the roebuck, and the great wild boar. Luckily these valuable men were replaced by such experienced and well-known characters as Frank Poppleton, formerly a Senior Warden in Uganda's National Parks, and Pat Hemingway, the American professional hunter turned biologist who is a character in his own right – without always having to be referred to by visiting journalists as the son of the man who wrote *The Snows of Kilimanjaro*. There have been many others besides these; British, Germans, Americans, an Italian; too many to mention

---

* Later David Anstey became Warden in charge of the Awash National Park in Ethiopia. In 1972, he succeeded the author as Chief Game Warden of Malawi.

by name, but all doing a job that is vital to the survival of the wildlife of Africa.

*

But on the 18th of June 1965, while I was flying high above the Nyika, deep in thought, much of this was still hidden in the mists of the future, while much of the past was already forgotten – even by those who were aware of the details. Then, at last, low on the horizon ahead of us appeared the glittering blue waters of the Indian Ocean; and as the plane banked and lost altitude for the approach to Mombasa, I craned my neck to catch a glimpse, through the port-side windows of the aircraft, of the coral-fringed coast to the north, with its thick green belt of bush and trees. There, a mere forty miles away, lay the Arabuko Forest, the scene, seventeen years before, of my first encounter with the African elephant, the animal which altered the course of my life.

PART FIVE

Afterword

*

CHAPTER 18

Taking Stock – 1987

"Writing about modern Africa is like trying to sketch a galloping horse which is out of sight before you have sharpened your pencil" – so wrote that famous authoress Elspeth Huxley, in a foreword to her highly acclaimed book *Forks and Hope*; Elspeth Huxley writes not only with shrewd insight but also with a deep personal knowledge of East Africa, and no truer words than these were ever penned.

Forks and Hope was published in 1964, a sad year for me since, as I have told in this book, it was then, after 17 eventful years, that my career in East Africa drew to a close and I sailed out of Dar es Salaam for the last time. Twenty-three years have passed since that sad day, and for East Africa as a whole, and more particularly for Uganda, they have been 23 turbulent and traumatic years, during which much murky and even literally blood-stained water has flowed down the Nile. Now, nearly a quarter of a century after the end of my service in East Africa, *The Shamba Raiders* is being re-printed and it was suggested to me that this would be an appropriate time to look back over what I wrote in the original edition, to think on what has happened in East Africa during the intervening years, and – most important of all – to try to take stock of the wildlife situation in Uganda, Kenya and Tanzania as it is to-day.

When I first thought about it, this idea appealed to me, but I soon realised that it presented problems. Over the last 23 years there have been so many dramatic happenings and far-reaching changes in East Africa, that to describe them adequately, even between the covers of a full book, would be a testing task for anyone. So, all I can do here is to generalise and summarise, which can sometimes be misleading, but I have done my best to get my facts as accurate and as up-to-date as possible. To the latter end, I have sought the help and advice of a number of knowledgeable people, notably Dr S. Keith Eltringham, Dr Hugh Lamprey and Dr Esmond Bradley-Martin, all of whom are men not only with long and wide experience of wildlife management in Africa, but who are also still very active in that field.

Keith Eltringham, currently Lecturer in Applied Biology, University of Cambridge, is an old friend and colleague of mine. One of the first directors of the Nuffield Unit of Tropical Animal Ecology in Uganda (now the Uganda Institute of Ecology), Keith is in great demand for consultancy and advisory wildlife assignments in Africa and he visits the main game areas of East Africa – particularly those in Uganda – every year, often to carry out aerial surveys of which, as a one time "Pilot-Biologist", he has much experience.

Hugh Lamprey, another old friend and colleague of mine, is also a Pilot-Biologist who has had a long and distinguished career in Africa. As I have told in this book, Hugh was not only my Biologist when I was Chief Game Warden of Tanzania, but also the man I selected to be the first Principal of the College of African Wildlife Management, at Mweka on Kilimanjaro, when I planned and launched the latter college. Later, Hugh became Director of the Serengeti Research Institute, after which he undertook wildlife research and advisory assignments in countries as far-flung as Senegal, Chad, Sudan and Kenya, on behalf of I.U.C.N., U.N.E.S.C.O., U.N.E.P. and W.W.F. At the time of writing Hugh is the World Wildlife Fund's "Regional Representative for East and Central Africa" and is based in Nairobi.

Last but not least, Esmond Bradley-Martin is the Vice-Chairman of the Survival Service Commission's "African Elephant and Rhino' Group", also with headquarters in Nairobi, and therefore a valuable source of information on the elephant and rhino' situations in Uganda, Kenya and Tanzania.

*

With Kenya, Uganda and Tanzania – the three countries of the original East African Community – all gaining their independence within a year or so of each other in the mid-sixties, that period marked the end of a colourful era in the game world of East Africa, but the long awaited granting of independence was not the reason that East Africa's game wardens, together with other seasoned supporters of the wildlife conservation lobby, entered the new era on the crest of a wave of high hopes, if not of euphoria. The reason for the optimism of the wildlife lobby was that – as I wrote at the beginning of this book – contrary to the forbodings of the pessimists, the new African governments had recognised and accepted with alacrity the fact that, as the basis of a tourist trade that was capable of enormous expansion, their countries' wildlife was one of their most valuable natural assests, and they had acted, or tried to act, accordingly. Alas, as the poet Robbie Burns would have it, "the best laid plans o' mice and men gang aft a' gley", and it was in Uganda first that things went wrong – and horribly wrong.

Tourism –' and wildlife-related tourism in particular – is a fickle and sensitive industry, quick to shy away from the slightest hint of political instability, and in Uganda's case less than four years after the Protectorate had been granted its independence, internal political troubles, long simmering below the surface, erupted violently. The cause of the trouble was the bitter personal rivalry between Milton Obote – then Prime Minister – and HH Sir Edward Mutesa, the Kabaka of Buganda, who was then the President of Uganda – and one of my keenest Honorary Game Wardens when I was Chief Game Warden of the Protectorate! But the savage and explosive manner in which this rivalry came to a head shocked the outside world.

I clearly recall the 24th May, 1966, the day I travelled to London Airport to board a flight to Uganda's administrative capital Entebbe, the first leg of my journey to Rwanda where I was due to carry out a wildlife management advisory assignment in the Parc National de la Kagera. On the way to the airport I bought an evening paper and from the front page banner headlines seemed to leap out at me; "KING FREDDIE UNDER ATTACK," they shouted, and the text went on to describe the attack on the Kabaka's palace that morning, an assault carried out by the 1st Battalion, Uganda Rifles led by Idi Amin, later to become notorious, then a Lieutenant-Colonel acting on the orders of Milton Obote. Twelve hours later, as I landed at Entebbe, the morning sky over nearby Kampala was darkened by the billowing columns of dense, black smoke rising from the Kabaka's palace. The Kabaka himself had fled, escaping to England by the skin of his teeth, but his people, the Baganda, never forgave Milton Obote, and from then on serious political trouble, arising from tribal differences and jealousies, continued to foment beneath the surface.

Four and a half years later, in January, 1971, Idi Amin, by then promoted to Major-General and Chief of Defence Staff, launched a successful coup while President Milton Obote was away in Singapore, attending the Commonwealth Prime Ministers' Conference. It is said that Idi Amin had discovered a plot to remove himself, and officers loyal to him, because he was of "the wrong tribe". Whatever the truth of the matter, Amin and his supporters – mostly Mahdi or Kakwa from West Nile Province – acted with typical ruthlessness and ferocity; a large proportion of the Acholi and Langi officers were murdered, or fled, and Amin – appointed President by "the soldiers" – clung on grimly to the reins of power for eight, blood-soaked years.

What has all this got to do with Uganda's wildlife? The answer is *everything*! To the outside world Idi Amin was a complex and macabre figure, a sinister and unpredictable clown who was a cruel and ruthless tyrant who ruled Uganda by a combination of primitive cunning, irrational impulse and unbridled savagery, with the result that the country rapidly lapsed into barbarism and near anarchy. With the consequent general breakdown of law and order, poaching increased and flourished and Uganda's previously spectacular and world-famous wildlife populations suffered accordingly, none more so than the elephant and the rhino.

However, even Idi Amin, who was a man of great vanity*, was sometimes sensitive to world opinion and there are a few things (but sadly few!) which can be said to his credit. For instance, as I have mentioned briefly in the body of this book, in September 1971, Amin cancelled the Obote government's grandiose plan for a hydro-electric scheme at the famous Murchison Falls, in the heart of the popular national park of that name, a scheme which caused a worldwide outcry because it was a purely prestige project that would have destroyed the spectacular and historic Falls merely to produce electricity for which there was no demand!

Again, three years later, on 3rd December, 1975, Idi Amin – reacting in typically violent fashion to international concern over the elephant situation in Uganda – issued a decree which ordered death by firing squad for anyone found guilty, by a judicial authority, of elephant poaching. In fact, the decree went further

*Amin assumed the rank of Field Marshall and awarded himself the V.C.; if pressed, he explained the latter away as being the "Lake Victoria Cross"!

370

for it also ordered that anyone found *in the act* of hunting elephant or shooting elephant would be shot on the spot! The slaughter of elephants stopped overnight, but the killing gradually crept back to its former level as poachers – lured by the world prices of ivory and rhino' horn, which had soared to the equivalent of £31 per lb and £240 per lb respectively – began to realise that the authorities, many of them corrupt and themselves involved in the illegal trade in ivory and rhino' horn, could not or would not enforce the decree. In fact, it is said that during Amin's regime his troops killed most of the elephants in the national parks to pay for the maintenance of the army! But it was not the ordinary forms of poaching that did the horrendous harm from which Uganda's formerly teeming wildlife resources were reduced to a pathetic shadow of their former glory: the holocaust was the result of total war, the invasion of Uganda by the army of Tanzania.

After Idi Amin's coup in January, 1971, Milton Obote had taken refuge with his friend President Julius Nyerere, in Tanzania, who had given him political asylum. Having his old enemy on his doorstep did not please Idi Amin and this led to much sabre rattling and contrived border incidents. Finally, in 1979, Julius Nyerere, tiring of these provocative irritations, launched the Tanzanian Army in an all out offensive designed to topple Amin and restore Obote to power in Uganda. The fighting raged over many of Uganda's finest game areas; the soldiers slaughtered game indiscriminately for food, for profit and as living targets on which to test their weapons; and by the following year, when Idi Amin and the remains of his ill-disciplined army had fled northwards and Milton Obote was back in office, much of Uganda's wildlife had been decimated.

According to Dr Keith Eltringham, a survey carried out in 1980 showed that, in the Queen Elizabeth National Park alone, the buffalo population had shrunk from 18,000 to around 3,000, hippo from 14,000 also to about 3,000, and elephants – which numbered some 4,000 in 1973, but had fallen to 1,200 by 1975 – had been reduced to a remnant population of little more than one hundred by 1980. Furthermore, with the virtual elimination of elephants from the park, the vegetation had changed considerably, with much more and thicker undergrowth and dense acacia woodland springing up on what was once open grassland. So much so, that the formerly spectacular concentrations of topi – an open grassland antelope here found at the southern end of the park – which had been savagely reduced from an original population of some 5,000 to around 500, in 1980 were seen to have to thread their way through the trees!

Elsewhere in Uganda the story was much the same, with antelope species reduced to a minimum and the total elephant population down to around 2,000 in the whole country. Worse still, the rhinoceros – both black and white – because of the insatiable demand and astronomical prices paid for its horns to make prestige dagger handles in North Yemen, and as an aphrodisiac and prized medicant in Asia, the Far East and China, had been exterminated. Needless to say, Uganda's tourist industry which, until 1972, had been the country's third most important foreign exchange earner after coffee and cotton, had collapsed years before.

Sadly, the overthrow of Idi Amin and the re-establishment of the Obote government did not bring peace and tranquillity, let alone prosperity, to Uganda. The government had a strong bias in favour of the Nilotic tribes of the north of the country and in consequence it was mistrusted, even hated, by the Baganda and the other Bantu tribes of southern Uganda; the Baganda, in particular, had never forgotten or forgiven Obote and his henchmen for what had happened to their Kabaka 15 years before. Covert resistance grew and it was not long before anti-government guerilla bands were operating in the countryside, bands which developed into the well-disciplined National Resistance Army (the N.R.A.) under the leadership of Yoweri Museveni, a force which eventually was to prove more than a match for the U.N.L.A., Obote's ill-disciplined Uganda National Liberation Army, a bullying mob, savage and sadistic, which practised intimidation and extortion and terrorised the countryside, committing atrocities reminiscent of the worst days of the Amin regime.

As the atrocities continued, so did Museveni's N.R.A. grow in strength and efficiency until, slowly but surely, the greater part of the southern half of Uganda had come under its effective control. In fact, by early 1985, virtually the whole of the south-western part of the country had become a no-go area for Obote's U.N.L.A.. Sadly for Uganda's wildlife, the influence and dominance of

Museveni's crusading forces did not extend to the country lying to the north of the Albert Nile: in that region, units of Obote's army, based in Gulu and Pakwach, remained in full control and the animals in the Murchison Falls National Park had suffered accordingly ever since 1980. During this period, poaching by U.N.L.A. soldiers was rife, and as their war with Museveni's N.R.A. gained momentum, the U.N.L.A. began training recruits in the Murchison Falls National Park itself and they were all fed on game meat!*

In July, 1985, the Obote government was toppled by an internal military coup, but peace was not restored to Uganda until Yoweri Museveni's National Resistance Army stormed Kampala in January, 1986. Although the peace was a fragile and uneasy one, Museveni then formed an entirely new government, with a brand new Ministry of Environmental Protection which took Uganda's national parks, game reserves and other wildlife areas under its protective wing. At the same time, the defeated and demoralised soldiers of the U.N.L.A. fled northwards, on their way looting everything they could carry from the safari lodges in the Murchison Falls National Park and destroying the remainder. Fortunately, at that time the Kidepo Valley National Park escaped serious damage for, by the time the demoralised troops reached the Kidepo, they were only interested in gaining the border to seek safety in the Sudan.

What is the wildlife situation in Uganda now, in 1987, and what of the future? Keith Eltringham, who did a survey in the Queen Elizabeth National Park recently, is cautiously optimistic about the main game areas in the southern half of Uganda, although he is uncertain about the north of the country. In the south the antelope species, he says, are breeding fast, and there is a healthy nucleus of the larger species of game, such as buffalo and hippo. He even saw a herd of forty elephants (a rare and unusual sight in recent years!) in the Queen Elizabeth National Park, and these great beasts appear to be slowly but surely infiltrating the park from across the nearby border with Zaire. He was also impressed by the effects on animal species of the very

* Professor Frederick I. B. Kayanja, Chairman of the Board of Trustees of the Uganda National Parks (and Deputy Vice-Chancellor and Professor of Veterinary Medicine at Makerere University), writing in *Swara*, the Journal of the East African Wildlife Society, in 1986.

noticeable change in the nature of the habitat in the park, a change caused by the virtual elimination of the previously great herds of elephants, with their destructive feeding habits. For instance, he saw many more Uganda kob than ever before, while in the hippo wallows he observed, for the first time, numbers of giant forest hog, a comparatively rare and normally shy species which I myself have never seen in that national park!

Elsewhere in Uganda the wildlife situtation is not yet clear because, in striking contrast to the south, at the present time that region of Uganda which lies to the north of the Albert Nile, and including most of the Murchison Falls National Park, can best be described as "bandit country", a no-mans-land with roving bands of well-armed, dissident soldiers, the savage remnants of the former armies of both Amin and Obote, raiding and looting virtually at will. In that region, Museveni's troops, almost all of them Bantu southerners like himself, are having an up-hill struggle trying to restore peace, law and order, an object which they can only achieve by defeating the elusive guerillas who infest this wild region of Nilotic tribes, an alien populace basically suspicious of and even hostile to the new regime. As a result (for what are euphemistically described as "security reasons"!) it is virtually impossible at present for any outside observers to visit and properly assess the wildlife situation in areas such as the Murchison Falls and Kidepo Valley National Parks. For instance, Keith Eltringham recently had to abandon, with great reluctance, his carefully laid plans to carry out an aerial survey of the Murchison Falls National Park; as he said at the time: "These guerilla bands are well armed and they could be anywhere. Therefore, as I would always be flying low on a steady course, the risk of being shot down by ground fire was just too great."

So, how does one sum up the present wildlife situation in Uganda, that beautiful and once peaceful country, Churchill's "Pearl of Africa", whose people were once happy and contented and the elephant reigned supreme? It is safe to say that, as long as peace continues to be maintained in the southern half of Uganda, in that part of the country there is real cause for hope, even for the elephant. In the north however, unless the last flickering flames of a long and tragic internecine struggle are smothered soon, the future for wildlife in that part of the country will be bleak. As for

Uganda's rhino – both black and white – it is clear that the long
day is already done; sadly, it is them for whom the bell tolls.

*

Compared with Uganda, over the last twenty-three years Kenya
has been a veritable "haven of peace", but that does not mean that
this dynamic and flourishing country, often held up as a shining
example to the rest of Africa, has not been without its own serious
internal problems. In fact, since independence Kenya, whose
government (unlike that of Tanzania) from the beginning
enthusiastically embraced capitalism, has had to face some big
challenges; and of these challenges none have been greater than
those arising from the problems of conserving and managing the
country's commercially valuable wildlife resources, a natural asset
which has long formed the basis of a flourishing and steadily
expanding tourist industry. In this sphere, the biggest and most
serious problem has been an alarming increase in highly organised
commerical poaching, particularly of elephant and rhino'.

Human nature being what it is and basically the same the
whole world over, in the countries of East Africa, after
independence, the heady and unaccustomed taste of new-found
power, together with the inherent temptations of authority, have
all too often led to avarice, graft and corruption in official circles,
sometimes in high places. In Kenya, as in Uganda and Tanzania,
in the first decade or so of independence this led, among other
things, to a massive increase in the age-old but largely illegal
trade in ivory and rhino'-horn. During this period, poaching of
elephant and rhino' increased by leaps and bounds until – often
with the help of false documents issued and stamped by corrupt
government officials – stocks of illegal ivory and rhino'-horn were
regularly being exported by the ton, sometimes in plane loads.

Reliable evidence suggests that the sad era of corruption in
Kenya reached its peak in the seventies, since when Kenya's
government, alarmed by mounting criticism both at home and
abroad and the consequent threat to its tourist trade, has made
valiant efforts to bring the situation under control. Although exact
dates are misleading, available statistics indicate that the worst
poaching of elephant and rhino' in Kenya took place in the period
from around 1975 up to 1980. In 1972, Kenya still had a massive
elephant population of some 165,000; to-day this population is

believed to number no more than 30,000 elephants, although ironically, in some areas such as the Maasai Mara and Amboseli, there is said to be a local surplus of elephant! The black rhino' situation is worse. In 1968, there were known to be at least 18,000 rhino' in Kenya; to-day there are no more than 500 rhino' left in the whole country and even these are under constant threat from avaricious poachers.

It was in 1977, that the Kenya Government first took really drastic steps to put its wildlife house in order. In that year Kenya set up strong, well equipped anti-poaching units, highly mobile teams designed to track down and eliminate the aggressive and well-armed poaching gangs (a large majority of them Somalis) and to seek out and bring to justice all members of the powerful illegal ivory cartel. In addition, with the object of improving efficiency and effectiveness, the government amalgamated the National Parks and the Game Department to form a new, unified "Wildlife Conservation and Management Department", in the Ministry of Tourism and Wildlife. Finally, at the stroke of a pen and with no prior warning, on 19th May, 1977, the government issued a decree banning all hunting in Kenya with immediate effect.*

The hunting ban was applauded by anti-field sports groups and the Kenya Government may have been pressurised by the blinkered but financially powerful total preservation lobby , but the reasons given for the ban were over simplistic and their validity open to question. The basic theory behind the ban appeared to be that if all legal hunting was banned, then anyone found hunting, or even if gun or rifle shots were heard, he or they must be a poacher and could therefore promptly be dealt with. Not surprisingly, both the ban itself and the summary manner in which it had been imposed caused a storm of protest, not least from that honorable and highly respected body " The East African Professional Hunters' Association", whose members and their safari staff had had their livelihood wiped out literally overnight.

Many experienced game wardens, as well as the professional hunters themselves, pointed out that the ban ignored certain

* The ban, which was extended a year later to cover all trading in wild animal trophies as well as hunting, was recently relaxed very slightly to allow licenced bird shooting only.

important facts. First, that as a result of the ban the former hunting zones, which were often important reservoirs or overflow areas for the game animals in neighbouring national parks or game reserves, and also earners of substantial amounts of foreign exchange from hunting licences and trophy fees, as well as from the many expenses connected with costly Kenya hunting safari, had immediately lost all economic value, so their retention as wildlife areas was at serious risk. Next, there was the indisputable fact, endorsed by experienced game wardens, that most of the professional hunters did a valuable job as "honorary game wardens", so much so that poachers gave areas occupied by legal hunting parties a very wide berth. Furthermore, it was important not to ignore the fact that the licenced hunters, unlike the poachers, only took a severely restricted number of carefully selected trophy animals and always attempted to kill them humanely.

Sadly, the protests of the professional hunters and their supporters fell on deaf official ears, and after the ban the poachers moved into the previously controlled hunting areas, slaughtering game indiscriminately, often by the most barbarous methods, thereby adding to the problems of the new and already sorely tried Wildlife Conservation and Management Department. For the professional hunters the outcome could not have been worse; for them, on 26th August, 1977, three months after the ban was announced, the Committee of the East African Professional Hunters' Assocation, under the veteran chairmanship of Tony Dyer, met for the last time. On the agenda in Nairobi there was only one item. The livelihood of the Association's members had been destroyed abruptly and without warning by the stroke of an official pen, which had thereby removed the Association's basic *raison d'être*. The discussions were brief, sad and to the point. Quietly and without fuss the East African Professional Hunters' Association was formally disbanded. Dedicated to maintaining the strictest possible code of sporting ethics and to working for the practical conservation of East Africa's valuable wildlife resources, a world famous and exclusive organisation, whose members for many years were so colourful and popular a part of the contemporary Kenya scene, faded unobtrusively into history. Many believed that the Association was the unfortunate victim of misguided policy; few do not regret its passing.

For Kenya the ban on hunting was an expensive move; it cost the country dearly in lost foreign exchange and it was three years before the mass tourist industry filled the gap left by the absence of the traditional, high priced hunting safaris. But Kenya's tourist industry as a whole, an industry which is based on the country's dramatic wildlife areas, has continued to grow at a surprising rate. In the first edition of this book, I commented that in 1963, the value of Kenya's tourist industry, in foreign exchange, was £8 million per year; by 1976 however, this figure has climbed to over £41 million; ten years later it had risen to a surprising £209 million per year, well above the value of tea and exceeded only by the export earnings of coffee, which topped the £230 million mark. But despite this success story, the game wardens and scientists are worried.

On the surface, which is what the tourist sees, the wildlife scene in Kenya looks set fair. Poaching, although not eliminated – which it never will be entirely anywhere as long as humans and wild animals co-exist in close proximity to each other – appears to have been reduced to what might be described as a more manageable level than for some years past. As a result, in the national parks and game reserves the numbers and species of animals on display, although not as numerous and spectacular as in days of yore, are still more than enough to keep all but the most critical and discerning tourists happy. Sadly, the great elephant herds, once such a common and dramatic sight, are now largely a thing of the past, but poachers now keep well away from safari lodges and the motorable tracks, in the vicinity of which animals tend to concentrate in consequence, to the benefit of the tourist.

On the administrative side, Kenya's new unified Wildlife Conservation and Management Department – in theory the most practical and effective organisation for managing a country's wildlife resources – after a bad start when it was widely accused of serious inefficiency, ineffectiveness and even corruption, has had a new director appointed in the person of the redoubtable Perez Olindo, the former Director of Kenya National Parks. Appointed early in 1987, by presidential decree, with orders to clean up the Wildlife Department, Olindo, a highly respected man of the greatest integrity, came in like a new broom and by all accounts he has already wrought near miracles in getting a moribund department motivated and into action again. However, there is another and more sober side to the coin, a side which reveals that there are a number of more insidious and in the long term more dangerous threats to Kenya's wildlife resources than poaching is ever likely to be; these are threats which have arisen as direct result of Kenya's biggest long term problem – that country's human population explosion.

There are a number of danger signs in the wildlife sphere. For instance, as Keith Eltringham points out, the change from traditional pastoralism to commercial wheat farming in the Narok area is going to have serious consequences for the animals of the Mara Reserve, as their normal range is thus being rapidly reduced. Shambas are also spreading into former prime wildlife areas, such as the Kitengela Reserve. The latter development means that the number of animals which used to move into the popular Nairobi National Park is also being greatly reduced. This pattern is bound to spread and, in fact, is already doing so, another recent example being the case of the Kora Reserve, the personal kingdom of that great "lion man" George Adamson of Born Free fame. The Kora Reserve, which is supported by the small Kora Trust (of which I myself am a Trustee) and the Elsa Trust, has recently been overrun by Somali nomads with their destructive herds of camels, goats and cattle but, faced with such a potentially explosive political problem, the Kenya Government has shown little stomach for a confrontation with the traditionally militant Somalis.

All in all, if I had to summarise, I would say that the future for Kenya's famous wildlife resources, on which that country's valuable and flourishing tourist industry directly depends, appears to be like the proverbial curate's egg, good in parts. With its human population explosion leading to ever increasing demands for more and more land for settlement and food production, the Kenya Government is faced with a difficult balancing act between conflicting problems; and, unless practical solutions are found and implemented, solutions which will almost certainly involve the firm grasping of some very controversial and probably unpleasant political nettles, it will not be long before it is discovered that this golden egg has become addled.

To prevent this insidious decline, draconian measures may well be called for. In the absence of such strong measures, the plains game (always resilient) and their predators will still survive for a very long time, albeit in steadily decreasing numbers, but for Kenya's once famous elephant herds the long term future will become increasingly precarious. As for the few remaining black rhinoceros in Kenya, as long as one ounce of gold can buy little more than one pound of rhino' horn on the world market, the future for this pitiful remnant of an almost prehistoric species will remain stark indeed. Everything depends on what the Government of Kenya is not merely willing but also able to do. The will appears to be there, the rest remains to be seen, but as long as Kenya continues to enjoy strong and pragmatic leadership, such as that of President Arap Moi, there is real cause for hope.

*

A quarter of a century has now passed since the former Mandated Territory of Tanganyika, the old German East Africa, was granted its independence. Under the visionary leadership of Julius Nyerere, first as Prime Minister and then as President, the Republic of Tanzania* followed a very different path from the Republic of Kenya, its former partner in the now defunct East African Community, and it is now generally accepted that, piloted by Nyerere, Tanzania took the wrong course. Julius Nyerere, an idealist and a dreamer who had been inspired by his visits to Communist China, shied away from capitalism and steered Tanzania into what, for Africans, were new and unchartered political waters. The outcome can only be described as calamitous.

The economic problems affecting Tanzania, over the last 15 years or so of Nyerere's term as President, were severe, partly due to his radical "African Socialism" policies – policies which were based on what he had seen in China – but also as a result of his early attempts at financial independence. Nyerere resented Nairobi's status as the recognised centre of the East African tourist industry, the focal point to which virtually all foreign tourists were drawn before visiting any other parts of East Africa; he also resented, with some justification, the fact that the long established and well organised Kenya based safari firms, which made maximum use of Tanzania's spectacular attractions,

* The name adopted after Tanganyika amalgamated with Zanzibar subsequent to the Zanzibar Revolution, followed by the mutiny of the Tanganyika Army, both of which occurred in January, 1964.

invariably met their clients and outfitted their safaris in Nairobi, thus leaving Tanzania with a pauper's share of the profits. So, late in 1977, with the object of making Arusha and Dar es Salaam, with their respective international airports, the bases for all tourist traffic in Tanzania, Nyerere ordered Tanzania's borders to be closed to all tourists from Kenya. The results were disastrous.

Prior to the border closure, the number of tourists visiting Tanzania was about half of the number recorded as visiting Kenya. After the closure however, the number of visitors to Tanzania slumped to less than one third of the Kenya figure and this discrepancy continued to increase until, in 1985, the Tanzania figure had fallen to as low as 58,000 visitors per year, compared to Kenya's figure of over 413,000. By then the financial difference was even more marked, with Tanzania recording a tourism related foreign exchange value of £8 1/2 million per year, compared with Kenya's dramatic figure of £209 million! In fact, by this time Tanzania was in dire financial straits.

With very little money and a corresponding loss of morale, both Tanzania's Wildlife Department and its National Parks could achieve very little and poaching virtually got out of control. In 1978, an aerial survey of the 20,000 square mile Selous Game Reserve revealed a massive elephant population of 110,000 animals; a similar survey carried out in 1986, indicated that in eight years this figure had been halved to 55,000, a staggering loss from poaching of nearly 7,000 elephant a year. In the same period, the black rhino' population of the Selous fell from an estimated 3,000 to what is believed to be little more than 500 rhino', while in the Serengeti National Park elephants were reduced from around 4,000 to a mere 400 (a 90% loss) and rhino' from 300 animals to a pitiful remnant of six endangered individuals.

The accuracy of some of the Selous aerial counts may be suspect, but very large numbers of elephant and rhino' carcases have been found in the Game Reserve by foot patrols, indisputable proof that, over a very long period, this vast reservoir of elephants has been subjected to intensive and systematic poaching by determined and well organised commercial ivory poachers. Furthermore, it is important to realise that the above statistics are just examples of the extremely serious commercial poaching trend which has been affecting the whole of Tanzania for a number of years. Another example is that of the buffalo population in the northern extension of the Serengeti National Park, a population which has been reduced from 25,000 buffalo to a mere 1,500 animals over the same period. Perhaps the saddest loss was the killing, in 1971, of one of the biggest tuskers that has ever been recorded; this old bull elephant, whose enormous tusks were each over nine feet long and over two feet in girth, and weighed 198 lbs and 204 lbs respectively, is believed to have been shot in the Ruaha National Park.

In welcome contrast to all these depressing statistics, it is reported that the wildebeeste population in the Serengeti ecosystem has increased to a staggering total of 1,600,000 animals, a figure which undermines the fact that the species which are the main targets of the poacher are those the trophies of which have considerable commercial value outside Africa. It is well known that, over the last ten years, the supply of tusks for the mainly clandestine ivory trade from Africa to the Far East, has been kept up at a high level, with the poacher in the field making as much as £12 for every pound of ivory that he poaches – a total of £240 for one 20 lb tusk alone – and of course with the fence or middleman receiving considerably more. In fact, it is also known that a well organised illegal trade in ivory is still flourishing under the management of a variety of unscrupulous businessmen assisted, it is believed, by corrupt politicians.

In the early seventies, Kenya was a prominent source of illegal ivory and it was during this period that 80% of the Tsavo National Park's elephants were poached. However, in 1977, when the Kenya Government's efforts to combat this problem finally met with considerable success, many of the ivory poachers moved south to operate in the Selous Game Reserve and the Luangwa Valley in Zambia. It is widely accepted that the main operators in the field are Somalis, working in association with unscrupulous local politicians and corrupt government officials, while most of the illegal ivory and rhino' horn is known to have been exported through Burundi, as it still is.

However, Burundi is not the only outlet for the illegal trade. Container-loads of ivory from Tanzania have also been intercepted in Kenya and in Holland, while on one occasion, when a tanker lorry, on its way from Dar es Salaam to Burundi, crashed near Mikumi 120 miles from Dar es Salaam, spilling its load all over the road, the load was found to consist of hundreds of pieces of elephant tusks! In many countries, the current laws and regulations governing the export and import of ivory, make this type of brazen and audacious smuggling all too easy. C.I.T.E.S. (the " Convention of International Trade in Endangered Species") is making tremendous efforts to bring all legal ivory trading under effective control, to achieve which it is attempting to get all the countries concerned to set and control really strict quotas of exports and imports of ivory. The Convention is achieving some success, but there still remains an enormous loop-hole through the illegal ivory trade and Tanzania is still in the front rank as far as the latter is concerned. Nevertheless, and despite the country's many . other daunting problems, all is not now doom and gloom in Tanzania, for the closing months of 1985, heralded what might fairly – if rather poetically – be described as a new dawn for Tanzania, preceded by a sad sunset reminiscent of a Greek tragedy.

In October, 1985, Julius Nyerere, the idealist and visionary who had created T.A.N.U. (the original "Tanganyika African National Union"), guided his country into independence, and led Tanzania first as Prime Minister and then as President for a quarter of a century, retired from the Presidency and faded quietly into the background. By the time Nyerere vacated the leadership however, the bottom had fallen out of Tanzania's economy, its wildlife-based tourist industry was in tatters, morale in the country was low, and it was clear that on all counts, and despite his personal sincerity and integrity, Nyerere's dreams had ended in nightmares, while his experiment in African Socialism had proved a costly failure.

On 4th November, 1985, Nyerere was succeeded by his former Vice-President, Ali Hassan Mwinyi, a Zanzibari. The new President, a realist and a pragmatist who realised that the African temperament is more inclined to favour capitalism than socialism, wasted no time in tackling Tanzania's crippling problems, but first of all he acted promptly to change the country's image. For a start, quietly and without fuss the name of Tanzania's ruling party was changed from the "Tanzania African National Union" (T.A.N.U.) to "Chama Cha Mapinduzi" (C.C.M.), which being translated means the "Party of the Revolution" – a singularly appropriate choice in view of the new President's Zanzibar background – while the tiller of the ship of state was swung firmly over so that its bows were pointing well to starboard of its previous course, to head steadily for the glittering shores of capitalism. Although the country's economy is still very weak, the results in two years have been encouraging, particularly in so far as Tanzania's valuable wildlife resources and their long term management is concerned.

Before the year 1985 drew to a close, the Director of Tanzania's National Parks had been replaced, the new incumbent being Daniel Babu who is widely reported as doing a praiseworthy job, as a result of which, with greatly increased morale, the efficiency and integrity of the Parks' staff is said to have improved considerably. Although it is early days yet, this development, following hard on the heels of the re-opening of Tanzania's border to tourists from Kenya,* bodes well for the future of Tanzania's national parks themselves, their spectacular wildlife, and the country's related tourist industry. Late in 1986, the Wildlife Department and the "Tanzania Wildlife Corporation" (T.A.W.I.C.O.)** were the next to attract the attention of the new broom, when the local press, waking up to the terrible poaching situation in Tanzania, blamed both the Wildlife Department and T.A.W.I.C.O. for gross dereliction of duty, corruption and mismanagment. As a result, a government enquiry was held into the affairs of both organisations and, although the findings have been kept secret, a new minister to oversee wildlife matters was appointed from among the top ranks of C.C.M. politicians.

The new Minister, a Mrs Gertrude Mongella, acted swiftly to clean up the mismanagement and tackle the poaching problem. To begin with, because it was believed that a lot of elephant were being killed illegally to support the long established trade in ivory carvings, the local ivory carving industry was closed down abruptly, and for the first time in eight years really vigorous anti-poaching patrols began operating in the Selous Game Reserve with money provided by the Tanzania Treasury – after much table thumping by the new Minister! According to recent reports, the

---

* The reopening of the border, a bitter pill for Julius Nyerere to swallow, was one of his last despairing bids to halt Tanzania's steady economic decline by attempting to salvage the country's tourist industry.

** Originally named the "Tanganyika Wildlife Development Company", a government owned tourist safari company conceived and started by the author early in 1964.

result was most encouraging in that poaching was almost stopped in the Selous, but this intensive effort used up all the Tanzanian funds in four months, since when great efforts have been made to keep up the campaign and obtain the necessary funding – hopefully with the aid of outside sources – for the poachers are undoubtedly just biding their time to resume their lucrative illegal operations.

The need for the efficient management and effective protection of the Selous Game Reserve is only one of the serious wildlife problems faced by Tanzania, but it has probably become the single biggest. The level of poaching in the Selous Game Reserve in the decade from ·1977 onwards, within which period, as I have observed earlier, 55,000 elephants are believed to have been poached, was on the face of it horrendous and certainly very serious. However, it is important to consider this whole matter in its true perspective, for it should be remembered that the Selous, with an overall length from north to south of some 200 miles and an average width of around 100 miles, is a vast area of 20,000 square miles of wild, remote and largely trackless bushland literally swarming with elephants and other game, in all one of the largest wildlife sanctuaries in the world. In my day as Chief Game Warden of Tanzania, when my department was obliged to kill on average upwards of 3,000 elephants every year on crop protection, a large proportion of these animals came out of the Selous Game Reserve which often seemed to be bulging with elephants. As I have mentioned before, the most recent aerial count, undertaken in 1986, recorded a population of 55,000 elephants in the Selous, which gives an average of 2.75 elephants per square mile; taking into account the size, the feeding habits and the amount of food required by these great beasts, by any reckoning that is still a lot of elephants for any stretch of country to maintain.

It is also of interest to note that the multi-use wilderness area project for the Selous Game Reserve, a project involving strictly controlled hunting and game viewing in most of the 20,000 square miles of the Reserve, is still functioning as planned and launched by myself, with the able assistance of Brian Nicholson, way back in 1964. Even in those days, it was clear that any wild areas as large as the Selous could not survive the ever-increasing threat of human encroachment unless, in some way, they could be shown to have an alternative economic use. On the grounds that it was too remote for the bulk of tourists and too difficult to protect and manage on their limited budget, the National Parks had declined to accept responsibility for the care and protection of this great game reserve; I had therefore had to think up an alternative plan, a scheme in the planning of which I had to bear in mind the oft' forgotten fact that the enormous Selous Game Reserve covers some 6% of the total land area of Tanzania, and that therefore, for the long term security of this great game reserve as demands for land inevitably increased, it was essential to be guided by the wise dictum of that famous ecologist the late Sir Frank Fraser Darling: "Conservation Through Wise Use."

So, early in 1964, after much heated argument and strong opposition from certain other wildlife interests, a government-owned company, the "Tanganyika Wildlife Development Company" (or T.W.D. for short) was formed with its headquarters in Dar es Salaam and myself seconded from the Game Department to act as its first General Manager, my initial brief being to develop and manage the Selous Game Reserve for all aspects of tourist hunting and game viewing. Like a number of the Game Department's more radical and unusual ideas, the launching of this project (financed by a massive bank overdraft!) had some hilarious and bizarre aspects, with a number of nail-biting crises, the full story of which must await another day; but in the end even the harshest critics had to admit that the Chief Game Warden's "mad idea", developed by the indefatigable Brian Nicholson, was at least a qualified success.

Now managed and controlled (in theory at least) by T.A.W.I.C.O., the successor in name to T.W.D. and T.W.S., the Selous Game Reserve – despite the vociferous local press accusations of mismanagement and corruption, in addition to the serious poaching problem – is bringing in a very healthy two million dollars (or about £1,250,000) in foreign exchange each year. To achieve this, the whole of the Selous is divided up into 47 controlled hunting blocks, two of which have been excised in the northern sector for game-viewing tourists and two others in the eastern sector for research, while three of the four permanent hunting camps are located on the banks of the Rufiji River, with the fourth camp at Beho Beho, near the site of Selous' grave in the northern part of the Reserve.

In addition to managing the Selous, T.A.W.I.C.O., which is now based in Arusha, also has the responsibility for the administration of hunting licences throughout Tanzania, as well as for the supervision of certain commercial game cropping schemes in various parts of the country. The importance of T.A.W.I.C.O. to the rational conservation of Tanzania's wildlife resources should not therefore be under-estimated, which highlights the fact that, when it comes to the questions of efficiency and integrity, it is equally important that T.A.W.I.C.O. should be seen, in the eyes of the general public, to be like Caesar's wife – beyond reproach! In view of the variety of temptations inevitably faced by T.A.W.I.C.O.'s staff, to cynics such perfection may appear to be an Utopian dream, but it is still a target to be aimed at and the new Government of Tanzania has shown both its muscle and its determination to put its country's house in order. This latter fact has already attracted the attention of the big international aid organisations such as the British O.D.A. and the American U.S.A.I.D. as well as B.M.Z., N.O.R.A.D., and the E.E.C. all of whom are beginning to take a great interest in conservation programmes in Africa, and who are already circling Tanzania like a flight of expectant fairy godmothers, with their hands deep in their bulging purses, the modern equivalent of the traditional magic wand. According to experienced observers on the spot, the results, even at this early stage, are encouraging, as Tanzania has now embarked on an "Economic Recovery Programme" linked to an Agreement with the International Monetary Fund, one of its implications being that the country is focussing more sharply on the priority of the tourist sector and on the need for conservation of wildlife.

*

Before I can conclude my stocktaking, there are two subjects which still remain to be reviewed, one is the current state of wildlife research in East Africa, the other is the present condition of wildlife management training in the same region, both of which are important matters that are vital to the long term interests of the wildlife resources, not merely of Tanzania, or even of East Africa, but of the African continent as a whole. Among the fluctuating political fortunes and even turmoil which have bedevilled the three countries of East Africa during the last quarter of a century, wildlife research is one activity that has not only remained virtually unscathed, but has actually progressed, sailing stubbornly on like a well-found ship in troubled waters. Even in Uganda, where a comparison with a wave-lashed rock in stormy seas would be more appropriate for its often beleaguered wildlife research unit, the Uganda Unit of Tropical Animal Ecology,* in the war-torn Queen Elizabeth Park, has continued doggedly to pursue its essentially practical scientific work, the applied research whose aims are to find feasible answers to the increasingly complex and difficult problems which continue to bedevil the task of conserving and managing Africa's still incomparable wildlife resources, threatened by a steadily shrinking environment. In search of these elusive answers, many scientists of different nationalities have worked with the Uganda research unit over the years, and in 1986, it proudly celebrated its Silver Jubilee.

In Tanzania, Uganda's wildlife research counterpart was the Serengeti Research Institute, which was established in 1966. Sited at Seronera, in the heart of the Serengeti National Park, its first director was Dr Hugh Lamprey, my Biologist when I was Chief Game Warden of Tanganyika and the man who, four years earlier, I had persuaded to accept the daunting task of running my favourite "brain child", the College of African Wildlife Management, as its first Principal. In Kenya, at this time, the often controversial Tsavo Elephant Research Project was initiated under the very able directorship of Dr Richard Laws, and overall this period was a time of rapidly expanding wildlife research in East Africa, with the production of a great deal of good quality field work in all three countries. This important research work still continues, with the majority of the permanent scientific staff now consisting of highly trained and dedicated Africans; and a number of notable scientific books and papers, on wildlife biology, have been written by scientists working from the three separate East African research institutions. Furthermore, in Tanzania, where the research administration has recently been reorganised and expanded, there is now a "National Serengeti Wildlife

* Originally named the "Nuffield Unit of Tropical Animal Ecology" which was started in 1961, its first director being Dr Richard Laws, who was succeeded in 1966, by Dr Keith Eltringham; it finally became the Uganda Institute of Ecology.

Research Institute", with headquarters in Arusha under the control of a Director General, and there are a number of subsidiary wildlife research centres in the field, mainly in national parks.

All in all, for wildlife research in East Africa, a field of research which attracts keen interest not only in scientific circles but also among the general public world-wide, the future looks to be full of promise. However, with wildlife management, as with all scientific disciplines, the value of applied research is nullified if there are insufficient trained professional and technical staff to implement the findings and recommendations of the scientists. Hence the need which arose in East Africa, as independence for the three countries rapidly approached, for properly established facilities to train Africans as game wardens and rangers, an urgent need which led me, in 1961 to 1963, to conceive, plan and finally to launch the College of African Wildlife Management at Mweka, on the slopes of Kilimanjaro. As I have described in Chapter 16, because of a quirk of fate the whole process of planning, funding and then physically creating this training college, which was a revolutionary idea in 1961, became a race against time, a race in which, until the closing stages, I was a lone runner.

When it was finally launched in 1963, and for a long time afterwards, the College of African Wildlife Management at Mweka was not only the first but also the only establishment of its kind in the world; its success as a centre for practical training, first under the able leadership of Dr Hugh Lamprey and then under Tony Mence, my former Deputy who succeeded Hugh as Principal, attracted a host of international aid organisations, all keen to get in on the act. For me however, after the College was well under way, my reward was the one so often experienced by the pioneer. Deliberately or by accident, I found myself eased into the sidelines by the powers that be and I soon discovered that, although my personal interest in Mweka remained as enthusiastic as ever, I no longer had any offical or formal connections with the College, even in an honorary capacity; as the conceiving and creating of the College of African Wildlife Management was one of the highlights of my career as a game warden in Africa, and arguably the most important thing I have personally achieved in a life which has been rich in variety, this was a bitter disappointment to me.

Years later, I was shown what is purported to be an "official history" of the College at Mweka, a story in which the events leading up to the creation of the College are gilded and glossed over, leaving the reader with the impression that the College of African Wildlife Management came into being in a vague form of immaculate conception, inspired by several fairy godmothers in the shape of certain international aid organisations. Perhaps memories are short or, since truth is said to be often stranger than fiction, perhaps the true story of how the College came to be created, and of my own leading role in its conception and creation, are a little too colourful and bizarre to be considered respectable!

However, and despite my personal disappointment, I have retained a very keen interest in the College at Mweka. Sadly, I have been unable to re-visit the College since I flew back there, to attend the very first graduation ceremony, in June, 1965, on my way to a wildlife advisory assignment in Bechuanaland;* but from all accounts, over the last 25 years graduates from Mweka have played a very important role, often a key role, in the management of the wildlife resources of a great many African countries. In fact, there is hardly a single country in English speaking Africa which has not had students trained at the College of African Wildlife Management at Mweka, and the College has frequently been held up as a shining example of one of the real success stories of post-colonial Africa. All this has given me immense pleasure and personal satisfaction.

From time to time, I have received personal reports on the progress of the College from Hugh Lamprey, Tony Mence, Keith Eltringham and others. As recently as April, 1987, Hugh Lamprey wrote to me and said "I visit the College from time to time as a member of the Governing Board. The present Principal is Bakari Mbano, and the Deputy Principal is John Boshe; they are both very able men who are assisted by eleven Instructors, all of whom are Tanzanians. There is also one expatriate biologist, an American. I meet ex-Mweka students in all the countries I go to in Africa, many in top positions in their parks and wildlife departments. The College has a tremendous reputation and is still doing a very good job. On my last visit to Mweka, there were students from more than a dozen countries attending the two and three year certificate and diploma courses, while in the

* Now Botswana

post-graduate diploma course there was one Nigerian, one Ethiopian, one American – and eight Cubans!"

Dr Keith Eltringham, who was commissioned by the World Wildlife Fund, in agreement with the College authorities, to visit Mweka in April, 1986, on a consultancy to review the syllabus and the training programme of the College of African Wildlife Management as an independent and unbiased observer, recently gave me his views on Mweka. He told me that he had stayed at the College and that he had therefore obtained a good insight into its affairs, describing it to me as "a lively place", remarking that he had noticed that the students included one from Japan and one from Hong Kong! He spoke highly of the teaching standards and the only real criticism he voiced to me was that, in his opinion, the teaching had become rather too academic and that he felt that more field training was needed. This comment interested me greatly because, way back in 1963, when I was discussing the very first training syllabus with Hugh Lamprey, Hugh and I had been in full agreement that the training supplied by Mweka had to be mainly in the field, with a firm backing from the classroom and the lecture hall!

In 1988, the College of African Wildlife Management at Mweka is due to celebrate its Silver Jubilee, but in the 23 years up to 1986, a total of 1,552 students from 31 countries spanning four continents attended courses at the College, most of them graduating to become holders of key wildlife posts in their countries of origin. Of these countries, 19 have been in Africa, the remaining 12 being Australia, Columbia, Cuba, Denmark, Hong Kong, Japan, Nepal, Panama, Singapore, Sri Lanka, the U.S.A. and the United Kingdom. This is an impressive record and although Mweka still flourishes, it is beginning to suffer from financial problems, like so many institutions in Africa.

The 19 African countries concerned are Tanzania, Kenya, Uganda, Zambia, Botswana, Zimbabwe, Malawi, Nigeria, Rwanda, Gambia, Ghana, Sudan, Somalia, Ethiopia, Egypt, Liberia, Sierra Leone, Cameroon and Mozambique.

In the case of Mweka, its financial problems have been exacerbated by what appears to have become a rival training institution on Lake Naivasha in Kenya. Originally started as a school to train staff for the tourist industry, personnel such as tour operators, drivers, guides and rangers, the Kenya project has recently been expanded to provide courses for game wardens. With its cheaper (subsidised) fees and easier access to supplies and equipment, the Kenya school is beginning to attract some of the students who hitherto would have gone to the College at Mweka. To counter this challenge, Mweka has decided to try to diversify its own activities; and in view of its past impressive record as a training institution which filled a very important gap, just in time, and has continued to fill this gap successfully for a quarter of a century, there are few who will not wish this College well for the future.

*

The purposes of all stock-taking is to establish facts, and as I have lifted the covers to reveal what has happened to the wildlife scene in East Africa over the last 25 years, one major factor has become increasingly apparent – that in one way and another, from ivory poaching to crop protection, the African elephant has continued to dominate the overall scene, straddling the stage like some mammalian colossus, as these great beasts have always done since time immemorial. Certainly, if it was not for the fact that there are many thousands of elephants in East and Central Africa even to this day, still raiding shambas and still being hunted and poached for their ivory, *The Shamba Raiders* would never have been written, while the greater part of my own life would inevitably have taken a very different course.

Forty years have now passed since, in the dense forests of Kenya's Coast Province, I first came face to face with an African bull elephant, and over this troubled period the world, and the African scene in particular, has changed dramatically. For the elephant this change has not been for the better. Recognised experts, such as Drs Keith Eltringham, Hugh Lamprey, Richard Laws and Iain Douglas-Hamilton, are in general agreement that over the last 15 years or so the elephant population in Africa has been reduced by two-thirds, from a dominant population estimated at anything up to one and half million, down to often beleagured remnants totalling no more than five hundred thousand.

Dr Richard Laws, the first Director of the Unit of Tropical Animal Ecology in Uganda, and later the leader of the research project investigating the problem of the apparent over-population of elephants in the Tsavo National Park in Kenya, has summed up the present elephant situation in a few well-chosen words: "In Africa, the distribution of man and elephant populations has changed from one characterised by human islands in a sea of elephants, to increasingly small islands of elephants in a sea of people." Without the elephant the African wildlife scene would seem empty indeed, a landscape strangely devoid of character, but as my stocktaking has revealed, the threat to these great beasts comes not from the legitimate hunter, but from the avaricious commercial ivory poacher, together with the demands of an exploding human population hungry for more land.

Happily for me, in the days when I was a game warden in Uganda and Tanzania, and later in Botswana, Rwanda and Malawi, the elephant situation then was very different from what it is to-day. At that time the problem was not that there were too few elephants, but too many; large herds of these great animals often filled the landscape, sometimes stretching to the horizon, and African folk-lore was full of tales of legendary elephants, ancient bulls with tusks so long that they swept right down to the ground, leaving tell-tale grooves in the soil when these great beasts were weary and their massive heads drooped. Some of these tales were true and in 25 years in Africa, both as a game warden and as a hunter, I had the good fortune to meet up with several of these mighty tuskers, secretive beasts often accompanied by one or more mature young bulls as sentries and bodyguards.

A few of these mighty but ancient tuskers were loners, and recently, when the ivory poaching situation in East Africa became so bad, the memory of one of these great beasts inspired me to write some evocative verses, a reaction which I attribute to that strange mixture of respect and affection which the true hunter has for his quarry, not forgetting that so many of the old time game wardens began their careers as elephant hunters. I entitled the verses *An African Night*, and now, as then, I hope that they will remind all lovers of the African wilds of the ugly menace of the commercial poacher. For me the verses are a small token of my deep respect and appreciation of the animal to which I owe so much – the African elephant.

The Ivory room, Dar es Salaam.

The author at his home in Herefordshire, 1987.

An African Night

Across the moonlit bushland came a lion's moaning roar,
The distant screams of elephants, a leopard's rasping saw.
At the water-hole below me there was scarce a sound until
Its peace was rudely shattered by hyaenas on a kill;
Their frenzied madman's cackles would have made a
   banshee shiver,
While those raucous, grunting bellows came from hippos in
   the river.

As I sat beside my camp-fire, its warming, flickering glow
Cast leaping, dancing shadows that wandered to and fro,
'Till imagination kindled and beneath the nearby trees
A stealthy, slinking movement brought my rifle to my knees.
But a moonbeam like a searchlight showed a jackal on the
   prowl,
Frustrated, hungry, searching, he departed with a howl.

Like diamond studded velvet far above me stretched the
   sky,
And across this star-lit backcloth the nightjars glided by
With trailing, fluttering pennants, unlike any other bird,
Their softly whispering pinions so quiet and seldom heard;
Yet they were also hunters, alert and on the seek,
Their gentleness deceptive, catching moths in gaping beak.

Then suddenly I heard it, that sound which brings a thrill
To the soul of any hunter, whatever grade his skill.
Like muted, rumbling thunder, or a giant feline purr,
   'Tho the mighty beast which made it was not adorned with
   fur.
I held my breath and listened for the sound to come again,
With adrenalin a'pumping speeding up my pulse and brain.

The noise was not repeated, but there came a different sound,
A rending, tearing, crashing – as a thorn tree hit the ground.
When the splintering subsided came yet another tone,
A steady, rhythmic chomping, massive jaws on wood like
   bone.
But still the beast was hidden by the shadows of the trees,
And still I tensely waited with my rifle on my knees.

My patience was rewarded, for like some giant snake,
Curling high above the thorn trees, yet another branch to
  break,
There rose a questing tentacle, a pachydermal trunk
So massive that I wondered could I possibly be drunk?
I looked again, this time the moon revealed a thrilling
  sight,
A fleeting glimpse of ivory – but could my eyes be right?

Then noiseless as a shadow and with cushioned, silent tread,
Out into the clearing stepped a shape all peasants dread,
A towering, massive elephant so tall it blocked the sky,
With tusks so long, so thick, so white, my throat and mouth
  went dry.
It was an ancient, mighty bull which hunters long had
  trailed,
A local native legend which I too had sought but failed.

One moment it was there – and then, as silent as it came,
The beast had gone, I knew not where, the jackal back again.
I waited for the dawn to break and at the sun's first gleam
I woke beside my camp-fire – so was it all a dream?
But no, around my camp-site the evidence was there,
The mighty tracks like giants' plates, the thorn tree
  smashed and bare.

With hope renewed I gathered up my rifle, pack and bearer,
The tracks were clear, we followed fast, our quarry ever
  nearer.
As noon approached the sun beat down, the pace we set was
  testing.
Excitement grew for well we knew our bull would soon be
  resting.
And so it proved, with sudden shock, in a fig-tree's spreading
  shade
We found our bull, his heart quite still – from a drop-spear's
  poisoned blade.

Index

397

Tanganyika Game Department, 83, 208, 257, 308; author as Chief Game Warden, 83, 281, 315-6, 320 *seq.*; annual total of elephants shot, 209; changes in, 313, 315, 321-2, 324; and national parks, 321; 'game regions', 322, 324; and training school, 322, 324, 326 (*and see* College of African Wildlife Management); proposed unified 'Wildlife Service', 332-4; Africans as game wardens, 330-2, 345, 356-62

Tanganyika Wildlife Development Company (now T.A.W.I.C.O.) 347, 347n, 384, 384n, 386-7

Tangi, River, 300

Taru Desert, 352

Tatam, Jane (Managing Director, Ashford Press Publishing), vi

Taunton Rotary Club, 257-8

Teare, Philip (Game Warden of Tanganyika), 207-8

Technical Co-operation, Department of, 340, 340n, 342, 344

Temple-Perkins, E. A., 154, 154n

Tengeru, 313, 321, 322

Territorial Imperative, The (Ardrey), 309

Tewa Saidi Tewa (Tanganyika Minister for Wildlife), 327n, 330

Third International Conference for the Protection of the Fauna and Flora of Africa (Bukavu 1953), 283

Thomas, Keith (Assistant Chief Game Warden, Tanganyika), 322, 324

Thomson, Joseph, 252-3

'Tippu Tib' (slave-trader), 353, 354, 355

Topsell, Edward, xiv

Torit, 251

Toro District, 141, 162, 198, 206; Game Reserve, 169

Toro, Omukama of, 273

Train, Judge Russell (founder of the African Wildlife Leadership Foundation), 337-8, 337n, 344

Treen, Chris 254

Trenchemer (yacht), 246

'Triumph of Science, The' (Owen), 348-50

Tsavo, River, 352

Tsavo National Park, 20, 49, 68, 382, 392

Tsetse Control Department, 214, 217, 225, 243, 244, 312-3, 344

Turkana tribesman, 211, 230, 242, 250, 251, 253

Turkwell, River, 210

Turnbull, Sir Richard (Governor of Tanganyika), 325-6

Uganda: geography of, 72-3; game conservation problems, 73-81, 88 *et seq*; damage by raiding elephants, 75, 78-81, 88-121; tsetse fly, 74-5, 78; ivory trade, 76, 122-37; appointment of game rangers, 79; creation of 'Elephant Control Department', 79-80; author's first elephant hunt in, 88-121; buffalo problems and hunting, 139-153; and national parks, 256-303; and hydro-electric scheme, 284-5; new game laws, 313

Uganda Game Department: author becomes Assistant Game Warden in, 3-17, 81; his work in, 50 *et seq*; creation of, 65, 79-81; official attitude to, 65-7, 80, 180, 182-4, 214, 216, 243, 260-1; problems and limited facilities, 70-2, 80, 156, 179-86; traditional titles in, 81-4; change of titles, 83-4; trouble over rifles supplied to, 118-21; and ivory permits, 123, 125-31; Pitman's work as Chief Game Warden, 174-8; author as Chief Game Warden, 178, 179, 185 *et seq.* and 393; and fisheries, 181, 182, 290-9, 307; and poaching problem, 188-206, 251-4; annual total of elephants shot, 200; and national parks, 256-78, 279-90, 299-303, 304-9; reorganisation, 305-8; and Fulbright scientists, 308-13; and hippo reduction, 309-12

Uganda Institute of Ecology (Nuffield Unit of Tropical Animal Ecology), 368, 388n 392

Uganda National Parks Act (1952), 277

404

Uganda National Parks Committee, 259, 260-7, 274
Uganda National Parks Organisation: administration of, 286-7, 289-90; relations with Game Department, 287, 302-3, 305-7; separationist policy, 306-7; and hippo over-population, 309-12
Uganda Railway ('the Lunatic Line') 354
Uganda Wildlife Development Ltd, 347n
United Nations Development Programme, 345, 347, 356n
United Nations Special Fund, 362

Verdier, Dr Jacques (Scientific Secretary C. S. A.) 326, 334, 343
Victoria, Lake, 50, 73, 90, 187, 274, 297, 307, 320, 353
Villiers, Marjorie (Harvill Press, Collins), vi
Virunga Volcanoes, 73
Vivers, 'Red' 161

Waliangulu tribe, 14, 114n; and illegal ivory, 21, 23-37, 39, 46-9; poisoned arrows, 21, 21n, 46, 200
Wamala, Lake, elephant hunt round, 88-117
Wanderings of an Elephant Hunter, The (Bell), 209, 227
Wankie Game Reserve, 188
Warija, William (game guard), 253-4
Wasanya tribe – see Waliangulu

Wayne, John (film star), 325
Weitz, Dr Bernard (Lister Institute, London), 213
Whelen, Colonel Townsend, 248
Wild, John (Senior Assistant Resident,Masaka), 144
Wildlife Management and Conservation Department, Kenya, 376-8
'Wildlife Service', proposed, 285, 289, 332-4
Williams, 'Elephant Bill', 208
Willingdon, Lord (President of the Fauna Preservation Society), 274, 274n
Winds of Change (Macmillan), 54
Wissmann, Major Hermann von, xvii
World Wildlife Fund, 269
Worthington, Dr Barton (as one of Africa's pioneer wildlife scientists), 259, 259n
Wright, Inspector Ernest (Kenya Police), 34-6

Yellowstone National Park, 256

Zambezi, River, 187, 188
Zanzibar ('Island of Cloves'), revolution 347; centre of ivory trade 355; amalgamation with Tanganyika to form Tanzania 380n; home of Tanzania's current President, 383
Zaphiro, Captain Denis (Senior Game Warden, Kenya), 81-3